THE NATURE

OF

HARMONY AND METRE

THE NATURE

OF

HARMONY AND METRE

BY

MORITZ HAUPTMANN

TRANSLATED AND EDITED

BY

W. E. HEATHCOTE, M.A.

GYAN

Published by

GYAN

Gyan Publishing House
5, Ansari Road
Daryaganj, New Delhi-110002
Phone: 011-47034999, 9811692060
E-mail: books@gyanbooks.com

Distribution Network
gyanbooks.com
India, USA, Canada, UK, Australia

ISBN: 978-93-6208-257-2 (HB)
First Published, 1888

2nd Impression 2024

Printed at: Gyan Press, Delhi.

THE NATURE OF HARMONY AND METRE
Author: MORITZ HAUPTMANN

HARMONY AND METRE

THE NATURE
OF
HARMONY AND METRE

BY

MORITZ HAUPTMANN

TRANSLATED AND EDITED
BY

W. E. HEATHCOTE, M.A.

LATE FELLOW OF TRINITY COLLEGE, CAMBRIDGE

LONDON
SWAN SONNENSCHEIN & CO.
PATERNOSTER SQUARE
1888

AUTHOR'S PREFACE.

THE knowledge to be acquired by him who is desirous of becoming a practical musician has been amply set forth in many treatises. Few have attempted to examine how the laws of music depend upon principles of the human mind, and how that form of musical expression which is true and correct must also be that which is natural to mankind, which is conformed to human reason, and which is consequently open to universal comprehension. Researches of this character will, as a rule, find less general acceptance than if they were directed towards strengthening the powers of execution, or towards refining the taste and the judgment. The beginner in music is absorbed in studies of a practical tendency; the mature musician is devoted to the exercise of his profession. They rarely find time, and have little inclination, to reflect upon principles for the truth of which it seems to them that instinctive feeling is a sufficient assurance. Occasionally, however, a desire is manifested for information as to the ground of certain inevitable axioms; and we are asked to assign a reason for rules whose validity is unquestioned, but which for the most part remain without demonstration. To such desire the present treatise is designed as the appropriate response. May it meet with the approval of all those who concur in, or will follow out, its arguments! It does not contain a practical method of instruction in harmony and metre, but is an enquiry into the nature of musical and metrical art.

M. HAUPTMANN.

LEIPZIG.

TRANSLATOR'S PREFACE.

THE following translation was undertaken with the view of rendering more accessible a work that possesses great interest both for music and metaphysics. For music, because, independently of the theory involved, it contains a clear and compact account, written by a skilful musician and experienced teacher, of the doctrine of harmony and metre; in which the received rules are reduced under general principles, while upon particular points new and unexpected light is frequently cast. For metaphysics, because it is an application of Hegel's method of philosophy to a concrete subject, that has, like logic, the peculiar advantage of standing by itself and of being comprised in a comparatively narrow compass.

It has been endeavoured to represent the original in as plain and literal language as possible, carefully avoiding all arbitrary interpretations. Also it did not seem that anything in the shape of a commentary or notes accompanying the text would be likely to be of use. For Hauptmann does not assume in his readers a knowledge of metaphysics, nor anything beyond technical acquaintance with music. It is conceived, however, that to readers unversed in metaphysics the method of reasoning may present, at the outset, some difficulty. The Translator has therefore ventured to prefix a short introductory essay, which may perhaps serve to give a general idea of the scope of the work, and of the nature and intention of the arguments employed in it, and at the same time elucidate certain special instances and expressions. The proof-sheets have been submitted to the criticism of Mr. H. Keatley Moore, B.A., B. Mus., who, besides revising in many respects the musical phraseology throughout, has also kindly made numerous suggestions and corrections, which have greatly added to the value of the translation.

114 EBURY STREET, S.W.
June 1888.

CONTENTS.

II. METRE.

III. METRICAL HARMONY. HARMONIC METRE.

A SHORT SKETCH

OF THE

LIFE OF MORITZ HAUPTMANN.

BY PROFESSOR DR. ALFRED SCHÖNE.

Translated from the Preface to 'Briefe von Moritz Hauptmann an Franz Hauser,' edited by Prof. Dr. Alfred Schöne. Leipzig: Breitkopf and Härtel. 1871.

MORITZ HAUPTMANN was born in Dresden on the 13th of October, 1792. His father, who was a provincial architect, recognised the exceptional talents of his son, and developed them by careful and judicious education. Inclination for music was early manifested by the boy, but up to his 19th year he was receiving complete technical training as a future architect, besides making zealous studies in mathematics, natural science, and languages. Without doubt this familiarity with architecture brought incalculable benefit to Hauptmann in his later labours in musical theory, to say nothing of the delicate understanding for the fine arts which he owed chiefly to these studies of his youth. At the age of 19 he turned wholly to music, and in 1811 went to Gotha, where he had instruction from Spohr in the violin and composition. In the very next year he entered the Dresden Court band as violinist, and in 1813 held during several months a like position in the Vienna Theatre orchestra, at that time conversing much with Carl Maria v. Weber, with Meyerbeer, and with Spohr, who occupied the post of conductor. Returned to Dresden, he accepted in 1815 an appointment as music master in the house of the Russian princess Repnin, and in that capacity passed five years in Moscow, Pultowa, Odessa, and St. Petersburg. After Hauptmann had returned in 1820 to Dresden, his teacher and friend Spohr, who had meanwhile become conductor in Cassel, engaged him as violin-player in the Electoral band, and for full twenty years the great man remained in this modest situation. Yet his name soon became known in wider circles. His two great masses, several sonatas for violin and piano, violin duets, some sacred choral pieces (among them his famous 'Salve Regina'), an opera 'Matilda,' secular song-music for one or more voices (as, e.g., the sonnets of Petrarch, 'Amor timido,' 'Anacreontiche,' and others), and some lesser pianoforte pieces met, if not with universal and sudden acclaim, yet with marked recognition from the best and ablest musicians, and gradually gathered round his name a small, steadily increasing, company of admirers and friends of his music. Nor did he meet with less acknowledgment as a teacher of musical theory. The number of his pupils was over 300; and, while thus perseveringly busied in teaching, he was developing that insight of genius into the essence of musical theory, which he has set forth in his book ('Natur der Harmonik und der Metrik,' Leipzig, Breitkopf and Härtel, 1853) and in smaller essays connected with it. Thus gradually he won the reputation of the most notable theorist and teacher of his time, and when in 1842 the post of Cantor at the Thomasschule, hallowed for ever by J. Seb. Bach, at Leipzig fell vacant, through Mendelssohn's influence Hauptmann was called to this honourable position, and was at the same time appointed teacher in the Conservatorium, then about to be founded. His mind quickly made up, Hauptmann left his quiet sojourn at Cassel, which he had broken only in 1829 by a journey to Italy and in 1842 by a visit to Paris. He was accompanied to his new home by his wife, Susette, whom he had married in 1841; she was a daughter of Hummel, Director of the Academy in Cassel. On the 12th of September, 1842, Hauptmann entered upon his office in Leipzig. Happy in his wife, whose great talents for music and fine art were the ornament of his house, and in his three children, in friendship with a circle of like-minded worthy families, conversing personally and by letter with many of the most eminent men in art and science, loved and honoured by the daily increasing band of his scholars, full twenty-five prosperous years of unenfeebled activity were allotted him. It was not until the end of the year 1866, shortly after a beautiful celebration of his silver wedding, that a bodily weakness set in, which rapidly gained ground and made the last days of his life burdensome. On the 3rd of January, 1868, he closed his tired eyes for ever; but in the recollections of his friends his memory will endure as one of the best and most noteworthy men that Germany has produced.

INTRODUCTORY ESSAY.

BY THE TRANSLATOR.

ALTHOUGH music itself is ancient, yet its modern European form is recent and of plain origin. The source of modern music is two-fold: Church and secular; of which Church music represents the more ancient phase, though both doubtless were in their beginning the same. Modern harmony, counterpoint, modulation, all the formal part of modern music, takes its rise from the Church chorale. And while Church music served as the mould, secular music furnished the material; so that rhythm, and those forms of music which are characterised by rhythm (e.g. marches and dances), are rather due to secular music.

Similarly, among forms of composition the fugue belongs principally to the Church style, and the sonata to the secular; the sonata being distinguished by multiplicity of contents, though its general course of modulation is not different to that of other forms of music.

Now the science of music is concerned more with the form than with the materials. Therefore the influence of secular music is regarded rather as falling in with the tendencies of modern music than as guiding them.

With the progress of music a system of rules for composing

was gradually formed. At first harmony was simple, and simple rules sufficed. Afterwards new effects were discovered, which made new rules necessary and also modifications of the former ones. To take an early example from Hauptmann: at the time of Palestrina Seventh chords were not used, or very rarely, in vocal counterpoint; later it was discovered that under certain restrictions they might be freely used with advantage. But at the same time the employment of this greater dissonance was the reason for certain other rules regarding the more delicate leading of voices in harmony being discarded; the introduction of the greater contrasts made the lesser unimportant. The final result was a body of rules, consistent indeed and not arbitrary, inasmuch as they formed in the aggregate a system, but still only gathered from experience and not illuminated or governed by any philosophic or scientific explanation. Various attempts have been made to supply such an explanation; but the doctrine of harmony, though empirical, is simple, and the explanations mostly added intricacy without helping practice. Many partial or particular explanations have been given, that are interesting historically, and have also left their impression upon the musical system; but of none of the older theorists can it be said that he formed a system to supersede all others, or gave more than a partial glimpse of the central truth pervading harmony.

Hauptmann's 'Nature of Harmony and Metre' is a philosophical explanation of the received laws or principles of the art of music, aiming at equal simplicity with the laws themselves. It explains them by showing that the various rules and principles are derived from one law that pervades the whole; also that the gradual development of music historically is the gradual embodiment of that law, and so may be said to be due to it; also that every single phenomenon in music is a perfect instance or embodiment of the law.

The treatise is written in the Hegelian philosophy. It may be compared to the 'Logic' of Hegel, which it resembles in method and in plan. In both works a large body of received rules and principles, recognised as forming a system, but inadequately explained hitherto, are established upon a philosophical basis and shown to depend upon a law. Both start from a simple beginning, from which the more complicated conceptions are shown branching out. This development (by which is not meant only development in time or by succession) is seen to follow a uniform law, by the operation of which the process of development is separated into stages; and each stage is marked by the accomplishment or completion of some particular notion, which then appears as including within it all previous notions completed in previous stages.

Recognition of the law referred to, which will presently be enunciated, is characteristic of the Hegelian philosophy. It was not, however, an invention or discovery of Hegel's. In one form or another it was known to and stated by many previous philosophers and metaphysicians. And in the form now to be noticed it has been stated as plainly by Goethe as by Hegel. But it is called Hegelian as having been made formally the basis of a system by Hegel, and by the school of which he is the chief representative.

The law is enunciated thus by Hauptmann: 'Unity, with the opposite of itself, and the removal of the opposite: immediate unity, which through an element of being at two with itself passes into mediated unity.' Here three stages or epochs in the process of thought are marked out: a stage of simplicity or unity; a stage of division or separation; and a stage of reconcilement or restored unity.

In speaking of the process of thought no contrast is intended between thoughts and things. All things are regarded as thought, and this triple organisation is attributed to concrete things no less than to abstract thoughts and notions. Thus for a first idea of the kind of triplicity that is meant we might instance the seed, the growing crop, and the harvest; the beginning, middle, and end; the power, the fulcrum, and the weight; the premise, the argument, and the conclusion. Now to learn or follow out any of these is a process; but when the process is completed, then the several elements appear as factors in a higher notion, in which, moreover, the process is surveyed as a whole. It is not known that a grain of corn is a seed until it is known that there will be a harvest from it. Also a conclusion does not satisfy until it is seen to follow from the premise, and premise, argument, and conclusion to form one coherent, necessary whole.

To consider more closely the three stages of thought, or, as it might be said, of our knowledge of things.

I. Anything is said to be 'unity' when it is perfect and simple ('in se ipso totum teres atque rotundum'), having no parts, or at least only such as are discerned to be necessary, not distinguished as parts, as when, e.g., a picture is viewed without reflecting on the parts of it or the reasons for their being such and such. Of this kind are the notions of 'up' and 'down' before the question arises of how much up and down; or when the branch of a tree is said to be at right angles to its trunk, which further reflection shows to be quite indefinite. So to say the sun rises in the east might seem either a definite statement or an indefinite, according as the quarter of the heavens or the point of the compass is thought of. But the later notions are not in reality more precise than the earlier, though they are apt to appear so; just as a sum is not made more precise for being stated in pence rather than in pounds. These are notions gained by reflection, which have not as yet undergone further reflection. In language they are also represented by general terms, as when a 'chord' is spoken of, meaning a chord in general, which was once a concrete thing, though now by reflection become abstract.

Therefore when musical sound, as the Octave, is said to be unity, we are not to think of it existing then as it does now, and capable of being distinguished into chords, notes, or scales. We are going back to a time anterior to all that—to a time when there was neither chord nor scale, when sound was indeed perceived as musical, but without further difference. For in the progress of music the law (viz. of unity, difference, and union) is the form that generates the notes; it is the cause of their existence and anterior to them. Musical pitch, tone, or quality of sound, which depend upon the triad, must not be thought of as existing before the triad exists, and still less as contributing to the formation of the triad. Therefore, in the beginning, musical sound must be thought of as existing indeed, but without difference; that is, as if every musical sound were understood as being the same.

Even the Octave in the triad of Octave, Fifth, and Third is not strictly the prime unity of all; for the Fifth and Third are also the prime unity (being modes of it) just as much as the Octave is. But within the triad the Octave represents the prime unity; for it is the prime unity appearing as such within the triad.

The distinction here pointed out arises merely from considering the higher unity as produced from the prime unity in a successive process: first Octave, then Fifth, then Third, which is the union of the two former. This implies a distinction between the prime unity, that exists first, and the Octave, that exists concomitantly with the Fifth and Third. In reality there is no successive process; but the intellect, in considering things as finite, necessarily assumes one. It follows that when an assumed prime unity—e.g. the triad—has through an intermediate process given rise to a higher unity—e.g. the key, a triad with its subdominant and dominant—then the chords of the subdominant and dominant are triads no less than the tonic triad, and the notion of triad becomes an abstract one. It has become abstract to the intellect because parted from it by an act of reason. For the process of unity, difference, union represents to the intellect the act of reason.

II. In the second factor, of division, difference, or separation—the Fifth in music—the immediate unity of the first factor is broken up; immediate unity is as it were perceived to be no limit for thought. It is not lost, but becomes doubtful and unreal; it is and is not at the same time. It becomes two, or at two, in itself; by which is not meant that it becomes two numerically, two separate, distinct unities, but that division or twoness appears in each element and every part of it. Thus twoness appears in musical sound when it is perceived to have 'sides' or double meaning, to be different in different directions. In the completed musical system this is represented principally by a note and its Fifth; but more generally by any two notes that are different. For the interval of the Fifth is the type of difference; and thus in music the Fifth, the type of difference, is present wherever sounds are considered as different. So in geometry a direction in a plane is defined principally with reference to two directions that are at right angles to one another, but more generally to any two directions.

III. The third factor is that of union or reconciliation. In the second factor the unity of the first was not lost; it only became troubled, that is, contradictory and opposed to itself. And so in the third factor the opposition is not lost, but reconciled. Fusion takes place. The contradiction is removed by being made reasonable. The Fifth is unreal, because in it there is opposite, unreconciled meaning. The Third brings back reality, for now the opposite becomes complementary meaning in a higher notion.

In the completed musical system this is represented principally by a note and its Third. For the Fifth is the direct opposite of the note; but the Third, holding the middle place between the note and its opposite, is their bond of union. The incompatible natures of the note and its Fifth are reconciled by a third nature partaking of both. Hauptmann takes the example of an end and a beginning. End and beginning are incompatible natures, but are reconciled in the nature of middle, which partakes of the nature of end and also of the nature of beginning, or more truly *is* both end and beginning. There are, then, beginning, end, and middle, factors of a higher nature.

But more generally the nature of the Third appears in any note that is considered as having relation to another. For one note is the same as another in so far as it is its Octave, and different to it in so far as it is its Fifth; but union of sameness and difference constitutes the nature of the Third. So a direction in a plane is defined by considering how far it coincides with a given direction and how far it is at right angles to it. In music the Octave is present wherever sounds are considered as the same; the Fifth is present wherever they are considered as different, and the Third wherever they unite sameness with difference. In other words, the Octave expresses sameness or identity; the Fifth, difference; and the Third, unity of sameness and difference.

A chief hindrance to understanding the Hegelian process comes from considering the three elements, through which the higher notion is manifested, as three distinct separate things, whereas they are more truly sides of the same thing: the higher notion is viewed on three sides before it can be seen through and viewed as a whole. For it might be supposed that there are a great number of particular things or substances, and that these 'combine chemically' (a comparison sometimes used of the Hegelian process) to form new notions; as if out of the great crowd of things a negative could always be found for any given positive, and then the two combined. But the true view is that the negative is produced out of the positive; or rather, positive and negative appear together in the prime unity. So that the better comparison is found, e.g., in the nature of dimensions, where a point or line considered at first *per se* is afterwards found to involve or generate the notion of space, and can then only be recovered out of space by a mental effort, so as to appear abstracted from it. Here space is not combined out of a number of points in space; but the notion of space is generated from the notion of point, which in space appears as abstract position. True that on the piano a note, its Fifth, and its Third are three distinct sounds, but that is because the way in which they have come about is left out of sight. Being themselves the fruit of previous thought, the embodiment of a whole history of music, the notes of a keyboard now stand ready-made in a system taken for granted like the alphabet, or the multiplication table in working arithmetic. They are thus for use in music, but music must not be founded on them. And so the question is not merely of combining them; for they are made so as to combine; but of combining them afresh, so that they transcend their nature. Thus every advance in music brings about advance in the construction of instruments, which are, so to speak, the register of results already attained in music. For every instrument is the evidence of its own use; as the story seems to imply, of the wise man who having been shown a chess-board and men discovered their use by meditation.

It remains to speak of the triad, the completed notion, in which the three elements appear united into one. In Hauptmann's words, the unity which at first was simple and immediate has become a mediated unity. To explain this let us consider the notion of musical sound. This may be defined as sound capable of being used as a means of expression. It is the first glimpse of music appearing in sound. Now at first musical sound is a simple notion; all musical sounds are the same. Afterwards there may be musical sounds that are musical and musical sounds that are not musical, e.g. concords and discords. So that the triad, the law of musical sounds, is to music what musical sound is to sound generally; for in it musical sound is doubly musical: as if we should represent musical sound by x, and the triad by $x{\cdot}x$, the x of x. Thus musical sound is reflected in itself; that is, musical sound becomes intelligible, is understood, by means of musical sound, or, as Hauptmann says, is mediated by itself. And this process of doubling upon itself, or specialisation, takes place continually in all parts of music, making it into an organic whole.

We have, then: first, musical sound appearing in sound; next, musical sound separating into concord and discord; lastly, the reconciliation between concord and discord, in view of which discord is more properly termed dissonance. Now the opposition between consonance and dissonance is analogous to that between musical sound and sound generally—noise. And what answers then to the resolution of dissonance is the whole development of music, or, as it is sometimes said, of the musical idea. There is no special charm in music not common to all sound; but the discovery of the charm is reached through music. Music is, therefore, in Spohr's phrase, the consecration of sound; it constitutes the demonstration that all sound is musical. The advance of music is marked by the gradual transformation of discord into dissonance. The meaning of discord is found, and it becomes the complement, the other side, of consonance. And in this notion is explained the term so often used by Hauptmann of the **meaning** of a sound or combination of sounds. For every sound employed in a particular way has to justify its existence; it has to contain in itself the reason for its being such as it is. Its existence involves a doubt or riddle and its solution. De Quincey speaks somewhat similarly when he describes 'the questions' in music 'asked and answered in a deep musical sense.'

Thus far has been considered the triad in music as the embodiment of a certain law. This, in its abstract statement, is claimed for the expression of the general process of thought: it is the shape taken by all thought, just as syllogism is the shape taken by all argument. Now, as in argument it is not usual to put forward the form of the syllogism, so neither does the form of thought lie nakedly upon the surface. Thought laid open to the intellect takes of itself this form; but the laying open is a kind of dissection, and rests upon a fiction. And so we see in Hegel that the abstract form of the law is not much appealed to; the natural process of thought is followed, and takes of itself the proper form. In Hauptmann the form of the law is made more prominent, and we are constantly shown the same process repeated in new material. The reason for this is partly that the symmetrical construction of the musical system had to be accounted for. It was known that every chord, every scale was based upon a fundamental note, and that modulations followed the same intervals that the notes of melody do; besides many other symmetrical relations, which, natural as they may now seem, were yet discovered only gradually and with difficulty. The outline of the system being, therefore, known, it remained for Hauptmann to show the connexion of the parts.

The object of knowledge, as Hauptmann tells us, is recognition of the particular in the universal and of the universal in the particular. Here a distinction may be made between **universal** and **abstract.** The latter is ordinarily used as a term in the common logic. In logical abstraction things are compared, and the qualities in which they differ are rejected. Thus the higher conceptions are always emptier and emptier, and the highest abstraction is nearest nothing. The term **universal** in Hegelian metaphysics has the opposite meaning to this. There the higher notion is such as to unite and include the opposite qualities of things; it is fuller in contents than the lower or particular, and the particular is regarded as a limitation of the universal. In the common logic the particular=the general + a difference. In Hegelian logic the particular=the general under a limitation. There is a very real distinction whether the abstract is thought of as emptier than the concrete, the universal than the particular, or whether as fuller of contents. The views are, in fact, opposite, and their reconcilement is found in that way of thinking so often brought forward by Hauptmann in the course of his work, when he says that the universal must be thought of in the particular, and the particular in the universal; which leads ultimately to abolition of the antithesis between universal and particular.

The following is meant as an illustration: The modulation of a piece of music may be represented in a series of chords. These are considered as the groundwork of the composition; as if a sketch or outline of the whole were laid down, and afterwards filled in, just as variations may be considered as filling out or giving greater detail or finish to a more simple air. The chords are in a way the abstract or general form of the piece: they certainly cannot be said to be the general notion or idea of the piece; still they may be taken as symbolising it. Now in one view the chords are simpler, less important than the piece, because the details are taken away; to the finished picture they are the sketch or outline, and may be filled up too in various ways. Herein the distinction is apparent. If we conceive the general form as emptier, then it may be filled up in different ways indifferently; but then that is because it is conceived inadequately. To conceive it adequately is to conceive it as capable of generating not merely this particular, but also an infinite number of other particulars. Now writing down the chords that underlie a piece of music is a more or less mechanical process. But to attain to the conception of the true form underlying a piece of music is to see it identical with an infinity of other pieces, and to know the general form as something of infinitely greater dignity and fulness than the particular piece. But, again, to know adequately the particular piece is also to know the general form in it. Then the general form appears in an individual shape, in which the other individual shapes are latent but effective; as when a solo occurs in an orchestra and the other instruments produce as much effect by being missed as when actually sounding. It certainly seems paradoxical to say that a simple succession of chords, such as a hymn-tune, has not less fulness and complexity than a long and complicated piece. But if development can take place towards without—that is, in the apparently complicated structure—so it must also take place towards within—that is, in the meaning, the expression of the single notes.[1] No doubt the progress in both directions is correlative. To contrive a large structure of musical notes is also to see more meaning

[1] Thus in beginning algebra the first result of putting letters for numbers seems merely the substitution of vagueness for precision; and not until later is perceived the increase of power that comes from using and comprehending the general values.

in the single elements; and if the outwardly more complicated form be chosen, this may be merely from the necessity of building, so to speak, from the ground, the general level of appreciation of the time, however deep the foundation might be laid. For where thoughts are to be communicated, over-simplicity fails equally with over-complexity. Thus in speech a meaning might have to be conveyed in phrases, for which in other circumstances words would have sufficed. And if there is no merit in intricacy, there is also none in simplicity: the value of each is the same; the only question is of means of expression. Though it might be said that outward complexity rather facilitates execution, as lending mechanical aid; but here the gain is apparent rather than real.

There is therefore a notion of progress both extensive and intensive. It aims at knowing more difficult things, but also at knowing easy things better. That is to say, it must be directed towards things past and things remote as well as towards things present and at hand. For to the mind as well as to the eye things appear simple by reason of remoteness. And it is not enough to understand a thing by its elements, which are the most remote parts in it, and most buried in the past. In proportion as anything is better understood there must be corresponding revivification of its elements; as complete command of an instrument may be shown in touching a single note.

It therefore follows that the explanation which starts from a simple beginning ought not to be regarded as mere development from a fixed base. Every enlargement of the system is attended by corresponding intensification of the germ from which the system springs; and if the first or parent notion be called most abstract, then the notions developed out of it may be said to form its better understanding. Hence comes Hauptmann's caution against supposing that the first notion or the first law can be from the beginning understood and then the later notions deduced from it. If the first notions were adequately understood then the rest would be self-evident; as it is said that the propositions of Euclid were self-evident to Newton. But in the process of learning the conclusions react upon the premises; and the growth of the argument makes it strike deeper root continually.

What has here been said principally with reference to notions whose connexion is demonstrated, will partly apply also to notions in which a connexion is merely shown by way of analogy. For instance, when Hauptmann finds in space an analogy to time and then speaks of the 'time of space,' he does not mean that time is a mode of space, nor any actual time in space, but only that there is something in space (a mode or property of space) that is to space what time is to the universe, that contains real space and time. The 'time of space' is a property of space; actual time is not so. So 'space of time' is not space, but a particular kind or mode of time. Though, on the other hand, if by time we mean the real notion, the idea of time, it might be said that 'time of space' is the real notion, the idea of time, appearing in space, just as 'time' is the real notion appearing in the phenomenal world or universe, and that in this sense the two are identical. An easier instance is found in considering the bass part of a piece of music. It is a doctrine of Hauptmann's that the bass part is earlier than the parts that lie above, that it exists before them and must be supposed that they may exist. On the other hand thorough bass is primarily regarded as the art of making a bass or accompaniment to a given air, and in this way the bass comes last into existence; also historically the air is prior to the bass, which involves harmony. Hauptmann's meaning, however, is seen when we recognise that the earlier forms of music, the choral and the simple arpeggio often repeated, have later found their proper place in the bass part. Of these early forms the meaning belongs rather to the past than to the present; now they are hardly to be recognised as 'tunes;' and in a piece of music they gravitate to that part of it which is representative of or symbolises past time. Here, therefore, that which in development is latest, in the completed notion symbolises the earliest. So in poetry Night is said to follow Day, and yet Night is representative of the ancient time, the survivals or superstitions of which are often found placed in it. Not that the bass part in its simplicity is equivalent to the ancient music; compared to that it is as a fossil to the living animal. For modern music accomplishes by means of a multiplicity of parts and many adjuncts no more than ancient music accomplished. And the bass no longer lives as a separate thing; the life having partly gone out of it, it now forms the standard, the skeleton for the rest. Thus in the bass we have, not ancient music, but only so much of it (that is, of the spirit of it) as agrees with the parts of music that are more peculiarly modern. There is an analogy in history; for past manners and customs survive as a basis, retaining only so much of their former meaning and reasons as agrees with the present time. And earth itself, which serves as the general foundation, is also made out of the perished forms of things past.

In estimating the value of Hauptmann's own explanation

something may be said of the arithmetical theorics which he regarded as unsatisfactory.

The system of music is wonderfully symmetrical. Yet its development has never been ruled by considerations of outward symmetry, but only by the feeling or intuition of what is right in music. Sound having been made the vehicle of expressing ideas, a symmetrical construction has resulted: symmetry has unconsciously been attained. Now, it was very early observed that the notes of the common chord stood somehow connected with simple numbers. It was therefore natural to suppose that the symmetry of numbers and the symmetry of music stood also in some close connexion, so that numbers might be traced in music and music in numbers. The arithmetical explanations were therefore attempts at showing likeness between systems that had developed independently. It was assumed that music depended somehow upon numbers; it was left out of sight that the likeness might be due to some common law of growth. The central fact was taken, that the notes of the common chord correspond with the numbers 3, 4, 5; whence it was sought to show analogy between all notes and all numbers. Here was what Bacon calls an 'anticipation of thought,' a hasty induction springing from an insufficient basis. It is not enough to say that the numbers 3, 4, 5 do in fact 'correspond with' the notes of the chord; the fact should have been shown rooted in some higher notion. The ratios 3 : 4 : 5 have meaning in numbers; so have the notes *C—e—G* in music; to show correspondence between 3 : 4 : 5 and *C—e—G* without showing identity of meaning is as if the same combination of letters without regard to the sense were shown to exist in different languages in order to found a theory of the derivation of one from the other.

Now in Hauptmann's work the whole development is traced inside music. Though illustrations and analogies are made use of, yet nothing is founded on them. The system is as self-supporting as, e.g., that of geometry; it is a simple unfolding of the musical notion. But the principle of development is not peculiar to music; it is the same everywhere. If, then, numbers combine, following the same laws as notes, analogies necessarily arise. For the course of development is logic operating upon the initial unit, the 0 from which the science in question springs. Thus the explanation of music goes back to the time when there was no music, only sound. Sound is the element in which the universe of music is generated. And numbers combining also into a universe by the same law, there will be a likeness of correspondence between the two, but not likeness of identity; because, though the two universes are the same, yet they subsist in different elements. As in arithmetic 3=3 in the abstract, but in the concrete 3 and 3 may be of different denominations.

Hence it is that numbers and symbols generally may be taken to represent musical sounds. For while a single note may be represented arbitrarily by any mark whatever, more perfect symbolisation requires that there shall be a system of symbols connected by a principle of generation to represent a system of notes also connected by a principle of generation. The systems correspond as wholes, and also in their single parts, and there is life in the symbols not less than in the things symbolised. Parallel with the history of the development of music we may expect to find a history of the development of its written characters, both of independent growth, yet representing one the other.

Now as music stands to its written characters, so it will also stand to other arts and sciences. Every notion that arises in music will have its analogies in other sciences, and then the question arises of interpretation: how far it will be possible to pass from one to another, e.g. from algebra to music, applying a knowledge of the general structure of any one science to interpret the general structure of another, as if in a kind of comparative anatomy of sciences. With the view of music as a pure science it is evident that music no more needs to be explained by mathematics than geometry does. Nevertheless results have followed the application of geometry to physics, and of algebra to geometry; and mathematical analysis applied to music, and not merely to its physical basis, might be equally fruitful. But the ultimate end is unity, and unity may be reached in two ways, either by finding that any one science, e.g. mathematics, includes all others under it, or else that the ultimate highest notions of any one science are the same in all. Now the knowledge of any particular branch of music deeply entered upon leads to that general knowledge of music in which all the branches converge and coincide. And so it might be supposed that the general knowledge of music followed as a pure science might ultimately lead to a point whence it should be seen to be identical with the general notion of science. And, indeed, Hauptmann's work is directed towards no less than this; provided that what in the book is explanation can be translated into actual experience.

W. E. H.

AUTHOR'S INTRODUCTION.

IT WAS ALWAYS THE CUSTOM to begin text-books of Thorough Bass and Composition with an acoustical chapter. In it the relations of the intervals are set out in known manner by the number of the vibrations or length of the strings: the ratio of the Octave as 1 : 2; of the Fifth, 2 : 3; of the Fourth, 3 : 4; of the major Third, 4 : 5; of the minor Third, 5 : 6; of the major Second, 8 : 9 and 9 : 10; of the minor Second, 15 : 16.

In the ratio of the vibrations the larger number belongs to the higher note of the interval; in the ratio of the lengths of strings the higher note is denoted by the smaller number.

Most theorists then find in the numbers 1, 3, and 5, in their doubles, powers and reciprocal products, the determination of all harmonic relations of notes.

Some seek it in the progressive arithmetical series from 1 to 16, and place the notes under the members of the series, thus:

1	2	3	4	5	6	7	8	9	10	11	12	13	14	15	16...
c	c	g	c	e	g	b♭	c	d	e	f	g	a	b♭	b	c

The notes set against the numbers 7, 11, 13, and 14 certainly do not correspond to the true intonation; *b♭* appears too flat, *f* too sharp, *a* too flat again.

This necessitates modification of the degrees in question; they must be raised and lowered, whereby occasion is taken for speaking of the difference between a natural system of notes and an artificial one, as of the difference between a savage condition and a civilised.

Many authors have believed that they must continue further the above series and assign to the new numbers which enter, and are not already designated from the series 1–16, the chromatic notes intermediate to the diatonic. Then in the former series they allot to the number 11 the note *f*♯ instead of *f*, so as to be able to claim the latter for the number 21, and *f*♯ for the number 22:

16	17	18	19	20	21	22	23	24	25...
c	c♯	d	d♯	e	f	f♯	g♭	g	g♯

Excepting the note *g*♯, which in this series is determined by the number 25, not one of the determinations here corresponds to the true ratio of these chromatic degrees.

Of the theory which seeks to trace the reason of all harmony in the so-called partial tones heard at the same time, we have only to remark that even if, when a note is struck as Root, its twelfth and the tenth of its Octave are the notes which make themselves heard most distinctly as sounding with it, still the other notes of the series—the series, namely, as continued *ad inf.*—are just as much to be called partial tones, and must be included in the notion of the notes heard at the same time. Indeed the degrees determined by the numbers 7 and 9 can often be heard sounding quite clearly.

Besides, even if the consonance of the notes corresponding to the first four numbers is alone considered, as being that which is most distinctly heard, still this yields only the harmony of the major triad. The minor triad can indeed be discovered in the continued series; it occurs first in the combination of the numbers 10, 12, and 15, as *e*, *g*, *b*. Since, however, it here does not proceed directly from the unity first assumed as Root, and also would compel the omission of the intermediate numbers 11, 13, and 14, it has been believed according to this system that there is less justification for regarding the minor triad as a natural product and of equal rank with the major triad, and the minor triad has been called 'artificial' in contrast to the 'natural' major triad.

If, then, we may disregard this partial-tone theory, so also does the theory previously represented, according to which it is thought that the key to harmony is found in the continued arithmetical series, reveal even in this first assumption decided untruth and disagreement with the structure of what is musically natural.

Better capable of being maintained is the view that all our harmonic determinations are produced from the numbers 1, 3, and 5, their doubles, powers, and reciprocal products. This assumption contains nothing that contradicts reality, but has in no way led to a further explanation of harmony.

In the numerical series resulting from these conditions:

1	2	3	4	5	6	8	9	10	12	15	16	18	20	24	25···
c	c	g	c	e	g	c	d	e	g	b	c	d	e	g	g♯

the inharmonic notes of the arithmetical series are certainly excluded. But it produces those harmonic notes only which lie on the upper, dominant side; the Fifth below can never appear in it. Further, it does not at all afford any rigidly definite determination of the triad, nor yet has any striking distinction been pointed out for consonant and dissonant intervals. For if such distinction is to be grounded merely upon the more or less 'simplicity' or 'comprehensibility' of the relations of sound, as has so often been said and repeated, it needs only the smallest perception to discover that the difference between consonance and dissonance is not one merely of degree. We hear the notes of the ratios 2 : 3, 4 : 5, 5 : 6, as consonant intervals, as agreement of the several pairs of sounds; but the notes of the ratios 8 : 9, 9 : 10, 15 : 16, as intervals decidedly **not** consonant, **not** in agreement, which cannot persist in sounding together, as the first-named intervals can. Thus the question cannot be only of **more** or **less** comprehensibility, of a no more than **quantitative** distinction between the ratios of these intervals; a **qualitative** distinction must be traced.

Now where these first determinations are yet to seek, we certainly cannot expect a theoretical establishment of harmony in the wider sense, an establishment of the laws governing the connexion and succession of chords, from such data only as the acoustic ratios.

And so we see that the introductory chapter on acoustics in the text-books is always entirely left behind in the subsequent doctrine of chords or harmony. That chapter is prefixed as a beginning to the book; its contents, however, can in no way count as an introduction to the doctrine, as a principle from which the subsequent matter is developed in a natural course. Neither the truth nor the falsehood of the acoustical presuppositions has any further influence upon the doctrine itself; although in view of the untruth and half-truth of these presuppositions this can only redound to the advantage of the doctrine.

It will always, however, be an indefensible position, that a doctrine of this kind has two beginnings: one left behind, given up, and one carried on.

To take up the neglected beginning and present it in a sense such that it may be a real beginning, leading up to where the practical teaching of harmony and composition begins, and that as a real beginning effective in every further formation it may therein be, and be seen to be, but a development or further ramification of itself—this is the aim of the present attempt.

The contents of this book do not run counter essentially to any practical method of composition, so far as its teaching is right. But still less should they run counter to that, which to sound human perception seems musically sound and natural; which, if not always and everywhere in the rules of the text-books, we at least meet with always and everywhere in sound compositions.

All that has already been theoretically demonstrated and experimentally verified of the physical doctrine of sound and intervals will here be assumed as known. We shall also assume acquaintance with the general field of practical music, as a whole and in its particular parts: practical knowledge of harmony and metre in all elements of their outward manifestation, as also knowledge of the usual technical terms for all the objects entering upon these fields. For our intention is not to instruct in these things upon the lines of their outward occurrence or their use in art, or with a view to these. For this purpose there is no lack of more or less good and thorough works of every sort and kind. Rather it is our intention to seek a natural establishment of the laws governing harmony and metre, the principle from which the manifold expansions in all directions issue determined from within, and developing are shaped into the phenomena known to us and again addressing us inwardly.

This shaping principle must in every element of its operation always be, and remain, the same in itself. In the broadest relations of the expanded musical work, so far as it is one whole, as in the narrowest particular, the smallest member of it, in all elements of its harmonic-melodic, as also of its metrical-rhythmical existence, there will always be only the **one** law to be traced for its right and intelligible construction. Again, this law cannot be exclusively musical, but it is rather the wholly universal law of construction, which operates everywhere, in that operation of it which attains to musical, i.e. harmonic-melodic, metrical-rhythmical, manifestation.

Music is universally intelligible in its expression. It is not for the musician only; it is for the common perception of mankind. Moreover music is not of radically different quality in popular tunes and in fugues of Bach, or symphonies of Beethoven. The contents of the complicated work of art may make it difficult to be understood, but the means of expression are always the same, and singly are intelligible universally. Through them the greatest, as well as the smallest, piece of music speaks to us, is imparted to us, in a language whose words and grammar we are not first obliged to learn. The triad is consonant for the uneducated as well as for the educated; the dissonance needs to be resolved for the unskilled as well as for the musician; discordance is for every ear something meaningless.

In no other kind of perception are the first elements of expression given and apprehended with such mathematical determinateness as in the acoustical. A practised eye is needed to judge the correctness of optical determinations and relations; of the acoustical, every sound ear is an unerring judge. To pronounce upon the purity of musical intervals requires no technical skill; the feeling for it is born in us, is given in the nature of humanly reasonable existence.

That which is musically inadmissible is not so because it is against a rule determined by musicians, but because it is against a natural law given to musicians from mankind, because it is logically untrue and of inward contradiction. A musical fault is a logical fault, a fault for the general sense of mankind, and not for a musical sense in particular. The rules of musical phrase carried back to their essential meaning are only the rules for what is in general commonly intelligible, and in this meaning may be comprehended by everyone, since they appeal in him only to that which is known to all.

The notion of an artificial system of notes is a thoroughly worthless one. Musicians were not able to determine intervals and invent a system of notes, any more than grammarians to invent the words of the language in which they speak, and the constructions they use in explaining constructions. They speak with the language, which the general sense of mankind makes. Now as speech does not consist in placing words together, but in setting them asunder, which in the thought are one, so also musical expression, which in succession and simultaneous sound is set asunder in notes, is only one in the contents of the musical thought which is to be uttered: its single elements are only members of an organic unity. Of conventional determinations for chords, for the arrangement of a key or scale, of arbitrary alterations, raisings and lowerings of the naturally given degrees, although such phrases are often employed by otherwise intelligent people, there can be no mention when we proceed rationally.

That which does not rest upon determination universal and everywhere valid, cannot be everywhere and universally understood.

That which is musically right, correct, addresses us as being humanly intelligible.

That which is faulty does not address us as the expression for something faulty, but it addresses us in fact not at all; it finds no sympathetic resonance in our interior. We cannot understand it, for it has no intelligible sense. If incorrectness could be the expression for what is faulty, for what is bad or ugly, then it would not have to be excluded from the means of æsthetic representation. But a painter would never think of carrying out an artistic conception by intentional wrong drawing, no more can a musician apply what is incorrect to the purpose of delineating characteristically; as the story is told of a composer, who thought that the words, 'There is none among us that doeth good,' were nicely expressed by a row of parallel Fifths. Here it is only the composer who does not do good; every Fifth by itself does quite what it ought.

Rightness or correctness of phrase is the condition under which generally a sense can be uttered.

This rightness, i.e. reasonableness of the shape taken by music, has for its law of formation Unity, with the opposite of itself and the removal of the opposite:—immediate unity, which through a moment of being at two with itself passes into mediated unity. There must always be the repetition of this process on that which is assumed as immediate unity or given as the result of a previous process. Thus the unity of sound correlated with itself gives rise to the triad, and the unity of the triad correlated with itself to the key. But sound itself is also already such a unity, that has gone out of and been correlated with itself; as all that is real always contains, or is, being within itself and being outside itself as one.

To try to set the full notion of this shaping process at once in a clear light would be labour in vain. But in the course of the following investigations it will, we dare to hope, be made out in its working more and more clearly, and be established as the ruling principle, as the essence of every intelligible formation, and at the same time as the right understanding of the same.

At the beginning the reader may perhaps wish and expect that things, which at first are simply enunciated, should be dwelt upon more minutely, and proofs brought to support them; as, e.g., when it is said 'there are three intervals: Octave, Fifth, and Third,' or when it is said of these intervals that 'they are unchangeable' —without further justification or explanation, why only three intervals are named, and why just these three, and why they are called unchangeable; for we know of more intervals, and of many changes in them. So too the meaning involved in the acoustical ratios of these intervals is at first only just stated as shortly as possible; and a minuter explanation at the first entrance of this subject might be all the more desired, as this way of thinking is, in the theory of music, not one already known, and may seem difficult on first being approached.

But further progress, with the expansion of the material, never ceases bringing up occasion of returning back upon these first determinations, and of explaining them by tracing them in their effects. Besides, the sense, which is hardest to grasp in the greater simplicity of the phenomenon, of its own accord lays itself open to easier understanding in the subsequent unfolding of the principle at first tightly packed in the germ.

We cannot deduce the law of a progression from one single member, but only from the succession of members. If we know the progression, then the single member may be known to us also as having come into existence in the series, and carrying in itself the conditions of its coming to be. So is it also with this law of ours, which rules in music. It is depicted for clear recognition only in the series of the functions, in which it attains to reality. Afterwards, the single element of its working, seen in the series of effects, from which the whole arises, will also become of easier comprehension.

For the first step it will only be requisite to acquire an inward conception of the notion of the formative process in its wholeness, in the unity of its three elements, with which we become acquainted in their first utterance as the intervals of the **Octave**, **Fifth**, and **Third**. This notion is and remains everywhere the same, in every formation and transformation. It is the notion, that something, which at first subsists for intuition in immediate totality (Octave), parts from itself into its own opposite (Fifth), and that then this opposite is in its turn abolished, to let the whole be produced again as one with its opposite (Third), as a whole correlated in itself.

Going into the universal sense of this notion, we shall soon be obliged to grant, that it no less than comprehends in itself the elements altogether of all knowing, and that anything further for knowledge is not conceivable;—just as simultaneous sound admits no consonance beyond the intervals of the Octave, Fifth, and Third, which further consideration may show us to be related to the notions of feeling, understanding, and 'felt understanding,' i.e. as **feeling, intellect,** and **reason.**

It may be well to say a word beforehand in justification of the way of representing notes by letters, which has been adopted here as serviceable. For at first sight it certainly seems as if the usual notation, which recalls our knowledge of music, and which we are accustomed to read as the equivalent sound, must convey more. Nevertheless it is useless for our purpose.

Written notes distinguish the degrees said to be enharmonically different, e.g. *c* and *b*♯, but they do not distinguish degrees different in the well-known ratio 80 : 81. They make no difference in the symbol for the Third of a Root and for its fourth Fifth, e.g. for *e* as the Third of *C*, and *E* in the series of Fifths *C—G—D—A—E*.

How essential this distinction is, and important to the notion of the system of harmony, and how necessary it is also in the notation, will be made clear by the contents of the following book.

There a Third-note is denoted by a small letter, a Root- or Fifth-note by a capital; e.g. the major triad of *C* in the first position is *C—e—G*; its second position is *e—G—C*; its third position is *G—C—e*.

It will want only a little practice for the distinction brought out by this notation between Third-notes and Fifth-notes to be perceived, both by the eye and also intuitively, in the meaning it has for harmony.

That which is contained as **harmonic** determination in the three intervals of Octave, Fifth, and Third and their mutual relations, **that,** in its abstract meaning, we see taking shape in **metrical** determination as two-, three-, and four-membered time-unity.

So too the opposition in the musical notion of major and minor, upon which we cannot now enter further even by way of allusion, is repeated in metrical determination as metre which begins with the arsis and metre which begins with the thesis, and as trochaic rhythm and iambic rhythm ; for the three elements of determination must reappear in every manner, rhythmically as well as metrically.

The metrical-rhythmical shaping process will then have to be combined with the harmonic-melodic. In this a determination of the one does not necessarily call for the corresponding determination of the other ; for the same succession of harmony can assume very different metrical shape, and the same metrical arrangement can be embodied in harmony very differently. Only in the element of dissonance a closer relation enters between the metrical determination and the harmonic.

Now the diversity of shape must be infinite, first in each sphere by itself, the harmonic as well as the metrical, and next in the combination of the two spheres. Therefore it must not be expected that a theoretical explanation is about to be given of every possible particular phenomenon. But when the general notion has laid open the course, upon the whole, of the train of construction, then it will be easy to obtain by it a solution for every single case in its particular occurrence. Our aim is principally explanation showing the general in the particular, and the part only in relation to its whole. And our examination of the particular can go no further than is requisite for the explanation of the general in it, but leaves it, when the determination for its kind has been found, to special and practical treatment of a different scope, which we are not now to engage in.

So too a last ending of the doctrine in itself is not possible. Its end is the notion, gathered up, of the whole ; in which the notion lies extended, while it is also contained concentrated in every single part of it. However far the doctrine is continued, however far off its end is put, it always remains unending. Of its nature it must remain so, if it is to unfold and show organic working and weaving in living growth.

As organic doctrine has no end, so also it has no determinate beginning. Both are to be looked for everywhere, and to be found nowhere; for what is outwardly most outward, or inwardly most inward, is in itself only one and the same thing. Thus a theory of the objects in the field of music, such as begins here with examining the phenomenon of sound, might just as well start from a metrical manifestation of the notion, or from the last rhythmical, the trochaic dactyl, so as in progression to arrive last at that which is here treated first, the phenomenon of sound. In the organic notion every beginning is also an end, and just for this reason the notion is finite-infinite, because in it every end is also a beginning: the germ is only contained in the fruit, and the fruit can only have come from the germ. So metre teaches us, that the close falls always upon a metrical first element, that the end must always be a beginning again.

We must distinguish this manner of theoretical contemplation from the theory which bears immediately upon practice: the theory of harmonic and metrical shape in itself from the theory of the art of composition.

For the active business of art, theoretical knowledge and understanding of the inner finite-infinite unity, or of the substantial essence of the phenomenon with its intellectually distinguished elements, are not a necessary requirement; as science in general is not necessary to art and its flourishing.

Consciousness of theory in the act of poetical production, which is rooted in feeling, and creates and forms in inward delight, is not even conceivable.

Not abstract theory alone, but also theory of art is excluded from consciousness in that act.

A work of art both in music and painting is called a 'composition.' The artist composes, puts together, notes or colours. After an inward image he composes an outward one to agree with it, which is able by its effect to call up the original again in our interior. The choice of notes and colours is guided and determined by the inward image, that the total effect may correspond to it as closely as possible. The artist may not be asked to account for the nature of his means of representing, or of the inward image itself; but if this is felt as a harmonious whole, then only by tones of sound or colour harmoniously joined can it be represented outwardly and communicated to us through the senses. To the inward thing thought only an outward thing thought can correspond, and for this the individual must be compacted and bound up into a whole, just as it would have been produced from that whole. Only as having come from unity can anything again become unity, and only as unity can anything speak to us as feeling and thought.

A person ignorant of music is able, though the keyboard is strange to him, to pick out on it the notes of a chord or melody, whichever he has in his mind, without in the least knowing the meaning of the notes in harmony. A musician knows notes and chords, understands their meaning in harmony, knows rules for harmony and melody, metre and rhythm, for musical form in every sense, but it is nothing of all this that guides him in poetical production, and makes him find the right expression for his thought. With him, just as with the ignorant person picking out his chord or his melody upon the notes of the piano, it is the desire of making the outward representation in agreement with something felt inwardly, so as to be the very thing itself.

Knowledge of art-theory may help technical acquirement, and generally endow the artist with that thorough education which renders him a master; in actual production it has no immediate share. At least the artist will not turn to Knowledge, until immediate Power leaves him, until the right will no longer come to him unsought, and he is obliged to seek clearness as to his own unclearness.

Those are not the happiest moments of producing, nor yield the happiest results; they take their turn however, driving the uninstructed to despair of success, the instructed to reflection and conscious contrivance of his end.

Here too technical knowledge stands nearer to practice, bears more immediately upon it, than general knowledge or knowledge of the general: the rule is consulted sooner than the law. Yet knowledge of the law is as able to lend clearness and certainty to technical knowledge, as that to help actual practice.

It is hoped that to scientific knowledge in the field of music the present treatise may be an incitement and a beginning.

I.

HARMONY

SOUND.

1. WHERE **sound** is to be produced, there is required (1) an elastic, stretched, uniform material, (2) and trembling or vibrating movement thereof. The parts of the body moved are then alternately in and out of their state of uniform cohesion. The instant of **transition** into this state of equality or inner **unity** is that, which by the sense of hearing is perceived as **sound.** It is the **coming to be** of the **being** which subsists absolutely during rest, and which is alternately abolished and restored in the elastic movement.

2. Not **being in self**, or dead persistence in rest, nor yet **being out of self** in the motion, is sounding; but **coming to self.**

3. Sound is only an element of transition from arising to passing away of the state of unity. Quickly succeeding repetitions of this element make the sound appear continuous.

4. We distinguish high and low sounds, and it is known, that the difference of height and depth stands in relation with the quickness of the vibrations. But greater quickness, or a greater number of vibrations following in a given time, cannot be the true cause of greater height in the sound, if, as stated above, the sound is contained in one element of a single vibration, and only repeated in the succeeding ones. For repetition more or less quickly of the same thing does not change it.

5. Determinate pitch of sound is rather the manifestation of a determinate degree of **tension** present in the elastic material. And we can regard the tension as **an effect of force fixed in a resistance,**

which is expressed in sounding as **greater**, in relation to the resistance, in the **higher** sound, and **less** in the **deeper**.

6. The same force in a quantitatively different resistance, or quantitatively different force in the same resistance, will equally produce difference of pitch. For pitch expresses only the relation of the two conditions combined: of the **force** as **active**, and the resistance or **mass** as **passive**. Thus the sound of a stretched string is raised either by shortening the string or by increasing the weight which stretches it. And since these conditions are quantitative, this can be done in determinable degrees and proportions.

7. Sound exists as a phenomenon through a material means; to its production there is requisite a body specially conditioned, and elastic vibratory movement of that body. But sound in its essence is not contained in the material as an utterance of qualitative attribute. What we perceive as the phenomenon of sound is only the coming into being of the abstract inner form of unity in the material, of equality recovering in the elastic movement from inequality. So too the determination of pitch is not contained in quantities of force or mass determined in themselves, but only in the abstract relation in which these factors stand to one another.

8. For the relations of sound and their harmonic meaning the particular way in which the different degrees of pitch are reached, makes no difference. It may be done by increasing the force or by diminishing the mass: either by stretching a string with a heavier weight, or by shortening the string stretched with the same weight. It is known that for double tension of a string there is wanted, not double weight, but quadruple, sc. in the duplicate ratio, and for triple tension nine times the weight; but the half of the string, in which, as in every single part, the whole of the stretching force is effective, contains in proportion twice as great tension as the whole does, and the third part thrice as great, which is ex-

pressed in the sound.[1] Consequently the quantitative determinations of sound are most simply considered in differences of quantity of sounding material at a constant tension. For to obtain them expressed in differences of the stretching force, we must use magnitudes which are squares and roots.

But it will soon appear, that the harmonic determinations of sound do not at all consist of complicated numerical relations, and that even the few numbers required impart definite musical character to the corresponding sounds in virtue, not so much of their numerical, as of a more general signification.

9. A sound of definite pitch we shall call a **note**, and relations of notes **intervals**.

MAJOR TRIAD.

10. There are **three** intervals directly intelligible:

I. **Octave.**

II. **Fifth.**

III. **Third** (major).

They are unchangeable.

I. The **Octave**: the interval in which the **half** of a sounding quantity makes itself heard against the **whole** of the Root, or fundamental note, is, in acoustic determination, the expression for the notion of **identity, unity** and **equality with self. The half determines an equal to itself** as other half.

II. The **Fifth**: the interval in which a sounding quantity of **two-thirds** is heard against the Root as **whole**, contains acoustically the determination that **something** is **divided within itself**, and thereby

[1] The tension is measured by the energy of the stretched string; in the half or third part of the divided string the tension, or energy, per unit of length remains constant.—TRANS.

the notion of **duality** and inner **opposition.** As the half places outside itself an equal to itself, so the quantity of two third-parts, heard with the whole, determines the third third-part; a quantity to which that actually given appears a thing **doubled,** or **in opposition with itself.**

III. The **Third**: the interval in which a sounding quantity of **four-fifths** is heard with the **whole** of the root. Here the quantity determined is the fifth fifth-part, of which that given is the **quadruple,** that is, **twice the double.** In the quantitative determination of **twice two,** since the double is here taken together as unity in the multiplicand, and at the same time held apart as duality in the multiplier, is contained the notion of identification of opposites: of **duality as unity.**

11. The **Octave** is the expression for **unity**; the **Fifth** expresses **duality** or **separation**; the **Third, unity of duality** or **union. The Third is the union of Octave and Fifth.**

Before union separation must exist, and before separation unity The Third fills out the emptiness of the Fifth, for it contains the separated duality of that interval bound up into unity.

12. With the three intervals here named the **major triad** is known to be given. But if the determinations of Fifth and Third take place upon a **Root,** then the **Octave** is no longer of essential importance; for the Root must in itself answer to the notion of definite unity, if upon it the Fifth, as interval of duality, and the Third, as interval of union, are to be determined. Therefore the conditions of the notion of consonance are completely fulfilled in the combined sound of Root, Fifth and Third.

13. In the notion of the unity of the three elements of the triad there is contained in brief all determination which underlies the understanding, not only of chords as the simultaneous union of notes, but also of melodic progression and succession of chords, and also, as will be shown later, the requirements of laws of metre and

rhythm. Every note of a musical phrase is Octave, Fifth or Third; every chord in union with others, and every rhythmical metrical element, has its intelligible meaning in the notion of the three foregoing determinations. They must, however, be comprehended as being of a nature wholly universal, and not merely as intervals of notes. Rather the determinate character of the latter is itself given by the universal meaning of the triad notion, whose contents here with quantitative determinations in the element of sound attain to sensible intelligible expression as the chord.

14. Of the meaning of **unity** and **opposition** we have to say, that under unity is to be understood **being one with self**, without distinction; under opposition, **being different to self.** The sense of opposition that is to be comprehended here, is, not that something is different to something else, but that it opposes itself as other to itself. The first is only a difference, but not opposition; intellectua opposition can only proceed from identity.

15. We can regard an object in its immediate wholeness, and comprehend the notion of this wholeness; this is the unity of the **Octave.** We can then regard the object distinguishing; e.g. form from contents. Now the intellectual opposition is not at once found in the fact, that the form is distinguished from the contents. But when to the form with its contents we oppose, as other determination, the contents with their form, then the same object appears in the distinction under opposite determinations, or as opposed to itself. This is the duality of the **Fifth.**

But in this opposition reality issuspended; for that is not contained in the separation of the two determinations, but only in their united simultaneous existence. When that which is **opposed to self** in the determination by distinction, is taken **at once** and **in one**, this corresponds to the notion of real being.

For the phenomenon of sound this is expressed in the **Third** which makes heard **the separate united.** In it duality has become unity, not in the sense of immediateness, which the Octave offers, but in the union of the opposites conceivable in it: derived, organic or real unity, such as is felt in the triad, as against the immediate wholeness of the Octave and the separated opposition of the Fifth.

16. That a construction of fundamental intervals going further than that now laid down is impossible, is clear theoretically from the nature of the notion. For all possibility of determination must necessarily be exhausted, when anything has been traced and recognised (I.) in its totality as a whole, (II.) in its separated opposites, (III.) in the union of the opposites into a whole. But it is also confirmed practically; because not only does the triad not allow of more consonant notes being added to it, but also, generally, any note in relation to another can only be understood as meaning one of three intervals of the triad. This will appear later in the construction of the scale.

MAJOR KEY.

17. As soon as the triad in its three elements has been shaped into a membered whole, it has again become **unity**, and passes entire into the meaning of **Octave.** This must then split up anew into its **Fifth**, and in its **Third** be restored again to concrete unity of a higher order.

18. The **Fifth**-notion for the Octave unity of the triad again consists in its splitting up within itself, or coming into opposite determination to itself. This is fulfilled by means of two other triads, that of the **subdominant** and that of the **dominant**, of which the first contains the Root of the given triad as Fifth, while the other contains its Fifth as Root. In this way the triad first assumed comes into opposition or contradiction with itself. For it has become dominant chord itself in the first position, and subdominant in the other, and

thus changed in itself from independent **Octave unity** into meaning **Fifth duality.**

19. The **Third**-notion, uniting, or removing the contradiction, then causes the opposite determinations, in which the triad is parted from itself, to be taken up into it both at once, and the passive '**being** a dominant' to fuse with the active '**having** a dominant;' so that the two unities, which make the triad two, are placed outside it as a duality, of which it is itself the unity: **unity of a triad of triads.**

20. The finished notion of this organic figuration, this triad of higher order, whose Fifth is found in the separation of the subdominant chords, and its uniting Third in the chord of the tonic, as correlated and correlating, determined and determining, we call a **Key.** It contains the elements of triad construction quite in the same sense as the triad itself does; it is only the triad appearing in a higher rank.

21. Not to weary with too abstract conceptions, what has hitherto been said may be made evident in the following way of representing it.

Let the triad with reference to the inner succession of its determinations be denoted by:

I—III—II;

let I—II signify the **Fifth**; III, the **Third**, as union of I—II.

If we denote, now and afterwards, the Root and Fifth by capital letters and the Third by small ones, e.g.

I—III—II
C e G,

then the Octave unity, the original independence, of the chord *C—e—G* is removed in the notion of key, because its Root *C* appears in the chord of the subdominant, *F—a—C*, as Fifth, and its Fifth *G* in the chord of the dominant, *G—b—D*, as Root.

I—III—II I—III—II
F a C e G C e G b D
I—III—II I—III—II

This is the **Fifth**-notion in the key, its splitting into two, which shows outwardly in the disconnected chords of the subdominant and dominant, *F—a—C, G—b—D,* but essentially consists in the contradiction of the double meaning of the unit chord, *C—e—G.*

To take at once, or conjointly, that which in the Fifth-notion is **set asunder**, answers, here as well as in the chord, to the notion of the uniting **Third.** There the Third-meaning does not lie in the separate note, which forms the interval of a Third with the Root, in the note *e* of the triad *C—e—G,* but in the removal in it and through it of the opposition of Root and Fifth. And so here in the key, what we have to think of as answering to the notion of Third is not the uniting triad separately, but the **union** itself.

First the given triad is **unity, Octave** ; then through its two dominant chords it falls apart within itself into opposition, **duality,** and becomes **Fifth** ; lastly it is restored as uniting **Third** element in the correlation of the other two, as higher unity, as unification or **unity of union.**

I
I — III — II
C e G
I —— II
I—III—II I—III—II
F a C e G C e G b D
I—III—II I—III—II
I — III — II
I—III—II I—III—II
F a C e G b D
I — III — II

22. To understand such a scheme rightly, let it be observed once for all, that by the symbol I—II is expressed, not a **first** and **second**, but the **standing apart** of opposite determinations, and by III, not a **third** or **triple**, but the **coming together** of the same. The organic property of a membered whole can never be represented exhaustively, either by symbols and numbers or by words; it can only be spiritually indicated to intellectual feeling, i.e. reason, that meets it halfway, and has the power of reproducing alive the living thought conjured into symbols, numbers, and words. For if in things surpassing utterance we would cleave only to the literal meaning, contradiction and doubt would rise everywhere, but never the living sense. The notion of union in the sense of the Third is an **infinite**. The acoustical '**twice two**' of the interval of the Third contains **duality**, or separation of unity, in its '**twice**' of the multiplier, just as much as it contains **unity**, or union of duality, in its '**two**' of the multiplicand. Were the last, **union**, alone contained, then its other, **separation**, would be wanting; union would still have its opposite outside of itself, and would thus be again only a one-sided determination. This of itself would be against the notion of the Third, which does not **exclude** opposition, but **includes** it. Now because this notion has to unite both union and separation, it can only be fulfilled in endlessly continued passage into contrary and comprehension of all opposites. Thus it must be conceived as an infinite process, and consequently as the notion of eternal becoming, living, or being real. This is **Nature**, who, produced as duality from the prime unity, and busied continually in making her opposites be absorbed into one another, is live being itself and **reality**.

23. The effect of Octave, Fifth and Third is determined for our perception quite as unambiguously as are the quantitative relations from which they proceed. It behoves us therefore to conceive the relations, which are communicated to us sensibly through the medium of sound, in their mental meaning, as we have tried to do

above; but the result of the trial must, in the fundamental meaning of explanation, always be again tested by feeling the effect that these intervals have upon us. For where what is thought contradicts what is felt, there it can only be untrue. If by theoretical explanation the Octave were found as the expression for a manifold, the Fifth as the expression for union, or the Third as the expression for separation, such a theory must at once be decisively refuted by the impressions that these intervals excite in us. But that the Octave should strike our feeling as unity, the Fifth as separation, hollow emptiness, the Third in the Fifth as a satisfying perfect contentment, the very meaning correspondingly found for the ratios, may itself supply another such contenting Third between **felt** and **thought**.

24. In the **chord** the determinations of Fifth and Third are taken upon one and the same unity; therefore there is nothing to prevent its intervals from being **simultaneous.** They are elements of a single existence. But the advance to the **key** begins with the contradiction of this singleness, because the reciprocal relation of Root and Fifth is removed by the dominant chords. Whereby the quiescence of the chord changes to motion, and the simultaneous becomes **successive**; because for simultaneousness it is a contradiction for the Fifth of a Root to be Root of a Fifth; a contradiction for **simultaneousness**, which we learn later to be the essence of dissonance, but which in the opposite of simultaneousness, **succession**, is none, because it is resolved by the Root **becoming** Fifth, or, contrariwise, the Fifth Root. Thus the key can be set out harmonically only in **a succession of chords.**

25. The notion of the triad determines first the intervals to form the chord, and next the chords to form the key. Similarly it may take the **key** as Octave unity, and proceed with it to Fifth- and Third-determination in the same sense as in chord and key construction.

26. The key arose, when the given triad, after coming into opposition with itself by the subdominant and dominant chords, comprehended in itself the opposition as unity, and thereby became tonic.

27. Opposition or Fifth-meaning for the key, which as yet subsists in absolute unity, is found in its taking on one or the other dominant meaning through subdominant and dominant keys; that is, in its becoming, as a **key**, a dominant to its subdominant and subdominant to its dominant.

28. The two opposite determinations attain unity by determining becoming determined; that is, by the middle key passing from the determination of **being** dominant to one key or the other into that of **having** one and the other key as dominants. Taking them together thus again answers to Third unity of the three keys. The middle key is shown as **tonic**, or middle of a system of keys, whereby to its inner determination there is added its outer one of being **principal** between **secondary keys**; just as the chord, when determined in itself, could only by secondary chords reach the determination of being the principal chord in the key.

29. This **triad of keys** has a link, or element of relationship, in the tonic triad of the middle key, which appears in it as tonic chord, in the subdominant key as dominant chord, and in the dominant key as subdominant chord:

I — III — II

B♭ d F a C e G b D f♯ A

I—III—II   I—III—II   I—III—II

I—III—II   I—III—II

30. The linking of chords started in the single key, may be continued in both directions without end. Now each triad, as it occurs in successive order, is necessarily determined as middle to two secondary triads, just as happens in key-union with subdominant and dominant. Thus the keys too appear linked endlessly

to one another. But to a higher unit notion than that of the key itself, it can never come; no more, indeed, than the triad can receive any addition in itself. For the latter contains the complete development of the triad notion **inwards**, and the key contains it **outwards**; the triad as simultaneity at rest, as **chord**, the key as simultaneity in motion, as **chord succession.** Besides, the last formation does not go beyond the notion of the key; it only confirms it, as being one key determined among others. To a determination of keys going further than that of the two dominants there would be wanting the direct reference to the unity originally taken. And things distinguished must necessarily have something in common, if one is to be able to gather them up into a notion, or to pass continuously and intelligibly from one to the other. For the understanding of change, or passage in general, can only be contained in change taking place upon something that **remains**: not in another being other or different to one, but in **one** itself becoming **other.**

MINOR TRIAD.

31. The determinations of the intervals of the triad have been hitherto taken as starting from a positive unity, a Root, to which the Fifth and Third are referred. They may also be thought of in an opposite sense. If the first may be expressed by saying, that a note **has** a Fifth and Third, then the opposite meaning will lie in a note **being** Fifth and Third. **Having** is an active state, **being** a passive one. The unity, to which the two determinations are referred in the second meaning, is passive: in opposition to the **having** of the first idea we find the second, **being had.** The first is expressed in the major triad, the second in the minor.

In the latter the relation of (major) Third holds between the middle and upper notes, and therefore the two intervals of the chord are conjoined, not in the **Root**, but in the note of the **Fifth**. In the major triad *C—e—G*, *C——G* is Fifth, and *C—e* Third; in the minor triad *a—C—e*, *a——e* is Fifth, and *C—e* Third. But in the last the common element for both determinations is contained in the note of the Fifth; therefore that note, being doubly determined, may be negatively considered as doubly determining, or as the negative unity of the chord. Therefore the symbol II—III—I seems not unsuitable for the minor chord.

32. In the natural infinite series of notes, written by the ratios of vibration:

1	2	3	4	5	6	7	8	9	10	11	12	13	14	15	16	17	18 ...
C	C	G	C	e	G	.	C	D	e	.	G	.	.	b	C	.	D ...

we find the major triad first occurring under the numbers 4 : 5 : 6, as *C—e—G*, the minor triad under the numbers 10 : 12 : 15, as *e—G—b*. If the series were carried on further, we should see every member of it that answers to a multiple of 4, bearing the major triad, and every multiple of 5 that is divisible by 2, bearing the minor triad, in the same proportion as the first ones above. E.g. *G—b—D* as 12 : 15 : 18 = 4 : 5 : 6, *b—D—f*♯ as 30 : 36 : 45 = 10 : 12 : 15.

33. The three members of the proportion in the minor triad, 10 : 12 : 15, can be reduced to smaller numbers, if we separate the two ratios 10 : 12 and 12 : 15 from one another; for then they can be expressed singly by 5 : 6 and 4 : 5. These ratios remain the same, if we substitute the expressions $\frac{1}{6} : \frac{1}{5}$ and $\frac{1}{5} : \frac{1}{4}$; for 5 : 6 is as $\frac{1}{6} : \frac{1}{5}$ and 4 : 5 as $\frac{1}{5} : \frac{1}{4}$. But by the last notation the proportion 10 : 12 : 15 has been expressed in smaller numbers $\frac{1}{6} : \frac{1}{5}$

$\frac{1}{5} : \frac{1}{4}$ and

a common middle term found; and the proportion $\frac{1}{6} : \frac{1}{5} : \frac{1}{4}$, or abbreviated $\frac{1}{6:5:4}$, may now be taken for the minor triad. In this expression we get the numbers again, but in contrary order, of the proportion of the major triad, which may be denoted by $\frac{4:5:6}{1}$. Also the two may be expressed as positive and negative powers, for there is

$$\underset{C\quad e\quad G}{4:5:6} = \frac{4:5:6}{1} = \left(4:5:6\right)^{+1}.$$

$$\underset{e\quad G\quad b}{10:12:15} = \frac{1}{4:5:6} = \left(6:5:4\right)^{-1}.$$

34. Thus the essential meaning of the minor triad must come to light, let the expression be of what kind it may, if only it is taken back to its essential contents. And with this we gladly leave symbolisation by numbers, which may indeed afford an interesting play of combinations, but offers no nearer opening towards the nature of things. It does not make the notion easier; rather it can only represent it veiled. For the notion is contained in determinations far simpler and more direct, those general terms of **unity**, its **becoming two**, and the identifying of both as **union**.

35. The minor triad, as an inverted major triad, must, in its meaning of being considered to originate from a negative unity, consist of a construction backwards. Referred to the unity C, the major triad is

I — II
C e G
I—III

The minor triad of the same unity C as negative, that is, as Fifth determining Root and Third, is

II — I
F a♭ C
III—I,

which is the same as if we put

F a♭ C
I — II
I–III.

In the major triad the unity is the positive which **determines**; in the minor triad it is the positive which **is determined.**

36. The minor triad thus being of passive nature, and having its starting-point above (not its most real starting-point, yet that which is determined as unity), and forming from it downwards, there is expressed in it, not upward driving **force**, but downward drawing **weight, dependence** in the literal, as well as in the figurative sense of the word. We therefore find in the minor chord the expression for **mourning**, the hanging boughs of the weeping willow as contrasted with the aspiring arbor vitæ.

MINOR KEY.

37. The system of the major key contains the minor triad in a secondary meaning, that is to say, in the middle of each pair of major triads: (1) of the subdominant chord and the chord of the tonic, (2) of the chord of the tonic and the dominant chord.

The simultaneous existence of two triads with a note in common of itself makes a contradiction; because then opposite meanings in two directions are attributed to the note **at once**, which it can only receive **successively.**

I—III—II I—III—II
F a C e G b D
I—III—II

But the contradiction, which would lie here in *C* or *G*, is called forth only by the extremities of the two chord dualities, in *C* by *F*——*G*, and in *G* by *C*——*D*; it is not contained in their middles, *a*—*C*—*e* and *e*—*G*—*b*, because *a*——*e* and *e*——*b* as Fifth-determinations, and *C*—*e* and *G*—*b* as Third-determinations, find their unity in *e* and *b*, passive it is true, but not self-contradictory.

38. Thus there is a motive for linking the minor triads together in just the same way as we found for the major triads:

...d F a C e G b...
II—III—I
II—III—I II—III—I

But if we tried to gather up a triad of minor triads into chord union, there would still be nothing at all answering to the notion of a minor key. Such a series of minor chords would always seem a mere result of the series of major chords. It can never come to have independent value, because there the positive unity for the minor chord is wanting. The minor key, like the major, can only make its determination of effect in issuing from the positive triad notion. Therefore the minor chord, as a denial of the major, must begin by really premising the thing itself, of which it is a negation; for a thing, to be real, cannot issue from negation without positive premise. The element of negation may, however, be taken as **principal determination**; that is here as **tonic, middle** of a key system, whose dominant will then be a **major** chord, the premised positive, and its subdominant a **minor** chord. For in the negative generation, where the triad determination originates in the **Fifth**, the minor chord is the beginning of a series of **minor** triads continued without limit towards the subdominant side; just as the positive, where the triad determination issues from the root, is continued towards the dominant side in an infinite **major** series.

39. In

I—III—II
G b D

there is given the **positive** triad notion for the unity *G*; in

II—III—I
C e♭ G

the **negative** triad notion for the same unity *G*.

In

I—III—II
C e♭ G b D
II—III—I

both determinations are contained joined; and in

II—III—I I—III—II
F a♭ C e♭ G b D
II—III—I

the second determination, the negative of the first positive one, is placed as **tonic**, or principal element of a key, whose contents accordingly are the minor triad of C, with the minor triad of F for its subdominant chord, and the major triad of G for its dominant chord. In this formation we recognise the key of C minor in its natural and self-determining conditions.

40. Here the process of the formation is shown unfolded in time; but, like that of the major key, it is only the concrete expression of a fixed thought. In the system of the major key the thought is, that I changes into II; in the system of the minor key, that +I changes into −I. Both originate from the positive unity; but there the notion of the change is that positive one becomes positive other; here it is that positive one becomes negative one. The former contains the opposition of being and becoming, the latter the opposition of being and not being. The former is life

carried onwards in another, the latter is solitude and narrowing down to self.

41. The major key will pass into other keys. The minor key is isolated, without the power of passage into others. With the major notion a system of keys could be marked out, containing a principal key, as middle, with its secondary keys; and afterwards each secondary key could in turn appear as principal with secondary keys, without contradicting the conditions belonging to the first as a key. But the notion of separation, out of which the minor key proceeds, is in principle against the notion of unity belonging to the major system. Secondary minor keys would make the fundamental conditions upon which the principal minor key rests, to be no longer of effect, and thus would abolish the principal key itself.

				II—III—I			I—III—II				
Key of C minor:				F	a♭	C	e♭	G	b	D	
						II—III—I					

	II—III—I			I—III—II			
Key of F minor:	B♭	d♭	F	a♭	C	e	G
			II—III—I				

	II—III—I			I—III—II			
Key of G minor:	C	e♭	G	b♭	D	f♯	A
			II—III—I				

The key of F minor, as subdominant of the given key of C minor, contradicts by its dominant chord, *C—e—G*, that which is here taken as the principal thing, the negation, *C—e♭—G*, of the positive unity, *G—b—D*; the key of G minor, as dominant of the given key, contradicts by *G—b♭—D* the positive unity itself.

42. The series of chords belonging to the notion of the major key continues in like form without limit, as a chain of major triads;

the series belonging to the notion of the minor key starts from an element of contradiction, and forms a chain of major triads in one direction, and a chain of minor triads in the other.

A. *Series for the Major Key.*

II I-III-II I-III-II I-III-II I-III-II I

I-III-II I-III-II I-III-II I-III-II I-III-II

...A♭ c E♭ g B♭ d F a C e G b D f♯ A c♯ E g♯ B...

B. *Series for the Minor Key.*

I-III-II I-III-II

I-III-II I-III-II I

...A♭ c♭ E♭ g♭ B♭ d♭ F a♭ C e♭ G b D f♯ A c♯ E g♯ B...

II-III-I II-III-I II-III-I

I II-III-I II-III-I

MINOR-MAJOR KEY.

43. In the minor key the negative element, the negation of the positive, or major, triad, which is assumed first, is determined to be the principal thing, the middle or **tonic**. But we may also conceive the notion of the key-system, so that it shall contain the negation, the minor triad, as essential determination, yet not give it prominence as principal element, i.e. not place it in the middle of the system. Then the positive, or major, triad represents the middle, and its negation, the minor triad, occupies the place of **subdominant** chord. For the dominant chord there results, by continuing the positive series, evidently a major triad.

By this there is formed a key-system, which contains in essence and effect the major and minor notions joined. We get then those harmonies of the major key, in which the **minor Sixth** asserts itself.

If in the series above for the notion of the minor key we put the positive triad *G—b—D* middle, the system takes the following shape:

II—III—I   I—III—II
C   e♭   G   b   D   f♯   A
I—III—II

Although it is unusual for the **minor-major** key to be formally made the basis of a piece of music, yet it occurs used in the course of one not rarely; oftener in the sentimental style of modern music than in the older. Wherever the diminished chord of the Seventh is resolved into the major triad as tonic, there this key is present; in fact it is then contained in its whole compass in the notes of the two chords. Similarly, so far as its principal contents, in the plagal close from the minor triad of the subdominant to the major triad of the tonic. This key has the diminished triad upon the second degree, the augmented triad and augmented chord of the Sixth [1] in common with the minor key; only here the chords are not referred to a minor triad as tonic.

44. When we speak here of the diminished chord of the Seventh, of the augmented chord of the Sixth, also of other intervals besides those named at first and explained, that is because we assume practical knowledge of these chords and intervals, as to their effect and outer properties. Their relation to the notion of the key could not up to now be explained, for we have been speaking of consonant formations alone. From the very beginning only three directly intelligible intervals have been named, and it was said of them that they are unchangeable—cannot, that is, be sharpened or flattened. The explanation of the notions which are expressed by the relations

[1] See pars. 60–62, and the beginning of par. 236.

in sound of these intervals, must bring the proof of what we say: namely, that anything else than one of the elements, which appear in the notion of a note as Octave, Fifth and Third, but are universally elements of the notion for all intellectually felt, i.e. reasonable knowledge, is in itself nothing that can be known directly. Therefore a **minor** Third referred to a Root has no more claim to be regarded as a direct interval, than a **diminished** or **augmented** Fifth has; or than have Seconds, Fourths, Sixths and Sevenths with all their different properties.

Now it would be very uncomfortable and roundabout always to describe people by their relationship, or by the degree of their descent from the first human pair, and we prefer calling them by their Christian or surnames. So here, for shorter description, it will often be good to use as names the terms 'minor' Third, 'diminished' and 'augmented' Fifth, and others, which describe the intervals outwardly. And as at any rate the expressions 'Third,' 'Fifth' and 'Octave' are already taken from numbers of degrees of the scale, so, when we are only concerned to describe outward distance, other, indirect intervals may also be named upon the same system.

DIMINISHED TRIADS.

45. In the linked series of keys, the major key can pass into either of the secondary keys related to it by the tonic triad, viz. those of the subdominant and dominant, by the tonic triad itself taking on dominant meaning in the one case, subdominant in the other. But for the notion of succession this is a twofold, opposite determination, and answers to **Fifth**-meaning. It is a motion diverging outwards; and with it, if we regard the rest of the key in its limits as answering to unity or **Octave**-meaning, there must be

found a motion converging inwards, a passage **into self**, answering to **Third**-meaning.

We can picture the idea of something passing into self by thinking of a finite straight line bent into a circle with its beginning and end united: **finite** as **infinite**, or **infinite** in **finite**.

Absolute finiteness would be suggested by the limited line; absolute infinity by the line running on without limit. The first is the limited key without passage into itself; the other is its progress into the keys linked in a chain without limit, each newly arisen dominant becoming in its turn a tonic.

46. As an effect of sound, the notion of the key passing into itself is expressed in the chords which contain the union of the Fifth of the dominant with the Root of the subdominant: the so-called diminished triads. Now the combination of sound in these chords rests upon a double basis, upon the dominant and subdominant; they must therefore always be dissonant.

The notion of dissonance cannot yet be entered upon more nearly; only it may be observed in passing, that the expressions sometimes used in Germany of '**well-sounding**' and '**ill-sounding**' for '**consonant**' and '**dissonant**' must be held quite inappropriate. On the other hand the verbal sense of the latter terms contains a perfect description: the character of consonance is determined sounding **together** in the harmony, and of dissonance determined sounding **apart**. A consonance may sound ill in a place where a dissonance is needed, and where a dissonance sounds well.

The Third and Fifth of the dominant triad can unite with the root of the subdominant triad to form a diminished triad; so can the Fifth of the former with the Root and Third of the latter. E.g. in the key of C major, *b—D|F, D|F—a*; in the key of C minor, as also in the minor-major key with the same name, *b—D|F, D|F—a♭*; chords which, because they include the limits of the key, have the property of closing it up into itself. The tendency of such chords, the reason for their arising, and their mental meaning, we shall afterwards see; here they are only to be regarded in themselves as combinations of sound.

47. The chord upon the Fifth of the dominant of the major key, *D*|*F—a*, must not be confounded with the minor triad, *d—F—a*; which, transgressing the lower limit of the system of the key of C major, is formed from the Third of *B*♭ with Root and Third of the major triad of F. And in general notes of the same name distinguished by capital and small letters in the notation which we use here for chords, must not be taken to be the same. The mechanical structure of our keyed instruments with its enforced equal temperament ignores this distinction, equally with the so-called enharmonic difference. The ordinary musical notation, too, while it has a difference of symbol for notes enharmonically different, does not distinguish notes different in the other meaning. It has only **one** sign for the Third of the scale of C major, and for the Second of the scale of D major, supposing the latter to have the second degree of the scale of C major as basis: that is, it has the same sign for *e* and *E*. Therefore it may well be, that, from want of care in practical study, musicians themselves are often unaware of the difference, although when it comes to the question as to which of the two meanings is to take effect, instinct will always make it be perceived clearly enough.

48. What temperament does for instruments with fixed tones, equally distributing these differences wherever they occur, can have no influence upon the essence and meaning of the intervals. The tempered Fifth is not meant to be heard as a flattened Fifth, nor the Third, which is in the temperament too sharp, as a sharpened Third; the intervals are meant to stand for true. Singers do not temper; as we shall see in the construction of scales, they have nothing to determine their intonation but the Fifth and Third, and they try to take their intervals perfectly true to them. The basis

of temperament is certainly nothing else than the using of one and the same note in several meanings; whereby there is confused not only the enharmonic difference, e.g. *b*♯—*C* (125 : 128), but also that other which exists between the major Third and the fourth Fifth of a Root (80 : 81).

49. Thus we find the Third *e* under the number 5 in the natural series (par. 32). For *E*, as fourth Fifth from *C*, we get (3^4) the number 81. And if *e* be raised to the corresponding octave (5×2^4), there is found for it the number 80, different therefore to that for *E* as Fifth. But how great or small the difference is does not matter so much as that there is a difference, and that in the number 81, as a power of 3, Fifth-generation may be recognised, but in 80, a product of 5 into a power of 2, Third-generation.

50. Where intonation is free, not fixed, there is never any reason for not making the intervals keep perfectly true. For inside a key, in the compass of three united triads, notes **of the same name** with different meanings do not occur; a key does not even contain two **chromatically** different notes. And **enharmonically** different notes lie in their real nature so far apart, that it is not possible for them to meet together in harmony.

51. If the dissonant triad, which has the **Third** of the dominant for Root (e.g. in the key of C major, *b*—*D*|*F*) is named diminished, then we can use the same term for the triad upon the Fifth of the dominant, *D*|*F*—*a*. For by what has gone before, *D*——*a* is no more a Fifth than *b*——*F* is. Both chords have a duality of basis; the subdominant and dominant: *F* and *G*. So in the minor key with the triads *b*—*D*|*F*, *D*|*F*—*a*♭.

52. Thus the **major system**

dim. minor dim.

D/F—a—C—e—G—b—D/F

major

contains three major, two minor, and two different diminished triads.

The **minor system**

dim. major aug. major

D/F—a♭—C—e♭—G—b—D/F

minor dim.

contains only **one** major triad of the first order, that of the dominant. A second is found as intermediate chord between the two minor triads of the subdominant and tonic. Further there are contained in it two diminished triads, on the Third and Fifth of the dominant, made up of notes of the two dominants, as in the major system; and lastly the so-called augmented triad, upon the minor Third of the tonic, a chord which expresses most harshly the twofoldness of its nature. Thus in the minor key there are three different dissonant triads; for the two diminished triads contained in it are not of like structure, any more than those upon the same places in the major key. Both rest upon the double basis of subdominant and dominant, but differ between themselves in taking more or less from one or other of the triads of the two bases: *b—D/F*, *D/F—a♭*.

53. But in the augmented triad *e♭—G—b* the middle note, *G*, is in itself decided duality; it is determined differently in two directions, as positive Root and negative at the same time:

III −I
+I III

In the diminished triads the dissonance consists in **two** notes not being unity; in the augmented triad it is contained in the inner duality of **one** note.

THE KEY-SYSTEM STRETCHING OUT, OR IN TRANSIT, TO DOMINANT OR SUB-DOMINANT.

The Triads joining the Limits, or Diminished Triads, of this System.

54. All the triad harmonies have now been pointed out which are found either inside the limits of the major and minor key systems, or at the meeting of the limits. There still remain to be mentioned the triads which arise from joining the limits, when the key system is shifted on through one member of the triad series (A and B, par. 42) in the subdominant or dominant direction, when it encroaches, that is, on one side or the other. The system is not thereby enlarged; it cannot be enlarged, for what it gains upon one side it must lose again upon the other, and so keep, as what its notion includes, contents of no more than three adjacent triad formations. But besides, by such shifting to the next member of the series on one side or the other, the existing key is not yet removed; for one dominant determination still remains. Suppose the step taken to the subdominant side, the Third of the dominant remains; or to the dominant side, the Third of the subdominant remains. Either of these still prevents the tonic triad from giving up its determination as principal chord.

55. Such a shifting must not, however, be regarded as a mere mechanical treatment of the fixed progression of chords; it can only rest upon a mental inner foundation. Besides, the progressive series of fixed, determinate chords has not, strictly speaking, its counterpart in reality; it is a means of depicting simultaneously something that in reality developed successively.

56. If in the key of C major the note *f*♯, Third of the dominant Fifth, enters, then in this there is at once expressed an inclination

towards the dominant side, a desire of making the dominant chord take tonic meaning. But just in measure as this is attained, the leaning to the subdominant side must have lessened ; in the same degree as the dominant side comes forward, the subdominant side must recede: the centre of gravity of the equilibrium between the two will turn to the side towards which the key receives a preponderance.

Supposing the centre of gravity in the system

F—a—C—e—G—b—D

to consist of the tonic **Third**, as middle of the middle chord, binding element of the tonic triad binding the dominant triads; and supposing that the note *e* is now equally inclined to move towards *F* and towards *D*; then, when the note *f*♯ enters the system, i.e. when the Third of the dominant of the key of G major is touched, as in

a—C—e—G—b—D—f♯,

the centre of gravity occupies no longer its former place, but is situated in that element of the tonic triad which belongs to the triad the Third of whose dominant has appeared, namely, in the tonic **Fifth** as Root of the dominant triad. But the *G* here does not enter in full tonic meaning. For with the entrance of the Third of the dominant Fifth, *f*♯, the key has only given up *F*, the Root of the subdominant triad, but not the minor triad of *a* formed from its Third *a* and the tonic Third-interval *C—e*; and this triad because of its Root *a* does not belong to the key of G major. The minor triad of *e* is now the triad of reference, and its Third *G* the middle of the system both by outward position and by inward meaning. Before, the middle note *e* was in equal degree urged towards the limit notes *F* and *D*; now it is *G*, that can be determined to move towards *a* or towards *f*♯. Upon the entrance of the Fifth of the dominant triad of the key of G major, the subdominant triad of the key of C major is wholly given up, because the note *A* excludes the subdominant

Third *a*. Then the tonic major triad of C will have become subdominant chord, and the middle of the system will lie in the Third *b* of the G major triad, now become tonic. The same process would result in reversed order, supposing the tendency turned towards the subdominant side. With the entrance of the Third of the major triad on *B♭* the chord *d—F—a* would take subdominant meaning, and *e—G—b* dominant meaning; and C, as middle of the middle triad *a—C—e*, would be determined as the middle of the system. By the entrance of the Root *B♭* the key of F major would be fully established, because then the tonic C major triad would itself have become dominant triad; and then the middle of the system would be settled in *a*.

DIMINISHED TRIADS OF THE KEY-SYSTEM IN TRANSIT.

(*a*) **In the Major Key.**

57. To learn what chords arise from the sounding together of the limit notes, when the system reaches out to one side or the other, we now go back to the two series A and B (par. 42), and begin with the march of the major system towards the dominant side, whereby the key of C major takes up the Third of the dominant Fifth, *f♯*, and leaves out the Root of the subdominant, *F*. The chords of the joined limits will then be: *D—f♯/a* and *f♯/a—C*; different in nature and effect from *D—f♯—A* and *f♯—A/C*, the chords which would be found in the key of G major.

If the system of notes is shifted through one member towards the subdominant side, then *d*, the Third of the major triad on *B♭*, comes forward, while *D*, as Fifth of *G*, is at the same time shut out. The combinations joining the limits are now the chords *G—b|d* and *b|d—F*; to be distinguished from *G—b—D* and *b—D|F*, as contained within the limits untransgressed of the C major system, and formed by joining them.

58. The reception of the Third note, which lies below the system, ought certainly by parity of reason to let the key continue; for the reception of the Third which lies above, does not make it cease. But the change itself, the difference between *D* and *d*, cannot be brought out in the same way as that between *F* and *f*♯. The Root *B*♭ must have entered before *d* can be shown decisively as not *D*. But with *B*♭ the key of *F* is determined, and that of *C* made to cease. Therefore, because the note gained by the move cannot be determined but by the note lying underneath that, the chords belonging here must be referred no longer to the given key, but to its subdominant. Thus *b|d—F* and *G—b|D* no longer belong to the key of C major, but are seen to be produced by the stretching out of the F major system, again towards the dominant side. Then the chords *G—b|D* and *b|d—F* have the same relation to the key of F major, which *D—f*♯*|a* and *f*♯*|a—C* have to the key of C major, and can no longer be regarded as derived from the latter key.

(*b*) In the Minor Key.

59. The minor key-system, from reasons which lie in its different nature to the major key, can suffer shifting to the subdominant side only under very narrowing circumstances. The reception of a member of the subdominant series would be an attack upon the positive premise, that from which the generation of the key has proceeded; it would rob the dominant chord of its Fifth, and the first chord to appear on the dominant side would then be the augmented triad, a chord of most marked duality. Therefore the triads *G—b—d*♭, *b—d*♭*—F*, which arise in the C minor system by the move towards the subdominant side, will

always attach themselves rather to the F minor key in the move towards the dominant side.

60. By shifting to the dominant side, there are found, following the former process, two chords containing an interval of diminished Third. E.g. in the series B, supposing the outlying note, *f*♯, above the Fifth of the dominant, received into the C minor system, and *F* as Root of the subdominant chord thereby shut out, then the chords of the joined limits are: *D—f*♯/*a*♭, *f*♯/*a*♭*—C*. From these combinations the so-called **chord of the augmented Sixth** is derived, which indeed makes its leading note strongly perceived as the Third of the Fifth of a dominant chord.

61. Therefore, in the minor key as well as in the major, the only triads joining limits, which are of real use, besides those belonging to the closed system, are the ones that can be produced by taking in the nearest member on the dominant side.

In the key of C major: *D—f*♯/*a*, *f*♯/*a—C*.
In the key of C minor: *D—f*♯/*a*♭, *f*♯/*a*♭*—C*.

The particular conditions governing the position of the intervals of the two last will be found later on. Every harmonic combination, whatever the shape it takes outwardly, can be produced only from inner determinations; and, to conceive a chord theoretically, it must be looked upon, never as an aggregate of notes, to which sharps and flats may be applied at pleasure, but always as an element of development in the notion of organic reality.

(*c*) In the Minor-Major Key.

62. The minor-major key is in its subdominant and dominant chords of like structure with the minor, and, when continued further in both directions, must also lead to like—on the subdominant side to minor triads, on the dominant side to major. Therefore, for join-

ing the limits of its system, either stretching out or closed, it can only contain the same chords as the system of the minor key; for in them the dominant chords alone have share.

SCALE OF THE MAJOR KEY.

63. The ancient, now somewhat antiquated, dispute or doubt, whether harmony or melody has precedence in music and must be taken to have arisen earlier, keeps about equal pace with that other, whether the chicken comes first, or the egg. That practical music had historically to begin with melody, one-part song, it is safe to assume; but it is also certain that all melodic intervals are only harmonic determinations, and that these neither are, nor can be, other than what we have pointed out above. Even a child singing has in its unconscious feeling nothing for determining the intervals of its artless song, but the **Octave, Fifth,** and **Third**; every note of a melody is one of these three intervals to a unity that connects the melodic notes.

64. First we can think of the **melodic** principle abstractly, as **what moves**; opposite to it the **harmonic** principle as **what fixes.** The former, also, as the tendency to go out of a subsisting state, but with no further determinations in itself; these it gets from the harmonic elements.

65. If we imagine a sound gradually rising from the tonic of the major key-system, and if we regard its starting-point as the first degree, then its second degree, as a harmonic-melodic determination, will be found in the Fifth of the dominant, which is the Second of the tonic; the third, in the Third of the tonic; the fourth, in the Root of the subdominant, as Fourth of the tonic; the fifth, in the Fifth of the tonic; the sixth, in the Third of the subdominant, as

Sixth of the tonic; the seventh, in the Third of the dominant; the eighth, in the Octave of the tonic itself. This is the series in which the ascending motion of a sound in itself undetermined meets on its way the intervals of the key, and by them is determined into degrees.

66. The scale makes the harmonic intervals appear in its degrees in an order that with each new element of the succession contradicts the notion of **simultaneousness.** The second degree belongs to a different triad to the first, the third to a different one to the second, and so on. But it is just this that corresponds to the essential meaning of the **notion of succession,** which requires a **one-after-the-other**—i.e. **after one, another.** But for the **one-after-the-other** to be a real connected succession, there must be, besides its difference, also a unity, a common, binding element; which, if the transition be pictured as happening in space of time, as being the **end of one,** is made also the **beginning of the other.**

67. For the first progression of a Second in the scale of C major, from *C* to *D*, the connecting unity is contained in the note *G*. *G* is at first the Fifth determined from *C*, and then becomes the Root determining *D*. The melodic progression here is in fact intelligible only as an expression for the transformation which goes on in *G*, out of one meaning into the opposite one. In the next progression of a Second, from *D* to *e*, *G* passes out of Root-meaning back into Fifth. The step *e*··*F* is determined in like manner upon the Root *C*. It is the same with the steps *F*··*G*, and *G*··*a*; in these progressions *C* changes between Root- and Fifth-meaning. But from the sixth degree to the seventh, from *a* to *b*, in so far as the two notes are contained in the key as Thirds of the subdominant and dominant chords, such a connecting note to explain the passage is not to be found. For the triads of the subdominant and dominant are disjunct; they have no common element by whose transformation the step *a*··*b* could be given. Therefore between these two

notes, referred to these two chords, there may be felt a division, which makes the passage difficult; for it is in fact not to be called a passage, but rather a leap. The distance between these two notes, in their quality of Thirds of the subdominant and dominant triads, seems to be greater than that of the previous steps of a Second; and yet it is equal to the distance between the first and second, or between the fourth and fifth degrees: described by the ratio of vibrations it is 8 : 9. But these ratios of numbers throw no light on the meaning of the intervals. We cannot pitch the Seconds *C··D* and *F··G* by the ratio 8 : 9, nor the Seconds *D··e* and *G··a* by the ratio 9 : 10, nor yet *e··F* and *b··C* by 15 : 16. Indifferent to the measure of the outward distance, be it greater or smaller, we get them determined only through change in the meaning of a connecting member. And so too the step from the sixth degree to the seventh can be yielded as intelligible succession only by means of some such mediation.

68. Here too a mediation is found; not indeed in the unconnected principal chords, but in the chords of secondary order, namely, in the two conjunct minor triads of the system, which have the Third of the tonic for a common note: *a* is Root to *e*, and *e* determines *b* as Fifth. Therefore the succession *a··b* is made possible by the change of *e* out of the meaning of Fifth into that of Root. The last step *b··C* is referred to the same note; *e* then returning to Fifth-meaning. The last passage might indeed also be given through the note *G*; here, however, for the succession of the three last notes the first meaning is the one of principal account.

69. Thus the whole scale is formed: in its first, second, and third degrees, on the **Fifth**; in its fourth, fifth, and sixth, on the **Root**: in its sixth, seventh, and eighth, on the **Third** of the chord of the tonic; each of these three elements of the principal triad strikes out of Fifth-meaning into that of Root and then back again to Fifth-meaning as at first.

```
II  I  II      II  I  II      II  I  II
 \___ ___/      \___ ___/      \___ ___/
     G              C              e
  ___ ___        ___ ___        ___ ___
C .. D .. e    F .. G .. a    a .. b .. C
I   II  III    I   II  III    I   II  III
```

70. The discontinuity which has always been felt between the two notes of the sixth and seventh degrees of the scale, supposing them to be referred to the subdominant and dominant chords, and the obstacle thereby opposed to their following one upon the other, was the reason why in the earlier **solmisation** it was not attempted to group together more than the first six notes of the scale, being those which afford a continuous succession. Then further progress was gained by letting the so-called **hexachord**, with its well-known syllables *ut re mi fa sol la*, begin with either the **Root**, or the **Fifth below**, or the **Fifth above**, of the key:

```
        15 : 16      8 : 9   8 : 9 : 10
8 : 9 : 10   8 : 9 : 10 15 : 16
C   D   e    F   G   a   b   C   D   e...
ut  re  mi   fa  sol la
                    (B♭)
             ut  re  mi  fa  sol la
                 (A)
                 ut  re  mi  fa  sol  la
                 8 : 9 : 10
                             ut  re  mi...
```

But in this way, supposing the hexachord starts from the **Fifth above**, the fifth, sixth, and seventh degrees of the scale of the Octave appear as first, second, and third of the hexachord, *ut re mi*; and the sixth and seventh are no more in the ratio of 8 : 9, but in the ratio of 9 : 10 like *D*··*e*. The sixth note of the original scale is thus no longer *a* the Third of the subdominant, but *A* the Fifth of *D*; whereby the scale reaches out into the territory of the key of G major. But if the hexachord begins with the **Fifth below**, then the sixth and seventh degrees of the scale of the Octave become third and fourth of the hexachord, and the progression *mi* · · *fa* is then that of a minor Second *a* · · *B*♭, whereby again a new key is touched, that of the subdominant, F major. Therefore, while the sixth degree of the scale of the Octave is pitched as *a*, when it means *la* or *mi* of the hexachord, and as *A* when it means *re*; so the seventh degree varies, accordingly as it gets the meaning of third or fourth, *la* or *mi*, of the hexachord scale, between *b* and *B*♭, between *B* **durus** and *B* **mollis.** The first, agreeably to its 'hardness,' was drawn square, ♮, *B* **quadratum**, a character related to, and meaning the same as, ♯ and ♮; from the last of which probably has come the *h* introduced in the German notation only, and standing in the succession of notes quite out of alphabetical order. It is seen that the discontinuous juxtaposition of the Third of the subdominant and the Third of the dominant, which is found interrupting the progression in the Octave scale, could not occur in the hexachord system, nor could singers have been encouraged to attempt it.

71. Through the connexion explained above, which takes place by the minor triads of the key, it is indeed made possible for these notes to succeed one another. But the meaning which they have as intervals of the minor chords is only a secondary one. And here their principal meaning as Thirds of the subdominant and dominant triads will all the more count, because the sixth degree following upon the fifth enters with Third-meaning already. It might seem that a determination for the passage from this point to the Third of the dominant could be found in the diminished triad of the seventh degree; but then we have only to remind ourselves that this chord is itself one of twofoldness or division, and that the name of triad is given it, not as meaning a concrete unity, but only as to

a combination of three notes. A real connexion for the succession of those two degrees is only given by the Third of the tonic.

72. The descending scale is determined by the same conditions of succession as the ascending, and contains accordingly the same series of notes in reversed order. If in the ascending scale we must take **force**, manifested in the rising pitch, to be that moving or melodic principle of direction which is by the harmonic elements determined into degrees; so now it is **weight**, drawing downwards and deepening, to which is due the formation of the melodic series in the reversed direction.

73. By the expression **melodic**, in the meaning which is here intended, there will always be understood successive onward motion of sound tending upwards or downwards. In melodic succession, even of intervals that are harmonically simultaneous, the voice has to go over all that lies between in its harmonic elements, in order to reach the more remote interval. The progression *F··b* as Fourth in the key of C major, the so-called **Tritone**, contains the same difficulty of passage, as that from the sixth degree to the seventh, where these are taken as Thirds of the subdominant and the dominant; although here there is no change of chord, because both notes belong to the chord *b—D/F*. But the change is contained in the melodic passage, which can only take place through the intermediate space with all its harmonic determinations; here therefore through *F··G··a··b*, where the division between *a··b* stands again in the way, as unmelodic. The same notes *b··F*, as diminished Fifth, offer no hindrance to melodic succession; because the passage *b··C··D··e··F* is continuous in all intermediate elements. All **augmented** intervals will be found for this reason **unmelodic**, but in their inversion as **diminished** intervals they will be **melodic**, i.e. continuous.

SCALE OF THE MINOR KEY.

74. The scale of the major key is a successive presentation of the harmonic determinations of the major key-system, in which it is completely contained. Each melodic degree is determined by a harmonic element out of the system closed off in itself.

75. The minor scale up to its sixth degree can be formed quite in the same way as the major, because in it, too, the first three degrees are made continuous by the Fifth, and the following three by the Root. Now in the major scale the sixth and seventh degrees were at first shown divided; and it was only in virtue of a subordinate connexion of chords that a succession of the two degrees was made possible. So too in the minor scale we come upon the same division in the same place; but here we are not offered the same means for a union, even for one of subordinate meaning, as in the system of the major key. In the major system the Third of the subdominant can be formed into continuous succession with the Third of the dominant by means of the Third of the tonic, which stands to the former in the relation of Fifth, to the latter in the relation of Root. But in the minor system this intermediate member is not present so as to form a connecting link, because the minor Third of the tonic does not stand to the major Third of the dominant in the relation of Fifth. Rather, the augmented Fifth between the two notes expresses most marked separateness: determination of a **positive** Root as **negative** simultaneously. Thus a melodic connexion of these two degrees is in no way granted in the minor system. It is impossible to pass in continuous progression **from the sixth degree**, as minor Third of the subdominant triad, **to the seventh**, as major Third of the dominant triad. That stands in melodic connexion only with the **fifth** degree; this only with the **eighth.**

76. If the seventh degree, the Third of the dominant, is to be reached, and further progress in general made possible, then the fifth degree must be followed by a note other than the sixth of the key. This must be one lying **outside** the system and connecting the fifth and seventh degrees, and can be no other than the Fifth of the Fifth of the dominant chord; which as sixth degree forms the passage to the seventh of the key, because now the fifth, sixth, and seventh are given by transformation of the Fifth of the dominant triad.

77. In the C minor key-system the melodic succession can move on through *C·· D·· e♭·· F·· G* in unimpeded connexion; the first three degrees being made upon the dominant *G*, the last three upon the tonic *C*, as in the major system. But if after the fifth degree *G*, we take *a♭*, which follows still based upon *C*, as sixth, then from this point return to *G* is alone possible, but not advance to *b*. For the triad *G—b—D*, to which *b* belongs as its Third, is not connected with the triad *F—a♭—C*, whose minor Third *a♭* has entered as sixth degree, by any common note through which the passage could be made intelligible. The connecting link between *G* and *b* can only be determined by the Fifth of the dominant, *D*, whose Fifth *A* provides the passage from *G* to *b*; and consequently the note *A*, lying out of the system though it does, will take its place in the scale as sixth degree, after which the seventh and eighth follow in unimpeded succession.

78. Now if in the ascending minor scale progress was impeded from the sixth degree to the seventh, then in the descending scale there will also be no connexion found between the seventh and sixth degrees. As there the minor Sixth could not form the passage to the major Seventh, so here the major Seventh cannot lead into the minor Sixth. The Octave, however, finds a note to conduct it to the minor Sixth, again outside the system, but this time upon the subdominant side. While in ascending the Fifth of the dominant

had to become Root, in descending the Root of the subdominant must become Fifth ; the former change provided the intermediate step to the major Seventh, the latter change provides the step to the minor Sixth degree.

79. In the C minor system the melodic progression ascending from the fifth degree was found in the succession :

G
G··A··b··C ;
D

the first three notes as determinations upon the Fifth of the dominant, the two last upon the dominant itself. Here the passage from *G* to *b*, which *a*♭ did not furnish, had to be formed by another middle member, *A*. Descending, a continuous passage has to be found from *C* to *a*♭, which is not possible with *b*. Therefore *C* and *a*♭ are referred to the subdominant triad, upon the Root of which, *F*, Fifth-determination passes then by means of *B*♭. Thus the descending succession will be :

C
C··B♭··a♭··G ;
F

the three first notes determined upon the Root of the subdominant chord, the two last upon the tonic.

The whole scale of C minor, ascending and descending, consists accordingly of the successions :

C G	C
C··D··e♭··F··G··A··b··C,	C··B♭··a♭··G··F··e♭··D··C
G D	F G
(ascending)	(descending).

80. That here or elsewhere there can be no mention of degrees

arbitrarily sharpened or flattened, need not be said or repeated after getting thus far. Again, it lies in the notion of the key-system, that the major Sixth of the ascending minor scale cannot be major Third of the subdominant triad, nor the minor Seventh of the descending minor scale minor Third of the dominant chord ; for both are by the organisation of the system impossible, they contradict its fundamental conditions.

81. This account of the construction of the minor scale in its three last degrees has been compressed as much as was possible, and yet has proved lengthy. But the thing itself has only been given in strict necessity, as the course of degrees formed in the nearest possible connexion. The gap of the **major key** is linked by the **middle** of the system ; in the **minor key** it is linked by the two **ends.** In this linked succession, the minor key again puts forth its divided nature ; while in the linked succession of the major key there is expressed the nature of unity.

SCALE OF THE MINOR-MAJOR KEY.

82. The scale of the minor-major key ascending will move like the major scale through the tonic major Third up to the Fifth ; its progress beyond will be that of the minor scale. It has no major Third on the subdominant, and therefore in its last degrees requires the same connexion by the Fifth of the dominant. And in descending, as with the minor scale, its passage can only be made continuous by means of the subdominant Root.

The major scale being formed of the series of notes

C‥D‥e‥F‥G‥a‥b‥C, C‥b‥a‥G;‥F‥e‥D‥C,

then the minor-major scale compared with it in

C··D··e··F··G··A··b··C, C··B♭··*a*♭··G··F··e··D··C

has *A* for its sixth degree ascending, *B*♭ for its seventh descending.

83. The following is a representation of the melodic succession of the scales according to their harmonic determinations, which may serve for a general view of the exposition above given :

Harmonic Determination for the Melodic Succession in the Major Scale.

I—III—II I—III—II

I—III—II

F a C e G b D

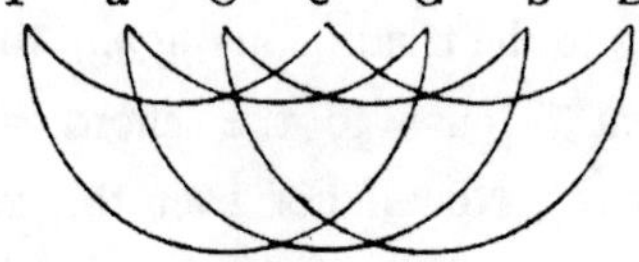

Harmonic Determination for the Melodic Succession in the Minor and in the Minor-Major Scales.

II—III—I I—III—II

II — I II—III—I I — II

B♭ (d♭) F a♭ C e♭ G b D (f♯) A

(I—III—II)

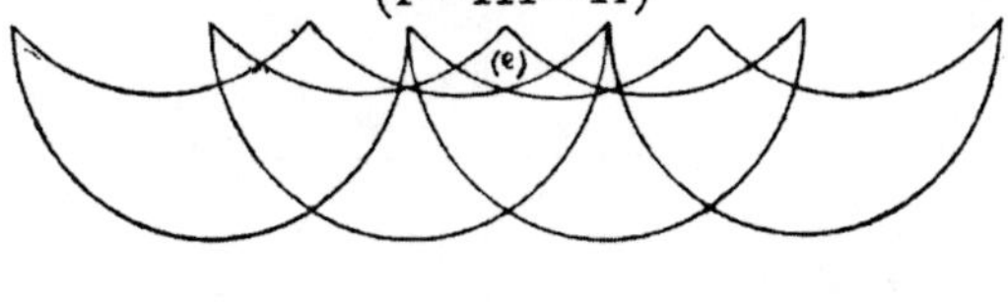

84. The minor key has sometimes been called an '**artificial**' one, in opposition to the major, in that case called '**natural.**' In

the first place it is difficult to see what can have been meant by this expression used to describe a system so directly rooted in feeling, and one in which so many popular songs move. But secondly, the system of the major key is no more naturally given than that of the minor key is artificially made. Both are forms humanly animate and self-generating, i.e. reasonable being and coming-to-be in sound and determinations of sound; something higher than 'naturally given' or 'artificially made.'

85. Nature gives determinate notes in a series, which indeed includes the elements of the triad among its members, but not in the sense of a determination complete in itself, in which sense alone it can have musical value for us. We must come to the infinite progression of the natural series of notes having already in our mind the notion of the chord, if we want to find out the members in it which belong to the triad. But again the progression soon goes beyond what belongs to the chord and has intelligible meaning in harmony. Now if not even the triad is given in the natural series as particular determination, much less is the system of the key so given. For even by its material contents, because it contains an element formed backwards (the subdominant chord), the key-system cannot be given in a series which naturally is formed only forwards. The arithmetical note-progression starting from *C*, even if continued to infinity, will never generate the note *F*, nor its Third *a*. These are no more possible for it than are *e*♭ and *a*♭, Thirds of the minor key.

CHORD SUCCESSION.

86. In the scale we considered a sound rising from below upwards, whose progress, in itself unbroken, is divided into degrees at the points where it meets the harmonic elements of the key; and we have shown how this is done, both in the major key and in the minor, preserving continuity of succession. The elements of the chords were taken as determining the degrees; but the order in which they succeed one another was given by the assumed direction, ascending or descending, of the moving sound. In **chord succession**, which consists of a simultaneous advance of several parts, other conditions of melodic movement will enter. We now get a **Harmony of successions** as a **Succession of harmonies**, and thereby again **opposites made into one**, the notion in its essentiality of all that is **real**: that is, we have the higher **Third**-notion of real harmony, whose **Fifth**-notion had to deal with the opposites separated; for previously we have only had **chords** determined in themselves, and melodic progression determined in itself as the **scale.**

87. The succession of two **triads** is again only intelligible in so far as both can be referred to a common element which changes meaning during the passage.

88. Two triads can be different: (*a*) in **one** note; (*b*) in **two** notes; (*c*) in all **three** notes. Starting from the middle of the major system, from the tonic triad, the triads which differ from the first in one note will be the two minor chords of the key; in two notes, the subdominant and dominant chords; in three notes, the two diminished or limit-joining chords.

In passing from the tonic to one of the minor triads, of the three parts which form the chord only **one** will have to move melodically, while the other two remain, changing the harmonic meaning of their notes.

The passage from the tonic to the subdominant or to the dominant triad makes **two** parts move melodically; the third part remains, receiving a new harmonic meaning.

In the passage from the tonic into one of the diminished triads, all **three** parts move; and of them one must spring through a harmonic interval to a note serving to connect the chords, the other two receive the melodic progression of a Second.

The first and second of these kinds of progression connecting chords are self-evident, so far as is now necessary, being those which lie nearest to hand. The third requires explanation.

89. Two triads lying wholly outside each other (such, namely, as have no common connecting note whose transformation into another meaning might give the understanding of the passage), require to be mediated by that triad, lying between the two, of which the first of the two unconnected triads contains two notes, and the other one note. And the passage from the first into the second cannot take place otherwise than in so far as the first has already this preponderance of community with the intermediate triad, and may therefore be put for it. Or, the progression from the first of the unconnected triads to the second is the same as it would be from the mediating triad to the second.

90. In the system of the C major key

D/F—a—C—e—G—b—D/F

the diminished triads *D/F—a* and *b—D/F* are separated from the triad of the tonic *C—e—G*, and therefore the passage from the latter to either of the former is only possible by the intervention of a connecting link. But the tonic triad contains two notes of each of the two minor triads; and again, the minor triads, each in its own direction, are joined to the corresponding diminished triads by one common note:

C—e—G C—e—G

a—C—e e—G—b

D/F—a b—D/F,

and the passage from the triad *C—e—G* to *D/F—a* must here be taken to be equivalent to the passage from *a—C—e* to *D/F—a*, and the passage from *C—e—G* to *b—D/F* equivalent to that from *e—G—b* to *b—D/F*.

91. Thus the three kinds of harmonic melodic triad progression within the C major key, starting from the chord of the tonic, will be :

I. To the triads with **two** common notes, the two minor chords:

From *C—e—G* to *a—C—e*,

in the position *C—e—a* $\binom{6}{3}$,

from *C—e—G* to *e—G—b*,

in the position *b—e—G* $\binom{6}{4}$.

II. To the triads with **one** common note, the subdominant and dominant chords :

From *C—e—G* to *F—a—C*,

in the position *C—F—a* $\binom{6}{4}$,

from *C—e—G* to *G—b—D*,

in the position *b—D—G* $\binom{6}{3}$.

III. To the Thirds **without** common note, the two diminished triads :

From *C—e—G* to *D—F—a*, as if
(*a—C—e*)

from *a—C—e* to *D—F—a*, therefore

in the position *a—D—F* $\binom{6}{4}$.

From *C—e—G* to *b—D—F*, as if
(e—G—b)
from *e—G—b* to *b—D—F*, therefore
in the position *D—F—b* $\binom{6}{3}$.

92. A second chord, or chord of succession, in every kind of mediated progression, supposing the first to have appeared in primary triad form, will assume a position of its intervals different to the primary one. It will be either a chord of the **Sixth-and-Third**, or of the **Sixth-and-Fourth**; for its position is not independent, but conditioned by the succession.

93. If the triad progression is to be carried on further from these secondary positions of the chords, and if the triad next following is related in two notes or in one note, then the melodic progression of the parts is self-evident. For the portion common to the two chords remains in its place, and the different portion can be reached by progression ascending or descending through a Second. But if the following triad be disjunct, then the secondary chord must itself first be referred to some primary chord related to the new chord to be taken; and the progression from the secondary to the new chord can only take place as if from that primary chord, which the secondary is considered to follow.

94. Now a secondary chord can always be derived from two different primary chords; first from that which has the lowest note of the secondary as its Root, and next from that which has the highest note of the secondary as its Fifth. E.g. the chord of the Sixth *C—e—a* can have arisen either from the triad *C—e—G*, or from the triad *D|F—a*; the chord of the Sixth-and-Fourth *b—e—G* from the triad *b—D|F*, or from the triad *C—e—G*. The triad which is to follow, and which is by hypothesis disjunct from the secondary chord, will in each case decide which of the two derivations is to be taken.

95. In the third kind of the above progressions, from the tonic

triad to the diminished triads, from *C—e—G* to *D|F—a* and *b—D|F* (by which for the first there ensues the position *a—D—F*, for the second the position *D—F—b*), it is true that the position of Sixth-and-Fourth *a—D—F* has as a fact been produced from the primary *a—C—e*, and the position of Sixth-and-Third *D—F—b* from *e—G—b*. But these derivations are not in themselves determined by the secondary chord forms, which can equally be referred in *a—D—F* to the primary triad *b—D|F*, and in *D—F—b* to the primary triad *D|F—a*. For the passages from these triads taken as primary bring out the same secondary positions of the two chords as we found for them from *a—C—e* and *e—G—b*.

96. The existence of this double derivation of every secondary position of a chord furnishes the mediation for the progression from it to the disjunct triads on either side.

97. The disjunct triads on each side of *D|F—a* are now *C—e—G* and *e—G—b*; those on each side of *b—D|F* are *a—C—e* and *C—e—G*. From the position *a—D—F*, mediated through *a—C—e*, there ensues for the C major triad the Six-Four position *G—C—e*, and for the e minor triad, mediated through *b—D|F*, the Six-Four position *b—e—G*. But the last triad can also be mediated by *a—C—e*, whereupon the Six-Three position *G—b—e* is obtained for the same chord. From the position *D—F—b*, mediated through *D|F—a*, is produced the a minor triad in the Six-Three position, and mediated through *e—G—b*, the C major triad also in the Six-Three position *e—G—C*. Here too the a minor triad can also be mediated through *e—G—b*, and receives then the Six-Four position *e—a—C*.

98. We see that the diminished triads brought from their secondary position back to the triad of the tonic, from which they came, can neither of them lead again to the primary position of that chord; and manifestly a triad in primary (or root-) position can

never be followed by a conjunct triad also in root-position. And if two triads can never follow immediately one upon the other in primary form (which would in fact contradict the notion of following), but in every case from a primary chord proceeds a secondary, and from a secondary a primary or another secondary, then not only is it impossible for two parallel Fifths to follow one upon the other in mediated progression, but also the succession of so-called **hidden** Fifths, the progression of two parts by similar motion to the Fifth, cannot occur in a strictly mediated connexion of chords.

99. The prohibition of Fifths, which causes such perplexity to the beginner not yet clear in harmony and to the amateur, and so often turns their finest inventions to water, is unnecessary for the master of harmonic phrase. Given right feeling of what progression is, and parallel Fifths are self-excluded. Where there is a parallel Fifth, hidden ever so carefully, the meaning will always sound through, that here is a second triad trying to make itself again beginning against a first which is placed beginning. This selfishness of the chord destroys the unity of the phrase. It is forbidden to write consecutive Fifths and Octaves; with equal right, since both are of bad effect. But the cause of the bad effect is not the same in both cases: in the succession of **Fifths** we miss unity of harmony, in the succession of **Octaves** difference of melody. Therefore to double in Octaves two parts which make no claim to difference is always permissible; but to progress in parallel Fifths never, for unconnected harmonies cannot but be foreign to rational artistic design. However, this can be said in such strictness only of an immediate succession of true Fifths, where the parts progress through a Second and the notes have chord-meaning. Such a succession does not occur in clear and correct phrase. To admit its lawfulness when thrust away under many parts is the same as to defend a lie told under compulsion.

100. The succession of chords, as presented above, is still con-

fined to the linking of harmonies, and exhibits the triads merely in the abstract sense of following one upon another, according as one arises out of another. But every chord, the position of whose intervals has been conditioned by a preceding chord, must, when present, also put in its own claim to a dignity of **independence**, a firm footing for itself. This it gets by the **Root** as basis or **bass**, and may also have it in the **Third** placed as lowest note; because the Third, comprehending in its essential meaning both Root and Fifth, contains the former, although in combination. But a triad-harmony, in which the **Fifth** is lowest or bass note, has not this independence. For the Fifth is just the decided opposite of the Root, and, placed in the bass, will therefore mark the chord as decidedly **not** having a footing of its own.

101. A succession of chords which, starting from the triad, is continued in **three** parts, will therefore need a **fourth** part to serve as basis for the chords; that so a foundation for the independent presence of each of the members of the succession may be provided, wherever such foundation is not contained in the position of the chord necessitated by the succession. But now, after that the notion of succession has been received, there can be no mention made of providing single chords which lack foundation with bass notes having no connexion between themselves. That would offend against the notion of succession, which admits of nothing isolated. Rather this part, while having its own relation to the others, must also in itself answer to the conditions of correct progression.

102. It has been said that, besides the Root, the Third of the triad can also serve as lowest or bass note to a chord, but not the Fifth, as being the exact opposite of the Root. Therefore those of the chord-connexions shown above, in which the Six-Three position appears, but not the Six-Four position, do not necessarily need foundation upon a fourth part. They already form in three-part harmony a phrase in which each chord can maintain itself in the shape which

it takes in the progression. Therefore the succession *C—e—G ...D—F—b···e—G—C* is admissible without a fourth part. But not the succession *C—e—G···a—D—F···G—C—e*; because the second and third chords contain as lowest part the Fifth, which is not suited for bass. Here a fourth part is required to add the Root or Third underneath, that the chords may be made to tread firmly. To avoid like progression with parts already present, it will take as lowest the course *C··D··e*; and the phrase of this succession is therefore in four parts: ***C***—*C—e—G*···***D***—*a—D—F* ···***e***—*G—C—e.*

103. The strict phrase of successive harmony, even when we regard it in a succession only of triads, for the present neglecting the four-part chord of the Seventh, is thus essentially four-part. It is a union of four melodic series, of which three are given by the triads passing into one another, while the fourth provides with a basis the chords not based in the passage.

104. In formal self-determination such as this, by which a succession of chords may grow only under bound necessity, shooting out one might even say like a mineral crystallisation, without any freedom or choice, there would indeed be offered a very cramped material for musical composition. Its productions in these fetters would be like the Egyptian sculptures, of which the proportions were prescribed with such strict precision, that two statues of equal height, finished by different sculptors, had also to be exactly the same in all their parts. But what is here shown is only the very directest and nearest union of chords, as it would be formed obeying the inner law of succession alone, without the intervention of any other determination whatsoever. The organism being first framed according to law, afterwards admits of a freer, nay, of the freest movement of its limbs inside the regularity. But now it is the regularity that we are principally concerned with, to find it out and observe what in the very first place it demands. Its formation

under other conditions will be understood the easier when we know the direct requirements.

105. Here the passage into conjunct and disjunct triads has been considered starting only from the triad of the tonic. But in the continued series each subordinate triad too may appear in primary form, as, e.g., in the series *C—e—G*···*C—e—a*···*C—F—a*··· *D|F—a*···*D—F—b*···*D—G—b*···*e—G—b*···*e—G—C*···*e—a—C* ···*F—a—C*, and so on, where the triads *D|F—a*, *e—G—b*, *F—a—C* appear in the first position, as well as the tonic triad *C—e—G*, from which the series starts; therefore each subordinate triad may as primary also become the starting-point, and the passages into the other triads will then be formed, in the analogy of the relationship, quite like those which start from the triad of the tonic: the passage from *D|F—a* to *F—a—C* like that from *C—e—G* to *e—G—b*, from *D|F—a* to *e—G—b* like that from *C—e—G* to *D|F—a*, and so on.

106. In the minor key, supposing the chord-union goes on inside the system and may not, as with the scales, reach out beyond it, between the Third of the subdominant and the Third of the dominant the progression will always be met by the impediment of the melodically discontinuous **augmented Second.** It cannot be gone round, but must be overleapt, and stamps the nature of the system in itself conceived in inner disunion. The passage from *C—F—a♭* to the triad of the seventh degree *b—D|F* can only lead to the position *D—F—b*. Proceeding from *C—F—a♭* to the primary position *b—D|F* would avoid the step of the augmented Second; but this form of chord-succession contains no inner union; as the hidden Fifths of the outside parts from *C——a♭* to *b——F* prove.

DISSONANCE.

107. **Dissonance is melodic succession sounded simultaneously.**

If in the C major key the note *C* should be followed by the notes *e*, *F*, *G*, or *a*, then we do not call it a melodic succession in the sense here intended; because each of these different notes forms with C a triad interval in direct or inverted position, and therefore has to it essentially **harmonic** meaning. Only the **Second** then, ascending or descending, can be counted an essentially **melodic** interval, and that in its meaning of succession, as we have seen it in the scale. The Second, both as simultaneous sound and as succession, is not a directly intelligible interval. By the ratios 8 : 9, 9 : 10, and 15 : 16 the feeling has no determination given to it for pitching any one of these distances; any more than we can find the intonation for many ratios lying between, as 6 : 7, 7 : 8, 10 : 11, 11 : 12, 12 : 13, 14 : 15. But it has already been made evident in the scale that the ratios of these outward distances do not at all come into question in determining Seconds, and that this determination is solely and wholly brought about by the transformation in meaning of a third note.

108. The progression from the first degree of the scale to the second is determined upon the dominant, which passes out of Fifth-meaning into Root-meaning. If then both degrees are heard at once, or if the first continues sounding against the second when that has entered, the harmonic meaning of the Second-interval with regard to the dominant will be: that the dominant is **simultaneously Root** and **Fifth.** This is a contradiction if the double meaning is taken as **persistent.** It may, however, be contained in the note as a **passing** meaning, supposing that in passing from one meaning to the other the note gives up the first, not simultaneously with the actual passage, but later. Consequently dissonance requires a time

precedent and a time subsequent for the justification of its existence, namely, a precedent time of **preparation** and a subsequent time of **resolution.**

109. In the explanation just given, dissonance has not yet appeared in the meaning of **Seventh** in a **chord of the Seventh.** Rather we recognise here the so-called **suspension.** Nevertheless the determinations which are universally valid for all cases of dissonance in simultaneous sounds are already contained therein: that (1) a dissonance can only be produced from a succession, and that (2) wherever a dissonance occurs, the understanding of the dissonant interval is to be found, not in the immediate relation of the two notes which sound dissonant to one another, but in an element lying outside of them, which by their simultaneous sounding is determined to twoness.

CHORD OF THE SEVENTH.

110. The chord of the Seventh is the sounding together of two triads joined by a common interval. It is formed by the passage from one to the other, so that the first persists along with the second.

111. The triads lying nearest the principal triad and joined to it by two notes are the minor triads of the key. The passage out of the C major triad into the a minor triad, keeping the first on with the second, gives the chord of the Seventh *a—C—e—G* in the position of Six-Five-Three, *C—e—G—a.* The passage from the C major triad into the e minor triad under the same conditions gives the chord of the Seventh *C—e—G—b* in the position of Six-Four-Two, *b—C—e—G.* For there *G* goes to *a*, here *C* goes to *b.*

Here we have the sounding together of each of two successions, where chord-progression is meant; where we had it before (par. 108), it was in the meaning of mere melodic note-succession. For instance, in the sounding together of the Second *C—D*, the sense of the dissonance is, that *G* is determined at once as Fifth and Root. But here it is, that the middle interval of the chord of the Seventh (*C—e* in the chord *a—C—e—G*, and *e—G* in the chord *C—e—G—b*) has the double determination of belonging at one time to different triads, and, as of course follows, to each triad in other meaning. For *C—e* is Root and Third in the C major triad, and Third and Fifth in the a minor triad; *e—G* is Third and Fifth in the C major triad, and Root and Third in the e minor triad.

112. In the dissonance of the **suspension** the twoness of meaning is contained in a doubly determined **note**; in the dissonance of the **chord of the Seventh** in a doubly determined **interval**. In the chord of suspension *G—C—D* the note *G* stands in its double meaning in contradiction with itself; and in the chord of the Seventh *a—C—e—G* the middle interval *C—e* contradicts itself in its different determination with respect to the two joined triads, and similarly the interval *e—G* in the chord of the Seventh *C—e—G—b*.

113. Generally, then, to the notion of dissonance, as being in itself an opposition, there must be again attributed the meaning of **Fifth**, after the universal sense of the interval; the consonance which forms the preparation for it has the meaning of **Octave**; and the consonance re-established after resolution the meaning of **Third**. Thus harmony gains with dissonance its perfect notion of consonance; for without dissonance consonance remains fixed in the immediacy of Octave unity, and cannot reach recognition of itself in the notion of the Third.

114. But before we speak of the resolution of dissonance, we have to consider whether chords of the Seventh can result also from other kinds of triad-progression.

115. We have seen that chords of the Seventh are formed when the progression from the tonic triad to one or other of the adjacent minor triads is taken sounding all together, and similar chords will be produced if, starting from any other triad of the key, the passage from it into the next adjacent triads above or below is taken sounding all at once. Thus the joined succession of *a—C—e* ··· *F—a—C* appears as the chord of the Seventh *F—a—C—e* in the form *a—C—e—F*; *F—a—C* joined with *D|F—a*, as the chord of the Seventh *D|F—a—C* in the form *F—a—C—D*; or *e—G—b* joined with *G—b—D*, as the chord of the Seventh *e—G—b—D* in the form *D—e—G—b*; *G—b—D* joined with *b—D|F*, as the chord of the Seventh *G—b—D|F* in the form *F—G—b—D*; and so on.

116. Only those triads which have a harmonic unity, i.e. a common interval, can be taken together at one time: therefore only two triads which are related in two notes. For the passage into the **nearest** is the only immediately intelligible progression. The passage from *C—e—G* to *F—a—C*, which leads to the position *C—F—a*, is a compounded one, and consists of the progressions *C—e—G*···*C—e—a*···*C—F—a*. Both progressions can happen at once, but the second cannot happen before the first or without the first (*C—e—G*···*C—F—G*), as the first can before the second or without the second. Similarly with the succession from *C—e—G* to *G—b—D* which (in *b—D—G*) is compounded of the successions *C—e—G*···*b—e—G*···*b—D—G*. There the passage must lead through the a minor triad, here through the e minor triad. If we wished to think of an immediate passage from the triad of the tonic to the subdominant or dominant triad and to take it all together in a single chord, then the first—to the subdominant—would be heard in *C—e—F—G—a* sounding all at once, and the other—to the dominant—in *C—e—G—b—D*. The former contains the union of *F—a—C—e—G* in the form of the immediate succession

of the two triads *C—e—G* and *F—a—C*; the latter in like manner the union of *C—e—G—b—D* as immediate succession of the triads *C—e—G* and *G—b—D*. The untruth of such a process is at once expressed as **discordance** in the combinations *C—e—F—G—a* and *b—C—D—e—G*.

The way in which such groups as *F—a—C—e—G* and *C—e—G—b—D* can have intelligible meaning, under particular conditions as to the position of their intervals, as so-called '**chords of the Ninth**,' does not belong here.

117. The passage from the triad of the tonic to a dominant or subdominant chord takes place through the intermediate minor triad: from *C—e—G* to *F—a—C* through *a—C—e*; therefore in the progression *C—e—G*···*C—e—a*···*C—F—a*. Here the first step in the voices is *G*··*a*, and the second is *e*··*F*. *F* makes *G* impossible in the union of triads, but not *e*, for *e* belongs to the triad *a—C—e*, which is conjunct with *F—a—C*. Therefore the passage from *C—e—G* to *F—a—C* can be shown, consistently with right progression, only in the chord *C—e—F—a* formed by taking together the last members of the succession *C—e—a* and *C—F—a*. Similarly the passage from the triad of the tonic to that of the dominant, from *C—e—G* to *G—b—D*, mediated by the minor triad *e—G—b*, in the chord *b—D—e—G*.

118. We see that passages even into distant-lying triads, when shaped into harmony of the Seventh, can only take triads together which are closely joined. The passage from *C—e—G* to *F—a—C* gives for its chord of the Seventh the union of the triads *a—C—e* and *F—a—C*, and the passage from *C—e—G* to *G—b—D* for its chord of the Seventh the union of the triads *e—G—b* and *G—b—D*.

119. It may have been perceived from the way in which harmonies of the Seventh arise, so far as we have yet gone, that one note cannot by ascending move on to another, that lasts, so as to

be dissonant with it, namely, as if the Seventh should enter to the Root in ascending motion; but that the Seventh issues in descending motion from the same note that must become Root of the chord of the Seventh. For when the Seventh enters later than the Root—that is, when the upper triad is joined to the lower—the progression which is given by the natural succession happens so that the Root of the lower triad moves downwards into the Fifth of the upper (which forms the Seventh) as into the degree melodically nearest. But when the dissonance is produced by ascending motion, i.e. when the lower triad follows the upper, then the note, which enters in dissonance with the note that lasts, can only be Root of the lower triad, and the Root also of the chord of the Seventh. Therefore when the empirical rule says that the Seventh, when not prepared, shall only be struck after the Root or its Octave, that is quite an organic requirement. The chords of the Seventh in which the diminished triads share are excepted from this rule. We shall see that the reason of the exception may be apprehended as easily as the reason of the rule.

120. Generally there is no rule, which has not its reason in some law of organism. But the rule does not trouble itself to show the reason of what it orders, is often, indeed, unconscious of it; and since it has in eye only the outward show and not the essence of the thing, so for every differing side of the phenomenon, it is itself different. But organic law is the soul, the inward living unity itself: it does not receive its determinations after the outward show; rather it produces them.

121. Triad-progression in itself we found to be of three kinds or grades of relationship; it must now be shown to be triple with respect to combinations into chords of the Seventh.

A triad can pass

(1) Into another triad lying next it, i.e. joined to it by two

common notes; e.g. the tonic triad into one of the two minor triads:

C—e—G···C—e—a, C—e—G···b—e—G.

(2) Into another joined to it by one common note; the tonic triad into the dominant or subdominant triad:

C—e—G···C—F—a, C—e—G···b—D—G.

(3) Into one wholly separate; the tonic triad into one of the two diminished triads:

C—e—G···a—D—F, C—e—G···D—F—b.

How the first two kinds of passage behave with respect to union into chords of the Seventh has been shown above. Now it remains to examine the third kind: the formation of chords of the Seventh belonging to the passage from one triad into another which is disjunct from the first.

122. Starting from the triad of the tonic, the first kind of progression leads to one or other of the minor triads, and joins the tonic triad and the minor triad into a chord of the Seventh. The second kind leads through the minor triad to the dominant (or subdominant) triad, and binds this intermediate minor triad and the dominant (or subdominant) triad together into a chord of the Seventh. The third kind, progressing in like manner, takes its way through the minor and dominant (or subdominant) triads to the diminished triad, and this last joined to the dominant (or subdominant) triad is heard as a chord of the Seventh. For simultaneous chord-union, as we have seen in passages of the second kind, only takes place between the two last triads related by a Third.

Therefore the passage of *C—e—G* to *D|F—a* will produce the chord of the Seventh *D|F—a—C*, and the passage of *C—e—G* to *b—D|F* the chord of the Seventh *G—b—D|F*, both in a position of their intervals answering the conditions of succession.

If we consider the mechanism of this formation it is

(1) Towards the subdominant side:

C—e—G . . . C—e—a . . . C—F—a . . . D/F—a = C—D—F—a.

(2) Towards the dominant side:

C—e—G . . . b—e—G . . . b—D—G . . . b—D/F = b—D—F—G.

123. For triad-succession in itself, apart from its relation to the formation of chords of the Seventh, there can be no mention of taking this triple contracted advance for the link between two disjunct triads; for the fourth triad contains no longer a note of the first, by which it could be seen that the formation of the fourth triad is transformation from the first. Disjunct triads can only be joined to follow immediately upon one another when the triad we start from is replaced by another related both to it and to the unconnected triad. In the passage from *C—e—G* to *D/F—a* the triad *a—C—e* linked the succession, and in the passage from *C—e—G* to *b—D/F* the triad *e—G—b*. In this way Seventh-construction going to the diminished triad of the subdominant side

C—e—G
(a—C—e) . . . a—C—F . . . a—D—F

gives the position *a—C—D—F*; and to the diminished triad of the dominant side

C—e—G
(e—G—b) . . . D—G—b . . . D—F—b

the position *D—F—G—b*. For there the note *a* from the substituted a minor triad, here the note *b* from the substituted e minor triad, supplies the link for the last member.

The above succession, which unites the third and fourth triads of the series into a chord of the Seventh, also contains in it one note of the initial triad. We see, however, that in this advance the first and last triads come to stand side by side in the primary position, for we get towards the subdominant side :

C—e—G . . . C—D—F—a ;

and towards the dominant side :

C—e—G . . . b—D—F—G.

As applied to the particular cases denoted here, i.e. in the passage from the tonic triad to the upper or lower diminished triad, there is nothing felt wrong in the progressions. But suppose we wanted to make the formation universal, and to apply it to Seventh-construction starting from any other triads, taken primary, of the key. For with the first two grades of the progression this did happen, and was allowed by sounding right. E.g.

(1) Towards the subdominant side :

D / F—a . . . D—e—G—b,
e—G—b . . . e—F—a—C,
F—a—C . . . F—G—b—D, &c.

(2) Towards the dominant side :

D / F—a . . . C—e—G—a,
e—G—b . . . D—F—a—b,
F—a—C . . . e—G—b—C, &c.

Thus the progressions carried towards the subdominant side seem to sound right ; but of those towards the dominant side only the first, leading from the tonic triad to the upper diminished triad, remains fit for use unconditionally ; all the others on that side have something that goes against the grain. Here we again meet the practical rule already touched on : that in chords of the Seventh the Seventh must be prepared ; and the exception to the rule : that in the chord of the dominant Seventh the Seventh may enter free when the Root is held. The reason for this exception, and why progressions where the triads stand side by side in primary position (just as they do in those towards the dominant side) may be used towards the subdominant side without producing the effect of consecutive Fifths, cannot be yet explained. We must first examine the resolution of dissonance with its essential conditions, and the nature of those chords of the Seventh which contain union of limits, above all of the so-called chord of the dominant Seventh. Till now this last has only appeared as a chord among other chords in the series of harmonies of the Seventh. But it is, as we know from experience, strongly distinguished by its peculiar character from all other chords of the Seventh.

124. First we shall once more place together in a general view the three kinds of triad-progression, with reference to the Seventh harmonies thence arising, in the order previously adopted for chord-succession in itself, without simultaneous combination.

I. Chord of the Seventh, produced by the passage from one triad into another joined to the first by **two** notes.

(*a*) From the tonic triad to the minor triad of the subdominant side, i.e. from *C—e—G* to *a—C—e*:

$$\underbrace{\text{C—e—G}\ldots\text{C—e—a}} = \text{C—e—G—a.}$$

(*b*) From the tonic triad to the minor triad of the dominant side, i.e. from *C—e—G* to *e—G—b*:

$$\underbrace{\text{C—e—G}\ldots\text{b—e—G}} = \text{b—C—e—G.}$$

II. Chord of the Seventh produced by the passage from one triad into another joined to the first by **one** note.

(*a*) From the tonic triad to the subdominant triad, i.e. from *C—e—G* to *F—a—C*:

$$\text{C—e—G}\ldots\underbrace{\text{C—e—a}\ldots\text{C—F—a}} = \text{C—e—F—a.}$$

(*b*) From the tonic triad to the dominant triad, i.e. from *C—e—G* to *G—b—D*:

C—e—G . . . b—e—G . . . b—D—G = b—D—e—G.

III. Chord of the Seventh produced by the passage from one triad into another **not joined** to the first.

(*A*) Linked by the intermediate triad.

(*a*) From the tonic triad to the diminished triad of the subdominant side, i.e. from *C—e—G* to *D|F—a*:

C—e—G
(a—C—e) . . . a—C—F . . . a—D—F = a—C—D—F.

(*b*) From the tonic triad to the diminished triad of the dominant side, i.e. from *C—e—G* to *b—D|F*:

C—e—G
(e—G—b) . . . D—G—b . . . D—F—b = D—F—G—b.

(*B*) In the succession of triads without substitution of a linking chord.

(*a*) From the tonic triad to the diminished triad of the subdominant side, i.e. from *C—e—G* to *D|F—a*:

C—e—G . . . C—e—a . . . C—F—a . . . D—F—a = C—D—F—a.

(*b*) From the tonic triad to the diminished triad of the dominant side, i.e. from *C—e—G* to *b—D|F*:

C—e—G . . . b—e—G . . . b—D—G . . . b—D—F = b—D—F—G.

RESOLUTION OF DISSONANCE.

(1) In Suspensions.

125. The resolution of the dissonance of suspension consists in the removal of the double meaning, which by the dissonance of two notes to one another is produced in a third note, and the substitution of a simple one in its stead.

In the dissonance first adduced (par. 108), *C*——*D*, the relationship of the two notes is contained in the note *G*. But here by *C* and *D* sounding together *G* is determined to be at once Root and Fifth :

I—II
C G D
I—II

This double sense neither allows the interval *C*——*G* to coalesce by the Third *e* into a triad, nor the Fifth *G*——*D* to be united by the Third *b*. But union may follow at once, as soon as either hindering note is removed. If *C* gives way, then the union of the Fifth *G*——*D* occurs in *b* ; if *D* gives way, then the Fifth *C*——*G* unites in *e*. The entrance of the Third *b* is here a natural consequence of the removal of the Root *C*, just as the entrance of the Third *e* is a natural consequence of the removal of the Fifth *D* ; *b* unites the Fifth *G*——*D*, *e* unites the Fifth *C*——*G* But neither union could happen in the presence at the same time of *C* and *D* ; because *G* meaning Root is contradicted by *C*, and meaning Fifth by *D*. Therefore when *C* passes melodically to *b*, the interruption of the unity of *G*——*D* is removed, and the union of the Fifth at the same time effected. Similarly when *D* moves to *e*, *G* enters into an uninterrupted relation with *C*, and is joined with it into a whole.

126. But of the two resolutions the first, with the progression

F

C··*b*, is the one principally required here, and for this reason: *G* in the preparation by *C* begins with meaning **Fifth**; but as element of a succession it must next become something else than Fifth, and so must become **Root**. Therefore *C* must proceed to *b*, and not *D* to *e*, that the dissonance may be satisfactorily resolved and the required unity effected.

127. This is the dissonance of suspension, in which the note which is the link and is differently determined by the two dissonant notes itself takes part in the combined sound, or when not actually present can be added mentally. In the above example *G* is **Fifth** in the preparation, **Fifth and Root** in the dissonance, **Root** in the resolution. It passes from one simple meaning through double meaning into the other simple meaning.

128. The combined sound *D—e* expresses the arrested passage of *G* from Root-meaning into Fifth-meaning, with a tendency to decide for the latter by *C—e*. The combined sounds *F—G* and *G—a*, as passages determined upon the Root *C*, will in like manner lead to the resolutions *e—G* and *F—a*. The Second *e—F* finds its resolution *D—F* by *b* as link of the dissonance; the Second *a—b*, the resolution *G—b* by *e*; and the Second *b—C*, the resolution *a—C* by *F*.

129. The dissonance *D—e* may, however, be also referred to a linking *a*, *G—a* to *D*, *b—C* to *e*, always according to the sense in which a linked progression is contained in the dissonant interval, and according as it is really intended. The resolution will happen always in like form; but the resolved note will thereafter differ in its chord-meaning; it will be respectively the **Root** or the **Third** of the triad of resolution. So, e.g., the dissonant interval *D—e* referred to *G* as link will lead to the C major triad, and the resolving *C* will have Root-meaning. But if the same dissonance *D—e* is referred to *a* as linking note, then the resolution leads to the minor triad on *a*, and the resolving *C* is Third.

A note resolving downwards can arrive at Fifth-meaning only if the other note of the dissonance moves upwards at the same time.

(2) In Chords of the Seventh.

130. In the dissonance of suspension the dissonant chord may be taken as already essentially that which results after resolution; except that it contains a jarring element to be purged out. With the **chord of the Seventh** it is otherwise. That consists of a combination of two triads, which cannot pass into consonance by the advance of one part alone.

131. In the chord of the Seventh the note linking the dissonance, which appeared in the suspension and was determined to be at once Root and Fifth, is not as yet present; it has to be sought out.

132. Here, too, the linking note must be **Root** to one of the dissonant notes and **Fifth** to the other.

In the chord of the Seventh it must enter instead of the middle ambiguously determined Third-interval, and the resolution will then follow upon it and by it, as with suspensions. For by this link of the dissonance entering instead of the inner Third-interval, the chord of the Seventh has in fact become a chord of suspension.

133. The resolution of the dissonant interval in the chord of the Seventh can happen simultaneously with the entrance of the linking note, or it can follow later. The latter is the treatment, where the Seventh keeps on as a suspension before resolving. Here we have the process in detail, while in the immediate resolution of the chord of the Seventh we have it contracted.

134. E.g. in the chord of the Seventh *e—G—b—D*, as twofold chord made up of the triads *e—G—b* and *G—b—D*, the notes *e* and *D* are as yet without relation to one another. The required note, which brings about the relation, is here *a*, to which *e* stands as Fifth,

D as Root (in the sense in which *D*——*a* counts as a Fifth in the key of C major). Thus the note *a* must enter instead of the Third-interval *G*—*b*, whereby instead of the chord of the Seventh *e*—*G*—*b*—*D* there is produced the chord of suspension *e*—*a*—*D*. And now the linking note *a* can substantiate either Fifth-meaning against *D* or Root-meaning against *e*, both of which meanings are now contained in it at the same time. Therefore either *e* will go on to *F*, or *D* to *C*; and from *e*—*a*—*D* there will arise either *F*—*a*—*D* or *e*—*a*—*C*. It was found above that in the chord of suspension the last resolution, where the linking note receives Root-meaning, is the one principally required; and that is now too the case. In the dissonance *D*—*e* the *e* has more power to last on and push *D* from its place, than *D* has to hold out against *e* and force it to advance. But in the chord of the Seventh the demand for the Seventh to proceed downwards is less pressing than when the suspension is required to be resolved in that motion. According to the foregoing explanation of the preparation and resolution of the dissonance of suspension the necessity for such progression lies principally in the note which is the link and doubly determined in the dissonance, requiring a different meaning in the resolution to that which it had in the preparation. Now, as link in the chord of the Seventh, it has the opposite determinations immediately upon its entrance; for when the chord of the Seventh *e*—*G*—*b*—*D* is replaced by the chord of suspension *e*—*a*—*D*, the linking note *a* in the latter acquires the double meaning at one and the same instant. Therefore it may decide subsequently as well for one as for the other.

135. As the one motion or the other, ascent of the Root or descent of the Seventh, leads alike to unity or determinateness, so if the two parts are mutually repelled, if *e* goes to *F* and *D* to *C* simultaneously, that will also work a resolution. Then *a* comes out of the doubt of being Fifth, or Root to the certainty, in *F*—*a*—*C*, of becoming Third.

136. But the resolution of the dissonance can, and for the most part will, happen simultaneously with the entrance of the linking note; so that in the above example the triads of resolution *e—a—C*, *F—a—D*, and *F—a—C* will follow the chord of the Seventh *e—G—b—D* immediately, without pausing upon the half-way chord of suspension *e—a—D*.

137. This resolution of the chord of the Seventh, in which the direct opposition of Root and Fifth is established in a note entering to link the dissonance, and then in it decides for one or the other simple meaning or for the meaning of Third, we may regard as the principal form; namely, because, by the entrance of the note which links the dissonance and takes the place of the middle interval, the triad twoness is removed and the consonance can enter unhindered.

138. When it was said above (par. 131) that in the chord of the Seventh the two dissonant notes as yet wanted connexion, what was meant was the want of that antithetical relation, which is present in the chord of suspension, and in the chord of the Seventh after the connecting note has entered with its simultaneous Root- and Fifth-meaning. An antithetical relation, but not of strong opposition, between the dissonant notes of the chord of the Seventh may, however, be found already in the chord itself. Not that of a note being determined as at one time **Root** and **Fifth**, but of its being determined as at one time **Root** and **Third**, or **Fifth** and **Third**. This determination is already contained in the two notes of the middle interval referred to the dissonant extremes. In the chord of the Seventh *e—G—b—D*, chosen above as example, *G* stands in a consonant relation to *e* as well as to *D*, but to each of the two notes in a different chord-meaning. So *b* stands consonantly to *e* as well as to *D*, and again is differently determined to the two notes. *G* is Third of the triad *e—G—b*, and Root of the triad *G—b—D*, but it must become Fifth of the triad *C—e—G* if resolution is to be effected by means of it; for the dissonance *e—G——D* can only

be resolved into *e—G—C*. On the other hand, *b* is Third of the triad *G—b—D* and Fifth of the triad *e—G—b*, but must become Root of the diminished triad *b—D|F* for the resolution to be determined upon it. For, again, *e——b—D* can only reach resolution in *F—b—D*.

139. Here, since the dissonant interval can be referred either to one or to the other of the middle notes of the chord, we see that the double determination is indeed doubly present. For the lower note of the middle interval is Third of the lower triad and Root of the upper, while the upper note is Fifth of the lower triad and Third of the upper.

Now because the resolution can only be effected with respect to one of the two middle notes, the other double meaning remains unresolved. The other note in which the double meaning is still contained has, however, as good a right to have it remedied, as the one for which that has been done. But instead of receiving satisfaction it is compelled to move forwards; unless, indeed, it will persist as new dissonance in the consonance which has followed the resolution of the one note. To this, however, not having been properly cared for in the state of dissonance, it will show greater inclination than to moving onwards. Thus the resolution of the chord *e—G—b—D* upon the Third *G*, easily produces a new chord of the Seventh *e—G—b—C* instead of the triad *e—G—C*; and the resolution of the same chord upon the Fifth *b*, easily produces the chord of the Seventh *F—G—b—D* instead of the triad *F—b—D*. In fact by mere reference of the dissonance to one or the other middle member of the chord of the Seventh the triad twoness is not yet removed. It was removed in the other resolution of the chord of the Seventh previously shown; and there, as in the chord of suspension, a more decided restoration of consonance followed.

140. Thus in the second manner of resolution one of the middle parts of the chord of the Seventh is held, and the progression is determined upon it, while the other, if it does not endure and become new dissonance, has to proceed to one and the same note with the

part resolved. Besides this we have yet to mention a third kind, which proceeds in respect, not of one of the two middle notes, but of both at once, as an interval which remains and changes meaning; because from twofold meaning, to which in the dissonance it is determined, it arrives at simple by melodic advance of the dissonant parts.

141. This is that resolution in which the interval of the minor Seventh is by divergent progression of both the extreme parts enlarged to the Octave, with which the persistent middle interval must stand in consonant relation: e.g.

G—b—D—F . . . f♯—b—D—f♯

or *G—b♭—D♭—F . . . G♭—b♭—D♭—G♭.*

This resolution can therefore only occur for chords with a minor Seventh, in which the diminished triad takes part; because only these can fulfil the conditions of the resolution. It must be observed besides, that here the resolution leads into another key, because it can only happen by chromatic progression of one of the two parts. Now chromatically different notes never lie inside the same key.

142. In the first example above the sense of the resolution is, that the middle interval *b—D*, which by *G* and *F* is determined to have a double chord-meaning, receives a simple meaning by the progression of the two mutually dissonant voices to the Octave *f♯—f♯*. In the second example the case is similar. The middle interval *B♭—d♭*, which in *g—B♭—d♭—F* has double meaning, in *G♭—b♭—D♭—G♭* is not different as it is an interval, but only as it means part of a chord. *B♭/D♭* would be different as an interval from *B♭—d♭* or *b♭—D♭*, as will be understood from what was said earlier.

143. This kind of resolution is less in use than any other. (For the succession of chords derived from the b minor key-system stretching out to the dominant side, namely *g—B—d—e♯*... *F♯—B—d—F♯*, cannot be confounded with the succession *G—b—D—F*...*f♯—b—D—f♯*.) Yet it was necessary to adduce it, that all possible forms might be surveyed together. And now

it results, that the dissonant interval may pass in its resolution into each of the three intervals of the triad.

(1) Into the **Third**; when one of two parts dissonant as a Second moves in resolving away from the other: the Seventh moving downwards **or** the Root upwards.

(2) Into the **Fifth**; when both parts dissonant as a Seventh move in resolving towards each other: the Seventh moving downwards **and** the Root upwards.

(3) Into the **Octave**; when both parts dissonant as a Seventh move in resolving away from one another: the Seventh moving chromatically upwards and the Root diatonically downwards, or the Root chromatically downwards and the Seventh diatonically upwards.

144. Thus every kind of melodic progression (not by springs) in the dissonant parts, which leads them away from or towards one another into one of the three triad intervals, contains the possibility of a resolution of the chord of the Seventh, and the resolution can be brought about:

(1) by a new note,
(2) by one of the two middle notes,
(3) by both.

145. The general scheme of the resolution of dissonance, as hitherto discussed, can be tabulated in the following form. But herein we take no count of difference in the triads combined, namely as they are major, minor, or diminished; we denote only the combination itself. That two triads of the same kind can never be shown united, is self-evident from the organic connexion of chords and from the nature of the key-system.

The diminished triads are also counted as organic chord-formations. The chords of the Seventh *G—b—D*|*F*, *b—D*|*F—a*, *D*|*F—a—C*, though printed with the elements from the dominant and subdominant chords separated by a line of division, are none the less grounded as combinations of triads. The chord *G—b—D*|*F* cannot have organic meaning as a union of the dominant triad with the subdominant Root, nor the chord *D*|*F*—*a*—*C* as a union of the dominant Fifth with the subdominant triad. Only things of like kind can be united. With the triad only the triad can enter into union, but not the single chord-element, the solitary note. The first of the two chords of the Seventh contains the union of the triad *G*—*b*—*D* with the triad *b*—*D*|*F*, the second contains the union of the triad *D*|*F*—*a* with the chord *F*—*a*—*C*. At the same time the interval of disunion *D*|*F* still has its meaning, and will always distinguish the chords of the Seventh in which it takes part essentially from the rest. But the particular attribute does not shut them out from the general determination, which, as chords of the Seventh, they have in common with the others.

146. The dissonance as **suspension** is in general notation either

$$(a)\begin{cases}\text{I—II} & \\ & \text{I—II}\end{cases} \text{ or } (b)\begin{cases}\text{III—II} & \\ & \text{I—II}\end{cases}.$$

For *a*, resolution may happen in two different ways; namely, the double meaning in $\begin{cases}\text{II}\\ \text{I}\end{cases}$ may be determined to I or to II.

For *b*, only one kind of resolution is possible; that is, for $\begin{cases}\text{II}\\ \text{I}\end{cases}$ to give up the I; because the Third (III) contained in the combination has already pronounced for the meaning II, not being able to progress melodically without coming into dissonance with the middle note. Thus the resolutions for *a* will be:

$$(\alpha)\begin{cases}\text{I—II} & \\ & \text{I—II}\end{cases} \qquad (\beta)\begin{cases}\text{I—II} & \\ & \text{I—II}\end{cases}$$

$$\text{III——I—II} \qquad \text{I—II——III,}$$

the resolution for *b*:

$$\begin{array}{l}\text{III—II}\\ \qquad\text{I——II}\\ \text{III—II—I.}\end{array}$$

147. The first form, $\begin{cases} \text{I—II} & \\ & \text{I—II} \end{cases}$, gives the so-called chord of the Fifth and Fourth, in which the Fourth is contained as suspension of the **Third** (Resolution *a*). The reason why the resolution *β*, in which the Fifth must be considered as a suspension of the Sixth, is not normally effective, has been mentioned earlier (par. 126).

The second form, $\begin{cases} \text{III—II} & \\ & \text{I——II} \end{cases}$, gives the suspension above the **Root**: the Seventh as suspension of the Sixth in the chord of Six-Three. A suspension over the **Fifth** as dissonance will not be found until the chord of the Seventh; in the triad, as Sixth, it is neither dissonant against the Root nor against the Third; the Sixth added to the Root and the Third only forms a transposed triad, of which it is itself the Root, the Third being Fifth and the bass Third. But in the chord of the Seventh a suspended Sixth is in fact again a suspended Fourth in the upper triad.

148. The dissonance of the chord of the Seventh may be expressed generally in the form

$$\begin{cases} \text{I—III—II} & \\ & \text{I—III—II} \end{cases}$$

The resolutions of the chord of the Seventh we have seen to be of two essentially different kinds. The **first** is, that instead of the inner interval of the chord there enters a new note mediating in itself between the two dissonant notes; resolution then follows as in the chord of suspension:

$$\begin{cases} \text{I—III—II} & \\ & \text{I—III—II} \end{cases}$$

$$\begin{cases} \text{II——I} & \\ & \text{II——I} \end{cases}$$

The **second** is when the mediation of the dissonance is found in the contents of the chord of the Seventh itself.

A. In one (*a*) or else in the other (*β*) of the two middle notes:

$$(a)\begin{cases}\text{I—III—II} \\ \quad\quad\text{I— III—II}\end{cases} \qquad (\beta)\begin{cases}\text{I—III—II} \\ \quad\quad\text{I— III—II}\end{cases}$$

$$\begin{cases}\text{I—III} \\ \quad\quad\text{I ——— II}\end{cases} \qquad \begin{cases}\text{I ———II} \\ \quad\quad\quad\quad\text{III—II}\end{cases}$$

With *a* the chord again acquires the meaning of a suspension; the resolution here is:

$$\begin{cases}\text{I—-III} \\ \quad\quad\text{I——II}\end{cases}$$
$$\text{III— II —I}$$

with *β* the resolution is:

$$\begin{cases}\text{I ——— II} \\ \quad\quad\quad\quad\text{III—II}\end{cases}$$
$$\text{II——I— III}$$

B. If the resolution is to be determined in respect of both middle notes at once, taken as an interval, so that this middle interval persists and becomes consonant in the chord of resolution, then that again may happen in two ways, according to the quality of the triads combined in the chord of the Seventh:

$$(a)\begin{cases}\text{I—III—II} \\ \quad\quad\text{I— III—II}\end{cases} \qquad (\beta)\begin{cases}\text{I—III—II} \\ \quad\quad\text{I— III—II}\end{cases}$$
$$\text{II——I— III——II} \qquad \text{I——III—II ——I}$$

In (*a*) the Seventh moves chromatically upwards, in (*β*) the Root chromatically downwards. Here the middle interval in the chord of the Seventh has the double meaning $\begin{cases}\text{III—II} \\ \text{I— III}\end{cases}$; in the first resolution (*a*) it decides for I—III, in the second (*β*) for III—II.

The last kind of resolution of the chord of the Seventh requires chromatic progression, and thereby brings about a change of key.

Yet other ways of resolution will have to be cited, in which chromatic changes enter; but of these the fitting place is not found till afterwards. For they give rise to a union of chords of the Seventh following immediately one upon the other; and that is a succession which ought previously to be considered in itself, as coming organically into existence.

PROGRESSION OF PARTS IN SEVENTH HARMONY.

149. The progression of the Seventh in giving rise to harmony of the Seventh cannot be other than it is in triad-succession. For harmony of the Seventh is really nothing else than such succession gathered up into a chord; and, as we have already seen, it can only contain two conjunct or rather two overlapping triads.

In the passage from *C—e—G* to *G—b—D*, the note *b* to be understood must mean advanced *C*, and *D* advanced *e*. *D* cannot be derived from *C*. That would express immediate passage from *C——G* to *G——D*, such as occurs in scale construction. But chord passage from *C—e—G* to *G—b—D* can only happen by means of *e—G—b*: as *C—e—G···b—e—G···b—D—G*; and the harmony of the Seventh produced from it can only contain the succession *b—e—G···b—D—G* united as *b—D—e—G*, in the same position and with the same progression of the parts as in the triad-succession.

150. Accordingly, when the Seventh enters to the Root already present, i.e. when the triad which lies uppermost is joined on to the triad next underneath, it can only issue from the Root of the lower triad; for no other part can melodically lead to the Fifth of the upper triad; and there can be no directly intelligible progression except that conceived melodically. That is, the Seventh

must issue as a Second from the Root of the lower triad, and thus form the Fifth of the upper triad, or *vice versâ*; because the change of chord consists in this difference alone. Where other progressions happen, or where the note gone over enters in another meaning in the new chord, there, in fact, combined successions are present: such that in them has taken place a double progression, a twofold change. So, e.g., in the succession *C—e—G···G—b—D* in the position *b—D—G*, where the root *C* has first advanced to the Fifth *b* of the triad *e—G—b*, and then the Root *e* of this latter to the Fifth *D* of the triad *G—b—D*. In Seventh-formation, then, the first and second or the second and third triads in the row must be joined, as *b—C—e—G* or *b—D—e—G*.

Wherefore, if the unprepared Seventh can only enter descending from the Root itself or its Octave, because the connexion of the triads produces it in this manner alone, it follows that for the Seventh to move ascending on to the Root must always be against the natural order of passage.

151. Let us now consider the opposite succession, that towards the subdominant side, i.e. leading from an upper triad to a lower. Here the Fifth of the first triad advances to the Root of the second joined closest to it. In the triad succession from *G—b—D* to *e—G—b*, which leads to the position *G—b—e*, *D* has advanced to *e*. The Seventh-harmony of this succession appears in the position *G—b—D—e*. Here the note added to the initial triad is **Root** of the chord of the Seventh. In the succession towards the dominant side it was its **Seventh**, as such the **Fifth** of the upper triad, and then by its nature a **second**, something that makes no beginning and that can only enter in succession to something gone before. Therefore the unprepared Seventh will not appear otherwise than struck after the Root or its Octave, and for this very reason, be it said in passing, preferably too upon that part of the bar which corresponds metrically to it, the **second** or so-called

'**weak**' part. On the other hand the Root of the chord of the Seventh, which is as well **Root** of the lower triad, has the nature of a beginning; it is in essence a **first**, something that can precede something else. The unprepared Seventh struck afterwards as in the succession *C—e—G···b—C—e—G* will always be heard as a part that has moved onwards; the Root entering to the prepared Seventh produces rather the effect of a fresh part added. The chord of the Seventh with prepared Seventh finds moreover its appropriate place upon the **first**, so-called '**strong**,' metrical member of the bar.

152. So too, taken quite generally, to any note held may be struck the next lying over it, but not the next lying under. The former is always a positive, a first, a **Root**; the latter a relative, a second, a **Fifth**. Therefore the form  is under all circumstances a right one; the opposite, , is admissible only under particular conditions. The simultaneous sound of two contiguous notes when the lower follows the higher can only appear in the form 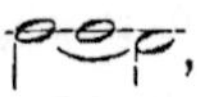, particular occurrences excepted.

153. From this it becomes manifest, why out of the successions above (par. 123) constructed into chords of the Seventh, from one triad into another not joined to it, those which lead to the subdominant side alone sound right; but those to the dominant side, with the exception of the first (*C—e—G···b—D—F—G*), cross-grained, disjointed, and 'Fifthy.' The succession from the triad *C—e—G* to the triad *D/F—a*, which there comes out as a chord of the Seventh in the form *C—D—F—a*, does not sound Fifthy, because there exists no necessity for deriving the note *D* from *C* or for hearing it as a *C* that has gone forward; as Root of a chord of the Seventh it can be just as well derived from the *e* of the C major triad, supposing that a natural progression should introduce it by this road. But taking the triad *D/F—a* first and letting *C—e—G* follow, whereby

the chord of the Seventh is produced in the position *C—e—G—a*, then in that case the Seventh *G* must either have arisen from the advance of *a*, according to which the triads *D/F—a* and *C—e—G* would stand next one another in Fifth-position, unlinked, and therefore not as a succession; or else in *C—e—G—a* the note *G* will be heard as an *F* moved onwards, that is, as a Seventh not derived from the Root of the a minor triad, but entering disjointedly; which, as has been shown, is inorganic, and must also sound wrong. Therefore, for all cases, Seventh formations going to disjunct triads lying beneath, i.e. in the subdominant direction, as

C—e—G···C—D—F—a
D / F—a···D—e—G—b
e—G—b···e—F—a—C, and so on,

in this form sound right; those going to disjunct triads lying above, i.e. in the dominant direction, as

C—e—G··· b—D—F—G
b—D / F··· a—C—e—F
a—C—e···G—b—D—e, and so on,

with the exception of the first, *C—e—G···b—D—F—G*, sound Fifthy or disjointed; in a word, wrong.

154. We have found that for the passing Seventh melodic motion descending from the Root alone accords with natural succession, and not motion ascending on to it; but that with the prepared Seventh the Root can enter either way. The explanation of those successions, where the Root of the lower triad cannot be derived from the Fifth of the upper, still remains to be given as regards their inner meaning. We mean those which, like *C—e—G··· C—D—F—a*, contain an apparent juxtaposition of two primary triads, yet do not give the effect of consecutive Fifths. We have indeed found, that here the note *D*, in respect of the construction

of the dissonance, may be as well derived from the Third *e* as from the Root *C*. But it has been also said, that the progression of parts in harmony of the Seventh can be no other than that in triad succession. Now if we make the Seventh-chord arise in the passage to the disjunct triad, as the Seventh-chords arose in the passage to conjunct triads, and therefore the above chord *C—D—F—a* in the succession

$$\text{C—e—G}\ldots\text{C—e—a}\ldots\underbrace{\text{C—F—a}\ldots\text{D—F—a}} = \text{C—D—F—a},$$

then the note *D* is by no means produced melodically from *e*. There is no possibility at all that it should have been so produced, because the harmony of the Seventh arises only from the union of the two last triads of the triple succession, *C—F—a* and *D*|*F—a*; but with the triad *C—F—a* the note *e*, Third of the C major triad, which in *C—e—a* lasted on as Fifth of the a minor triad, is removed. Even if we would derive the Seventh-harmony *C—D—F—a* from the a minor triad of the succession in the manner of chord-unions of the second degree of affinity (par. 91), *C* must still progress to *D*, *e* to *F*. Now apparent necessity for leading *e* to *D*, intentional working towards a set end, cannot be brought in here; because we are not now speaking of fine-art construction, but only of natural formations self-produced, without approach of individually determined will. Therefore the succession *C—e—G* ··· *C—D—F—a*, if justifying itself to the ear, must be explained from some other grouping than the one denoted above: $C\text{—}e\text{—}G\cdots C\text{—}e\text{—}a\cdots\underbrace{C\text{—}F\text{—}a\cdots D\text{—}F\text{—}a}$ $=C\text{—}D\text{—}F\text{—}a$; for that contains progression of Fifths *C—G*··· *D—a* between the first chord and the last.

SUCCESSION OF SEVENTH CHORDS.

155. In the second kind of resolution of the Seventh (par. 138) there is contained the germ of a continued series of joined Seventh chords. That resolution was effected by the intervention of one of the two notes of the middle interval of the chord. E.g. in the Seventh chord *e—G—b—D* the dissonance can be found as a double meaning either in *G*, as

I—II
e G D
III—II

or in *b*, as

I-III
e b D
I——II

and the resolution will in the first case be

e G C
III - II—I

and in the other

F b D
II—I-III.

In the first case the progression leads towards the subdominant side, in the second towards the dominant ; for in the first the Third of the lower triad, and in the second the Third of the upper triad, is the note which determines the resolution. But because in neither of these two determinations is the whole of the middle interval accounted for in the resolution, but only one or the other of its notes, therefore, as was earlier noticed, the slighted note is more inclined to stop in its place than to move forward to the restoration of consonance. It has no interest in the resolution. But so a new dissonance arises, because the note which moves to its resolution comes into dissonance with the note which stays, and that as Root or as Seventh of a new Seventh chord. For with the Seventh chord above, *e—G—b—D*, taking the *G* as link, the resolution *e—G—b—C* follows, and, taking the *b* as link, the resolution *F—G—b—D*; supposing that in the first case *b*, in the second *G*, stays in its place. With this, one Seventh-harmony has passed into another. If this succession be continued further in the same way, then, starting from the tonic triad, the following two series will arise :—

(1) Towards the **subdominant** side, when in the Seventh chords the **lower** note of the middle interval determines the resolution :

C—e—G ··· C—e—G—a ··· C—e—F—a ··· C—D—F—a ··· b—D—F—a···

(2) Towards the **dominant** side, when in the Seventh chords the **upper** note of the middle interval determines the resolution :

C—e—G ··· b—C—e—G ··· b—D—e—G ··· b—D—F—G ··· b—D—F—a···

In the first series may now be found that which by triad progression alone could not be produced, continuous succession from the first member to the fourth, from *C—e—G* to *C—D—F—a*; in which the Root of the triad *D|F—a* is produced, not by the ascent of *C*, but by the descent of *e*, which as Seventh of *F* had to resolve to *D*.

156. This series contains in each of its members a construction of dissonance following correctly from the member next preceding. The other, on the contrary, is at once manifested to be inadmissible in the succession from the second member to the third, because there the Seventh moves ascending on to the Root; now if not prepared the Seventh can only proceed from the Root. Therefore if the succession *C—e—G··b—D—F—G* commends itself as perfectly right to the ear, its construction is not to be

explained out of the second of the above series in the same way as the construction of the succession *C—e—G···C—D—F—a* is explained out of the first, in which every member stands in right succession with that which goes before as well as with that which follows. Here the process of construction must be otherwise derived. We shall return to it in considering the chord of the dominant Seventh.

157. Every succession from a triad to the disjunct triad upon the dominant side, except only that which leads from the tonic to the upper diminished triad, will also at once bring out the same incongruity in the construction of the dissonance as that just found in the example given ; as, e.g., *D/F—a···C—e—G—a, e—G—b··· D—F—a—b, F—a—C···e—G—b—C,* and so on. We always have to choose between hearing two triads moved side by side in primary position, and finding the Seventh ascend on to the Root. But the one and the other are alike against the nature of continuous progression.

158. The passage *C—e—G···C—D—F—a*, in the subdominant series above, stands in intelligible succession by its intermediate members *C—e—G—a* and *C—e—F—a*. Now this succession leads through two Seventh chords preceding *C—D—F—a*, and so joins the third Seventh chord in sequence with the first. Thus a series of Seventh chords progressing through the first, third, fifth, seventh members of the one above, must also be linked intelligibly. For from the third to the fifth, from the fifth to the seventh, there is repeated only the same relation of the first to the third.

159. The **first** series puts together in Seventh-harmonics a progression of triads related in the **Third**. In the **second**, which every time passes by a member of the first without stopping, we get as Seventh-succession a progression of triads related in the **Fifth**. The same follows if we progress through the second, fourth, sixth, eighth members. A **third** series, led through the first, fourth,

seventh, tenth members, contains in the succession from one member to another a contraction of three progressions; and can therefore, after the first step starting from the triad, no longer regularly appear to follow correctly. For such a progression brings with it the simultaneous advance of three parts by a Second, namely, continual passage into disjunct triads. This, it is true, may be correctly managed by means of intermediate triads (par. 90); but the course of the parts thereby necessitated comes into contradiction with that which the Seventh to be resolved demands here. It does so quite decidedly in the succession of the fourth, fifth, and sixth members of the series, as well as in those which correspond periodically with that place, where triads in primary position twice stand next one another. Therefore in this series those successions will alone seem right to the ear which answer to linked progression of disjunct triads and at the same time fulfil the requirements of dissonance.

160. The **first** series of joined Seventh-harmonies, progressing towards the **subdominant** side in triads related in the **Third**, is:

1.	2.	3.	4.
C—e—G ···	C—e—G—a ···	C—e—F—a ···	C—D—F—a ···
C	a7	$\mathrm{F}_{\not 7}$	D°_{7}

5.	6.	7.	8.
b—D—F—a ···	b—D—F—G ···	b—D—e—G ···	b—C—e—G ···
b°_{7}	G7	e7	$\mathrm{C}_{\not 7}$

The **second**, progressing in triads related in the **Fifth**:

1.	2.	3.	4.
C—e—G ···	C—e—F—a ···	b—D—F—a ···	b—D—e—G ···
C	$\mathrm{F}_{\not 7}$	b_{7}	e7

5.	6.	7.	8.
a—C—e—G ···	a—C—D—F ···	G—b—D—F ··	G—b—C—e ···
a7	D°_{7}	G7	$\mathrm{C}_{\not 7}$

The **third**, progressing in triads without direct relationship:

1. C—e—G ··· 2. C—D—F—a ··· 3. b—D—e—G ··· 4. a—C—e—F···

C D_7 e7 $F_{7\backslash}$

5. G—b—D—F ··· 6. G—a—C—e ··· 7. F—a—b—D ··· 8. e—G—b—C ···

G7 a7 b°_{7} $C_{7\backslash}$

the last offending against triad continuity in the successions 4–5 and 5–6.

161. To complete our view of the whole subject, the corresponding three series of joined Seventh-harmonies towards the **dominant** side shall also find place here; the stubborn succession of the same has already been discussed.

The **first** series, progressing in triads related in the **Third**, is:

1. C—e—G ··· 2. b—C—e—G ··· 3. b—D—e—G ··· 4. b—D—F—G ···

C $C_{7\backslash}$ e7 G7

5. b—D—F—a ··· 6. C—D—F—a ··· 7. C—e—F—a ··· 8. C—e—G—a ···

b°_{7} D°_{7} $F_{7\backslash}$ a7

The **second**, progressing in triads related in the Fifth:

1. C—e—G ··· 2. b—D—e—G ··· 3. b—D—F—a ··· 4. C—e—F—a ···

C e7 b°_{7} $F_{7\backslash}$

5. C—e—G—b ··· 6. D—F—G—b ··· 7. D—F—a—C ··· 8. e—G—a—C ···

$C_{7\backslash}$ G7 D°_{7} a7

The **third**, progressing in triads without direct relationship:

1.	2.	3.	4.
C—e—$\dot{G}$ ...	b—D—F—G ...	C—e—F—a ...	D—e—G—b ...
C	G7	F$\not 7$	e7
5.	**6.**	**7.**	**8.**
D—F—a—C ...	e—G—b—C ...	F—a—b—D ...	G—a—C—e ...
D^{o}_{7}	C$\not 7$	b_{7}	a7

The first two series are marked faulty by the entrance ascending of the Seventh. In the third, to this must be added the inconsequent progression of the disjunct triads, which in the progression towards the subdominant side was enough to prevent the series from subsisting without periodic interruption.

162. Thus altogether a sequence of Seventh-harmonies can be framed only to the subdominant side, because in that direction alone are the requirements of organically lawful succession corresponded to. And here in the first and second series it may be continued uninterruptedly, but in the third it is interrupted by Fifth successions, which set in periodically.

163. But a sequence in Seventh-harmonies towards the dominant side is self-contradictory. This series is really an inverted one. In the opposite direction, if the progression were from the third to the second, from the fourth to the third member, it would seem quite consequent; because then it becomes exactly a subdominant series, or a series in which the Third of the **lower** triad is taken as linking the dissonance. (In the dominant series it is the Third of the **upper** triad upon which the resolution follows.) So too the progression here from the fourth to the second, from the fifth to the third member, and so forth, would follow quite correctly.

164. Seventh-formation, when carried towards the dominant side, can only consist of mere triad-union, and not of linked Seventh chords, as found practicable in the direction towards the subdominant

side. Therefore upon the dominant side, only the passages into triads related in the Third and in the Fifth can be gathered up into a Seventh chord, but not the passage into a disjunct triad. Towards the subdominant side that also is a possible progression, linked, namely, by Seventh chords.

165. The possibility of framing dissonance towards the disjunct triads of the dominant side is not thereby unconditionally denied; only the combination cannot be reached by the linking drawn directly from this series. The succession *a—C—e···G—b—D—e*, which out of the primary position of the first triad is bad, will seem perfectly right out of the Six-Three position of the same, *C—e—a···b—D—e—G*; because here the chords *C—e—a* and *b—D—G* stand in right succession to one another, and the Seventh *D* is produced from the *e*. Similarly the Six-Four position of the first triad would afford a good progression.

166. Now if the succession *C—e—G···b—D—F—G* is found right to feeling, and yet cannot be linked by the series *C—e—G···b—C—e—G···b—D—e—G···b—D—F—G* (as the succession *C—e—G···C—D—F—a* is linked by the series *C—e—G···C—e—G—a···C—e—F—a···C—D—F—a*); and if further in this subdominant series every passage to a disjunct triad, as *D|F—a···D—e—G—b*, *e—G—b···e—F—a—C*, *F—a—C···F—G—b—D*, is right equally with the first, but in the dominant series, except the first, every other, as *D|F—a···C—e—G—a*, *e—G—b···D—F—a—b*, *F—a—C···e—G—b—C*, seems wrong; then the goodness of the succession *C—e—G···b—D—F—G* must by all means have its reason in something else than the linking derived from these series. Now simple triad-linking will bring about the union of the minor triad with the dominant triad. But from the Seventh chord hence arising *b—D—e—G* to the union of the dominant and the diminished triads in *b—D—F—G* there is required a progression of the *e* to *F*; and this makes the Seventh

enter ascending to the Root. This is what we hear in the succession *C—e—G···b—D—F—G*, where the entrance ascending of the Seventh does not strike the mind as being contrary to smooth progression. This smoothness is founded in the nature of the **chord of the dominant Seventh,** which results from the union of these two triads. We have now to consider this more closely, as the first of the three chords of the Seventh in which the limits of the key-system appear joined.

SEVENTH CHORDS OF THE KEY-SYSTEM PASSING INTO ITSELF.

I. Dominant Seventh Chord.

167. We have found the essence of harmonic dissonance in a contradiction, a double determination, that the sounding together of two dissonant notes produces in a third note. It is the simultaneous determination of a note to be Root and Fifth, Root and Third, or Third and Fifth. But decided opposition is only contained in the first determination. For the Third according to its notion unites Root and Fifth in itself, and therefore is not the opposite of one or other of these two triad elements in their separation, but rather only the opposite of the separation itself. Thus a completely satisfactory resolution of the Seventh chord could not be reached through one of the notes of the chord, which have only the imperfect opposition of the Third with one of the other two elements; but a fresh note had to enter instead of the middle interval, and then in it the two dissonant notes call forth the double determination of Root and Fifth.

168. This double determination of strong opposition is situated in the very origin of the key itself, when its dominant and subdominant are sounded at once; for then the tonic is at once Fifth of the subdominant and Root of the dominant:

I——II
F C G
I——II

This is the **Fifth**-relation of the two notes, which they have as regards the Root, and it splits the Root into opposite meanings. **Third**-relation (connexion in a chord) the dissonant notes find in the simultaneous union of the dominant triad with the diminished triad of the dominant side, *G—b—D——b—D—F*, as dominant Seventh chord,

I—III—II
G b D F
I—III—II

which for its resolution postulates that former Fifth-relation of the notes *F* and *G* in the Root *C*.

169. This Seventh chord has the same importance in the key as dissonance which the tonic triad possesses as consonance. The former refers unambiguously to the latter; for it is precisely the Root of the tonic triad itself, which is here set at two in itself by the two dissonant notes, and its unity restored by the resolution. Therefore it is that this Seventh chord leads to the perfect cadence.

170. Characteristic of the dominant Seventh chord, as also of the Seventh chord on the Third of the dominant, to be hereafter more minutely discussed, is the interval of the diminished Fifth, which in this harmony is contained between the Third of the dominant chord and the Root of the subdominant chord. If in the key of C major or C minor the notes *b* and *F* sound together, then *b* will want to move to *C*, *F* to *e* (in the minor key to *e*♭). Between *b* and *F* no triad unity is present; therefore to bring one about by the nearest way is what is wanted. But each note seeks to make itself felt, and so the note *F* draws *b* up to *C*, and the note *b* drags *F* down to *e*. In the minor key *b* will draw *F* to *e*♭, because *b* and *e*♭ stand by the augmented triad *e*♭—*G*—*b* in nearer chord-relation

than the notes *b* and *F* taken out of the separated dominant and subdominant triads. For even if the limits of the key-system are outwardly united in its passage into itself, yet the inward separation, the twoness of basis, will always prevent such a union from producing a triad unity, such as we have comprehended in the notion of the major or minor triad. The diminished triad *D|F—a* contains indeed in *F—a* the interval of Third, but not in *D——a* an interval of Fifth; the diminished triad *b—D|F* contains neither Fifth nor Third interval. Similarly in the two diminished triads of the minor key *D|F—a♭*, *b—D|F*, neither interval is contained; and, in respect of the Fifth, the difference in our notation of capital and small letters has already brought this prominently before the eyes. It is true that in the so-called augmented triad

III—I
e♭ G b
I—III

Fifth-relation of the outside notes is also not present, but then both are bound to the middle note in Third-relation. On the other hand the diminished triads contain only one direct relation between two notes, *D|F—a*, *b—D|F*, while the third stands in triad-relation to neither of the other two. Thus the dissonant augmented triad may still lay claim to a meaning of unity as against the diminished, and the interval *b——e♭*, against *b——F*, count as an approach towards unity, proportionably to the nature of the minor key.

171. Although the splitting in two of the principal triad is most strongly manifested in the Third of the dominant sounded together with the Root of the subdominant triad, yet it is also contained (and with the same meaning) in the Fifth of the dominant sounded together with the Root of the subdominant. Only the dissonance of these two notes is less plainly to be felt, because we may be tempted to confuse the Fifth of the dominant with the Third

below of the subdominant (e.g. in the C major key *D* with *d*); hence the chord *D*/*F*—*a*, where not determined by the context, may be easily taken for the d minor triad *d*—*F*—*a*, and in itself appears less like a diminished chord than the chord *b*—*D*/*F* does. In the minor key there is not room for this confusion, because there the difference of *D*/*F*—*a*♭ and *d*♭—*F*—*a*♭, which is correlative to **that in** the major key of *D*/*F*—*a* and *d*—*F*—*a*, is sufficiently distinct to the ear.

172. In the combined sound of the Third and Fifth of the dominant with the subdominant Root and its Third, in *b*—*D*/*F*—*a*, the limits of the key-system have come together. In this union *b*—*D*/*F*—*a* we must think of the key-system as **turned about upon itself**. The **boundaries** placed **united** as **middle** make the **middle** come out **divided** as **boundaries**.

F a C e G b D
(e) G—b—D/F—a—C (e)

Here the middle *b*—*D*/*F*—*a* as Seventh chord refers its dissonance *b*——*a* to the middle of the system, i.e. to *e*, the **Third** of the tonic triad, which from meaning union as Third

I—III—II
C e G

is by *b* and *a* brought into contradiction by meaning at once Root and Fifth.

I——II
a e b
I——II

173. The same applies to the minor key-system with regard to the Seventh chord *b*—*D*/*F*—*a*♭ and *e*♭, the Third of the tonic:

F ab C eb G b D

(eb) G—b—D/F—ab—C (eb).

174. Reference to the **Root** *C* in the dissonance *G*——*F* is a property of the dominant Seventh chord *G—b—D/F*, in the major as well as in the minor key; wherefore this chord, and not that just named, may rightly lay claim to the meaning of **principal Seventh-harmony.** Then the Seventh chord which stands opposite to the principal one, namely, *D/F—a—C* or *D/F—ab—C*, relates to the **Fifth** of the tonic triad. These three Seventh chords, standing in their dissonance in antithetical relation to the notes of the tonic triad, all contain the interval of the joined limits, *D/F*; they belong to the **transposed** key-system. The rest of the Seventh chords relating to notes outside the tonic triad are contained in the **untransposed** system.

175. The whole system of Seventh-harmonies is:

(**A**) In the major key.

b—D/F—a

e

G—b—D/F D/F—a—C

C G

e—G—b—D F—a—C—e

a b

C—e—G—b a—C—e—G

F D

(**B**) In the minor key.

b—D/F—ab

eb

G—b—D/F D/F—ab—C

C G

eb—G—b—D F—ab—C—eb

ab b

C—eb—G—b ab—C—eb—G

F D

176. Up to this we have considered the Seventh chord as merely a union of two overlapping triads, without heeding the particular quality of the triads so combined. But now that too must be investigated, and the meaning which it has for the character of the Seventh-harmony brought out.

177. The Seventh-harmonies of the untransposed key-system :

II–III–I F a C e, I–III–II	II–III–I a C e G, I–III–II	II–III–I C e G b, I–III–II	II–III–I e G b D I–III–II

each consist of the union of a major and a minor triad. The two notes forming the middle interval of the Seventh-harmony are contained organically in both triads, with different determination in each ; so that in the first and third Seventh chords they stand thus :

{ II—III
{ III—II
a C
e G

and in the second and fourth thus :

{ III—I
{ I—III
C e
G b

Here a combination of two real triads appears as harmonic union, dissonant in its outside members, which last do not bear to one another the relation of either of the three triad-intervals. This is the only dissonance contained in the combined sound.

178. But the Seventh chords which contain both the extreme notes of the untransposed system, *D* and *F*, together,

G—b—D/F, b—D/F—a, D/F—a—C,

and thereby define the transposed system, are of other nature and quality than those of the untransposed system. Here the dissonance does not so flatly consist in ambiguity of the middle interval, nor its manifestation merely in the sounding together of the outside notes of the Seventh chord. Indeed it is altogether untrue that in these chords there is found union of real triads.

We may be able to comprehend Seventh-harmony in general under the notion only of triad-twoness, and the dissonant triads may have, like the consonant, organic existence in that notion; yet still they have it but as dissonant chords, that are of their nature cleft, and not self-rounded in their component parts. In the first of the three Seventh chords above, *G—b—D|F*, which consists of the union of the triads *G—b—D* and *b—D|F*, the diminished triad *b—D|F* will surrender the component part of the G major triad, *b—D*, wholly to the latter triad on being joined with it: the Seventh chord *G—b—D|F* is heard as the dominant chord *G—b—D* together with the subdominant Root *F*. The second Seventh chord *b—D|F—a*, made up of the diminished triads *b—D|F* and *D|F—a*, makes itself heard as the sound of the Third and Fifth of the dominant together with Root and Third of the subdominant. The third Seventh chord, made up of the triads *D|F—a* and *F—a—C*, makes itself heard only as the union of the subdominant triad *F—a—C* with *D*, the Fifth of the dominant.

179. In the dominant Seventh-harmony *G—b—D|F*, the Seventh stands apart, and out of all real triad-relation to the chord. In the Seventh-harmony on the Fifth of the dominant, *D|F—a—C* (*D|F—a♭—C*), the Root stands similarly separate and out of triad-relation. In the Seventh-harmony on the Third of the dominant, *b—D|F—a* (*b—D|F—a♭*), the division is there in the middle of the chord; it falls asunder into two parts, of which the lower belongs to the dominant triad, the upper to the subdominant. Indeed all three Seventh chords take their contents from the dominant and subdominant triads alone, and are only distinguished by their taking

more or less from the one or the other; the first has for contents the dominant triad complete and the Root of the subdominant triad, the second has the subdominant triad complete and the Fifth of the dominant triad, the third has the Third and Fifth of the dominant and the Root and Third of the subdominant.

180. Now since the Seventh of the dominant chord is not related to any note of the triad lying underneath it, and since further it is decidedly a **Root** (of the subdominant chord), that is, a **primary**, of independent value, and not a **Fifth** such as are the Sevenths in the untransposed system, that is, a **secondary** getting its derivation from a primary, or Root—therefore this interval may enter to the triad ascending and descending alike, altogether freely, just as the Root of any Seventh chord might enter in ascending or descending motion or as a new part added to the triad. To the triad *G—b—D* as **dominant chord**, apart from any particular kind of melodic derivation, *F* the Root of the subdominant chord may enter, just as *e* the Root of the e minor triad related to it in the Third might do. And yet to *G—b—D* as **tonic triad**, *f*♯, the Fifth of the minor triad on *b*, cannot otherwise be added than as springing out of the Root *G*, just as to the triad *G*|*B*♭*—d* the Fifth *F* of the *B*♭ therein contained can as Seventh only be derived out of the Root *G*.

181. Thus the tonic triad, as well as any other that contains the Fifth of the tonic triad, may be followed by the dominant Seventh chord, and the Seventh may enter to the Root in as good succession ascending as descending. And thus the passage *C—e—G*··· *b—D—F—G*, which the ear allows to be right, while others like it, e.g. *D*|*F—a* ··· *C—e—G—a*, *e—G—b* ··· *D—F—a—b*, sound wrong, is really only a progression from *C—e—G* to *b—D—G*, and the Seventh *F* accompanying the last chord is derived ascending from the *e*: a progression that cannot occur with other passages of this form, because then the Seventh would want to be introduced descending, whereby parallel Fifths arise with the lowest part.

182. Now, with regard to the succession *C—e—G···b—D—F—G*, what determines *e*, the Third of the tonic, to split asunder and move simultaneously upwards and downwards, must be the tendency to gather up the key within its boundaries, to characterise it as a determined and sharply defined whole. The succession *C—e—G···b—D—G* does not so far contain any determination of the key; so too the succession *C—e—G···C—F—a* leaves the key still undetermined. In the former either *C—e—G* or *b—D—G* may be tonic triad, in the latter *C—e—G* or *C—F—a*; in that we can take *C—e—G* for subdominant triad, in this for dominant triad, quite as well as for tonic. If determinateness of key is to be expressed, if *C—e—G* is to be determined as tonic middle by one other chord, then the movement must not be to **either** the subdominant **or** the dominant side singly; it must be carried to **both** at once. **Beginning** and **end** united in time with the **middle** in immediate succession, this is the meaning of the double motion in the Third of the tonic, when it passes to the Root of the subdominant and the Fifth of the dominant at the same time. But in the chord-succession *C—e—G···b—D—F—G* this happens. The progression *e··F* takes on a tendency to the **subdominant** side, the progression *e··D* to the **dominant** side. But the tendency may be active towards both sides with equal energy, or with preponderating energy for one side or the other. In progressing from the tonic triad to the subdominant triad there arises the succession

I II
C—e—G···C—F—a,

and in progressing to the dominant triad the succession

II I
C—e—G···b—D—G.

The first is determined upon the Root of the tonic triad, the second upon its Fifth; because in the first the former passes out of Root-meaning into Fifth-meaning, and in the second the latter passes out of Fifth-meaning into Root-meaning.

183. In these successions the melodic progression happens so that *e* passes to *F* or *D*, *G* to *a*, *C* to *b*.

F—a—C—e—G—b—D.

184. If the motion turns to both sides with equal energy, then the tonic triad itself is quite dissolved in the passage:

F—a . . . b—D.

Here *C—e—G* passes into *b—D—F—a.*

185. If it presses preponderantly towards the **subdominant** side, then the **Root** of the tonic triad, as Fifth of the subdominant triad, will remain unmoved; it becomes the **Seventh** of the resulting Seventh chord:

F—a—C . . . D.

Here *C—e—G* passes into *C—D—F—a.*

186. If the inclination is preponderantly directed towards the **dominant** side, then the **Fifth** of the tonic triad, as Root of the dominant triad, will keep its place; it becomes the **Root** of the resulting Seventh chord:

F . . . G—b—D.

Here *C—e—G* passes into *b—D—F—G.*

187. The same process, employed upon the system of the minor key, gives results shown as follows:

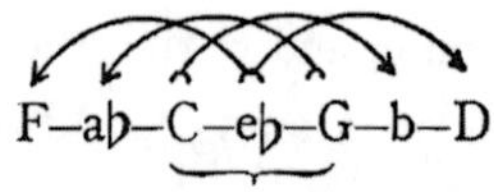

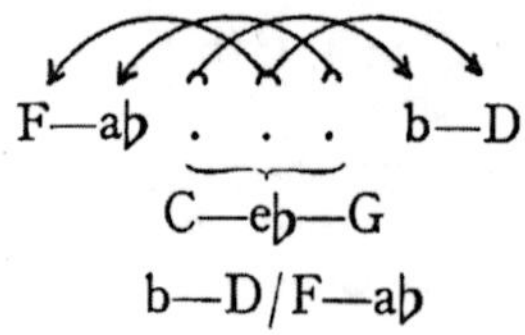

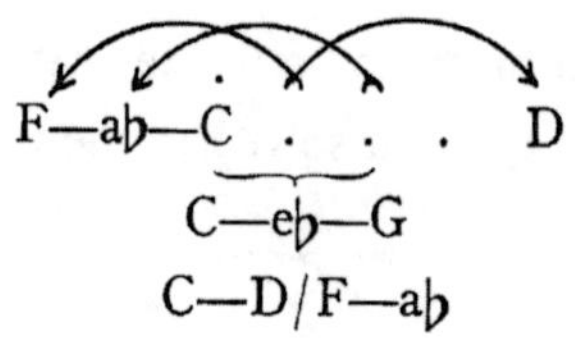

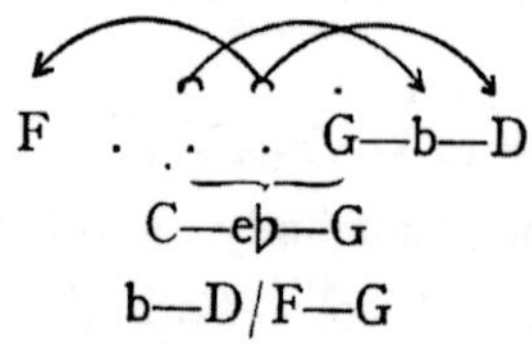

188. These three dissonance-determinations which arise out of the splitting asunder of the tonic Third and unite the dominant and subdominant sides, can, as being nearly related, pass into another easily in any order of arrangement.

189. All possible successions of these three Seventh-harmonies are contained—

I. For the **major key** in the series:

b—D/F—a···C—D—F—a···b—D—F—G···C—D—F—a···
1 —— 2 —— 3 —— 2 ——

b—D/F—a···b—D—F—G···b—D/F—a.
1 —— 3 —— 1

II. For the **minor key** in the series:

b—D/F—a♭···C—D—F—a♭···b—D—F—G···C—D—F—a♭···
1 —— 2 —— 3 —— 2 ——

b—D/F—a♭···b—D—F—G···b—D/F—a♭.
1 —— 3 —— 1

These chords always contain two notes, *D* and *F*, in common; therefore in every passage only one or two parts have to move, and, where they progress together, in parallel Sixths or Thirds. In itself, therefore, the progression of the parts cannot be faulty. The approach of the Seventh ascending to the Root, as it occurs in the successions 1——2, 3——2, and 3——1, might, in view of what has been said about the entrance of the Seventh, arouse theoretical suspicion. But the effect of these successions, although a little rough in 1——2 and 3——2 of the major key, may count as right; and their justification too in theory will result from the nature of the diminished triads *D|F—a* and *D|F—a♭*, as the free entrance of the dominant Seventh resulted from the nature of the diminished triad *b—D|F*.

190. In the successions 1——2 and 3——2 in both series we see *b* move to *C* dissonant against *D*; and in the succession 3——1 we find *G* going in the first series to *a*, in the second to *a♭*, both dissonant to *b*.

191. With the dominant Seventh chord *G—b—D|F* the excuse found for the same progression was: that the **Seventh** of this chord is a note not joined to the dominant triad, lying underneath it, not growing out of it, and therefore not claiming derivation from its Root.

192. With the Seventh chord *D|F—a—C* the **Root** is similarly a note parted off from the subdominant triad which lies above it; it does not enter into inner union with *F* and *a*. The note *C* ascending from the *b* finds in *D* no hindrance to its uniting with *F*

and *a* into the F major triad, such as a *C* ascending from *B♭* would find in *d*; where *F* and *a* belong to the triad *d—F—a* as Third and Fifth already, and the passage into the other meaning, in *C—F—a*, can only be gained by the progression *d·· C*.

193. Thus the successions *b—D|F—a···C—D—F—a* and *b—D—F—G···C—D—F—a* do not seem discontinuous or faulty to the ear; while, shifted into the territory of the F major key, with the minor triad *d—F—a* instead of the diminished *D|F—a*, as *B♭—d—F—a···C—d—F—a*, *B♭—d—F—G···C—d—F—a*, they prove inadmissible.

194. Far easier is it to enter into the meaning of these successions where they relate to the intervals of the minor key, as in *b—D|F—a♭···C—D—F—a♭*, *b—D—F—G···C—D—F—a♭*. Although the dissonant interval, as to its outward structure, is the same in these chords as in those of the major key, yet the effect of the dissonance is far less rough or hard. In this we once again find it confirmed, that the effect does not lie in the immediate ratio of the dissonant notes themselves, but is produced and receives its character from other relations. The reason of these chords being easier to understand lies in this: that the combined sound of *D|F—a♭* is heard distinctly as a chord of division, while *D|F—a* by its likeness to *d—F—a* may leave us in doubt as to which of the two chords is to count in the Seventh-harmony. Only in union with *b*, the Third of the dominant, is *D* distinctly determined as Fifth of the dominant; joined with *F—a* alone it may easily take on the meaning consonant to that interval; that is, it may change to *d*, the Third of *B♭*, and Root of the minor triad *d—F—a*.

195. Now the structure of the chords *D|F—a—C* and *D|F—a♭—C* being such as to make the entrance ascending of the Seventh seem lawful, so the like entrance for the Seventh *a* in the chord *b—D|F—a*, and the Seventh *a♭* in the chord

b—D|F—a♭, is, from the nature of these dissonant harmonies and their origin, not only admissible, but necessary. For as the Thirds of the subdominant and the dominant (*a* and *b* or *a♭* and *b*) cannot melodically pass immediately into one another, so too the Seventh *a* or *a♭* cannot descend from *b*, but must ascend from *G*.

The peculiar nature of these chords we shall now proceed to discuss.

II. Seventh Chord upon the Third of the Dominant.

(*a*) *In the Major Key.*

196. In the Seventh chord *b—D|F—a*, when the Seventh is not prepared, not only may the notes *a* and *b* not occur in the position of Second, but generally no note of the chord may lie above the Seventh *a*, or the harmony becomes of doubtful effect. In the interval of the Second itself, apart from the way in which the notes have come together, lies the meaning of a melodic progression fixed harmonically. Now we know that *a* and *b* cannot be melodically connected otherwise than through *e*, the Third of the tonic:

```
I——II
a    e    b
     I——II
```

But this mediation is decidedly contradicted by the combined sound *D|F*; and thus *a—b* sounding together as a Second contains, with regard to the harmony *b—D|F—a*, a contradiction, because *D|F*, denying the Third, does away with the mediating *e*, and makes mediation of the *a* and *b*, placed melodically next one another, impossible. It is not alone the relation in the Second of the two notes, as contained in the positions *D—F—a—b*, *F—a—b—D*, *a—b—D—F*, that sounds incorrect, but generally every position of the chord in which the Seventh is not the highest part. For then the interval between the Seventh and the next upper note of the chord will contain by implication the notes of the harmony that lie in between; just as every so-called **dispersed** or **open** harmony is for theory only a **close** harmony continued without being filled up. The interval *a*——*D* gives the feeling of *a*—*b*—*D*, and the interval *a*——*F* of *a*—*b*—*D*—*F*; whence it follows that if the Second *a*—*b* in this chord is not good, then neither the Fourth *a*——*D* nor the Sixth *a*——*F* can be so. Therefore, like the chord-positions above written which contain *a*—*b* as a Second, other combinations in which the Seventh *a* is not the highest part, as *b*——*F*—*a*——*D*, *b*—*D*——*a*——*F*, will in the sense of this harmony appear unnatural, though perhaps in smaller degree: and even where such a position is led up to by artistic treatment, there will always remain something strange about it.

197. The position of the intervals below the Seventh is subject to no restricting conditions; the single requirement is for the Seventh to be at the top. Like the position *b*—*D*—*F*—*a*, all those due to transpositions of the lower parts, as *D*——*b*——*F*—*a* and *F*——*b*—*D*——*a*, will also be well-sounding and fit for use, notwithstanding that the intervals *D*——*b* and *F*——*b* include *a*, the Third of the subdominant. This leads to a not unimportant observation, namely that all harmonic form shapes itself from below upwards, even in transposed chords which do not contain the Root as lowest part. In the chord *D*——*b*——*F*—*a* an intermediate *a* for the Sixth *D*——*b* is not expressed till afterwards, any more than in the chord *F*——*b*—*D*——*a* between *F* and *b*. Until the higher **later** part enters with *a*, so long those intervals belong to the chord *b*—*D*—*F* without Seventh. And even when the *a*, as Third of *F*, is added, it is only operative in its place **and upwards**, but does not serve for filling up gaps in the intervals **downwards**. Thus the interrupted position of the notes

D——b——F—a, and similarly any still wider separation or other transposition of the three lower notes of the chord, will always let the chord be recognised as *b—D—F—a*; the notes will be condensed upwards into the close position of the chord and understood collectively, but *F* will have no effect in filling up the gap between the deeper *D* and *b*, nor *a* in filling up that between *F* and *b*. On the other hand, if *D* or *F* were to come above the *a*, the deeper *b* would thrust its Octave in between *a* and *D*, and *b* and *D* each its Octave between *a* and *F*, to fill up; and in the position *b—D——a——F* we should listen to an effect partaking, in the interval *a——F*, of that produced by the position *a—b—D—F*. And as the latter actually contains in itself the Second *a—b*, so the former too will make palpable by implication the subdominant and dominant Thirds standing side by side discontinuously.

198. As, then, the notes *a* and *b* in the position of Second can only be linked through *e*, the middle of the tonic triad, and yet this linking is made impossible in a combination of sound that contains *D*|*F*; therefore the positions *D—F—a—b*, *F—a—b—D*, *a—b—D—F*, are in themselves really foreign to the key

I—III—II   I—III—II
I—III—II
F a C e G b D

in its inner transposition to

I—III—II I—III—II
(e) G b D/F a C (e)

If the interval *a—b* must find a link in *e*, that can only happen in a triad system in which the note can be had for linking; which in this case is the system of the A minor key.

II—III—I   I—III—II
II—III—I
D f A c E g♯ B

The chord is then, not *b—D/F—a*, but *B/D—f—A*. The effect of the latter we get every time that the Seventh is not the highest part in the Seventh chord *b—D/F—a*; the chord then changes into the meaning of *B/D—f—A*, and is thereby attached to the A minor key. The positions *D—F—a—b*, *F—a—b—D*, *a—b—D—F*, are heard as *D—f—A—B*, *f—A—B—D*, *A—B—D—f*, and their natural resolution is upon the E major triad. Besides, in the position of Second the unprepared Seventh resists being moved ascending to the Root—we may take for instance the progression *G · · a* in the key of C major: *D—F—G—b*··· *D—F—a—b*; while on the other hand the similar succession in A minor, *D—f—g♯—B*···*D—f—A—B*, forms quite a proper passage. But because the chord *B—D—f—A* can in harmony of the C major key by no means be intended, therefore every position of the chord *b—D/F—a*, which does not contain the Seventh at the top, is a normally unauthorised one. Here we are dealing with harmonic formation as it must be to be expressed clearly and plainly under all circumstances; for under particular conditions of different quality of voices, or derivation in the actual phrase, or of the context of the chord, such a transposed position of this chord may also be of certain and excellent effect.

(*b*) *In the Minor Key.*

199. In the minor key the place of the Seventh chord *b—D/F—a* is taken by the so-called **diminished Seventh chord** *b—D/F—a♭*. This in its organic structure has the same relation to the minor system as the former has to the major system. But the diminished Seventh chord is not liable to uncertainty in the meaning of its notes. As in the dominant Seventh chord, so too in the diminished Seventh chord, the peculiar nature is definitely expressed. Naturally there can be no mention here of so-called enharmonic multiplicity of meaning. In this chord,

even in a transposed position, as *D—F—a♭—b*, *F—a♭—b—D*, *a♭—b—D—F*, the interval of the Second *a♭—b* cannot give occasion for mistaking the meaning, because, as we have already seen in the origin of the minor scale, a melodic relation between the two notes can in no way be established. They do not require to be connected. The note *a♭* can only be derived melodically from *G*, and *b* only from *C*; a mediation for the passage of one into the other is not contained in the minor system, which sets out from the notion of division, and in its whole essence rests thereon. The system of the minor key, having the negation of unity for its principle, in the sounding together of its subdominant and dominant Thirds contributes to dissonance that which in this quality is most decided: the diminished Seventh chord.

200. We have seen how Seventh-harmony in general is formed by melodic progression in a union of triads. But as for the Seventh chord which in the major as well as in the minor system contains the Thirds of the subdominant and dominant in dissonance, there is a hindrance to its production, namely the harmonic separation of these notes, that prevents them from passing into one another melodically. To *a* ·· *b*, as well as to *a♭* ·· *b*, the element to link the passage and make it intelligible is wanting. For although in the major scale a link for the Second *a* ·· *b* was found in *e*, yet with the harmony *b—D*|*F—a* this mediation will not serve, because the tonic Third is taken away by the combined sound of *D*/*F*, and a thing cannot be affirmed and denied at the same time. But if the progression here, *a* ·· *b*, is not linked, then also the Seventh chord *b—D*|*F—a* cannot have come from the triad *D*|*F—a* followed by the triad *b—D*|*F*. For that succession cannot happen otherwise than with the progression *a* ·· *b*, or from *b—D*|*F* to *D*|*F—a* with the progression *b* ·· *a*; the first in the form *D*|*F—a*···*D—F—a—b*; the other, *b—D*|*F*···*a—b—D—F*. Both successions awake a sentiment for the key of A minor, in which

the step *A* ·· *B* may be linked in *E* without contradiction by the harmony *B*|*D*—*f*—*A*. Similarly in the key of C minor the Seventh chord *b*—*D*|*F*—*a*♭ is not to be derived from a union of passage between the triads *b*—*D*|*F* and *D*|*F*—*a*♭, which must appear in the forms *b*—*D*|*F*···*a*♭—*b*—*D*—*F*, and *D*|*F*—*a*♭···*D*—*F*—*a*♭—*b*. Indeed the separation, for melodic progression, of *a*♭ and *b* is still more decided than that of *a* and *b*; or rather it is quite absolute, because every link fails. Therefore, altogether, the Seventh-harmony *b*—*D*|*F*—*a*, or *b*—*D*|*F*—*a*♭, is not to be looked on as a passage, fixed, from one diminished triad into the other, but as a passage of the tonic triad into the subdominant and dominant triads **at the same time**: *C*—*e*—*G*···*b*—*D*|*F*—*a*; *C*—*e*♭—*G*···*b*—*D*|*F*—*a*♭ (pars. 182–187).

201. Were any other Seventh chord than this to be introduced with Root and Seventh unprepared, the contradiction would lie in the note that links the dissonance having opposite meanings at the moment of entering. But that in itself is contrary to the sense of a reasonable reality; the substance of which is, that the one meaning in its passage to the other is contained at the same time with it in the intermediate element. Being at two is not **an element to start from**; it can only be **an element to pass through.** But the understanding of the Seventh chord *b*—*D*|*F*—*a*, or *b*—*D*|*F*—*a*♭, does not at all depend upon the determination of a linking note as being at the same time One and the Other; for in the first chord the linking *e*, in the other the *e*♭, is taken away by the combined sound of *D*|*F* as unity. The intervals *b*——*a* and *b*——*a*♭ here are not dissonant in the meaning of a doubly determined unity, but because of *D*|*F*, which is twoness taking the place of unity. And as the dissonant combination *D*|*F* in following upon the tonic Third cannot have preparation, and does not need it, because in itself it expresses unambiguously the sense of an intelligible alteration, so too the Sevenths *b*——*a* and *b*——*a*♭, which depend upon it, can enter un-

prepared. The Seventh chord *b—D|F—a* can follow upon the tonic major triad *C—e—G*, and the Seventh chord *b—D|F—a♭* upon the minor triad *C—e♭—G*, without any unpleasant effect, such as results from every other Seventh chord introduced in this manner. For instance, the successions *D|F—a*···*C—e—G—b*, *e—G—b*···*D|F—a—C*, *F—a—C*···*e—G—b—D*; or *D|F—a♭*··· *C—e♭—G—b*, *e♭—G—b* ··· *D|F—a♭—C*, *F—a♭—C* ··· *e♭—G—b—D*, could not be written.

202. Of the restricted position of the intervals of the chord *b—D|F—a*, and the reason for the absence of these restrictions in the chord *b—D|F—a♭*, we have already spoken; and it will not be necessary further to explain why the Seventh chord *b—D|F—a*, in correct progression, can only be produced from a position of the tonic triad with the Fifth at the top; although the Seventh chord *b—D|F—a♭* may be derived from any position of the tonic triad. So that we may have the successions *e♭—G—C* ··· *D—F—a♭—b*, *G—C—e♭* ··· *a♭—b—D—F*, but not *e—G—C* ··· *D—F—a—b*, nor *G—C—e* ··· *a—b—D—F*.

III. Seventh Chord upon the Fifth of the Dominant.

203. For the Seventh chord *D|F—a—C* of the major key, the minor key contains the chord *D|F—a♭—C*. The former may be confounded with the Seventh chord *d—F—a—C*, the dissonant intervals *D|F* and *D——a* being really inclined to pass into the consonant ones *d—F* and *d——a*; but in the Seventh chord of like place in the minor key *D|F—a♭—C* this ambiguity is not present. On the other hand the latter has an outward resemblance to the Seventh chord *d—F|A♭—c* of the E♭ major key, answering to the chord *b—D|F—a* of the C major key. Position, and the treatment suited to the dissonance, will always make it easy to distinguish between the chords *D|F—a♭—C* and *d—F|A♭—c*, as well as between the chords *D|F—a—C* and *d—F—a—C*.

204. The structure of our keyed instruments it is principally that leads to the mixing up of such chords, and altogether that allows the unclearness of the harmonic notion to continue. In the heart of the thing itself, to determine the whole is also to determine with certainty each single part. But for the pianoforte the notes *b*♯, *f*♭, *G*, may be written to make up a well-sounding triad; clearly then a natural and systematic demonstration of harmonic laws ought not to be looked for on the keyboard. Where even the **enharmonic** difference has gone, which in writing and the names of notes is still preserved, there the diversity of notes called by the same names (as *D* and *d*, &c.) will be yet more certainly overlooked.

205. That the triads joining limits, and similarly the Seventh chords in which they take part, are the same in the system of the minor-major key as in the system of the minor key, is already known to us; their occurrence therefore in this system needs no particular discussion. The diminished Seventh chord here relates to a tonic **major** triad, while in the minor system it has relation to a tonic **minor** triad.

DEGREES OF DISSONANCE.

206. The difference in the dissonant effect both of the Seventh chord and of the chord of suspension depends principally upon the melodic relation of the dissonant notes in their position of **Second.** The more decidedly they contain the melodic progression in direct chord-union, the harsher will be the dissonance of the interval, harmonically separated, whilst simultaneously sounding. In the **scale** we found that progression by a Second was throughout made possible in the same way; but in the **union of triads** the progression was conditioned by simultaneous motion of several parts. Thus in the given key of C major a single part could move upwards

and downwards in the succession *C··D··e··F··G··a··b··C*; but in chord-union, where the triads *C—e—G* and *G—b—D* may not follow immediately but only linked in *C—e—G··e—G—b··G—b—D*, the very first melodic movement is not *C··D* but *C··b*, and the second is *e··D*; and even if both parts move at once, *C* is still related melodically to *b*, not to *D*, just as when they move successively, and *D* to *e*. But in the succession *C—e—G···C—F—a*, which consists of the contracted progression *C—e—G···C—e—a···C—F—a*, *e* will have advanced to *F* and *G* to *a*. Lastly, in the direct union *e—G—b···e—G—C*, *b* can only progress to *C*. Therefore the harmonic melodic degrees in the key of C major are *b··C*, *D··e*, *e··F*, *G··a*; and the steps *C··D*, *F··G*, *a··b* remain excluded from the progression of the parts in real triad-unions. These first become possible in the successions *D|F—a···F—a—C*, *G—b—D···b—D|F*, *b—D|F···D|F—a*, i.e. in triads of the transposed system, as: *F—a—C···F—a—D*, *D|F—a···C—F—a*; *G—b—D···F—b—D*, *b—D|F···b—D—G*; *D|F—a···D—F—b*, *b—D|F···a—D—F*; consequently the necessity for such progressions exists only outside the real harmonic unity. The steps *C··D*, *F··G*, *a··b*, placed as Sevenths in the chords *D|F—a—C*, *G—b—D|F*, *b—D|F—a*, are less harshly dissonant in proportion as they have less determination to pass melodically into one another in their position of Second. Melodic separation is most decidedly expressed in the minor system between the Thirds of the subdominant and of the dominant, in C minor between *a*♭ and *b*. And the less a relation of succession is called up in these two notes placed as a Second, so much the less harsh is their simultaneous sound in the Seventh chord *b—D|F—a*♭. Besides this chord (as well as *b—D|F—a*, which answers to it in the major system), when derived from the primary position of the tonic triad, was necessarily produced with both the diminished triads contained in it, *b—D|F* and *D|F—a*♭, also in the primary position; its dissonant notes being thus placed not as a **Second** but as a **Seventh**. The other Seventh chords, which arise from unions of triads related in the Third, can only be formed in an inverted position from the tonic in the primary position and contain the dissonant interval as a Second.

207. The above may stand as the reason for the mildest effect of dissonance being exerted by the diminished Seventh. The major Seventh must, on the other hand, be so much the more rough in dissonance in that its two dissonant notes have to one another the closest melodic relation, most strongly determining them to come in succession **one after the other**, and not to unite in sounding together **at one time**. Thus in the key of C major the Seventh chords *F—a—C—e* and *C—e—G—b* are the most dissonant, because they contain, fixed in simultaneous sound, the progressions *e*··*F* and *b*··*C*, which are strongly determined as melodic by triad-union.

208. Less dissonant than these Seventh chords and more dissonant than those previously named will be found the Seventh chords *a—C—e—G* and *e—G—b—D*. They contain in *G—a* and *D—e* as dissonant interval a progression belonging to direct triad-union, but not one melodically urgent to the same degree as the Seconds *e—F* and *b—C*, and in such less degree these Seventh chords too will be less harshly dissonant.

209. The degrees of dissonance of the Second are presented in the following order of ratios, advancing from the less degree of harshness to the greater:—

a♭ : b	=	64 : 75
a : b C : D F : G	=	8 : 9
D : e G : a	=	9 : 10
e : F b : C	=	15 : 16

210. What has now been said of the dissonance of the **Seventh chord** may be applied to the dissonance of **suspension** as well. That in both cases the difference of effect must depend, not upon the kind of dissonant interval alone, but upon the whole nature of the chord, it will hardly be necessary to observe. But it would require a special treatise upon suspensions and Seventh chords, if an explanation were to be given of all the characteristic peculiarities of dissonance. A few remarks only in this respect may still find place here.

First there is the particular quality of the combination of triads contained in the Seventh chords. In the major key they can only be formed from a major and a minor triad (*C—e—G—b*, *F—a—C—e*), a minor and a major triad (*a—C—e—G*, *e—G—b—D*), a major and a diminished triad (*G—b—D|F*), a diminished and a major triad (*D|F—a—C*), and from two diminished triads (*b—D|F—a*). To these the minor key adds further by its augmented triad (*e♭—G—b*) the Seventh chords of which that forms part (*C—e♭—G—b*, *e♭—G—b—D*), as well as the Seventh chords produced from the union of the major and minor limits (*b—D|F—a♭*, *D|F—a♭—C*), and the chords hereafter to be considered which arise from the union of the limits of the extended system. But besides this difference in the conditions of combination, which must impart different degrees of dissonance even to chords which have outwardly equal distance of Seventh, there is also the melodic relation of the dissonant notes to the notes adjacent on the outside of the simultaneously sounding interval of a Second, to influence the effect of the dissonance. A nearer melodic relationship to those neighbouring notes, because it makes easier the step to resolution, will also make the dissonance seem less harsh than when there is a wider separation between them.

Thus the dissonance of the Seventh chord of the tonic, *C—e—G—b*, is harsher than that of the Seventh chord of the subdominant, *F—a—C—e*; although the two Seventh chords in themselves are quite of like structure; and the Seventh chord of the tonic in the minor key, *C—e♭—G—b*, is harshest of all. For the progression to resolution in the first is *b··a*, 9 : 8, and in the second *e—D*, 10 : 9; while in the third it would have to be *b··a♭*, 75 : 64, which for melody is quite discontinuous. On this account the last chord cannot possibly be resolved inside the key and with a descending Seventh. Again, similar Seventh chords, as *F—a—C—e*, *C—e—G—b*, or *a—C—e—G*, *e—G—b—D*, are also of different effect by leading on resolution to different kinds of triads:

F—a—C—e···F—b—D,	C—e—G—b···C—F—a;
F_7 b°	C_7 F
a—C—e—G···a—D—F,	e—G—b—D···e—a—C;
a_7 D°	e_7 a

so that besides the degree of dissonance, and the progression of the parts in resolution, this condition of succession will also help to characterise the Seventh chord.

211. The examination and analysis of a given dissonance, together with all its attendant circumstances, may be laid down with perfect distinctness for each distinct individual case. On the other hand, it would be impossible to establish a general formula or comprehensive scheme for the occurrence of all possible phenomena. The manifoldness of the formation is infinite, even within the boundaries of what is determined by law. Manifold as are the ways in which the Seventh chord can be prepared and resolved even inside its key, yet the multiple meaning of the chord, its presence in more keys than one, as well as the modulation that may take place at the very moment of resolution, endow it with a wealth of possible developments, branching out so that, even if a classification were attempted, no general mental survey would be afforded. If from a knowledge of the structure of the human body and of the functions

of the muscles we can explain every motion of the individual members, that will content us ; we shall not set about finding a formula of motion for the expression of a series of changing actions.

Only those triads that are most nearly related can pass into one another, or be developed one from another, in a metamorphosis of triads according to the same elements of the notion from which the triad itself was produced. But the manifoldness of possible development and propagation is inexhaustible, and if we wish to escape indefiniteness, it will be just as requisite to consider each particular phenomenon in its own individual existence, and to allow it some special name, as it is to try always to have the whole in view, membership in which is the life of the individual, seeing that the whole is reconstituted a whole only through co-ordination of its parts. For as the life of the member is in the whole body, so the life of the whole body is in its members.

CHROMATIC RESOLUTION OF DISSONANCE.

212. As regards the progression of the dissonant notes, resolution of dissonance consists briefly in this : that by diatonic melodic motion of one or other of them, or of both, a relation of consonance, Third, Fifth, or Octave, in the direct or inverted position of the interval, is reached. Now we have already met with one kind of resolution, involving **chromatic** progression of one or other of the parts. It was that in which the interval of the minor Seventh passed into the Octave by the diatonic progression of one part and chromatic progression of the other (par. 140). But any chromatic alteration that, during the progression to resolution of one note of the interval, is effected in the other which does not move diatonic-

ally will be not inconsistent with the other kinds of resolution. The dissonance *C—D* is resolved into *C—e*, but it can find its resolution in *c♯—E* just as well; for the interval *c♯—E* is, like *C—e*, a consonant interval, i.e. subsisting in the triad. Thus too the progression *f♯–A–C–D* ··· *G/A–c♯–E* sounds right and agreeable. Similarly the dissonance *C—D*, instead of going to *b—D* or *b♭—D*, is also able by chromatic progression of the upper note to pass into *B—d♯* or *B♭—d♭*; and hence we perceive the admissibility and reason of successions such as, e.g., *f♯—A—C—D*··· *F♯—A—B—d♯*, and *F—a♭—C/D* ··· *F—a♭—B♭/D♭* or *F—a♭—B♭—d♭*. It will not be difficult from this process to explain the successions written below:

g♯–B/D–f ···	G–b♭–c♯–E ···	f♯–A/C–e♭ ···	F–a♭–b–D···
a···VII$^{\circ}_{7}$	d···VII$^{\circ}_{7}$	g···VII$^{\circ}_{7}$	c···VII$^{\circ}_{7}$
g♯–B/D–f ···	A–c–d♯–F♯ ···	a♯–C♯/E–g ···	B–d–e♯–G♯···
a : VII$^{\circ}_{7}$	e : VII$^{\circ}_{7}$	b : VII$^{\circ}_{7}$	f♯ : VII$^{\circ}_{7}$

In the first, the Root is lowered chromatically while the Seventh descends; in the second, the Seventh is raised chromatically while the Root ascends. The two successions are in reality no other than those which we obtained above in the progressions of harmonies of the Seventh by taking every alternate member of the descending and ascending series, the first as:

G—b—D/F ··· G—b—C—e ··· F—a—C—e ··· F—a—b—D ···

the second as:

G—b—D/F ··· a—C—D—F ··· a—C—e—G ··· b—D—e—G···

The last was seen to be only admissible in the Seventh chords of the transposed system, because in these alone can the Seventh move upwards to the Root; but in the above succession, which progresses only in diminished Seventh chords, it may be used without interruption.

213. There is something violent or forcible contained in these chromatic sequences, especially in the second of them ; but that lies in the continual change of key. A chromatic progression, as regards harmony, always leads into a new key-system ; and the above successions lead from one minor key into another—that is, from one isolated system into another. For, as we saw earlier, the minor keys are not linked together among themselves in the same way that the related major keys are.

Then, again, the stiffness of the progression of the parts in these successions is partly due to the notes which are combined. In the chord *g*♯—*B*|*D*—*f* of the first series, *g*♯ in union with *D* and *f* has far more inclination to move to *A* than to *G*. Similarly in the second series, *f* taken with *g*♯ and *B* would like to progress to *E* and not to *f*♯ The same constraint appears in the descending motion in *B*..*b*♭, in the ascending in *D*..*d*♯, so that in these successions of harmony not more than two of the four parts are ever allowed an unconstrained path : *D*—*f* in the first going to *c*♯—*E*, *g*♯—*B* in the second to *A*—*c*; but the other two are obliged to progress contrary to their free tendency. The reason why the second of the above successions progresses with still less readiness than the first we shall find opportunity for discussing when we treat of modulation.

THE ESSENTIAL DIFFERENCE OF SEVENTH-HARMONY OF THE UNTRANSPOSED AND OF THE TRANSPOSED SYSTEM WITH RESPECT TO CHORD-POSITION.

214. In the descending series of linked Seventh-harmonies:

C–e–G ···	C–e–G–a ···	C–e–F–a ···	C–D–F–a ···
	6	6	6
	5	4	4
	3	3	2

b–D–F–a ···	b–D–F–G ···	b–D–e–G ···	b–C–e–G
7	6	6	6
5	5	4	4
3	3	3	2

we see the four different positions or inversions of the chord produced from one another by the conditions of succession, and consequently justified in their effect.

While, however, the first position of the Seventh chord, which consists of Third, Fifth, and Seventh; the second, which consists of Third, Fifth, and Sixth; and the fourth, which consists of Second, Fourth, and Sixth, may be freely used even outside this strict progression in all cases where there is a suitable preparation of the dissonant interval, the third position, consisting of **Third, Fourth,** and **Sixth,** does not submit, even with preparation of its dissonance, to such unconditional usefulness. In the Seventh chords of the untransposed system the third position produces a feeling of something being upside down, unsupported, wanting **basis.**

In this inversion the **Fifth** of the Seventh chord, i.e. the Fifth of the lower of the two triads joined in the chord, has become deepest or bass part; in it therefore we have the **Six-Four** position of the lower triad, a position which, even as the inversion of a triad, can only be introduced when properly led up to, because the Fifth has, and in its sound expresses, a meaning opposite to that of the basis of the chord.

215. This position of the harmony of the Seventh can, however, enter, even apart from the connexion or derivation above, in the Seventh chords in which the limits of the key-system are heard sounding together: that is to say, in the dominant Seventh chord and in the Seventh chords upon the Third and Fifth of the dominant; but in the last with greater clearness only in the minor key, by reason of the ambiguity to which it is subject in the major key. Thus the Seventh chords of the **transposed** system, *G—b—D|F*, *b–D|F–a*, *b–D|F–a♭*, *D|F–a♭–C*, can appear in the inversions *D–F–G–b*, *F–b–D–a*, *F–a♭–b–D*, *a♭–C–D–F*, without tying the Fifth placed as bass; the others from the **untransposed** system, *F–a–C–e*, *a–C–e–G*, *C–e–G–b*, *e–G–b–D*, and *F–a♭–C–e♭*, *a♭–C–e♭–G*, *C–e♭—G–b*, *e♭–G–b–D* (the last two in so far as they ought at all to be introduced as harmonies of the Seventh), can only appear in the Six-Four-Three position with the bass note tied.

216. But if we ask for what reason the Seventh chords which belong peculiarly to the transposed system admit of an inversion that appears unsuitable to the Seventh chords of the untransposed system except where it has arisen by the conditions of a succession, the answer must be sought for in the notion of the transposition itself, (*e*) *G—b—D|F—a—C* (*e*). Because that which is pre-eminently **separated** is here placed together as **middle,** while the **unity of the middle** is separated and placed asunder as **boundaries,** therefore the whole transposed system, in everything that is referred to its middle or that participates in it, is a system of **dissonance.** Thus in this dual nature of the whole, the combined sound of *D|F*

must have, and maintain, the **meaning of unity**; so that the Seventh chords *G—b—D|F*, *b—D|F—a*, *D|F—a—C* are to be considered as **triads of absolute dissonance**, *G—b—Ð*, *b—Ð—a*, *Ð—a—C*, in which *D* and *F* must, for the meaning of the chord, count not only as unseparated but also as **undistinguished.** Accordingly the Fifth *D* of the first of the three Seventh chords above is in *Ð* at the same time the Root *F*; the Fifth of the second, *F*, has in itself Root-meaning; and the Fifth of the third, *a*, is in *Ð* also Third of *F* (being for the effect more clearly **not Fifth** in the minor Third *a♭*). But in these chords the Fifth does not receive the double meaning, as is the case in the rest of the Seventh-harmonies, through another triad joined to the first; rather it has it in the chords themselves, agreeably to their nature, as a meaning unseparated and undistinguished.

217. In the two last of the combined triads of dissonance of the transposed system, *b—Ð—a* and *Ð—a—C*, having ascribed Root-meaning to the *F* of the first and participation in Third-meaning to the *a* of the second, it would seem that we ought now to ascribe clear Fifth-meaning to the *a* of the first and to the *C* of the second. But the notes *a* and *C* do not originate as Fifths in triads of absolute dissonance; they are contained in them as real Sevenths, because this interval of the chord can never be anything but Fifth of the upper triad. Moreover, in virtue of the Seventh-meaning of the notes a preparation by tying is assured to them in every position, and therefore also when they appear as basis; and then the Six-Four-Two position of the Seventh chord, like the positions of Seven-Five-Three and Six-Five, may be used as freely in these chords of dual nature as in any other.

218. But the Seventh chord on the Fifth of the dominant will always in the major key maintain its dual nature with difficulty. The chord *D|F—a—C* is too liable to have its meaning changed into *d—F—a—C*, which does not annul the unity of *e*. Therefore

it is only in the minor key, where no such ambiguity is present, that this Seventh chord is capable of being inverted in the Six-Four-Three position, (*D*|*F*—*a*♭—*C* in the position *a*♭—*C*—*D*—*F*), or of appearing in other transpositions that contain the relative Fifth *a*♭ of the chord as bass; but *D*|*F*—*a*—*C* cannot appear as *a*—*C*—*D*—*F* (apart from the derivation of the note *a* from *b*, as in the succession *b*—*D*—*F*···*a*—*C*—*D*—*F*, or from its being tied, as in *a*—*C*—*e*···*a*—*C*—*D*—*F*).

219. For insight into the manner of chord formation and transformation, it is beyond everything essential that the thought of a complete and originally determined series of notes should be entirely dismissed. The chord is not determined by given notes, but they are themselves produced, i.e. determined harmonically, through the vital weaving and working of the chord-notion.

The harmonic thought itself, incorporated in these determinations of intervals, is as the soul that forms in them the body for itself. What distinguishes a **Third**-note from the **Fifth**-note of the same name, *d* from *D*, is not the trifling difference of pitch, but the quite different generation of the two. That *D* stands with *G*, *d* with *a*, in the relation of Fifth, that the one note belongs to the dominant side, the other to the subdominant, is their essential difference. Similarly *a* is distinguished from the *A* which forms the Fifth to *D*, and therefore cannot enter into any union with *D* as a Fifth. Therefore we do not hear **consecutive Fifths** in a succession like ***C***—*e*——*C*——*G* ··· ***D***—*F*——*b*——*a*, in which the meaning of the note *a* in the second chord is clearly expressed. But the opposite succession ***D***—*F*——*b*——*a* ··· ***C***—*e*——*C*——*G* we shall find to be inadmissible, because it contains in the outer parts, ***D***——*a*·· ***C***——*G*, similar motion from the interval *D*——*a* to the Fifth *C*——*G*. The difference between *a* and *A* will also be perceptible if we accompany the first four notes of the chorale 'Ach, Gott und Herr,' *C*··|*b*··*a*··|$\widehat{G}$, first with the harmony of the Roots ***C··/e··F··/C̑***, and then with the harmony ***C··/G··D··/Ĝ***. In the last the melody of the chorale *C··/b··a··/G̑* changes its Third-note *a* into the Fifth-note *A*, and the intonation of the note in singing will be otherwise determined (and sharper) than the intonation of the Third *a* in the triad *F—a—C*.

SEVENTH CHORDS WHICH ARISE FROM THE UNION OF THE LIMITS OF THE EXTENDED KEY-SYSTEM, AND SEVENTH CHORDS CONTAINING AN AUGMENTED TRIAD.

220. We have earlier spoken of a precession, a shifting on of the key-system for one member of the chord series (pars. 54–62), and have seen produced from it towards the dominant side, in the major key as well as in the minor, intelligible triads by union of its limits. The system of the key of C major

F—a—C—e—G—b—D

was thereby altered into

a—C—e—G—b—D—f♯;

and from the system of the key of C minor

F—a♭—C—e♭—G—b—D

there arose

a♭—C—e♭—G—b—D—f♯.

221. The triads produced by union of limits from this system extending towards the dominant side are, in the key of C major:

D—f♯/a, f♯/a—C; and in the key of C minor: *D—f♯/a♭, f♯/a♭—C.*

In the major key the chords *D—f♯/a, f♯/a—C* may be easily known and distinguished from the chords *D—f♯—A, f♯—A/C.* If in a harmonic progression the Third of the Fifth of the dominant, *f♯*, is led chromatically from the subdominant Root *F*, then, although it is not contained within the compass of the C major system, this *f♯* will not give the impression of the key of G major, so long as the subdominant Third *a* remains joined to it; as, e.g., in the harmonic succession:

a–C–F···a–C–f♯···b–D–G, F–a–D···f♯–a–D···G–b–D.

For this progression of *F··f♯* does not oblige the Third *a* to pass into the Fifth *A*. Consequently the chords *a—C—f♯* and *f♯—a—D* still participate in the subdominant side of the system of C major, which therefore still continues.

222. And so too the Seventh chords in which the interval of the joined limits, *f♯/a*, occurs may be produced naturally without transformation of the Third note 80 into the Fifth note 81; except the Seventh chord *b—D—f♯/a* (*b—D—f♯/a♭*), which will be spoken of later on. In sounding the succession *F—a—C—D··· f♯—a—C—D···G—C—e* the note *a* in the second chord need not give up its relation to *C* of minor Third below, namely 5 : 6.

223. But the chords of like position referred to the minor key, and to the major key with minor subdominant, *D—f♯/a♭, f♯/a♭—C*, must be considered more particularly, both by themselves and also as to the part they take in Seventh-harmony.

224. In the union of the limits of the closed system, both of the major and minor keys, there arises an interval *D/F* that does not correspond to the ratio 5 : 6 of the minor Third. The ratio 27 : 32, in which these notes stand to one another, is out of direct triad-reference. And from the union of the limits of the

major system extending towards the dominant side there results, in the combined sound of *f♯/a*, exactly the same interval and ratio 27 : 32. But in the joined limits of the minor system extending towards the dominant side, and of the system of the minor-major key, which, as regards the dominant and subdominant, is like it, we obtain the interval of the so-called **diminished Third**, *f♯/a♭*. The ratio of its vibrations is 225 : 256, as we easily find by taking twice the progression of a leading note; for

f♯ : G = 15 : 16
G : a♭ = 15 : 16
225 : (240) : 256
f♯ : (G) : a♭

In this combination of sound both notes, *f♯* and *a♭*, supposing the question to be of their melodic derivation, can only be referred to the note *G*; for in the minor key *f♯* cannot be led from the *e♭* lying below, nor *a♭* from the *b* lying above, because the augmented Second fails to be mediated as a passage.

225. Nor yet in the extended minor-major key

a♭—C—e—G—b—D—f♯

can the note *f♯* have come from *e*, major Third of the tonic. In the scale indeed a mediation (in *b*) for this step would be established by the Fifths

I——II
e b f♯
I——II,

just as in the closed system the step from the sixth to the seventh degree is mediated by the Third of the tonic in the same way. But in the harmonic progression, in the succession of chords, which is presented in triads related in the Third and not in the Fifth, the chord-connexion for this case could only consist in the overlapping of *f*♯/*a*♭—*C*—*e*. But here neither *C* nor *a*♭ affords a mediation for the passage, the possibility of which lies always in this: that a note which is in itself a triad element shall take on another chord-meaning. But neither *C* with *f*♯, nor *e* with *a*♭, has any meaning of harmonic unity.

226. Now the link for the progression *G*··*a*♭ is contained in *C*, and for the progression *G*··*f*♯ in *D*. Therefore for the double progression *G* must at the same time be referred to *C* as Fifth and to *D* as Root. For the combination of the diminished Third (*f*♯/*a*♭) to be produced, *G* ought to be **simultaneously opposite.** And it is this contradiction that is expressed in the effect of the diminished Third as a harmonic interval.

227. We have already become acquainted with one chord, for whose dissonant interval a natural position could only be found apart from the direct melodic relation of its notes. This was the Seventh chord upon the **Third of the dominant** in the major key, *b*—*D*|*F*—*a*, in which the Seventh must always be the highest part, to prevent its dissonant notes *b*——*a* from being transformed into the notes *B*——*A* of the key of A minor (par. 198). Something akin to this takes place with the interval of the diminished Third *f*♯/*a*♭. That stands here with both its notes referred melodically to the note *G*; it seems like a progression of *G*··*a*♭ and *G*··*f*♯ made at one time. But as such it also contains a contradiction; just as the Second *a*—*b*, which can melodically be linked only by the Third of the tonic, does in a harmony of the C major key, which, because it negatives the Third *e*, cannot therefore provide that link. Now here, placing the notes *b*——*a* as a **Seventh,** a direct melodic relation of the notes in the series

C

b··C··D··e··F··G··a

G

is not raised: *b* may be regarded as derived from *C*, and *a* from *G*;

and the interval as linked in the Root and Fifth—in the progression *C··b* by *G*, in *G··a* by *C*. And similarly with the interval of the diminished Third *f♯/a♭*; if the same notes be placed as an augmented Sixth *a♭—f♯*, with reference to a separate derivation,

$$\underbrace{G\cdot\cdot a\flat}_{C}\text{————————}\underbrace{f\sharp\cdot\cdot G}_{D}$$

it will likewise be no longer contradictory. For though the melodic derivation of the two notes is still from *G* only, yet it is not from the unison of that note, but from its doubling in the Octave: from one and another *G*, of which the lower or earlier is to be referred as Fifth to *C* and the higher or later as Root to *D*. And then the position which the dissonant notes *a♭——f♯* are found to occupy, is not such that they are turned melodically towards each other, but they are placed out of melodic relation. In the interval of the diminished Third, *f♯—a♭*, we hear the progression from the *G* which ought at once to be Fifth and Root; in the interval of the augmented Sixth, *a♭——f♯*, we hear the progression from the *G* which first was Fifth and then became Root.

228. Here again the one condition established for the position of the chord is, that in a combination in which these united boundary notes take part, they may appear only in the position of Sixth, and not in the position, either close or extended, of a Third.

229. The Seventh chords of the minor key in which the combination is contained are to be found on the Third and Fifth of the dominant and on the new note which has entered on the dominant side.

In the key of C minor they are

b—D—f♯/a♭, D—f♯/a♭—C, f♯/a♭—C—e♭

The two last, with the interval of the diminished Third in the position of Sixth, accost us as well-known harmonies; the middle one, *D—f♯/a♭—C*, is found also in the minor-major system upon the

Fifth of the dominant, and the last, as *f♯/a♭—C—e*, upon its Third. But the first, which seems as well authorised a construction as the others, nevertheless yields no intelligible chord from any transposition of its notes.

230. The combination *b—D/f♯—a♭* contains in *b* and *f♯* two **leading notes** at once. They are shown to be really such by the fact that both the one and the other in union with *a♭* can only move upwards: *b* can only lead to *C*, and *f♯* only to *G*. But *b* can only be maintained as leading note in combination with *F*, and *f♯* only in combination with *C*; the one in the chord *b—D/F*, the other in the chord *f♯/a♭—C*. The Seventh chords in which these combinations take part are in the one case *G—b—D/F*, *b—D/F—a♭*, and in the other case *D—f♯/a♭—C*, *f♯/a♭—C—e♭*. Therefore the Seventh chord *b—D—f♯/a♭* is self-excluded as containing an inner contradiction.

The same applies fully to the system of the major key. Here also union of the limits of the extended system can only give rise to the Seventh chords *D—f♯/a—C* and *f♯/a—C—e*, and not to the chord *b—D—f♯/a*. In its relation to the key of C major the note *f♯* is still to be derived only from *G*; and in the combination *b—D—f♯/a* precisely the same doubleness of leading note is found as in the chord *b—D—f♯/a♭*. What imparts to the chord *b—D—f♯/a* an appearance of admissibility, can be only the opportunity for confounding it with the Seventh chord *b—D—f♯—A*, in the key of G major upon the Third of the tonic.

231. Accordingly of the three Seventh chords in which the diminished Third takes part, only two are left as really possible and therefore **intelligible**: that upon the Third of the dominant and that upon the note which has entered the system: *D—f♯/a♭—C* and *f♯/a♭—C—e♭* (or, in the minor-major system, *f♯/a♭—C—e*), each of them with its diminished Third in the position of Sixth.

The essential dissonance of the first lies in *C—D*, and of the second in *e♭—f♯* (*e—f♯*). But besides that, both contain in the combination *f♯—a♭* the further dissonance of the joined boundary notes. There was this already in the chords with the combinations *D|F* and *f♯|a*; but here as *f♯|a♭* it is the more harshly pronounced, in that the expression of a note divided against itself is more decided.

232. The Seventh chord on the Third of the dominant in the system of the major key allowed only of a restricted position of its intervals. This was reduced to the condition of the Seventh having to be **highest part** in the chord; the other intervals might then be used in all transpositions. The chords with the interval of the diminished Third require that interval to be in the position of Sixth, and have their peculiarity brought out most clearly when the lower note of the interval of Sixth is in the bass. Nevertheless so long as the interval of separation keeps its position of Sixth, they will admit of another note of the chord being bass without becoming unintelligible.

233. Here too it must again be remembered that we are still speaking only of directly intelligible harmonic constructions, as presented in the natural order. For, as with the dissonant interval *b——a* in the Seventh chord on the Third of the dominant of the major key (*b—D|F—a*), which can only be used with the Seventh as highest part, if the effect is not to be ambiguous, and can yet under special conditions be used in the other position with excellent effect in good music; so also the interval of the diminished Third or Tenth can be used, in certain particular cases, in its untransposed form as part of the chords discussed here. In especial we find it very often used in new and the newest music as a means of producing a striking effect.

THE AUGMENTED TRIAD AND ITS OCCURRENCE IN THE SEVENTH CHORD.

234. In the system in extension of the minor key, the so-called **augmented triad** stands to the Seventh chord upon the Fifth of the dominant in a relation of harmonic opposition; in the key of C minor, *e♭—G—b* to *D—f♯/a♭—C*. In the system from the junction of whose limits this Seventh chord is formed,

a♭—C—e♭—G—b—D—f♯,

the dominant (*G*) of the key in its meaning of Root, determined at once positively and negatively, (in *G—b* and *e♭—G*), forms the middle. As in the closed system

F—a♭—C—e♭—G—b—D

the Third of the tonic, *e♭*, has its progression to the limits *D* and *F*, so here the dominant *G* must progress to the limits *f♯* and *a♭*; and thus for the augmented triad the Root *e♭* can only move to *D*, and the Fifth *b* only to *C*. Consequently there results the relation of succession *e♭—G—b ··· D—f♯/a♭—C*.

235. The parallel succession of two major Thirds, which in the progression of a major Second, *F—a ·· G—b*, would be discontinuous, is here continuous: the succession *G—b ·· a♭—C* or *e♭—G ·· D—f♯* being perfectly smooth. The linking takes place thus: the passage *G—b ·· a♭—C* is understood as *G—b ·· G—C ·· a♭—C*, and the passage *e♭—G ·· D—f♯* as *e♭—G ·· D—G ·· D—f♯*; that is, as a contracted double progression, in which the succession *G—b ·· a♭—C* finds its linking element first in *G* and then in *C*, while the succession *e♭—G ·· D—f♯* finds it first in *G*

and then in *D*. In the progression *F—a·· G—b*, however, considered as a succession of *F—a··F—b··G—b*, such a linking element does not exist, because *b* does not stand to *F* in any relation of unity.

236. In the organic construction of the minor key the augmented triad is found upon the Third of the tonic, and in the system of the minor-major key *F—a♭—C—e—G—b—D* upon the Third of the subdominant. In both cases its existence is implied in the notion of the key. But, besides that, it can also be produced in two ways by progression. Firstly, by raising chromatically the Fifth of the major triad, e.g. *E♭—g—B♭···e♭—G—b*, which denotes a passage from the region of the key of E♭ major into that of the related key of C minor. Secondly, by lowering chromatically the Root of the minor triad, e.g. *E—g—B···e♭—G—b*, which would here express a passage from the region of the key of E minor into that of the related key of G major with minor subdominant. That such a chromatic progression does not effect a distinct modulation into the other key is easily perceived. The key is notwithstanding awaked for the moment in the augmented triad, which contains precisely that notion of twoness :

$$\begin{array}{c} -\text{I} \\ +\text{I} \\ \text{G}, \end{array}$$

from which the minor key or the major key with minor subdominant alone can proceed.

237. The augmented triad forms part of the following harmonies of the Seventh :—

I. (*a*) The Seventh chord upon the Root of the minor key, e.g. in A minor,

A—c—E—g♯.

(*b*) The same, as Seventh chord upon the subdominant of the minor-major key; e.g. the chord just written, in the key

A—c—E—g♯—B—d♯—F♯.

In the latter indeed its appearance is more easily made possible, because there *g*♯, the Seventh dissonant to *A*, can be resolved on *F*♯; not by the linking of chords, for that does not exist in *F*♯|*A*—*c*—*E*—*g*♯, but by continuous melodic progression in the system. In the system of A minor, *g*♯ has no melodic progression to *f*; accordingly the resolution by means of the ascending Root can alone be used, which we have seen cannot make good a claim to principal importance. At the same time by this resolution there is always given the possibility of this Seventh chord in the minor key.

II. (*a*) The Seventh chord upon the Third of the tonic of the minor key, e.g.

c—E—g♯—B.

(*b*) The same, as Seventh chord upon the Third of the subdominant in the minor-major key; e.g. the chord just written, in the key

A—c—E—g♯—B—d♯—F♯.

III. The Seventh chord upon the Third of the tonic of the minor key in extension towards the subdominant side. E.g. in respect of the key of A minor,

c—E—g♯/b♭

from the system

b♭—D—f—A—c—E—g♯.

This last chord, because it contains the interval of the diminished Third *g*♯/*b*♭ in the union of the limits, can only be used when that interval is inverted as the augmented Sixth.

The Seventh chord which we obtain upon the Fifth of the tonic (that is, on the dominant) of this system, *E—g♯/b♭—D*, has the same form as that upon the Fifth of the dominant of the minor key in extension towards the dominant side; in this case, for example, the same chord would be given by the D minor system with the Third added beyond the Fifth of the dominant:

b♭—D—f—A—c♯—E—g♯.

The resolution expected, however, in the latter case is that into the triad of A major, and not that into the triad of A minor, as required in the first. This is for the same reason which, as we previously found, made the extension of the minor key-system towards the subdominant side seem barely admissible (par. 59). Even with the Seventh chord cited under III., *c—E—g♯/b♭*, the feeling of the key of A minor is almost entirely absent. We hear the chord much more as belonging to the key of F major; that is to say, in *c—E—b♭* we seem to have *C—e—B♭*, and in *g♯* a sharpened Fifth to the dominant *C*. For the system

b♭—D—f—A—c—E—g♯,

which has no complete dominant triad (though we have recognised this as the positive element of the minor key), is far more inclined to put forward its positive triads *B♭—d—F*, *F—a—C*, as its principal contents than the minor triad *A—c—E*. And so in this combination we become theoretically acquainted with a chord which frequently occurs in practice, **the dominant Seventh chord with chromatically sharpened Fifth.** The diminished Third which it contains subjects it to a restriction of position, by always requiring to be inverted.

CONCERNING THE SO-CALLED CHORDS OF THE NINTH, ELEVENTH, AND THIRTEENTH. PEDAL.

238. If it is only the most closely related links of a progression that can be taken together simultaneously as dissonance, and if therefore it is only two triads having a common interval that can unite to form a Seventh chord, then no combination going beyond the harmony of the Seventh is possible as a union of triads. As we have seen, the passage from *C—e—G* to *G—b—D* cannot be represented in a chord with the contents *C—e—G—b—D*, but only in the notes *b—D—e—G*; that is, in the union of the triads *e—G—b* and *G—b—D*. We have similarly seen the passages into the wholly disjunct triads, e.g. from *C—e—G* into *b—D|F* and *D|F—a*, always resulting in unions of triads most nearly related to one another: the first in *b—D—F—G*, the second in *C—D—F—a*. Therefore the so-called chords of the Ninth, Eleventh, and Thirteenth are self-excluded from the harmony of dissonance which springs from the union of triads.

239. To resolve the chord *G—b—D—a* or *G—b—D—F—a* let us make the note *a* descend to *G*. That by this no resolution of the dissonance *G—a* is effected is plain; for, considering the combination *G—a* in itself and keeping inside the key of C major, that could only consist in progression to *F—a*, to *G—b*, or to *F—b*. Consequently, in the passage *G—b—D—a*···*G—b—D—G* the lowest note of the first chord is entirely neglected in the resolution, and the dissonance *b——a* is alone taken into account, for which the resolution *b——G* is given. A direct harmonic reference between the outer parts is no more to be pretended in this chord of the Ninth

and its resolution than in the series continued in the descending sequence

G—b—D—a··· *G—b—D—G*··· *G—a—C—G*··· *G—a—C—F*···

of dissonance chords and their resolutions corresponding with the first. The Ninth *a*, which progresses to the Octave *G*, is resolved as Seventh of *b*, just as in the continued succession *G—a—C—G*··· *G—a—C—F* the upper *G* moves to *F* as Seventh of *a* and not as Octave of *G*. In the last succession we cannot hesitate to recognise a **pedal**, or **organ-point**, that is a series of chords under which is placed a note independent of them, and the first succession cannot possibly be taken in any other sense ; it is not a combination of two triads related in the Fifth (which, moreover, not being an immediate succession, could not coalesce in a chord), but is an independent chord of dissonance placed over a pedal note, whose resolution is determined in the chord itself and not referred to an outside basis.

So also with the other chords going beyond the harmony of the Seventh, which it is thought necessary to build up by a pile of Thirds. The chords of the **Eleventh** and **Thirteenth** are not established as formations of harmony in this sense. The chord of the Eleventh begins by excluding the Third ; the chord of the Thirteenth excludes the Fifth as well. This series of Thirds is in like plight with the arithmetical progression of notes, if we seek to trace in it the basis of our harmony. As there the notion of harmony guided us to select from the infinite series of numbers all that answered to itself and to reject the rest, so also with the edifice of Thirds there must be previous knowledge by which that is selected which is agreeable to the notion of harmony. This mechanical construction by Thirds does not, however, lead on to infinity, like the progression of notes in the arithmetical series of numbers. In the eighth member it coincides again with the starting note, for this is the Fifteenth or double-Octave of the Root :

G b D f a C e g

1 3 5 7 9 11 13 15

Otherwise we should doubtless be told of chords of the Fifteenth, Seventeenth, and so on, as well as of chords of the Thirteenth. Given a series containing all the notes of the key, it is certainly not hard to put together all the chords which can occur in that key, supposing one is free to make omissions at pleasure. Only after all no generative principle of harmony will have been demonstrated. In the newer theoretical works this mode of explanation has been quite abandoned; neither is it to be met with in the oldest works. It belongs to a middle period, and at present is only occasionally heard from teachers who had their education then.

SUSPENSION OF THE NINTH.

240. Only the dominant and tonic of a key can appear as basis of a pedal, because these two notes alone admit of a change of principal chords over them. It follows that not every dissonant chord in which a note suspended over the bass note of another part is resolved on the Octave of the bass note, i.e. a **Ninth**, is to be regarded as a pedal; for such a suspension may occur upon every degree of the scale. Rather the pedal here only shares in the property by which the deepest note of **every** harmony allows a suspension in another part. Thus with suitable preparation we find the chord *e—G—C—F* permitting the resolution of *F* to *e*, in this as well as in every other disposition of the parts lying above the bass note; not so if *e* were contained in the chord as an upper or middle part, and *F* at the same time as a suspension of *e*. Here

too the chord of dissonance *G—C—F* stands independently over the pedal *e*, and the resolution of its dissonant interval *G—F*... *G—e* takes place without finding that obstacle in the *e* of the deepest part as a pedal, which would be presented by the same note *e* placed in any other part.

241. The parts of a chord which lie above the bass note have the effect of a harmonic aggregate set against it. They may be transposed among themselves, and the chord is not essentially altered thereby. On the other hand it is of striking difference to the effect, which note of the chord is allotted to the bass part; whether the chord is built upon its Root, its Third, its Fifth, or its Seventh; whether it is triad, chord of the Sixth, or chord of the Sixth and Fourth; or in harmony of the Seventh, whether it is chord of the Seventh, chord of the Sixth and Fifth, chord of the Fourth and Third, or chord of the Second. So too a repetition above of the progression of the bass (Octave motion with the bass), is not admissible, though between the other parts it may occur, as we find it frequently used in the doubled parts of orchestral and pianoforte music. The bass note, even when it is not Root of the triad or Seventh chord, always remains the basis for the **position** of the chord. To repeat the progression of the chord in the upper parts, to let the basis be heard a second time in the middle of the harmony or at the top of it, like a foundation built upwards into the air, can only be the expression of something contrary to common sense and upside down.

242. It would also have equal unfitness if the harmony which stands over the bass note should contain contradictions in itself, i.e. unresolvable dissonance; that is, if a note of that harmony should be sounded in one part and suspended in another, and so at once be there and not be there, in the way in which it can be present in the bass and suspended in another part as a dissonance to be resolved against a third part.

243. When the suspension is contained in the bass itself, then the note upon which it is resolved cannot be allotted to any of the other parts. Here the basis itself enters into the meaning of the parts subject to harmonic conditions among themselves; it is dissonant with a part lying above it, and has to be resolved against that. But the note on which the resolution takes place, to be present simultaneously with the suspension, can only be the **deepest** part; it cannot therefore at the same time occur in the harmony itself. Besides, such an arrangement would again express the absurdity of a bass lying above the bass. And indeed wherever anything sounds bad or incorrect the reason of its unlawfulness should be sought, not in particular technical conditions, but in its contradiction of a truth and reality to be conceived as quite universal.

Here again we cannot now enter upon particular instances of exception to what has here been enunciated as universal, where that which has been explained to be unlawful becomes with full right lawful and capable of being used with excellent effect. For our purpose it is enough to set down that which is directly and universally valid.

PASSING-NOTES.

(*a*) **Diatonic.**

244. In pedal harmony, chords move independently over a sustained bass note. Similarly, if a chord be held, a part moving in melody can sound notes other than the intervals of the chord. These melodic passing-notes are none the less determined throughout by considerations of harmony, for no other determination of a note is conceivable. But the determination of the intervals of the melodic progression is independent of the harmony of the sustained chord.

Supposing the tonic triad to be sustained, and a part to move melodically in the diatonic scale, then its degrees are given by the different triads in the system of the key, just as if each note were accompanied by the triad to which it belongs in the linked succession. For no melodic note can receive definiteness otherwise than as it is conceived as the Root, Third, or Fifth of a triad.

(*b*) **Chromatic.**

245. In the same way the chromatic scale moving against the sustained triad can only be constructed independently of the chord, through unions in which the chromatic notes find their connected progression. This takes place in such a way that even the notes that coincide with the degrees of the sustained triad do not receive their meaning from that triad. They have the meaning which comes to them from the chords of the connected progression, which may coincide with the former meaning, but may also be different to it.

246. The chromatic scale in the system of the key of C major is formed in the series:

c ·· c♯ ·· d ·· d♯ ·· e ·· f ·· f♯ ·· g ·· g♯ ·· a ·· b♭ ·· b ·· c ;

or in the series:

c ·· d♭ ·· d ·· e♭ ·· e ·· f ·· f♯ ·· g ·· a♭ ·· a ·· b♭ ·· b ·· c.

In this way of writing the notes, without the distinction of small and capital letters, it remains undecided in what character they appear as chord-intervals. But a note raised chromatically can in the first instance only have the meaning of the Third of a dominant, i.e. the **leading note** of a major or minor key, which forms a **close** with the note next above it. These two notes stand to one another in the unchangeable ratio 15 : 16, while the chromatic progression, following the ratios of the diatonic degrees 8 : 9 and 9 : 10, can also vary between the ratios 128 : 135 and 24 : 25. To the first ratio, 128 : 135, correspond in the key of C major the chromatic progressions *C··c♯*, *F··f♯*, *B♭··b*; to the other, 24 : 25, the progressions *D··d♯*, *G··g♯*.

Accordingly we obtain the first of the chromatic scales written above in the following meaning:

c♯ ·· D, d♯ ·· E, F ·· f♯, G··g♯, a··B♭, b ·· C
15 : 16, 15 : 16, (128 : 135) 24 : 25, 15 : 16, 15 : 16,
(128 : 135) 24 : 25, 15 : 16, 15 : 16, 15 : 16, (128 : 135)
C··c♯, D··d♯, e ·· F, f♯ ·· G, g♯·· A, B♭ ·· b,

in which, as is evident, only the Root of the tonic triad keeps its place in the chord-meaning. The Third *e* and the Fifth *G*, coming after the leading notes *d♯* and *f♯*, appear with Root-meaning. Receiving thus harmonic melodic determination, they acquire in consequence a self-subsisting existence independent of the sustained chord; which is also acquired by every note foreign to the scale, or, generally, by every so-called passing-note of a part that moves melodically against a stationary harmony.

247. In the scale ascending by chromatically lowered degrees:

D♭··d, E♭··e, F ··f♯, G ··a♭, a ··B♭, b··C,
(128 : 135) 24 : 25, (128 : 135) 15 : 16, 15 : 16, 15 : 16,
15 : 16, 15 : 16,. 15 : 16, 15 : 16, 24 : 25, (128 : 135)
C··d♭, D ·· e♭, e ·· F, f♯·· G, A♭··a, B♭ ·· b,

the tonic elements *C* and *G* are transposed from Root-meaning and Fifth-meaning into Third-meaning, and appear themselves as leading notes. The tonic Third *e*, which in the progression by chromatically raised degrees acquired Root-meaning, here keeps its Third-meaning.

Either mode of chromatic progression can be used ascending and descending. It is an erroneous opinion that chromatically raised degrees belong exclusively to ascending motion, and chromatically lowered degrees to descending.

248. In both kinds of the chromatic scale a directly determined progression is contained only as follows :—

(1) In the relation of a leading note to the note lying above it, 15 : 16; whether the first is a note proper to the scale, or gained by chromatic raising, and whether the second is a note proper to the scale, or chromatically lowered :

c ·· D♭, c♯ ·· D, d ·· E♭, d♯ ·· E, f♯ ·· G, g ·· A♭, g♯ ·· A, a ·· B♭.

(2) In the chromatic change which transforms the major triad into the minor, or inversely the minor triad into the major : by chromatic raising, *e—G—b···e—G♯—b*, *b—D—f♯···b—D♯—f♯*; by chromatic lowering, *F—a—C···F—a♭—C*, *C—e—G···C—e♭—G*. This is the progression which we have denoted by the ratio 24 : 25. It is given by a comprehensible determination, in so far as it consists of an intelligible alteration, a becoming-other of the same thing : namely, when the relation of Fifth between two stationary notes passes from the positive to the negative meaning or the reverse.

249. There is another chromatic progression, marked with the ratio 128 : 135. This occurs in the scale produced by chromatic raising between the degrees *C ·· c♯*, *F ·· f♯*, *B♭ ·· b*; and in the scale by chromatic lowering in the two intervals last named, which appear there also, and in the interval *d♭ ·· D*. This progression is not one that is in itself comprehensible or directly intelligible. If the *c♯* that follows the *C* is to be related as leading note to *D*, the Fifth of the dominant, as is required, then this *c♯* may not be referred to the Fifth-interval *a——e* contained in the system. It may not fitly be considered as a transformation of the triad of a minor into the triad of A major. For then *c♯* could only lead to the *d* that lies below the system and not to the *D* that is Fifth of the dominant. The essential differ-

ence between these two notes we need not turn back again to explain. To get the leading note of *D* we must take, to the Root *C*, the Third not of *a* but of *A*; that is, the Third of the triad of A major in the chord-series *C—e—G—b—D—f♯—A—c♯—E*; a progression that, judged by the notion of intelligible succession, is quite without possible link. A like relation comes out in the chromatic steps *F··f♯, B♭··b, D♭··d*. We have denoted it by 128 : 135 because the Third of the third Fifth ($3^3 \times 5 = 135$) will compare with the Root raised into its neighbourhood ($2^7 = 128$) in this ratio of the numbers of their vibrations. The step *C··c♯* in the chromatic scale of C major, as well as others answering to the same ratio, thus remains undetermined in itself. The chromatically raised note can here be comprehended only in its relation of leading note to the note which follows it, and as determined from that. On the other hand, the passages *D··d♯, G··g♯*, and all progressions answering to the ratio 24 : 25 (which is found included within the limits of the Fifth, 20 : 30, as the difference between the major triad 20 : 25 : 30 = 4 : 5 : 6 and the minor triad 20 : 24 : 30 = 10 : 12 : 15), contain a determination in themselves. On this account they are easier to sing in tune than the intervals standing in the ratio 128 : 135, as may be confirmed by testing attentively the free intonation of the different chromatic degrees. For in the ratio 128 : 135 there is present only the relation of leading note to the note following, but no determination of the chromatic note with respect to the note started from.

250. The diversified and constantly changing meaning, which must be assumed by the determining notes in the chromatic progression, makes it more complicated and for free intonation harder than the diatonic. In the latter, as was shown above, the succession of the degrees is determined upon the elements of the tonic triad, without making a change of meaning for one and the same degree necessary; if we except the step from the sixth to the seventh degree, in which the sixth appears at first with the meaning of Third

of the subdominant, and then passes into the meaning of Root of the minor triad upon the Third of the subdominant. But in the chromatic scale, besides this change of meaning of the intervals, a change of key also enters with each of the determining notes; and, since no three successive degrees are ever contained within the same key, the inner structure of the whole succession becomes so crowded in its composition, that it is not surprising that a perfectly true intonation of chromatic progressions should be in many cases unattainable by singers not thoroughly grounded in harmony, who yet may be able to move with certainty in the diatonic scale. Thus often what is outwardly nearest fails to be taken with certainty, because the determination for it is neither unmistakably felt nor intuitively known.

251. The chromatic scale, whether progressing in sharpened or in flattened notes, contains seven degrees of the ratio 15 : 16, three of the ratio 128 : 135, and two of the ratio 24 : 25. But the ratio 15 : 16 is not a chromatic one, but diatonic. It answers to the progression of the leading note to the Octave of the Root; also in the minor key to the difference of the second and third degrees of the scale.

Where simply a nearest has to be added, there it will always be some such small **diatonic** degree. For the **chromatic** progression produces a **leading note** that takes us further, leading upwards in a sharpened, downwards in a flattened degree. Certainly in the two chromatic scales written above we meet with no *g*♭ or *a*♯, no flattened Fifth or sharpened Sixth, but in that which moves in sharpened progression there is *B*♭ the seventh degree flattened, and in that with flattened notes *f*♯ the fourth degree sharpened. The reason is that *B*♭ and *f*♯, and not *a*♯ and *g*♭, find as chord notes a determining element in the system of the key of C major. Nevertheless the melodic movement of *F*··*f*♯··*F* or *b*··*B*♭··*b* could not be justified to feeling. In the succession *F*··*f*♯··*G* only the degrees *F*··*G* and *f*♯··*G* are determined in themselves, and in the succession *B*♭··*b*··*C* only the degrees *B*♭··*C* and *b*··*C*; therefore the successions *F*··*f*♯··*F* and *b*··*B*♭··*b* fail of intelligible foundation. Here too *F* can only be related as leading note to a *g*♭ lying above it, and *b* to a leading note *a*♯ lying underneath it, and now *B*♭, which lies below the C major system, and *f*♯, which lies above it, enter as notes linking the steps *F*··*g*♭··*F* and *b*··*a*♯··*b*; just as before we found the sharpened sixth degree in the diatonic ascending minor scale, and the flattened seventh degree in the descending, linked by the boundary notes outside the closed system.

252. Thus the chromatic places between *F* and *G* and between *a* and *b*, determined only as *f*♯ and *B*♭ in the progressive arrangement, yet become *g*♭ and *a*♯ when the first is to join on to *F* and the second to *b*. But in all other places of the chromatic scale, which already in themselves furnish a double progression by sharpened and by flattened diatonic degrees, the relation of the leading note 15 : 16, and not the chromatic 128 : 135 or 24 : 25, is always given as the difference of two notes that hang together or desire to pass into one another by natural inclination. Properly chromatic degrees can only enter in a motion that tends onwards, e.g.

C··d♭··C··b··C··{d♭/c♯}··D··e♭··D··c♯··D··

{e♭/d♯}··e··F··e··d♯··e··F··g♭··F··e··F··f♯··

G··a♭··G··f♯··G··{a♭/g♯}··a··B♭··a··g♯··a··

B♭··b··C··b··a♯··b.

253. Manifestly the distance of the diatonic interval 15 : 16 is greater than that of either of the two chromatic intervals 128 : 135

and 24 : 25. Yet *c*♯ pitched as leading note in the succession *C*··*c*♯··*D* will seem higher than the *d*♭ in the succession *C*··*d*♭··*C*; consequently the chromatic interval *C*··*c*♯ seems to be greater than the diatonic *C*··*d*♭. In instruments with fixed and therefore tempered degrees of sound this must certainly depend upon an acoustical illusion, because they use the same note for *c*♯ and *d*♭. Singers and players on instruments with free intonation, however, will feel the necessity of actually taking the leading-note sharper than truth, but the minor second (which leads backwards) at a less distance than the ratio 15 : 16 assigns. There is here an endeavour to characterise the note in its interval-meaning, to enliven or animate the intonation. Intonation untempered, mathematically true, would be musically lifeless, and remain an unsatisfying means of expression. It would be like rhythm moving strictly in time to the metronome. The beat of the metronome to living performance seems at one time to linger, at another to hurry on, because in its mechanical strictness it cannot answer the light and shade of an animated rhythm. So too the intonation of characteristic degrees of sound will not be bound to mathematically determined pitch, but often deviate from it, pressing upwards or downwards. It must so deviate, if intonation itself is not to remain something merely determined mechanically, as it is in the fixed degrees of keyed instruments. But such departure from mathematical purity can only touch the interval of the Third, the interval which alone is changeable: not in the sense that it can become larger and smaller, but that by shifting chromatically it can pass from its relation to the Root into its relation to the Fifth, whereby the major triad is transformed into the minor; e.g.

C—e—G . . . C—e♭—G
I—III III—I

This passage, as well as the difference in general of the one and the other determination, whenever it receives a characteristic meaning, tends to acquire emphasis by intensified expression; and this happens in the sharpened pitch of the major Third and in the flattened pitch of the minor. None but the Third-meaning can give occasion for altering the mathematically true intonation. The interval of Fifth, as an invariable, must be pitched always with perfect purity. Similarly, nothing but the strain of a transition can bring about the alteration of the Third. Whenever the chord stands independent and at rest, then that interval too is pitched according to its acoustical determination.

254. The explanation of the chromatic progressions has kept us somewhat longer than the occasion seemed to require. But the opportunity has occurred of noticing the difference of the chromatic relations 24 : 25 and 128 : 135, the direct meaning of the first and the indirect meaning of the second; a difference that should be (but is not always) observed both in theory and in practice. The singer who pitches his voice, not by white keys and black ones, but by harmonic determinations alone, will not be able to take the apparently nearest, the chromatic degree, with certainty, if he be without feeling of the harmonic meaning of the note. In diatonic progression the linking of the notes is so simple, and up to the step from the sixth degree to the seventh so unambiguous, that a passage presents no difficulty. But in chromatic progression the conditions are complicated and often change, and in many places a singer may be in doubt whether he has to take a progression in the meaning of the ratio 15 : 16 or of 24 : 25 or of 128 : 135; so that here the intonation is less assured and is exposed to the vacillations which chromatic song-music so often experiences in performance. But the blame is not always to be put upon the singer. Far oftener it belongs to the composer, who should require from the singer 'nothing unintelligible, nothing unintelligently.'

MODULATION.

255. By changed meaning of the **note** is determined a new **interval**; and by changed meaning of the **interval**, a new **chord**. Similarly the changed meaning of the **chord** will determine a new **key**.

But the meaning of the **note** cannot be expressed in the note by itself, nor until the note sounds together with another note in the **interval**; nor is the meaning of the **interval** known until it sounds together with another interval in the **chord**. So too the meaning of the **chord** cannot receive its determinateness in the chord by itself, nor until it is placed with other chords in the **key**. And thus it comes round that for objective knowledge the **key** is what determines the meaning of the **chord**, the **chord** determines the meaning of the **interval**, and the interval the meaning of the **note**.

256. The triad of C major, which is **tonic** chord in the key of C major, is **dominant** chord in the keys of F major and F minor; **sub-dominant** chord in the key of G major; and chord of the sixth degree or Third of the subdominant minor triad in the key of E minor. And so universally; each of the three major triads of the major key, and each of the two major triads of the minor key, may take part in three major keys and two minor keys. Also each of the two minor triads of the minor key, and each of the two minor triads of the major key, may be parts of two minor and two major keys.

257. According to this, the major triad has fivefold meaning with respect to the three major and two minor keys to which it can belong; the minor triad has fourfold meaning with respect to the two minor and two major keys in which it takes part.

258. The diminished triad on the seventh degree forms an element of relationship only between the major and minor (and

also the minor-major) keys with the same name. The diminished triad on the second degree of the minor key is only contained again in the minor-major key with the same name. In the major key the diminished triad on the second degree, as is shown by its structure, can find place only in **one** system.

259. In the manifold meaning of the chord lies the possibility of passage from one key into another. But this possibility is not matured until the changed meaning has been put clearly forward by succession and combination of sounds, and until the new key to be occupied has been marked out in that whereby it is distinguished from the first. Thus the passage from the key of C major to the key of G major,

F—a—C—e—G—b—D
C—e—G—b—D—f♯—A,

linked by the triads *C—e—G—b—D*, can only be effected by the appearance of the Third of the dominant of the latter key, that is, *f*♯; the passage from the key of C major to the key of F major,

F—a—C—e—G—b—D
B♭—d—F—a—C—e—G,

linked by the triads *F—a—C—e—G*, only by introducing the sub-dominant Root *B*♭; the passage from C major to A minor,

F—a—C—e—G—b—D
D—f—A—c—E—g♯—B,

linked by the triads *F—a—C—e*, is only possible by sounding *g*♯, the Third of the dominant of the new key; and the passage from C major to E minor,

F—a—C—e—G—b—D
A—c—E—g—B—d♯—F♯,

linked by the triads *a—C—e—G—b*, only by *d*♯.

260. Accordingly, if we wish to make the dominant triad of the key of C major, *G—b—D*, which is also tonic triad of the key of G major, pass from the first meaning to the second, it can only be done by uniting the major triad on *G* with the major triad on *D* by placing these chords together:

C : I —— V
C–e–G ··· b–D–G ··· A–D–f♯
G : I —— V

In like manner the subdominant triad of the key of C major, *F—a—C*, will come to stand in the meaning of tonic triad of the key of F major, if we bring the subdominant triad of the latter key into union with it:

C : I —— IV
C–e–G ··· C–F–a ··· d–F–B♭
F : I —— IV

The minor triad on *e* contained in the key of C major as minor triad of the dominant side becomes tonic triad of the key of E minor when placed with the dominant chord of that key:

C : I —— III
C–e–G ··· b–e–G ··· B–d♯–F♯
e : I —— V

The minor triad on *a*, which lies on the subdominant side, becomes tonic triad of the key of A minor when placed with the dominant chord of that key:

C : I —— VI
C–e–G ··· C–e–a ··· B–E–g♯
a : I —— V

261. It must, however, be admitted that by these successions no

modulation into the new key has been effected such as to satisfy and land us safely in it. Although a chord has entered from its domain, yet the key itself still remains not definitely marked off in its boundaries. Scarcely more is felt than that the side or the direction is opened, towards which the modulation is about to turn. There is no firm settlement in a new key.

262. Among the harmonies of the Seventh we have seen one which is quite suited to determine a key in its principal elements, because its essential contents are the dominant and the subdominant in its dissonance and the Tonic in its resolution, thus comprehending in itself and the following chord the principal parts of the whole system.

This is the **dominant Seventh chord**, also named the **principal Seventh harmony**. As it has the property, in its dissonance, of causing the limits of the key-system to be heard in union, and, in its resolution, of establishing the tonic triad as middle of the system, it will, when introduced in natural connexion, announce the new key in a decided manner and allow it to enter with certainty.

263. Thus, take the two first passages above, *C–e–G* ··· *b–D–G* ··· *A–D–f*♯ and *C–e–G* ··· *C–F–a* ··· *d–F–B*♭, of which the first contains the transformation of the dominant chord, and the second the transformation of the subdominant chord into the tonic, whereby in the former a modulation into the dominant, in the latter into the subdominant key is stirred but not accomplished; the passage could have been made more decided by the dominant Seventh harmonies of the two keys.

264. In considering the harmonies of the Seventh, we found that the chord of the dominant Seventh, which consists of the dominant triad united with the diminished triad upon the Third of the dominant, is taken in right connexion if made to issue either from the tonic or from the dominant or subdominant triad (par. 181). Accordingly the tonic triad *C—e—G*, taken as subdominant triad of the

key of G major, or as dominant triad of the key of F major, may be followed immediately by the dominant Seventh chord of the one key or of the other. In this way, after resolution of the chord, the new key will not only be introduced, but also will be at once exhibited in its whole compass and firmly settled. Then the modulation is formed on the following plan:

(*A*) Towards the dominant side:

C : I
C–e–G ··· C–D–f♯–A ··· b–D–G
G : IV —— V_7 —— I

(*B*) Towards the subdominant side:

C : I
C–e–G ··· B♭–C–e–G ··· a–C–F
F : V —— V_7 —— I

The tonic triad gained, of the new key, can in its turn be transposed into either dominant or subdominant meaning; and then by the same modulation it will either lead back into the original key, or else one degree—that is, one key—further in the direction of the first modulation.

A. (1) Leading back:

C : I C : V —— V_7 —— I
C–e–G···C–D–f♯–A ··· b–D–G ··· b–D–F–G ··· C–e–G
G : IV —— V_7 —— I

(2) Leading onwards:

C : I
C–e–G ··· C–D–f♯–A ··· b–D–G ··· A–c♯–E–G ··· A–D–f♯
G : IV —— V_7 —— I
D : IV —— V_7 —— I

B. (1) Leading back:

C : I   C : IV —— V7 · — I
C–e–G ··· B♭–C–e–G ··· a–C–F ··· G–b–D–F ··· G–C–e
F : V —— V7 —— I

(2) Leading onwards:

C : I
C–e–G ··· B♭–C–e–G ··· a–C–F ··· a–C–E♭–F ··· B♭–D–F
F : V —— V7 —— I
B♭ : V —— V7 —— I

265. The modulations A (2) and B (2), if further continued in the same way, would lead into the keys which from time to time are the most nearly related in the two directions: the first, which takes the tonic triad in subdominant meaning, towards the dominant side; the other, which takes it as dominant, towards the subdominant side.

266. But we have to distinguish two kinds of modulation to remoter keys: **one**, that **advances** from one key to the other, altogether leaving the seat of the first and settling in the region of the second; the **other**, that **transforms** the key to another within its own boundaries.

267. Suppose we modulate, upon the plan given above, into a key of the third degree of relationship, from C major to A major or E♭ major; then we have progressed to the new key in one or other direction in the chain of triads:

E♭ A
A♭–c–E♭–g–B♭–d–F–a–C–e–G–b–D–f♯–A–c♯–E–g♯–B
C

The connexion with the original key here consists in the uninterrupted succession of related keys which has led from the first key to the last. But now the notes *c*, *g*, *d* in the key of E♭ major are not the same as those of like name in the key of C major, *C*, *G*, *D*; nor do the notes *A*, *E*, *B* in the key of A major correspond to those of like name in the key of C major, *a*, *e*, *b*. The note *F*, Fifth of the dominant in the key of E♭ major, and subdominant in the key of C major, is common to the two keys, and similarly the note *D*, Fifth of the dominant in the key of C major and subdominant in the key of A major, belongs in common to the two keys; yet upon this a relationship of key cannot be founded. For the key is a union of triads, and therefore for it the triad alone, and not the single note, can be an organic element of relationship. This the single note can be only for the interval, and the interval only for the chord.

268. But, according to this requirement of inner relationship—namely, for notes with the same name in two different keys to be the same with changed chord-meaning—we should be able by the chain of triads to arrive at no more than the keys that lie nearest, i.e. the keys of the dominant and subdominant. Even there the Fifth of the dominant (*A*) of the dominant key is shown to be different from the Third of the subdominant (*a*) of the original key; and in like manner the Third of the subdominant (*d*) of the subdominant key is different from the Fifth of the dominant (*D*) of the original key. But the demand for identity cannot extend to these notes, because they are produced by the entrance of a new Fifth-determination. The notes *a* and *D* in the system of the key of C major do not stand in true Fifth-relation; consequently the Fifth *D*——*A* of the key of G major cannot want to keep *a*, the Third of the subdominant of the C major system. No more can *D*, the Fifth of the dominant in C major, want to be taken for *d*, the Third of the subdominant in F major; because that must stand in Fifth-relation to *a*, Third of the subdominant in C major, and must

therefore be a different note from *D*. According to this the difference between *a* and *A*, or between *D* and *d*, should determine the modulation from C major to G major, or from C major to F major, as well as the difference between *F* and *f*♯ in the first case, or between *b* and *B*♭ in the second. But this difference of the Third-note from the Root- or Fifth-note with the same name, as it is ignored in our manner of writing music, so also in practical use is too little for a change of chord to be made clear by it. Unless *f*♯ is added, *a* will not pass into the meaning of *A*; and, unless *B*♭ is added, *D* will not pass into the meaning of *d*.

269. It is not merely through the greater quantity of like material that the keys of the Fifth above and below are most nearly related to the key assumed as tonic. They are much more essentially related in the sense that the tonic triad of the tonic key is contained as subdominant triad in the dominant key, and as dominant triad in the subdominant key; and similarly the tonic triads in the dominant and subdominant keys are respectively the dominant and the subdominant triads in the tonic key; and that therefore the relationship, the opposition of difference and equality, is here to be found in the principal element, the tonic triad itself.

270. With the two keys which follow in the progressive series, B♭ major and D major, the key of C major is related only in one subdominant or dominant chord: with the key of B♭ by the major triad of F; with the key of D by the major triad of G. In the tonic triad, the **principal** element, these keys remain strange to one another; **principally**, therefore, they are **not** related.

In the keys which follow next, which are more remote by a Fifth, even this subordinate relationship dies out, and the mutual reference of such keys, if considered only in this series, ceases entirely. The plan of modulation introduced above can, it is true, lead onwards to the remotest keys; only when even the third key is reached we are in a wholly strange region, out of all inner connexion with the first.

271. To this plan of modulation stands opposed that other kind, which does not consist in progressing to another key through the intermediate keys, but in taking what is common to the two keys to be united, and transposing it from the meaning which it has in the first into the meaning which belongs to it in the second. Thus the new key springs right out of the middle of the first.

272. Key-relationship must be sought principally in the tonic triad. For the dominant and subdominant keys it consists in this, that the **Root** of that triad can become **Fifth**, or its **Fifth** the **Root**, of the new tonic triad. Hence a relationship may also be contained in making the **Root** or **Fifth** of the tonic triad the **Third**, or its **Third** the **Root** or **Fifth**, of a new tonic triad. In this way reappear elements of relationship constituted by the tonic triad with remoter keys, which elements, if the keys were reached by **progressive** modulation, would have already left us at the third step. For—

(1) taking the **Root** in **Third**-meaning:

I

F—a—C—e—G—b—D,

III

D♭—f—A♭—c—E♭—g—B♭,

we have the identity of the notes *F*——*C*——*G* and *f*——*c*——*g* in the keys of **C major** and **A♭ major**;

(2) taking the **Third** in **Root**-meaning:

III

F—a—C—e—G—b—D,

I

A—c♯—E—g♯—B—d♯—F♯,

we have the identity of the notes *a——e——b* and *A——E——B* in the keys of **C major** and **E major** ;

(3) taking the **Fifth** in **Third**-meaning :

II
F—a—C—e—G—b—D,

III
A♭—c—E♭—g—B♭—d—F,

we have the identity of the notes *C——G——D* and *c——g——d* in the keys of **C major** and **E♭ major** ;

(4) taking the **Third** in **Fifth**-meaning :

III
F—a—C—e—G—b—D,

II
D—f♯—A—c♯—E—g♯—B,

we have the identity of the notes *a——e——b* and *A——E——B* in the keys of **C major** and **A major.**

273. According to this there now enters a nearer mutual reference between keys of the third and fourth degrees of relationship than is afforded by those of the second degree of relationship. We saw that the latter, being, as to their tonic triads, without anything in common, were in so far to be regarded as, in the principal sense, unrelated.

274. But if the relationship between the keys is to consist of the notes with the same name, the modulation must also be of such a kind that the notes in the two keys to be united do in fact remain the same, and that the keys which follow one upon the other do

really find their unity in these notes, as something that endures, though in changed meaning. That, e.g., in the modulation from C major to A♭ major we may see the identity of *C* and *c* (*C* being here opposed to itself as Root and Third) really preserved, and not, as happens in the passage through the series in succession of the united keys :

```
*                                                                                          *
C-e-G ... B♭-C-e-G ... a-C-F ... a-C-E♭-F ... B♭-d-F ... A♭-B♭-d-F ... g-B♭-E♭ ... g-B♭-D♭-E♭ ... A♭-c-E♭
C:I
F:V  —  V7  —  I
                B♭:V  —  V7  —  I
                                  E♭:V  —  V7  —  I
                                                    A♭:V  —  V7  —  I
```

obtain *c* the Third of the tonic triad of A♭ major as a note differing by 80 : 81 from the Root of the tonic triad of C major.

275. If instead of the passage just written we hear the following :

```
*                                                                                   *
C-e-G ... B♭-C-e-G ... a♭-C-F ... A♭-D♭-f ... A♭-B♭-D♭-f ... g-B♭-D♭-E♭ ... A♭-c-E♭
C:I
f:V  —  V7  —  I
                A♭ : VI  —  IV  —  II7  —  V7  —  I
```

which might certainly be very much contracted without loss of clearness, the identity of the note *C* in the first chord and *c* in the last is easily perceptible. The Root of the key of C major has here become Third of the tonic triad of A♭ major, the key of C major has passed into the key of A♭ major, without quitting and annulling the intervals which can remain common to both keys and in which their inner relationship is contained. If the passage to the key of E♭ major, related in this manner to the key of C major, is made by the following series :

```
C–e–G ··· B♭–C–e–G ··· a♭–C–F ··· A♭–B♭–d–F ··· g–B♭–E♭,
                            *               *
```

then in progressing from the third chord to the fourth there will be perceived an alteration in the note *F*, the passing of the Third-meaning into Fifth-meaning. For the transformation of the keys in the case before us is this:

F — a — C — e — G — b — D
B♭—d♭—F — a♭— C — e — G
(f)—A♭—c—E♭—g—B♭—d—F.

Here the permanent, binding element is the Fifth-interval, *C——G*, which belongs in the first key to the tonic triad, in the second to the dominant triad, and in the last, where it exchanges the positive for the negative meaning, to the minor triad on the subdominant side. But upon this enduring element the rest of the intervals of the keys are formed, following the assumption that the E♭ major triad shall contain as its Third the Fifth of the C major triad; and thus the Fifth of the dominant (*F*) of the key of E♭ major is a different note from the Root of the key of F minor, and therefore also from the subdominant Root of the key of C major. Certainly, by what was said earlier about the extension of the key-system, the transposed chord might also stand in the course of modulation as *A♭—B♭—d—f* with the Root of the key of F minor without losing its value as a dominant Seventh, which is sufficiently expressed in *A♭—B♭—d*. But the note *f* will be hard to maintain as not-Fifth against *B♭—d*; it will always tend to shift into Fifth-meaning (from 80 to 81).

276. These processes of modulation begin by taking the tonic triad of a major key as dominant triad of a minor key. By this turn of meaning we immediately gain a region lying towards the subdominant side, that in process of successive modulation could not be reached but by progression through three keys. Therefore the more distant keys that lie on this side are in general easily accessible in this way. For if by the triad of C major we are already landed in the key of F minor, then the passage into

the keys related to it may be effected in closest union by dominant Seventh chords linked and linking. Here, however, the question was only of modulation to the A♭ and E♭ major keys.

277. As the keys of A♭ and E♭ major contain a relationship with the key of C major in the Root and Fifth of its tonic triad, so we found the keys of E major and A major related with it in the Third. In the former cases the Root or Fifth of the tonic triad of one key is turned into meaning Third of the tonic triad of another. In the latter cases, inversely, the tonic Third of one key is turned into meaning Root or Fifth of the tonic triad of another. Modulation into the remoter keys of the **subdominant** side results when the dominant chord of a related **major** key is referred to the **minor** key of the same name. It will lead to the remoter keys of the **dominant** side if we refer the dominant chord of a related **minor** key to the **major** key of the same name.

Thus the tonic triad of E major may follow the dominant chord of the key of E minor; or the tonic triad of A major the dominant chord of the key of A minor:

C—e—G, C—e—a, B—d♯—F♯/A, B—E—g♯
C : I — VI
e : IV — V_7
E : V_7 — I

C—e—G, a—d—F, g♯—B—D—E, A—c♯—E
C : I
F : V — VI
a : IV — V_7
A : V_7 — I

278. But it is to be observed that modulation to the keys on the dominant side is always less easy than to those on the subdominant side. We remark this even in the modulations which are nearest, to the adjacent dominant and subdominant keys.

First the keys may be considered as members of a chain in the never-ending triad-propagation, and afterwards each single key as subsisting for itself. In the former case each key is a uniting middle member for two others adjacent to it on the two sides: in the latter the key does not pass into another; therefore it passes into **not-another**, i.e. into **itself.** We found that this passing into itself is expressed in the chords which contain the boundaries of the single key-system united. The separated key has its centre of gravity in the middle. In the chain of keys each key rests upon the one that has gone before it. But this is the key of the **subdominant**; for positive production, as an effect of **force**, is directed towards the **dominant** side, **upwards**. It raises a secondary, the **Fifth**, into a primary, the **Root**; it does not lower the primary into a secondary. The dominant key is one that has to be produced out of the tonic; it requires productive energy, needs an effort to make it come out of the tonic. On the other hand the subdominant is a key that precedes the tonic; to it, as a thing that has already been present and determined, the modulation easily descends. Therefore too a key is far less endangered in its tonic quality by the dominant than by the subdominant. For if the modulation turns so easily towards the subdominant side, it will yet more readily return from the dominant to the tonic, and be able to re-establish it as principal key after an excursion into the dominant. On the other hand, a modulation into the subdominant at once throws upon it the tonic character, which it requires new exertion to restore to the true tonic.

After more than a short stay in the subdominant key it will be almost a necessity to again touch the dominant; so that, returning from it to the tonic, the latter may be felt quite in its tonic meaning.

Thus, our regular modulatory form of pieces of music in the major key, which pass, in the middle of their course, into the dominant, is exactly that which fits with reason and nature. It is, speaking generally, going on, which from first to last cannot be going back, and therefore cannot lead to the subdominant. Retreating from the dominant to the tonic is going home. In the minor key the modulation leads regularly, not to the Fifth, but to the related major key. The minor key has no going onward; it is shut up in itself, and must first get rid in the major key of the fetters which hamper it, before it can gain freedom and outside alliance.

279. By the foregoing considerations, we see generally, that every key which, compared with another, contains chromatically raised notes, will be more exalted, tenser; and a key that is distinguished from another by chromatically lowered notes will seem depressed, quieter, less tense. Moreover, in this alone is to be found the much talked of **character** of the keys. That certainly exists; but it can only be **relative**, and not **absolute** for any single key, because each particular key by itself rests in its organisation quite on the same conditions as every other. And there is no absolute pitch; therefore no determination for the character of the keys can lie in that. A song in the key of C major is perfectly identical with the same song in D♭ major, if the latter be pitched to the same height as the former; for in its essence the one key is perfectly identical with the other. The characteristic determination lies in their relation to one another, sc. that the key of D♭ major has the Root of the key of C major for its leading note, and the subdominant Root of the key of C for the Third of its tonic; and that by the transformation of the Root-notes into Third-meaning all other elements of the key of C are chromatically lowered and turn towards the subdominant side, towards a region from whose standpoint the key of C major must itself appear exalted and tense. But the exact character of the difference between the keys of D♭ major and C major will also be shown in the key of D major taken with C♯ major—and similarly in E♭ major taken

with D major—and none of them can pretend to any positive character. In orchestral performance single keys can indeed take a peculiar colouring in the wind and string instruments; but this, depending only upon mechanical structure and special acoustical conditions in the different instruments, and not being founded in the nature of the keys themselves, cannot here be considered as essential. In pure vocal music there will be no desire to ascribe a particular character to single keys. There what is characteristic is to be found solely in their placing with other keys, in the bearings of their relationships, and in how far these are brought out in the modulation.

280. Succession of keys, like that of chords or single notes, can never happen otherwise than continuously. A key may be followed by the remotest possible, but only in so far as the chord from which the modulation to the new key takes place is either already present in it too, or at least belongs to a key most nearly related to the new one.

281. The passage from the tonic triad of C major to the D♭ major triad is only rendered intelligible by taking the former to mean the dominant chord of the key of F minor, whereby the D♭ major triad enters as chord on the sixth degree of that key.

282. Supposing the tonic C major triad to be followed by the B major triad, then in the former there is a change of meaning; it becomes the triad on the Third of the subdominant in E minor, in which the second of the three chords named is the dominant. But we know that the latter (the B major triad) regarded as simply a major triad can have four other meanings besides this. Here it belongs to the key of E minor. It is also contained in the keys of E major, B major, F♯ major, and D♯ minor; in the first as V, in the second as I, in the third as IV, in the fourth as VI. And just as the tonic triad of C major was determined to be the triad upon the sixth degree in E minor, in order that the B major triad might follow,

so now the B major triad, which, following upon the former triad, enters as dominant of E minor, may in its turn exchange this determination for another, and afterwards progress agreeably to the newly chosen determination.

283. Similarly in the succession first named of the major triads on C and D♭, the latter, besides that of *f* : VI, has also at disposal the meanings of D♭ : I, G♭ : V, *g*♭ : V, A♭ : IV; so that what follows further may be referred to the keys of F minor, D♭ major, G♭ major, G♭ minor, or A♭ major.

284. Thus to the initial chord, if it be major, a fivefold indication may be attributed; and if it be minor, a fourfold. A diminished triad has the various determinations pointed out above. Also the same Seventh chords appear in different keys with changed meaning, and thereby lead to different modulations.

Thus, even with the condition that the two chords in immediate succession shall belong to the same key, infinitely manifold change of key is still possible.

285. But also modulation may take place by chords belonging not to the same, but to very nearly related keys. Supposing the C major triad to be followed immediately by the triad of E major, of A major, or of E♭ major, then in these successions the two chords standing next one another are not contained in one key; as in all cases where chromatic progression happens, there the territory of another key is entered upon. In the first succession, *C—e—G···B—E—g*♯, the Third of the tonic triad of C major becomes Root of the dominant chord of A minor. In the second, *C—e—G···c*♯*—E—A*, it becomes Fifth of the dominant chord of D minor. In the third, *C—e—G···B*♭*—E*♭*—g*, first the positive state of the Fifth in *C—e—G* has passed into the negative *C—e*♭*—G*, and then the negative state of the Third *e*♭*—G* has taken on positive meaning, *E*♭*—g*. In the second element of the compound succession *C—e—G···C—e*♭*—G···B*♭*—E*♭*—g*, namely in *C—e*♭*—G*, no key is as yet determined for the minor triad on C; whether it

belongs to the key of C minor, G minor, E♭ major, or A♭ major, remains as yet undecided. Nevertheless the progression *e··e♭*, which presses towards *D*, and would seem to lead probably to *b—D—G*, speaks most for the first meaning and least for the last. The reversed succession *C—e♭—G ··· C—e—G* would make the second chord appear pretty clearly as the dominant triad of F minor.

286. By the feeling alone it may easily be perceived that the first of the chromatic progressions above, *e—G···E—g♯*, is far smoother, more pliant than the other, *C—e···c♯—E*. In the first, *g♯* is determined as Third by the *e* already present; in the other, *C—e···c♯—E*, no determination for *c♯* is given by *e*. The first progression is decidedly the chromatic difference of 24 : 25; in the second it is undecided whether *c♯* is to be referred as leading note to *d* or to *D*; whether the step shall enter in the ratio 24 : 25 or 128 : 135 (par. 250). It is true that the ratio 24 : 25 in itself no more contains a determination for the intonation of the chromatic progression than does 128 : 135. But the former expresses the difference between the major Third and the minor, and the intonation of the major Third is directly determined and grasped with certainty; while the other progression, 128 : 135, must first assume the note to which the chromatic note shall stand as leading note, and the leading note itself finds no determination in the notes of the given interval. Hence the **Fifth** of the major triad is always easier to raise chromatically than the **Root**, and therefore the passage

C—e—G ··· B—D—E—g♯ ··· A—c—E—A

proves smoother than the passage

C—e—G ··· c♯—E—G—A ··· D—f—A.

It may also be remarked that the note *E* in the last example, which here ought to remain identical with the *e* and maintain with *G* the interval of 5 : 6, is by the chromatically ascending *c♯* impelled to become rather sharper, namely to accord with the *E* of the series of Fifths, *C——G——D——A——E*, which in the dominant Seventh chord *A—c♯—E/G* forms with *G* the interval of 27 : 32. The triad *C—e—G* here in itself contains no determination for considering it as the dominant of the key of F major (which for the passage to D minor would be requisite); therefore the chromatic progression *C——c♯* will be referred only to the *D* contained in the system of the key of C major, whereby the Third of the major triad on *A*, as it stands in the series of Fifths, is taken. This, being too high for the *a* and *e* given in the key, must raise them to *A* and *E*, to bring about the consonance in *A—c♯—E*.

If we insert the major triad on *F* between the two first chords, and instead of the succession *C—e—G* ··· *c♯—e—G—A* ··· *D—f—A* take the succession *C—e—G* ··· *C—F—a* ··· *c♯—E—G—A* ··· *D—f—A*, then the Seventh chord *A—c♯—E/G* sounds smooth and perfectly pure; because now in the Third of the major triad on *F* there is given a determination for the step *C* ··· *c♯* But then we shall have obtained exactly that first succession, in which the **Fifth** progresses chromatically.

So too modulation to the key of the dominant is not to be effected by chromatic progression of the subdominant Root of the original key to the Third of the dominant of the new key, e.g.

F—a—C ··· f♯—A—C—D
C : IV G : V_7

but by taking the dominant Seventh chord of the latter after the tonic or dominant triad of the original key: e.g.

C—e—G ··· C—D—f♯—A
C : I
G : IV —— V_7

or:

C—e—G ··· b—D—G ··· A—C—D—f♯
C : I —— V
G : I —— V_7

The first modulation would always, in the interval *f*♯—*A*, have to alter the *a* of the key of C major into the *A* which is Fifth of the dominant in the key of G major. On the other hand, in the two last examples the note may at once acquire that meaning.

It is in such differences, outwardly small but inwardly important, that the reason must be sought why so many modulations, natural in appearance and into near keys, nevertheless keep something of harshness and constraint, and in vocal music refuse to be brought to satisfactory purity; while often others leading into the most distant keys turn out tractable and easy in performance.

287. The inner relationship of keys, it has already been said, can principally be determined only upon the tonic triad itself; which either in entirety, or in Root and Fifth, Root and Third, or Third and Fifth, or lastly in only one of the three chord-elements, discovers a relationship with another key. Thus its positive becomes relative, or a relative in it takes positive meaning in the other key; or lastly, a relative in the chord takes a new relative meaning in the new key. But this last is a less essential determination of relationship; since for 'another' to become 'other' can have but an indirect meaning for the 'one.' Therefore those relationships of keys, which indeed are connected with the tonic triad, but in which the change of meaning is from one secondary element into another—Fifth transformed to Third, or Third to Fifth—are of a less degree than those in which the primary element passes into the meaning of a secondary either in a positive or a negative sense, or a secondary changes into positive or negative primary meaning. Of the relationships founded upon change of meaning in single elements, the keys of A major, E♭ major, and E minor have a less direct bearing upon the key of C major than have the keys of E major, A♭ major, and A minor. In the first set the Third *e* is taken as Fifth,

III
C—e—G
A—c♯—E
II

the Fifth *G* as Third,

II
C—e—G
E♭—g—B♭
III

the Third as negative Fifth, and the Fifth as negative Third,

III II
C—e—G
e—G—b
II III

But in the second set the Third appears as Root, the Root as Third, the Root and Third as negatively Third and Root:

III	I	I III
C—e—G	C—e—G	C—e—G
E—g♯—B	A♭—c—E♭	a—C—e
I	I	III I

In the first the transformation acts on a relative and leads to a relative. In the second it is positive changing into relative or else relative into positive; whereby in each case there is always a positive actually present, either as determining or as determined.

288. The relationships in the minor key will be determined, not on the triad, its positive premise, but only on the negation of that triad, that is, on the tonic minor triad itself; for here the negation is what is principally meant. But where the negation has not the principal meaning, where the major triad is tonic chord and the minor triad only subdominant, as in the system of the minor-major key, there the relationships will be determined only upon the

tonic major triad. By change of meaning in the tonic minor triad of the key of C minor there result the relationships—

II III I
C—e♭—G
I III
E♭—g—B♭
III II
A♭—c—E♭
II
G—b♭—D
I
F—a♭—C

of the keys of E♭ major, A♭ major, G minor, and F minor. The key of G major is not related to the key of C minor. The G major triad is in itself already positive and of primary determination. But when it is confirmed as such, then the notion of the key of C minor is taken away; for the essential content of that notion is, that this triad presupposed positive is taken as negative. To the key of C minor, the key of G major with minor Sixth, which we term minor-major, alone can appear related; as also to the latter, taken as principal key, the key of C minor is in its turn related, which, however, does not stand in relationship to the key of G major.

To every key-system the opposite system with like name will always stand in near relationship; the minor key to the major with like name, the minor-major to the minor or major key with like name, and so too inversely. For here the transformation acts upon the tonic interval of Fifth, which passes from positive to negative or from negative to positive meaning, but in both determinations always contains at once the positive of the one and of the other.

I—II
II—I.

ENHARMONIC CHANGE.

289. Those passages which are founded upon so-called enharmonic change we can here only mention in passing, for they belong to the **tempered**, not to the **pure** note-system. So far as they may be possibly referred to the latter, they have already been included in what has preceded. Mostly they depend upon the diminished Seventh being identified with the major Sixth, or the augmented Second with the minor Third, e.g.

b—D—F—a♭ = B—D—f—g♯ = B—d—c♯—G♯ = c♭—d—F—A♭
C : VII°_{7} a : VII°_{7} f♯ : VII°_{7} e♭ : VII°_{7}

On this assumption every chord of the diminished Seventh lands us in four different, widely separated, keys. Three such chords, each looking four different ways, may be set out:

b—D/F—a♭, f♯—A/C—e♭, c♯—E/G—b;

whereby, if the proper Seventh chord be taken, modulation to the whole twelve keys of the tempered Fifth-circle stands open—to the major keys as well as to the minor, for we know that the diminished Seventh chord can be referred to a major triad as well as to a minor, and accordingly that the resolution *b—D/F—a♭ ··· C—e—G* is found no less frequently than the other, *b—D/F—a♭ ··· C—e♭—G* (par. 43). Besides these we know too the lawfulness of the resolutions *b—D/F—a♭ ··· C—F—a♭* and *b—D/F—a♭ ··· C—F—a* (par. 212). In the latter the Six-Four position of the resolving chord may draw after it progression to the triad *C—e—G* as dominant chord, and bring about the close in the key of F major or minor, which may thus be equally well reached either from the Seventh chord *e—G/B♭—d♭* or from *b—D/F—a♭*.

A diminished Seventh chord in any of its enharmonically different attitudes may always be derived unprepared from one of the three principal triads of any key. Consequently modulation into any major or minor key that may be desired is easy to accomplish by this method.

290. For so far as this way of modulation is believed to be authorised in assuming as identical, because of outward nearness, what is inwardly quite different and without relationship, it is as it were tainted with untruth, and we cannot rank the constructions, whose explanation has to be sought in such enharmonic changes, with those which depend upon an organic union. They have not a natural life, and exist only in the turbid element of the inaccuracy of tempered intonation. We have already perceived that in true harmony the difference between like-named Third- and Fifth-notes is found to be essential, and that these notes may indeed come into collision in chord-constructions, but can never stand indifferently for one another. But the difference of the enharmonically different notes, *b♯—C*, *c♯—D♭*, according to theory still less allows of their being identified; not because the interval of sound is greater, but that in their organic generation, the primary source of all note-determinations, there is no possibility at all of confounding such different degrees. Even if we will not abide by the positive series of triads

C..e..G..b..D..f♯..A..c♯..E..g♯..B..d♯..F♯..a♯..C♯..e♯..G♯..b♯..D♯

in which the enharmonically different note does not appear until the ninth member, and if we look for its nearest possible approach as given by the series

C..e♭..G..b♭..D..f♯..A..c♯..E..g♯..B..d♯..F♯

yet even then the inward gap between enharmonically different degrees still stretches out far beyond anything that can enter into mutual relation in harmony or melody.

291. It is not by any means true, however, that all enharmonic substitutions that occur in the writing of music are to be taken for changes of meaning in the above sense. More often it happens that a composer consciously or unconsciously puts one name for the other to lighten actual performance, for more comfortable fingering, and sometimes no doubt also from over haste or want of thorough knowledge of harmony, without intending thereby harmonically to alter the meaning.

But in vocal music it is never allowable to write an enharmonically different note instead of the right one, with the intention of facilitating intonation. If a progression is impossible to sing with the right notation, that is because the harmonic link fails. Difficulties in singing are not made easier by wrong notation. The minor Sixth is in itself an easy interval to sing, the augmented Fifth a very uncomfortable one. But when the latter is part of the harmony, a composer dares not write the easier for the harder, if he will not risk persuading the singer to attempt what is perhaps impossible.

292. In view of theory it naturally makes the greatest difference, whether from C major we modulate to the key of F♯ major or to the key of G♭ major; for the two last stand to the first in exactly opposite relation: *G♭* to *C* as *C* to *F♯*. Nevertheless in practice it often happens in pianoforte and orchestral music that one of the extreme keys is exchanged for the other. This is not always to be called modulation in the enharmonic way, for the enharmonic change of meaning can take place in this case either before or after the modulation. But so it may chance that a piece of music of some length with such enharmonic changes shall begin in C major, and close, according to the connexion of notes, in B♯ major or D𝄫 major, although the writing may show neither of these, but the original key. Then, however skilfully the whole may be composed in other respects, as regards the key it will always contain an untruth.

293. Music in performance passes in time before the hearer, and while it goes on we have sensibly before us only what hangs immediately together. This makes us overlook many faults in the form and conduct of a piece of music, which, if the whole were set out comprehensively or, if we may so say, architecturally to the inner sense, could not possibly be hidden. Crookedness, want of symmetry, disproportion, in visible objects that pretend to regularity, at once meet the healthy eye unpleasantly. Unfitness in modulatory arrangement, as well as in metrical relations of phrase, would be as easily perceived as faults in the immediate succession of chords, if it were not already in itself a harder task to glance over a whole of some magnitude in time with its parts, than to review in its proportions something made up of parts in space. Now there is such an architecture in music, and it consists principally in the regular structure, metrical and modulatory, of the piece; a requirement so essential that without it a composition has no pretence to art. For the first impression these conditions seem to be of less active influence. For we see productions shapeless, rhapsodical, without intelligent building up of periods, without organic unity of manifold contents, extort not seldom a brilliant success. But the works that have been able to keep in lasting favour have ever been such as, apart from characteristic peculiarities, apart from charm of melody and harmony, preserve order of rhythm and modulation; i.e. which wear their beauties set in the beauty of the whole, in the truth and reasonable conformity to law of a form in itself artistically valuable.

294. It is no more purposed to give lessons here on the practical handling of passages of modulation, than in the earlier investigations of harmonic combinations it was discussed how technically to apply them. That can by no means be expected in a treatise that represents chords exclusively in the closest position of their intervals and in progressions such as issue, without choice or guidance, merely from the most obvious requirements.

295. If determinations should be here given for the modulatory organisation of a piece, they could only be quite general. The particular form is determined by the particular contents; it is subject to principles of universal validity only in the broadest outlines and in the narrowest detail. Particular in universal (which is also universal in particular), i.e. individual, constitutes reality; of which the concrete existence is apparent to reason, but by the intellect can only be imperfectly apprehended, i.e. either in abstract universality or in abstract particularity.

296. That something leaves unity and enters into opposition with itself, and then that this opposition is done away with and linked into union, is the notion and explanation of all real coming-to-be and of all reasonable formation.

The harmonic succession of the triads **C** ··· **G** ··· **C**, or the three first notes of the melodic scale, *C* ·· *D* ·· *e*, which are based upon that succession, contain in the narrowest compass everything that normally lies at the bottom even of the broadest formation. What is here given within the key as chord-succession can but be repeated in the same sense, when the key itself is taken as the concrete element of unity, and the advance of construction made from it. Thus in the succession above, the secondary triad-element (the Fifth, *G*) is by the entrance of another triad changed to primary meaning; or, in other words, the change of meaning in the secondary triad-element produces another triad; and then the change back of meaning (*G* becoming Fifth again, as at first) reproduces the first triad, which before was absolute, but now is resultant. And when not an element of the triad but the triad itself as element of the key experiences a like transformation (i.e. starts as tonic, travels through dominant meaning, and finally re-enters upon tonic), the key will similarly be reproduced from its opposite, and derivative, instead of being, as at first, posited immediately.

297. Although there are pieces that take another course of

modulation, and that have not their principal division, the finish of their first part, in the dominant key, yet we may now set aside every divergent form as abnormal. The decidedly **other** key, which forms the **opposite** into which every piece of music must pass in the middle, is the key of the **dominant**; not the subdominant, for from the first an onward, not a backward, course should be taken. With the latter the beginning could only come upon an earlier beginning, and would then no longer be itself a beginning. If the modulation leads straight on to the subdominant, then the principal key appears itself as dominant; it loses the tonic character. By the key of the dominant the tonic is not only not endangered; rather this is the right key to settle it firmly. The principal key, coming after the dominant, is at once felt as tonic; after finishing in the dominant, the tonic can re-enter with full power.

298. There are small pieces too constructed all in the same key. They then have their harmonic opposition not in the key but in the chord; and what has just been said of the key is in this case true of the triad.

299. As a composition with modulation can be constructed in the tonic and dominant keys, but not in the tonic and subdominant, so one without modulation may be made with the tonic and dominant triads, but not with the tonic and subdominant, at least not in a natural manner. There the principal key, here the principal chord, would through the subdominant take on dominant meaning: that is, a meaning, not of setting out, but of going on. It would exchange the character of positive for that of relative.

300. But though the tonic key, as also the tonic triad, has in the first place to maintain positive quality, yet must not this positive continue absolute and given immediately. For then the condition of reality would depart, which requires that it should be derivative as well. Thus the tonic triad must be accompanied with its dominant and subdominant triads before it can receive full

meaning as at once source and offspring. For the subdominant chord has only positive meaning, and the dominant only relative; but the tonic has relative meaning to the first and positive to the other: it therefore comprehends in itself both determinations, being in fact determined on two sides and not, like the others, only on one. It is like the notion of the present, which between past and future is itself to the first a future and to the other a past, and thus at once future and past; and in this opposition held united in one it is the only time that exists really. So for the complete determination of tonic quality it is necessary to touch also upon the subdominant side. The succession of the major triads of C and G contains as yet no unmistakable establishment of the first as tonic, for it might as well be subdominant. But let the dominant Seventh chord *G—b—D|F* follow the major triad of C, and doubt as to the key will no longer be possible. For in the dominant Seventh chord dominant and subdominant are held united, and the resolving chord *C—e—G* demanded in the dissonance then enters as decided tonic. A more detailed and spread-out determination of tonic character would be given by the dominant and subdominant triads in succession preceding the close, or by the Seventh chord upon the Fifth of the dominant followed by the dominant Seventh chord, e.g. (marked with the Root-harmony)

$$\boldsymbol{C \cdots F \cdots G_7 \cdots C} \quad \text{or} \quad \boldsymbol{C \cdots D_7^{\circ} \cdots G_7 \cdots C}.$$

301. These successions establish the **chord** as tonic. With regard to the **key**, the condition that it must be established as on both sides derivative seems less pressing than the need felt within it of hearing the subdominant, as Seventh to the dominant triad. Nevertheless in a composition carried to any length the modulation would be felt to be wanting in completeness if keys lying **below** the principal one were not also brought in; if only chromatic **sharpenings**, and not chromatic **flattenings**, were found in it. For, taken generally, it is in this outward difference that the 'One'

and the 'Other,' the dominant and subdominant sides, must be shown, in phrase of the major key. But the first part of a piece, even when of larger compass, cannot in general be determined to manifoldness of modulation; because its business is merely the setting out of certain contents, in particular of a duality consisting of a principal and a subsidiary phrase, the first in the tonic and the second in the dominant. So that other keys, and therefore also those of the subdominant side, especially the subdominant key itself, cannot find a place until the subsequent working out, when the positive character of the tonic key has been established by its dominant.

302. In the universally valid, normal form of musical structure, so far as manifoldness of key upon the whole prevails there, everything remote in modulation, and especially everything directed towards the subdominant side, falls only into the second part of the whole; and there its place is before the re-entrance of the principal key, in which the principal and subsidiary phrases, which in the first part were held apart in Fifth-separation, now come together and are united tonically.

303. Although the principles which rule the arrangement of modulation are quite general and may be applied to every musical form, yet here, when we speak of a succession of principal and subsidiary phrases, of their Fifth-separation in the first part and tonic union in the second, we have principally in view that conception of a musical composition known as **Sonata-form.** This consists essentially of **homophonic** phrase with divided periods. It is opposite to the **Fugue-form**, which, woven **polyphonically**, less admits of a division of periods, or similarly of an abstract determination of the succession of modulation. And, generally, in the fugue, for reasons not now to be explained, no richness of modulation can be developed.

304. Exceptional arrangements of modulation could be caused

only if the principal key, instead of passing into the dominant, sought out one of the other relationships, such as we discussed earlier; always excluding those of the subdominant. Thus in **Beethoven** sometimes in major phrases we see the principal key turn to a major or minor key related in the Third, and the first section finished in that key.

305. The minor key has its principal relationship in the major key of its tonic Third, which passes from negative Third-meaning into positive Root-meaning, while the negative Root assumes positive Third-meaning (A minor, C major). This is the relationship most founded in opposition, and is therefore the one most universally applied. A relationship of opposition almost as decided the minor key finds in the major key of the Third of its subdominant, by the negative tonic Third receiving positive Fifth-meaning and the negative Fifth positive Third-meaning (A minor, F major). This relation too affords a form of modulation well approved for the first division of a piece. And it is of the first division alone that we speak here; because there only is found a more or less determinate opposition of related keys and the establishment of a second against a first. For the further carrying out of the modulation up to the re-entrance of the principal key no schematic determination of form can be given. It could be expressed only as obedience to general principles of modulation, and in æsthetic conditions, as also in the negative determination that keys wholly without relationship, which may be touched in passing, must not attain to being tonically established.

306. The minor phrases of earlier times usually pass from the tonic into the minor key of the Fifth. This is a relationship rather grounded upon the structure of the particular 'church modes,' as they are called, than in the nature of our more general musical system. There was also a special claim to it in the polyphonic manner of phrase; where if a theme in a minor key has to be

carried out, it can be transposed into other minor keys, but not into a major key without undergoing alteration.

CLOSE.

307. The title of this section may seem to indicate a conclusion of the doctrine of harmony; but that is not meant by it. Merely to gain an insight into the general principles of harmony has been the aim and object in our path hitherto. The conclusion of the doctrine is never attained. The end remains out of reach, if not sought in this, that in all and everything we come back again to the beginning.

Although, in what has preceded, the principal phenomena of harmonic combination, of the process for construction and reconstruction both in simultaneous and in successive sounds, as well as in successions sounding simultaneously, have been discussed, yet infinitely more might still be offered of interest for theoretical knowledge. This infinity cannot be exhausted. Everywhere the way only can be shown, how it leads onward in every direction, and where it must be struck for the investigation also of any single case, any particular instance. And the clue is to be found in following out that process of production which is illustrated in the present work, by steadily grasping the three factors of development in their simple abstract meaning, in their universal essentiality, and by analysing each composite whole in order to see it built up again from its parts by their union.

What is here denoted by the title is the musical close, the **cadence.**

The very essential **metrical** conditions which co-operate in the construction of the cadence must as yet remain unexplained; here we are dealing with the **harmonic** conditions alone.

308. The expression contains the sense of something having to be **brought together.** Thus the **close** really presupposes **separation.** Chords that are principally **united** can form no close when following one another. The tonic triad of the major key cannot unite with the two minor triads of the system into a close; their too near relationship is against such union. In the passage from *C—e—G* to *a—C—e*, or from *C—e—G* to *e—G—b*, no decidedly antithetical change of meaning takes place in the notes which remain the same, *C—e* or *e—G*. For the **Third** to become **Root** or **Fifth** is not for it to pass into its **opposite**, into what is quite **other** than itself. That can consist only in the **Root** becoming **Fifth** or the **Fifth Root.** The Third is in itself already Root **and** Fifth; if it becomes Root **or** Fifth, it only gives up one or other of the determinations contained united in it and reverts to the single one; it finds a decided opposite in neither of the two. That can only consist in one thing appearing as another that, before, it decidedly was **not.** Therefore a change of meaning sufficient to give the effect of a close cannot take place on the **Third,** but must go upon the **Root** or **Fifth.** Accordingly in the first instance they must be triads **related in the Fifth** that passing into one another can form a **close**:

C—e—G ··· b—D—G, G—b—D ··· G—C—e;
C—e—G ··· C—F—a, F—a—C ··· e—G—C.

309. But, again, wholly **disjunct** triads can also be united into a close in so far as they have the link of the triad that lies between, with which the initial triad is united in two notes. This linking triad stands to the triad, into which the succession is to lead, in Fifth-relationship, the relation of the close; and, since the passage can take place only from the linking triad placed instead of the initial triad, this succession also yields the close in Fifth-related triads. Thus the meaning of the close in the succession *G—b—D···* *a—C—F*, which consists directly of the succession *b—D|F···*

a—C—F, is that the Fifth *F* of the first triad, *b—D|F*, receives Root-meaning in the second, *a—C—F*. In the succession *F—a—C···D—G—b*, which is directly the succession *D|F—a···D—G—b*, the meaning of the close is that the Root *D* of the first triad, *D|F—a*, receives Fifth-meaning in the second, *D—G—b*.

Of the relative triad-value which the chords joining the limits have for their key, we have already spoken above (par. 145).

In the successions of Fifth-related triads this transformation to the opposite takes place in the common note itself:

II — I I — II
C—e—G···b—D—G, G—b—D···G—C—e.

Therefore of the three possible kinds of triad-succession, only that of **Third-related** triads remains excluded from those that form a close. The successions

III — II III — I
C—e—G···C—e—a, C—e—G···b—e—G

have no meaning as closes; they do not bring together what is essentially divided, decidedly antithetical. The tonic major triad allows the possibility of a coexisting minor triad, but not of a coexisting dominant or subdominant triad, or of a diminished triad.

Every other progression of triads than that of triads related in the Third will form a close, and likewise every resolution of the Seventh chord. For in the latter the resolving chord will always be related in the Fifth to one of the two triads united in the Seventh chord, or else disjunct from it.

310. But we have to distinguish two meanings of the word **close**: namely **bringing together** and **concluding**. The first is present wherever triads united in the Root or Fifth, or triads not directly united, follow one another.

The close as conclusion may also be considered in two ways: it may close altogether, or it may be such as to let an after-phrase

N

be expected. The former kind must lead from a dominant or subdominant chord into the tonic triad in its triad-position, in order quite to fulfil the sense that the beginning appears as the end, and that first and last merge in one another. Any other than the fundamental position of the tonic triad must have been brought about by some previous progression; it cannot be absolute beginning, and therefore also not closing chord. But it is alone the union with a dominant or subdominant chord, the change of tonic and dominant or subdominant triad, that in the close leads back into the **fundamental position** of the tonic triad:

(5/3) (5/3) (5/3) (5/3)
C—e—G···b—D—G···C—e—G, C—e—G···C—F—a···C—e—G.

The two diminished triads, which besides the dominant and subdominant triads may be united with the tonic in forming a close, lead, in consequence of their indirect progression, to a transposed position of the latter:

(5/3) (6/3) (5/3) (6/4)
C—e—G C—e—G
(e—G—b)···D—F—b···e—G—C, (a—C—e)···a—D—F···G—C—e;

the diminished triad on the dominant side to the **Six-Three position**, the diminished triad on the subdominant side to the **Six-Four position** of the tonic closing chord.

311. But the closing chord does not attain to full tonic establishment until its relation not only to the dominant **or** subdominant, but to **both** of them is brought out:

C—e—G···C—F—a···C—e—G···b—D—G···C—e—G,

or

C—e—G···C—F—a···b—D—G···C—e—G.

That here the subdominant precedes the dominant, is simply in agreement with the direct order, as the former is the earlier in the harmonic generation. Wherefore this form of close is the most universal and ordinary, and found repeatedly in the greatest compositions and in the smallest, in the trivial as well as in the most sublime. For composers of genius have ever least sought originality in oddness.

312. Nevertheless the form:

C—e—G···b—D—G···C—e—G···C—F—a···C—e—G,

in which the relation to the subdominant stands last, is also not less right. In the older music especially it is frequently used, where, moreover, it was naturally necessitated and brought about by the structure of some of the so-called church modes. We call this kind the **Plagal close.**

313. Under the notation:

C—e—G ··· b—D—G ··· C—e—G,
C—e—G ··· C—F—a ··· C—e—G,

might be conceived, not merely the form of a close, but also the notion of that progress of modulation and its return into itself which makes up the whole of a composition. Now by the requirements of modulation the first passage must be, not to the subdominant, but to the dominant; and when the tonic has been established from that side, then the subdominant too will be touched on.

Therefore the general form:

I——IV——V——I,

which places the subdominant before the dominant, is only good for the close: not as a scheme of modulation, not as a succession of **keys**, but only as a succession of closing **chords** inside the key.

314. When the dominant chord follows the subdominant:

F—a—C ··· D—G—b,

no sustained note which changes its harmonic meaning is present.

Union is therefore sought to be recovered by the entrance, simultaneously with the subdominant chord, of the diminished linking triad *D*|*F—a*, whose Root *D* becomes Fifth in the dominant chord:

I — II

F—a—C—D ··· G—b—D;

or by the Root of the subdominant chord continuing on into the dominant chord as Fifth of the diminished triad *b—D*|*F*:

I —— II

F—a—C ··· D—F—G—b

and forming with it the dominant Seventh chord which leads to a decided close. In the sounding together of the Third of the dominant and Root of the subdominant is contained the compulsion for the former to proceed to the tonic Root. Therefore also in the first form *F—a—C—D ··· G—b—D*, in which *F* and *a* go together to *G*, the note *F*, which now is not present as sustained into the dominant triad, will readily be added as a later Seventh to the chord, to drive the leading note upwards; so that this form of close even in four-part harmony surrenders the Fifth of the closing chord more readily than the Seventh of the dominant chord.

315. Already (par. 238) we have noticed the **Pedal**, though only to allude to it. Here too a detailed discussion of it cannot be undertaken. That belongs to the technical lesson-book. But so far as the pedal bears upon the close, something general may still be said on it.

316. The pedal can be established on two notes of the key-system: on the dominant and on the tonic. These two are pivots upon which a change of principal chords moves. Upon the dominant, the dominant triad changes with the tonic triad; and upon the tonic, the tonic triad changes with the subdominant triad. Such a simple change of triad and chord of Six-Four upon the two notes is indeed b no means what is imagined under the term pedal;

rather the web of harmony over such a sustained note may be most manifold. But those two chords are the fixed points for the passing harmonies, which are spun upon the dominant **before** the close, and upon the tonic **after** the close, in the one case postponing it, in the other to prolong and echo it. The pedal upon the tonic, which can only be formed **after** the close, is always to be regarded as an appendix or **Coda** of the piece or section closed; and here we have always to distinguish the **end** from the **close.**

The newer music is much more exhaustive in closing, in heaping on appended phrases, than the older. In old music mostly with the closing chord the piece too is at an end. But in modern music the close must often be sought a great way before the end. With the older close which has no coda it is almost always necessary to introduce a ritardando before the end, so as to prepare for leaving off. Otherwise the piece seems to close abruptly and unsatisfactorily.

317. In melodic progression, when a close is to be brought about, we see that the parts do not take the course that is suggested by the conditions of chord-union. The succession *G—b—D* ··· *G—C—e* makes the Fifth *D* of the first triad go to the Third *e* of the second, a progression brought about by triad-linking for the two chords, which are joined only in the Fifth, in this manner:

G—b—D ··· G—b—e ··· G—C—e.

But in closing, this part needs to pass, not to the Third of the tonic, but to its Root, to find there the rest not given in the Third. Now in essentially melodic phrases it is principally this Fifth of the dominant that precedes the closing note in the part that carries the melody. Thus the closes of chorales and popular melodies have this form in greatly preponderating majority; the melody closes with a passage to the tonic, not from the leading note, but from the Fifth of the dominant. In the harmonic close, besides the Fifth of the dominant, the Third of the dominant will appear, another part, and this also must proceed to the tonic. A third part will hold the dominant Root unmoved as Fifth of the tonic. Thus with these progressions the tonic triad will remain without a Third; for if the Fifth of the dominant does not progress to that note, no other interval of the dominant chord leads there. Hence the polyphonic music of the old time, which throughout is more melodically combined, less a succession of chords than a chord of successions, a sounding together of melodies, often closes without tonic Third. The dominant Seventh, which with us leads to the tonic Third, was still strange to that time, or at least unusual and of rare occurrence; as indeed was Seventh-harmony altogether—the dissonances of the old style are as a rule suspensions. When the top part has leading-note progression, an inner part will readily progress from the Fifth of the dominant to the Third of the tonic. With that melody in the upper voice the Third is not wanting even in the old vocal phrase, unless the tenor is obliged to close on the Root by the **Cantus firmus**, which in many cases it has to carry. In the minor key yet another motive comes in for not letting even an inner part close with the Third. It is that between the Fifth of the dominant and the minor Third of the tonic there exists leading-note relation. In the key, e.g., of C minor to the chords **G**...**c** such an inner part would receive the melody *D*··*e*♭. This taken in itself expresses, not a close in C minor, but one to E♭ major, the key of the Third. To avoid this the inner part here too goes better to the Root; or else instead of the minor it takes the tonic **major** Third. Thus in phrases of old music in the minor key we see the close, when not **without** the Third, always made with the major triad. But the reason is not to be sought in the minor triad having been deemed too little consonant for a closing chord; it could not in fact be introduced naturally if the melodic independence of the part was to be preserved.

318. In the major close the Fifth of the dominant should for

melodic determination of the close pass to the tonic; but, as urged by chord-union, it would rather progress to the tonic Third. Therefore it is brought by the two claims into division. It cannot do both at once; but it does one after the other. It lets the Third be heard struck into or out of it before going to the Root. It also repeats the Third struck afterwards, and with that there arises the **shake** upon the Fifth of the dominant, the ornament so long customary at the end of the old airs and solo pieces of every kind; which was therefore not a mere prettiness at pleasure, or fashion of the time, but given with the kind of close and a natural condition in it. Although the shake has its origin and proper seat upon this note, it can nevertheless occur also upon other notes; but, in obeying nature, only upon such as admit of a double progression, upwards and downwards. The upper note of the shake contains the first; the so-called turn belonging to the shake contains the second. The Sixth and Seventh degrees of the minor key-system allow of the shake only when the relations of passage for each are discovered outside the limits of the closed minor system: as we found them from the Octave downwards to the minor Sixth in the minor Seventh, and from the Fifth upwards to the major Seventh in the major Sixth. But in a harmony that contains both degrees united according to their determinations in the system, these cannot be had recourse to without violence. Thus in the diminished Seventh chord neither a shake upon its Root nor upon its Seventh is found natural. To the former the turn is wanting, to the latter the upper note of the shake; the one has the augmented Second below it, the other has it above.

319. To the close from the dominant or subdominant triad into the tonic is opposed the close from the tonic into the dominant or subdominant triad. With the former a whole is concluded, or the principal section of the whole which has established on its own behalf a key related to the principal one. The latter only marks the

fore phrase to an after phrase: not a period, only a clause. And as such a clause need not present a closing chord, it follows that the dominant or subdominant chord, due regard being had to its derivation, may there appear in one of its passing shapes. Besides this, the condition whereby the perfect close could only be led from either the dominant or the subdominant triad, here lapses, and the dominant or subdominant triad may issue from any succession that meets the case of a close. In the perfect close only the two cadences V···I, V···I; **G···C, F···C,** could be realised. But for the half-close upon the dominant and subdominant, besides the two cadences opposite to the two former, I···V, I···IV; **C···G, C···F,** these stand also at disposal:

II°···V, IV···V, VI···V;	D/F—a ··· b—D—G,
F—a—C ··· D—G—b,	a—C—e ··· b—D—G, and
VII···IV, V···IV, III···IV;	b—D/F ··· a—C—F,
G—b—D ··· a—C—F,	e—G—b ··· C—F—a.

Similarly this close may have its derivation from the triads that unite the limits of the key-system in extension; into the upper Fifth *f♯/a—C···D—G—b*, into the under Fifth *e—G/B♭··· C—F—a*.

320. We have yet to mention that form of close in which the dominant chord is followed by some other in place of the tonic triad expected. Such a succession is well known under the name of **False close.** Within the key this succession will be subject only to the principles which make up the general conditions of the close. It cannot lead to chords related in the Third. Thus, after withdrawal of the triad on the tonic *C—e—G*, there remain the triads *a—C—e, F—a—C, D/F—a*, into which the dominant triad *G—b—D* can pass so as to meet the conditions of a close: as in the successions .

V — VI	V — IV	V — II°
G—b—D···e—a—C;	G—b—D···a—C—F;	G—b—D···F—a—D;

where we still denote the triad-progression only in close three-part harmony, and neglect the consideration of one part serving as basis for the others; though this, in many cases, will itself take up one of the progressions governed by the succession.

Besides the false closes which are yielded within the key, a much larger number will be offered if the closing chord may belong to another key. Here every way stands open which the arrangement of modulation allows. We can ascribe to the dominant chord four other meanings in different keys, agreeably to which it can take the most manifold progressions. These will, however, be curtailed, both here and also in the false close within the key, when the chord leading to the close is not merely dominant triad but dominant Seventh chord; because then the progression in resolution of the Seventh receives determinations by which many of the otherwise possible successions are shut out. Instead of them, with the Seventh chord, there are now successions found suitable for a close which would not be so with the plain dominant chord: those, namely, which suit with the upper of the two triads joined in the Seventh chord. A false close in another key will by preference fall always upon one of the three principal constituents, tonic, subdominant or dominant, according to chord-union as issuing from the dominant or subdominant chord with or without Seventh, agreeably to the precepts in general of succession. The entrance of a new chord of the dominant Seventh, if it can be prepared in the chord preceding, is eminently fitted for determining the new key; because then the new leading note stands out clearly in its quality of Third of the dominant.

II.

METRE

METRE AND RHYTHM.

1. WE shall call the constant measure by which the measurement of time is made—**Metre**; the kind of motion in that measure—**Rhythm.**

2. The measure, as to outward structure, is found to be a **two-**, **three-**, or **four-**part unity. For the motion in that measure, it may in itself be infinitely manifold of shape; nevertheless as measured it can be understood only by the determinations that issue from the metrical notion.

3. And here we shall meet again with the same elements of the notion, by which the essence of the triad was explained to us: namely, those of the **Octave, Fifth**, and **Third**, taking these intervals in their abstract meaning, i.e. of unity, opposition, and unified opposition.

METRE.

I. Two-timed. (OCTAVE.)

4. For the beginning of metrical determination we must take an interval of time that at first is still undivided. Two successive audible beats, supposed one second of time apart, may be the sensible image of such an interval of time.

5. These two beats enclose only **one** space of time. But with the two beats we have, not one, but two times determined. With

the second beat, marking the end of the enclosed space of time, there is given the beginning of a second space equal in duration to the first. At the end of this second space we may expect a new beat, which, however, cannot happen earlier than at that point of time without causing an interruption, a curtailment of the time determined for us by the two beats. What is injured by a later beat happening out of time is not the actual interval of time bounded by the two original beats; for that in itself cannot experience disturbance from something that does not enter until it has expired. Yet we feel that a beat happening before the completion of the second space of time does disturb the metrical determination given by two beats. Consequently what is disturbed is not the enclosed interval of time simply, but the metrical unity made up of this and the interval which follows it.

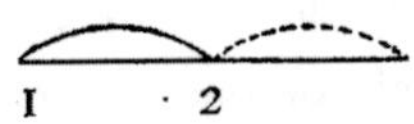

6. A **single** beat then cannot determine a space or magnitude of time. Rather it denotes only a beginning without an end. But with **two** beats following one another we obtain a **whole** determined in time, of which the space of time enclosed by the two beats is the **half**. The first metrical determination is not of a simple interval of time, but of a twofold or repeated one.

7. A simple time is not a metrical unit, and cannot stand as a metrical whole. A single thing in metrical determination has its meaning only as part of the whole, as **first** or **second**. For the metrical whole, from its first determination onwards, is an undivided double, a twin unity.

8. This first determination is to metre that which the **Octave** is to the intervals of harmony. The Octave too is in reality only a **half**; and in this meaning it opposes itself to its other self, i.e. the other half; and taken together with this other (the reflexion, outside, of itself), it 'then' fulfils the notion of **itself** as half of a whole.

II. Three-timed. (FIFTH.)

9. As **two** beats enclose **one** space of time, determine a second and join it to the first, so **three** beats, actually bounding **two** spaces of time, cause a third to follow as echo of the second. But this third part of that which is now to be comprehended as a whole of three parts does not stand in a relation of equality to the two preceding parts, but only to the second of them. It arises by echoing the second, just as we have seen the second arising as an echo of the first. And thus the second member of the three-part unity gets the double meaning of being second to a first and first to a second. But in the latter meaning, because it becomes first to a second, it is withdrawn from union with the first member, which is left standing solitary. **Separation of the unity** enters in the first pair. The **twin unity** becomes **twoness.** This and the contradiction of the double meaning in the second element is what we have already pointed out as the essence of the **Fifth.**

10. It is not as a succession of three members strung together that the three-part in time is metrically determined and intelligible. For then as a mere chain of members every other quantity, fivefold, sevenfold, elevenfold, would be so too. But its metrically intelligible sense is the interlacing of the twoness of the first and second members as first pair with the second and third as second pair; a formation in which the middle member of the three-part whole has the determination of belonging to both pairs, and, self-opposed, of being end or beginning.

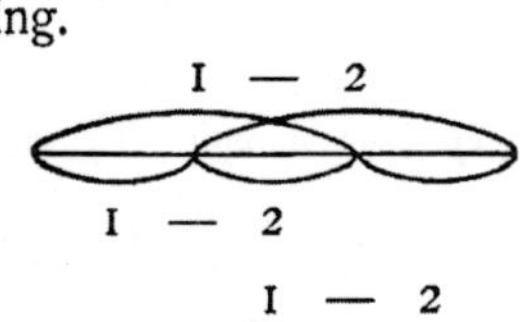

11. If a second is to be added to a first, then it cannot be otherwise than equal to the first; for unequals cannot be counted

together. In the three-part whole, to the first single part a part of double magnitude, or to the two first parts comprehended in unity a single part, would be opposed as other part. In neither case would the notion of equality in opposition be satisfied. That which is single can only have another single ; the pair can only have another pair, to be its other or second. Thus if the three-part unity is to admit of intelligible partition, the pair made up of the first and second parts of time can come into opposition only with the pair made up of the second and third parts.

12. In a succession of three equal elements of time *a*, *b*, *c* :

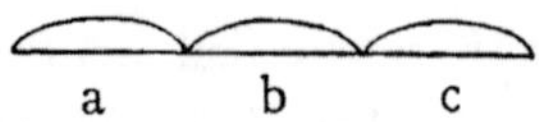

if the part *a*, as first, be taken single, then the second *b*—*c*, being double in magnitude and unequal to the first, for this reason cannot be a second to *a* ;

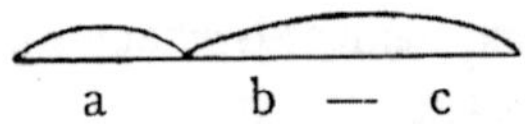

nor yet if *a*—*b* be joined to make a first, can *c*, being single, be second of this first.

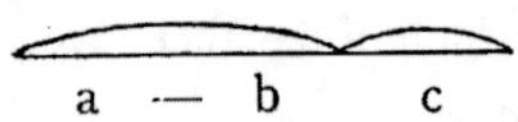

Only the double times *a*—*b* and *b*—*c* can here be opposed to one another as *A* and *B*.

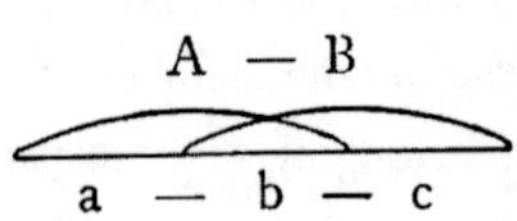

III. Four-timed. (THIRD.)

13. A fourth beat happening after completion of the third space of time now causes a fourth part of time to follow as echo of the third, which, at first itself preceded, now precedes, and has become a first with the fourth space as its second.

14. This last metrical formation, being four-membered, is twice-two-membered, and in this sense is **Third**. But in the course of its successive growth—and it is shaped in time, and therefore can have its nature and reality only in this process of becoming and having become—it is at the instant of its first determination two-membered, or **Octave**; next it becomes three-membered, or **Fifth**; and lastly four-membered, i.e. twice-two-membered, **Third**. To the last determination it cannot attain otherwise than by passing through the shapes proper to the first two. And thus on reaching the last it is a successive union, a union in time, of **Octave, Fifth,** and **Third: the metrical triad.**

15. The first beat gives us the **Root**, as yet undetermined in duration. The second gives us the **Octave**, the determinate time; the interval of time joined to its copy as metrically determined unity. With the third we have the copy of the second space of time, reckoning the second space now as a **first**; consequently the two first times, which belonged together, are now separated; the half is withdrawn from its whole, and there is the contradiction in the second time of being self-opposed, second and first, end and beginning. This is the metrical **Fifth**. The fourth beat causes the copy of the third element to come into existence, and the third, from being a second, to become a first. Thereby the second, which in its relation to the third was withdrawn from its union with the first, is restored to the first, and again becomes one with it. And now the first and second, being in a state of unity produced and derivative and no longer merely immediately given, have themselves become a first, that has for its second that like double unity of the third and fourth which is its copy. The whole has become also a part in the notion of the **Third**.

16. It is this inner reconcilement of separation in unity and unity in separation, the completed negation of every negativing excluding element, that speaks to us here in metrical determination

as the essence of the triad; but in combinations of notes as the perfection of harmony; and generally in any guise of phenomenon as the perfected notion of determinate reality.

17. Now in the processes of metrical formation there is one thing that must be kept in view as an essential condition to their right understanding. It is, that the changes happen upon a unity always one and the same. Otherwise a change, into another, could have no intelligible sense. Only in so far as a determination is imparted to the first metrical element by the later ones, have they a meaning of unity with it. The unity given undetermined by the first beat, is determined by the second, splits into twoness by the third, and passes by the fourth beat from twoness into unity of twoness. It is the passage from the feeling of the immediate whole, through the intellectual analysing perception of its members, to the intellectually felt, i.e. reasonable, notion of the whole in its memberment.

18. The four-part, then, as a musical measure of time is the metre which is perfectly determined in itself and independent, containing within it all elements of the notion of a membered whole, and needing no addition to complete its unity. For the unities of the metrical two-part and three-part taken alone are imperfect in inner determination of memberment. In the former the element of separation is wanting; in the latter the element of reunion. Both of them need to be repeated in order to find determination as part, as half, in the notion of unity of a whole of higher order.

THE DIFFERENCE OF TWICE-TWO-TIMED AND FOUR-TIMED METRE.

19. Two-part time repeated is always easily distinguished from time essentially four-part: the $\frac{2}{4}$ bar repeated, from the $\frac{4}{4}$ bar.

The first is only opposed as a whole to itself:

1 — 2 1 — 2

1 — 2

whereby the second and third times in succeeding are not united. The union is only between the pairs themselves and between the members of each pair by itself. But in four-part metre, whose full notion in fourpartedness is reached after passing though three-part,

I. II. III.

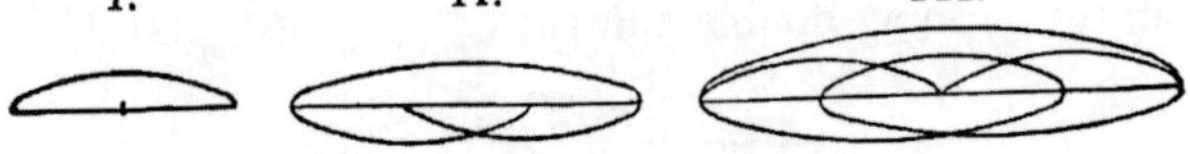

1 — 2 1 — 2 1 — 2

the third member is not merely a repetition of the first, as beginning in the second part; it has previously, in three-part time, also been the successor of the second member, relation to which it gives up only with the entrance of the fourth member; i.e. it gives the second member back again to its first, and causes the two to be united which at first were one and then separated.

20. Now it is true that the determinations of the metrical formation have their essential bearing upon the first pairs of members only. Yet the difference of two-part, three-part, and four-part division, as well as of four-part and two-part repeated, is represented also in the time-figures just as we have drawn them. Like the body showing the soul, or the outside of a thing showing the inside, so the figures show to what degree less or higher the unit-notion first posited is developed.

Thus the difference between two-part metre repeated and metre essentially four-part, which in outward compass are both alike, comes out clearly when we consider the two figures standing below, and compare them with one another.

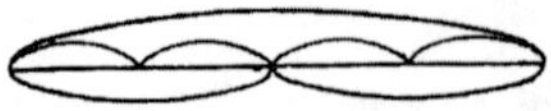

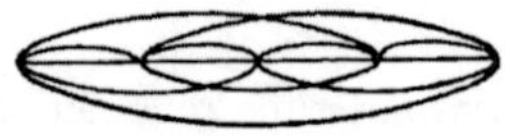

Here the eye tells us that the last as against the first is undivided in the middle, is organically richer determined, and more luxuriantly twined.

FIVE-TIMED AND SEVEN-TIMED FORMATION AS ARTIFICIAL AND INORGANIC.

21. The three-part metrical unity consists as to its formal structure of an overlapping double pair;

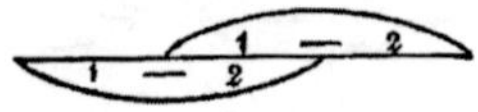

for the twin unity has here half gone out of itself, and taken its second element anew as first. Also the four-part begins a new pair with its third member without thereby denying the past existence of the union between the second and third members,

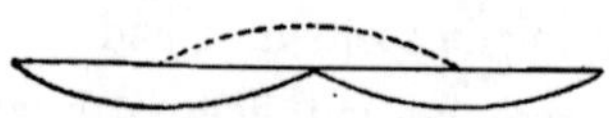

although that union is set in the background now that the united whole pairs are opposed. From this one might easily be tempted to advocate a construction carried on with overlapping pairs in the manner of the three-membered formation, so as by continued linking together of halves to give rise also to metrical unities of more than four times.

But we have seen how with the entrance of the fourth member the separation of the first pair, which sprang up in the third element of time, is annulled. The pair has again become **whole,** and therefore can now find its **second**, or opposite, only in the other pair, which is set quite outside it. So that such an articulation by halves can make metrical union only in **Three**-time. With the fourth time the determination of the whole in its parts is closed, and now to produce a further formation the whole must itself enter into the meaning of the part.

22. It will therefore be self-evident that anything extending beyond the fourth member, beyond the end of the second pair, can no longer exercise an influence upon the interior of the first pair, and therefore too can no longer stand to it, as such, in an organic relation of unity ; and that therefore a metrical formation going beyond the four-part lies outside the notion of unity, and consequently falls asunder into twoness. Anything metrically **five**-part cannot be understood otherwise than as artificially put together out of **two**-part and **three**-part, as 2 + 3 or 3 + 2,

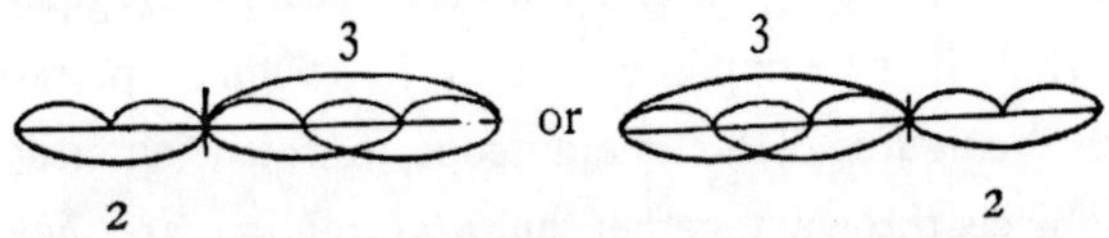

Similarly **seven**-part can only be metrically intelligible as artificially made up of **three**-part and **four**-part ; or else of **two**-part, **three**-part, and **two**-part ; as 4 + 3, 3 + 4, and 2 + 3 + 2.

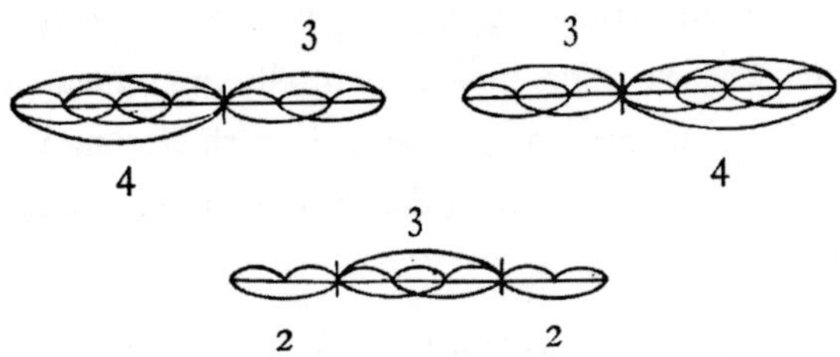

But such formations are by no means capable of being shaped into a metrical unity, as were those of two, three, and four parts. Not

having sprung out of organic determination, they will never seem more than artificially put together. Here the one is not followed by another of like quality, i.e. a second, as the first in its opposition. Instead of this there is another first, a new determination, which can only make another beginning, and not a succession to what has gone before.

In chord-union an immediate succession of two Fifths is self-excluded. In harmony taught rationally no special prohibition of that progression would be wanted, for between united triads it can never occur. Rather it marks discontinuous juxtaposition of two triads in the primary position, two beginnings placed next one another; and it is precisely this want of union that comes out so offensively in consecutive Fifths. So too a metrical formation placing two- and three-membered unities alternately makes us feel how rhythmically incongruous is the repeated shock of the new beginning which it causes at every change instead of steady progress.

23. Still a thing irregular in itself may yet form a regularly symmetrical whole if it be opposed to itself in a regular pattern. We see this in the figures of the kaleidoscope, in which the most heterogeneous objects thrown together quite at random are shown as a regular star by repeating them symmetrically about a centre. So too such metrical formations as the five-part and seven-part may attain to a degree of admissibility by being received as members into a metrical formation of a higher order and repeated; that is to say, when the evolution proceeds initially from them as from a given quality. But even in this use of them the feeling for unity is not fully satisfied, and less when the two-part or four-part precedes the three-part,

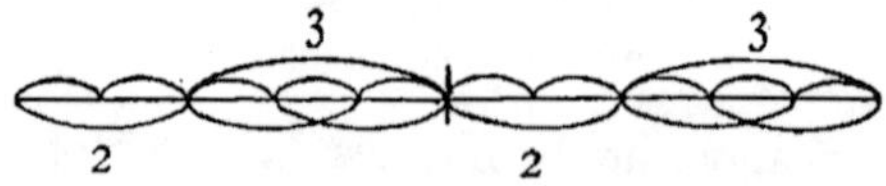

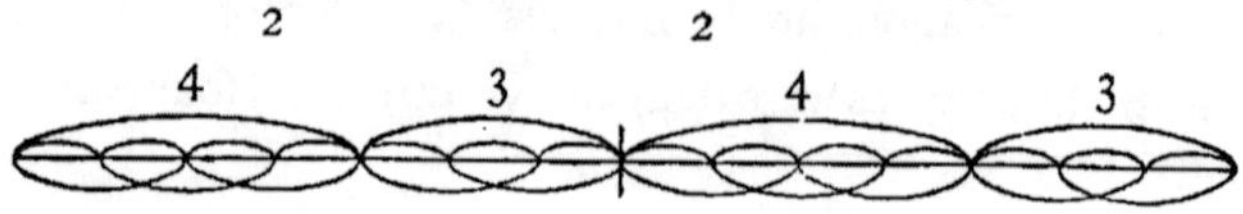

than when it follows it.

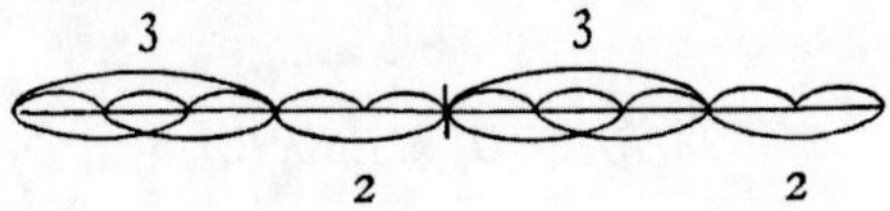

In the last form, after the termination in two- or four-part of the first member, it is easier to begin the second member again in three-part than it is in the first form to join the two- or four-part beginning on to the three-part end. Even by itself the five- or seven-part member is produced more readily when the crooked precedes the straight. The crooked, the three-part, contains the element of dissonance, which finds its resolution in the straight, the two- or four-part. Nevertheless such determination is too abstract for every case of concrete detail to be included in it. Formations of this kind, which spring out of an evolution, not that progresses steadily, but only that is steadily interrupted, regularly irregular, can never reveal a metrically healthy nature ; and they are as little suited to the continued time-measurement of a whole piece as diminished and augmented triads for carrying out its harmony. Attempts to apply composite bars in music are as a rule far more apt to impress us with the perverse eccentricity of the composer than with the naturalness of growth, in metrical structure, of the composition. Besides that such metres cannot hold out in five or seven parts for long, and usually soon pass again into two-, three-, or four-part measure ; so as to be resolved in a determination in itself intelligible, and therein to attain steadiness and quiet progress.

COMBINED METRE.

24. Now though such an artificial putting together of different metrical formations, i.e. the **addition** of them, has thus small power to form a metrical unity; yet on the other hand their **multiplication**, the combination in which something two-, three-, or four-fold is again taken two, three, or four times, and where the two-, three-, or four-membered unity becomes itself a member of a two-, three-, or four-membered unity of higher order, will always result in none but natural, easily-comprehended metres.

In the multiplication of the quantities of metrical determination, the quantity of the multiplicand is taken as unity, and in this quality is taken metrically double, triple, or fourfold together into a whole. Then every single element of such a combined formation, as member in a member, has its value with respect to the whole determined to it by the whole, and stands to every other member in a determinate reciprocal relation.

25. In a metre composed by addition of straight and transverse, e.g. in five-part, each single part has metrical organic determination only as either half of the two-part or a third of the three-part; it belongs to the whole not in the same quality: in one member of the compound metre it is different to what it is in the other. In the metre arising from multiplication of straight and transverse, in the six-part made out of twice three or three times two, every sixth part has its determination as a third of the half or half of the third of the whole—if we may so express it, as Fifth of the Octave or Octave of the Fifth of the Root of the six-membered metrical unity—and in each position it remains the same with respect to the whole. In the five-part each single part is Octave of the two-part, Fifth of the three-part; it is determined differently from two

different roots, and remains disparate in itself, an unresolved dissonance.

26. Thus besides the simple two-, three-, and four-part, further formations, metrically intelligible, may be constructed, by taking two-, three-, or four-fold as units again in two-, three-, or four-fold, namely:

$$2 \times 2, \quad 2 \times 3, \quad 2 \times 4.$$
$$3 \times 2, \quad 3 \times 3, \quad 3 \times 4.$$
$$4 \times 2, \quad 4 \times 3, \quad 4 \times 4.$$

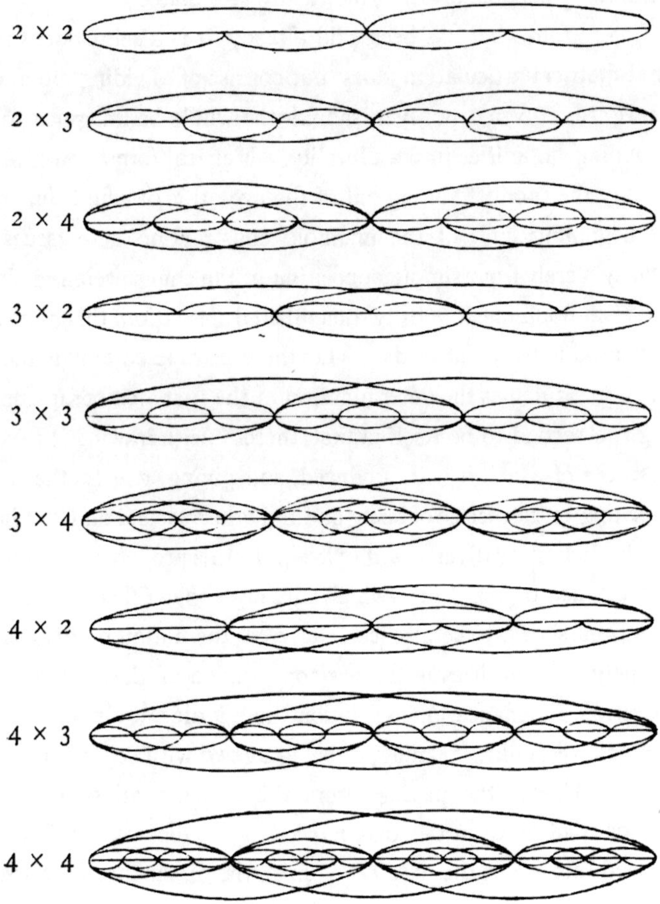

In these forms is necessarily contained everything that as metrical construction can be comprehended under the notion of unity. This in no wise limits us from giving wider scope to the whole of the formation or a more minute articulation to its parts. For we are quite able either to regard any one of the metrically combined forms of unity as being in its turn part or member in a new arrangement of higher order, in simple or combined form; or else to think of the part of any whole as being in its turn a whole, i.e. a unity capable of being metrically articulated.

27. From what has been said already, it is a self-evident result, that metrical articulation does not consist of dividing up a whole previously given; nor yet should the whole be imagined to be a grouping of unities into a plurality. Metrical formation is always simply the product sprung out of the evolution of a first time taken as beginning, and all the manifold construction here issues primarily merely from simple opposition of the thing premised simple, i.e. from doubling it. In two-membered formation, this opposition acts productively outwards. The three-membered annuls the production; it denies the determination of the first member in appointing the second to be itself a first, thereby withdrawing it from the first, out of which it was produced, and giving rise to the double meaning in the second of being one and other, second and first in self-contradiction, or diverse within itself. In this property we encounter the essence of the Fifth, which already above ('Harm.' par. 113) has been shown to be also correlative to the notion of dissonance; namely, inasmuch as in the harmonic union of the chords of preparation, dissonance, and resolution the middle one also contains the element of double meaning, of being at two with self, as the Fifth.

28. Thus in the passage from the major triad of C into the major triad of G, in the dissonance *C—D* prepared by *C* and resolved into *b—D*, the note *G*, to which the dissonance is referred, is

Fifth in the preparation, Fifth and Root in the dissonance, Root in the resolution:

II — I
II — I.

In the passage from the major triad of G into the major triad of C, in the dissonance *D—e* prepared by *D* and resolved into *C—e*, the note *G*, to which the dissonance is referred, is Root in the preparation, Root and Fifth in the dissonance, Fifth in the resolution:

I — II
I — II.

In both cases the middle element is oppositely determined in just the same sense as in the metrical three-membered unity:

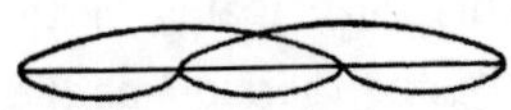

1 — 2
1 — 2,

which, as we shall shortly see, can also appear in the meaning of the first case:

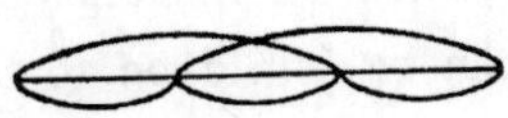

2 — 1
2 — 1

29. How in four-time the third element in the evolution annuls the separation of the first and second members, while in place of their first immediate oneness it now brings about the derivative unity of unitedness—all this has been explained in detail in what has gone before, and nothing more is necessary to be added here.

30. It is by no means the idea that we ought, in the metre divided into three parts, to listen for a Fifth of sound, or in the Fifth

for a dissonance according to the special musical notion; nor yet in the consonant chord which prepares a dissonance, and in the metre of two members, for an Octave, nor in the chord of resolution and in the metre of four members for a Third. But then in such identifications we have to seize upon and hold fast in proportionately greater generality all that is essential to the notion of these elements in their qualitatively different manifestations. So we may also discover the same determinations joined into unity of notion in subject matter seemingly yet far more remote. E.g., in the division of the notion of regular **extension** or of **space** generally, by considering its vertical dimension, **height**, as **unity**; its horizontal bilateral dimension, in every direction opposed to itself, **breadth**, as **duality**; and both united, as one in other, making a Third in which every element of duality participates in the unity and is absorbed in it, as **unity** of **duality**, and therefore as the **Third**, which completes the notion by being the union of height-unity, or **Octave**, with breadth-duality, or **Fifth**; that is, as the close of the determination of space. Therefore, as in the notion of completed space there is no longer room for a further determination to be added, and as no further consonance can be joined on to the triad; so too the metrical unity cannot extend beyond a fourth element of time without becoming again twoness in itself; and this we have seen in the metrical formation of fivefold falling apart into two- and three-fold.

ACCENT.

31. A first element of time, which metrically can only be the first of a second equal to it, is, in regard to its second, **determining**; the second is **determined.** A first as against its second has the energy of beginning, and consequently the metrical **accent.**

Accent of the Member.

(*a*) In the Two-timed Metre.

32. In the two-timed metre the first member is accented the second is without accent:

I — 2

(*b*) In the Three-timed Metre.

33. In the three-timed metre, as we regard its meaning up to now, the first and second members are accented, the last is without accent.

I — 2

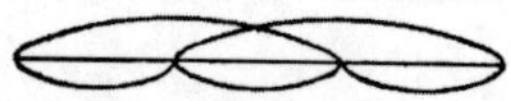

I — 2

I — 2

(*c*) In the Four-timed Metre.

34. The four-timed metre may not and cannot disown that union of the second and third members, which was constituted by the third portion of time in determining the second to be a first; even though such determination has been given up again with the entrance of the fourth member. Hence the second member must here receive another meaning than the one attributed to it in the two-timed formation. It cannot be altogether without accent, as in two-timed metre repeated; for what essentially distinguishes double two-timed metre from four-timed is that the latter has submitted to the determination of three-part time, and that from this third stage of its growth it contains the two halves of the whole, not merely as the first and second to be united, but as a thing already one in itself and knit together. Thus if the accent in double

two-timed metre can exalt only the first and third members, letting the second as well as the fourth drop altogether, yet in four-timed it cannot suffer the second member to recede, as against the first and third, in the degree in which the fourth recedes. It must bring out the value which, before the fourth entered, was attributed to the second in its relation to the third.

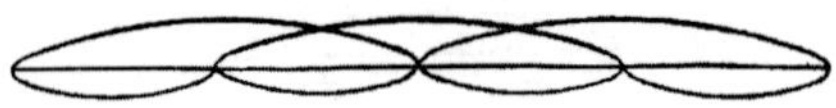

1 — 2 1 — 2

1 — 2

35. Here, then, three accented members follow one another; for as the first precedes the second as primary in the pair of members, so the second precedes the third, and the third the fourth.

COMBINED ACCENTS.

36. To this determination of accent, which only touches the members in the meaning that each has in its pair, must be added, when pairs are united, another of higher order: that, namely, for the pairs themselves. Everything that is to be comprehended in the notion of a succession partaking of unity can have but **one** beginning, **one** first, and not a repeated beginning nor several beginnings. And so in every order of the formation one member must be the first, and the member which follows equal to it must be the other; and should the formation be carried further, yet still these two united can but be again a first to a following equal member.

(*a*) Twofold, in Three-timed Metre.

37. The only metre without combination of several superposed orders is the **simple two-timed.** The **three-timed** metre contains

already a first and second of higher order; it has as members a first and second **pair** of members; only here they are not yet fully parted from one another, as in the four-timed. But the second pair, which begins in the middle of the first pair, has in respect of it the secondary meaning, just as the second pair has in the **double two-timed** metre. There the second pair is without accent as against the first; and so too the second member beginning in the middle of the first, both of the higher order, is without the accent belonging to **this** order. Consequently the second third part of the three-part metre receives only the accent which it gets by being first time in the pair of members of the **lower** order. This accent it has in equal strength with the first third part. But the first third part bears the accent of the **higher** order: that of the first of the **pairs**; and this it is that makes the first time of three-part metre stand out above the second in having the principal emphasis.

Thus in the three-timed metre the first time is strong of the strong; the second is weak of the strong and strong of the weak; the third is weak of the weak.

(*b*) **Threefold, in Four-timed Metre.**

38. The accents of the four-timed metre, in so far as the members of the formation in their pairs are concerned, have already been demonstrated: in this meaning the three first times are accented, the fourth is without accent. Taking the higher order into account in the three-timed metre, we have found upon the first time the accent of the first **pair** combined with the accent of the first **member** of the pair; upon the second, only the accent of the first **member** of the unaccented second pair; and the third time is without accent.

If three-timed advances into four-timed, and if four-timed is to be conceived as sprung out of three-timed and succeeding to it; then, agreeably to the notion, the 'one and other' of the last form can again be sought only in opposing to itself the three-timed.

39. As the three-timed contains a first and second of **two-time**, so must the four-timed, succeeding to the three-timed, consist of a first and second of **three-time**.

I

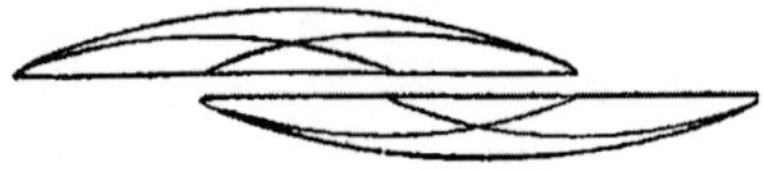

2

40. It is not this side of the organic structure of the four-timed metre that stands out in the effect as the principal division of it. **That** is rather the opposition, also contained in it, of the first and second halves of the whole: the twice-two, as in the double two-timed metre. It is, however, easy to feel how much closer is the linking of these two members in four-timed metre; which comes from the element of three-time and the union of this with itself, and is in fact the essential distinction between the four-timed formation and the double two-timed.

41. As regards the accent of higher order in the four-timed metre, it will result as different from that of the double two-timed. In the latter it is the second pair that is, as against the first, altogether without accent. Hence the third member only has the accent of being first in its **pair**. This in itself is equal to the accent of the first member in respect of the pair. For the accent of a member is independent of the meaning of the pair. It is **in its order** the same in an accented as in an unaccented pair; for it depends merely upon the determination of distinguishing a first above a second of the **same** order.

42. The four-timed metre in its derivation from the three-timed consists of three overlapping pairs,

of which the second is without accent as against the first, but the third must be accented as against the second; for that which has to follow a last can but be a new first.

This inverted succession will come up for detailed discussion later on, and its consideration is therefore deferred to that place.

Of the two three-timed unities which exist interlinked in the four-timed, the first is the accented one, and the second is without accent:

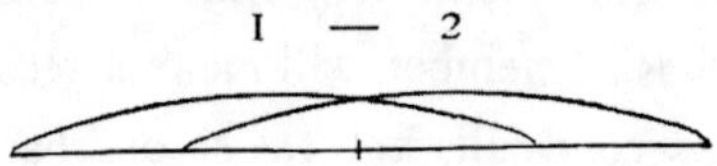

Again, in the first three-timed unity the first of the pairs joined in it is accented, and the second is without accent; in the second, which begins with an unaccented first pair, the second pair is accented:

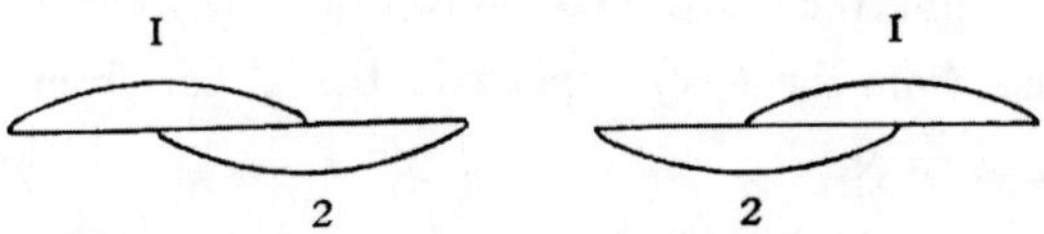

and by this determination the third as well as the first of the overlapping pairs receives an accent:

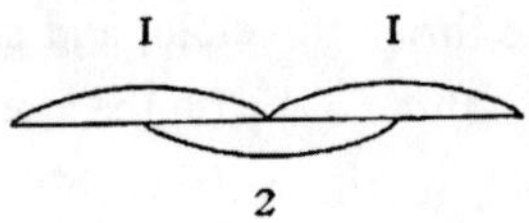

This accent will be increased, in the first pair, by the accent belonging to the first three-timed unity; it will thus be exalted above the second accent of like order; so that here, as in the twice-two-timed formation, the first pair is the accented pair, while at the same time full value is given to the accent which is due to the second half of the whole as accented pair in the second three-timed unity.

43. These determinations of thrice-two-timed and twice-two-timed combined in the four-timed metre may be thus summed up: The first member, besides its accent as member, which it has in like measure with the second and third, receives an accent as first of the

two-timed, and another accent as first of the three-timed, members. The second member has only the accent of first in the second unaccented pair. The third member, besides the accent of the first beat in the pair, receives that of the pair itself, which is an accented one. The fourth, because there is nothing left to which it can stand as a first, remains without accent. Thus the stronger accent of the first member will exalt it above the third, i.e. the first half of the whole will rise above the second half, while the accent of the second member, which it has as member, will make it recognised as a first of its order whose second falls into the second half of the whole; whereby both halves appear in an inwardly joined unity, and not merely strung together into a whole, as in the two-and-two formation.

This accent of the second member is the characteristic element for distinguishing the four-timed metre from the twice-two-timed: e.g. the $\frac{4}{4}$ bar from the $\frac{2}{4}$ bar repeated; the $\frac{12}{8}$ bar from the $\frac{6}{8}$ bar repeated, and so on.

44. Since no formation beyond the four-timed can afford a metrical unity, therefore the determination of accent closes here. Combined metres, as the twice-twofold, the twice-threefold, the thrice-twofold, and the thrice-threefold, and similarly the combination of the twofold and threefold with the fourfold, and of the latter with itself, will in each of the orders which exist interlinked in them follow the same determinations of accent which would be valid for them when standing alone. But the accent of the member will always be absorbed in that of the pair which stands over it, so that the latter gives the determination for the principal division into members; and the accent of the member in combined formations can only stand out in places where the pair itself has no accent; as, for example, in the second member of the three-timed and four-timed metres.

45. Perhaps this exposition of inward and outward metrical relation may seem far-fetched and artificial, importing into the matter

meanings and subtleties which do not lie in it, to gratify a theory set up. But if we consider the results produced from this seemingly too complicated procedure, nothing has been brought out but what rhythmically squares with our feelings and seems natural, nothing but what, in the sense of metre, comes naturally 'of itself.' And this indeed is the sole aim of these investigations: we wish to make clear in what sort and guise that is made which 'makes itself'—in the simplest thing as well as in the most complicated—or which is artificially made in the way we think natural when using art. The artist's endeavour can only be to make anything so that it may seem to have made itself. But, to enable him to accomplish this, the means for representing his thought must be universally intelligible, i.e. naturally given. A good musician will no more take pains to discover new chords and new varieties of accent than a painter will labour to invent a new shape for man, or to give man's form another set of members than that which it has received from God.

THE NOTION OF MAJOR AND MINOR IN METRICAL DETERMINATION.

46. What in harmony lies at the base of the opposition in the notions of **major** and **minor**, in metre serves to determine the emphasis of the **first** or **second** member of the pair.

In the major triad the element of unity is placed in the **Root** of the chord: in *C—e—G*, *C——G* is Fifth and *C—e* Third; both intervals have their meaning determined by *C*, and find in *C* the agreement of their sound. In the minor triad both intervals are referred to the note of the **Fifth**. In *a—C—e*, *a——e* is Fifth, *C—e* Third; here the note *e* is unit-element in the chord, and in it the sounds of the Fifth and Third intervals find agreement. Since both positive determinations meet in this note, we may also say that they issue negatively from it ('Harm.' par. 31). In this sense we have throughout denoted the minor chord as a negative triad: II—III—I. This elevation of the second element of the triad, making it a primary and converting the first to a secondary, will be expressed in metrical sense when the second and not the first member of the metrical pair receives primary or **positive** determination, and the first receives secondary or **relative**; i.e. when not the first but the second member is accented.

Then in the metrical notion of minor, as formerly we saw in the harmonic notion, the **duality of unity** will be expressed; the notion of major expresses the **unity of duality.** For the fact of emphasising the second member marks it out as a positive beginning; because an accented element can be nothing but the positive first of a second, since it is only in that quality that it receives an accent. And if the metrical dual unity corresponding to the notion of major contains a **first and second** as a whole, then the dual unity in the notion of minor must comprise a **second and first.** Also the metrical beginning, the accented, positive member, occurs in the second half; thus making it apparent that in the middle of the minor formation separates have been united.

ACCENTS PRODUCED FROM THIS DOUBLE DETERMINATION.

(*a*) **In Two-timed Metre.**

47. In the metrical positive or **major** unity a first is followed by a second:

1 — 2

in the metrical negative or **minor** unity a second is followed by a first:

2 — 1

In the first case the beginning, in the second case the end, stands out as the principal thing. It is seen that the first form has for its contents what is sole; the second, what was separated and is united.

(*b*) In Twice-two-timed Metre.

48. But now in combined metre, where the whole of a lower order is contained as part of a higher order, such a pair (either of one kind or of the other) may become member in a pair of higher order (again either of one kind or of the other); that is to say, the positive of the lower order in either the positive or the negative of the higher order, and similarly the negative of the lower order in either the negative or the positive of the higher order. In this way, if we place the two-timed as member in the two-timed metre, there arise four varieties of construction:

A. (*a*) positive in positive;
(*b*) negative in positive;
B. (*a*) positive in negative;
(*b*) negative in negative.

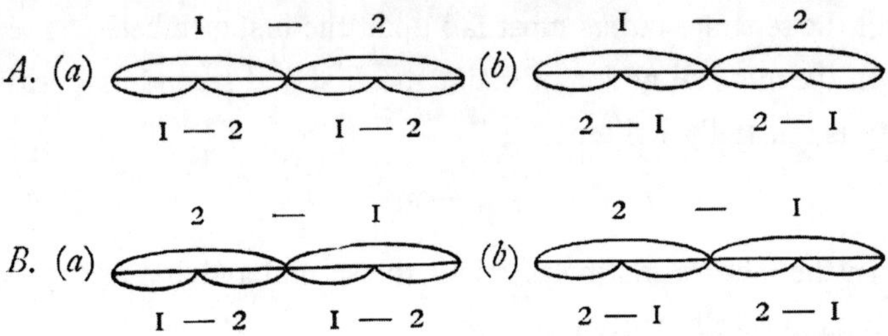

The principal accent, because it betokens the element positive to the highest power, must in such combined formations fall always upon the accented member of the lower order in the accented member of the higher order: in *A* (*a*) upon the first time; in *A* (*b*) upon the second time; in *B* (*a*) upon the third time; and in *B* (*b*) upon the fourth time. The subordinate accent belongs to the accented member of lower order in the unaccented member of higher order. This is in fact the accent of the lower order of members, which here stands out. It falls in *A* (*a*) upon the third time; in *A* (*b*) upon the fourth; in *B* (*a*) upon the first; in *B* (*b*) upon the second.

Musical notation comprehends the metrical two-, three-, or four-part unity within the compass of a bar. In combined metrical formations it is the multiplier that determines the principal division of the bar. The $\frac{6}{8}$ bar, as being of twice three parts, is ranked among two-part metres; the $\frac{12}{8}$ bar, which is of four times three parts, is four-part. The beginning of the bar is always determined by an accented element. But the most highly emphasised need not always be the beginning of the bar. There are also metrical formations in which the principal accent falls upon another member of the bar than the first.

49. The metrical forms considered earlier, before mention was made of the notion of minor in metre (the succession 2—1), all of them begin with the beginning of the bar; because in a combination of several orders with none but positive determinations the accents of all the separate orders must fall upon the first member.

In the metrical notion of major the first and second as positive unity is musically written:

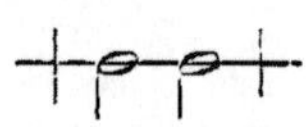

In the metrical notion of minor the second and first as negative unity is musically written:

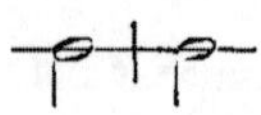

This beginning with the unaccented member is called the **up beat**.

50. The above four metrical formations we should not consider as four-timed, but only as twice-two-timed, according to the distinction that has already been made apparent between the two determinations. For they do but contain two-timed in two-timed,

without having passed through three-timed into four-timed; their fourfoldness is only repetition of the whole pair, whereby no separation of it is induced. These four formations, then, combined from the positive and negative meaning in the pair of lower order with the positive and negative meaning in the pair of higher order, will be presented in musical metrical notation as follows, the determination being that the principal accent [∧] must fall upon the accented member in the accented pair, and the subordinate accent [∨ or •] upon the accented member in the unaccented pair:

A. (*a*)

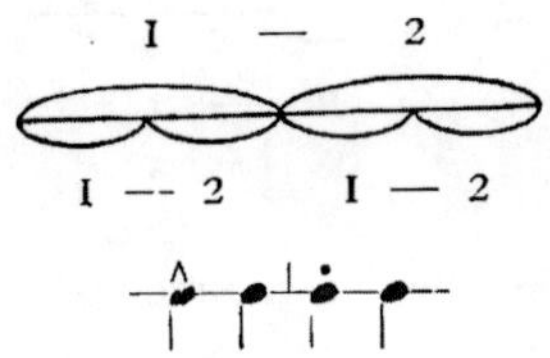

(*b*)

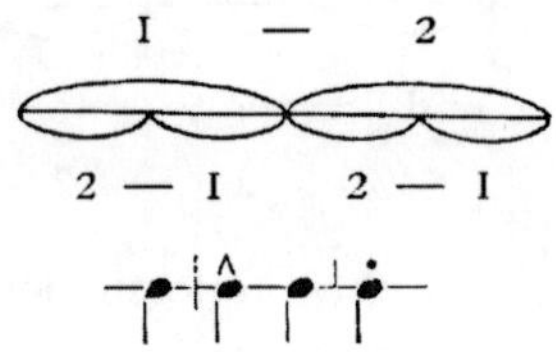

B. (*a*)

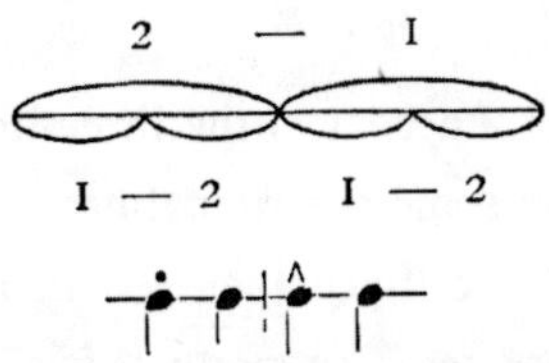

(*b*)

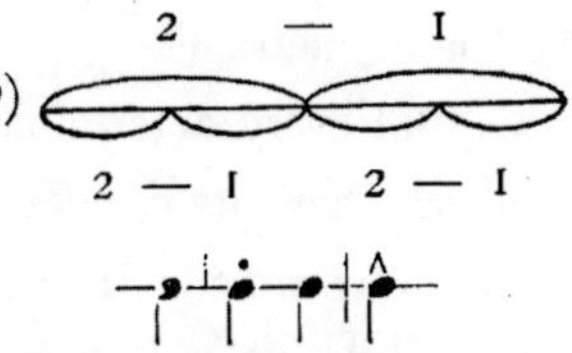

We find coincidence of the accented elements of both orders (i.e. the accent of the member in the accented pair), in *A* (*a*) upon the first time, in *A* (*b*) upon the second, in *B* (*a*) upon the third, and in *B* (*b*) upon the fourth.

(*c*) In Three-timed Metre, referred to Twice-two-timed.

51. The three-timed metre is already in itself a formation consisting of two orders united. It contains a pair of pairs, the second of which begins in the middle of the first:

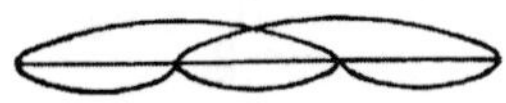

With this it has a double determination of accent: one for the single members in the pairs, the other for the pairs themselves. The pairs can here lie next one another, or rather overlapping one another, either in the positive succession as first and second, or in the negative as second and first :

1 — 2 2 — 1

Similarly the members may be related to one another either in positive succession or in negative:

1 — 2 2 — 1

1 — 2 2 — 1

From these different determinations for the members of the two orders there result again four different kinds of accentuation in the three-timed metre.

52. But every determination of accent in the three-timed metre will always have its derivation in some determination of accent in the twice-two-timed. For the three-timed metre is in fact a contraction of the twice-two-timed, or, more properly, it is a twice-two-timed metre imperfectly spread out.

Thus the twice-two-timed positive determination of accent:

1 — 2

1 — 2 1 — 2

is presented in three-time in the following involved shape:

1 — 2

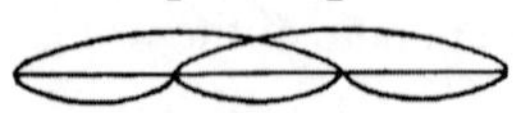

1 — 2

1 — 2

where the accented member of the second pair coincides with the unaccented member of the first. And similarly every other form of accent in twice-two-timed metre is translated in like sense into three-timed; and the combinations of accent placed side by side in what follows as twice-two-timed and three-timed must mutually correspond to one another.

A. (*a*) Positive of the lower order in positive of the higher:

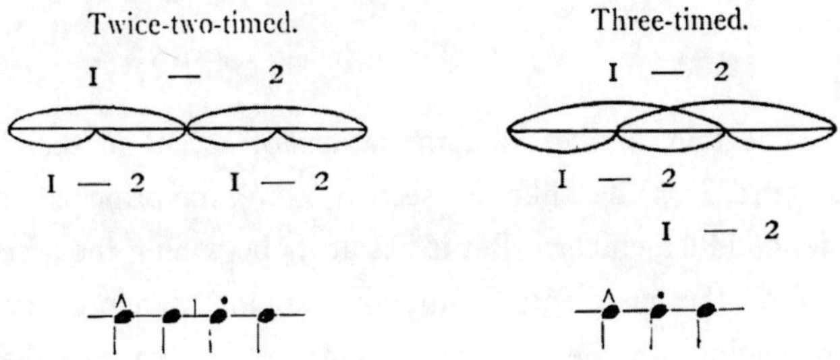

(*b*) Negative of the lower order in positive of the higher:

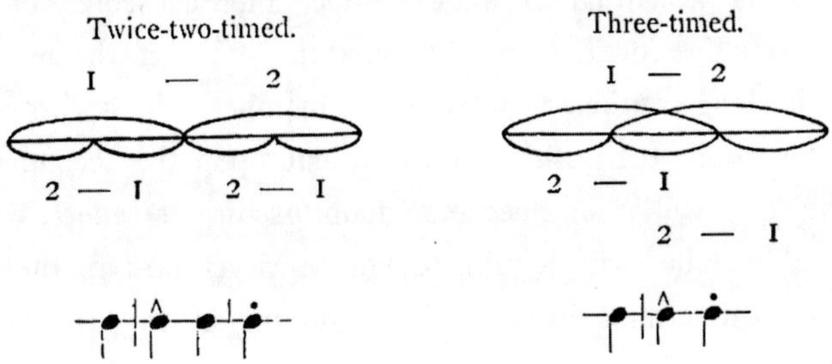

B. (*a*) Positive of the lower order in negative of the higher:

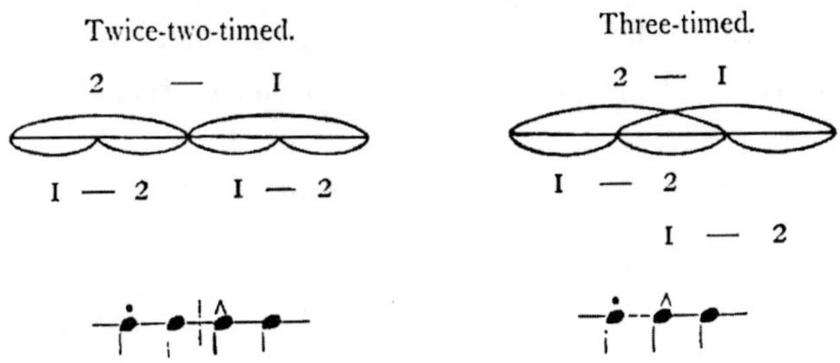

(*b*) Negative of the lower order in negative of the higher:

Twice-two-timed.

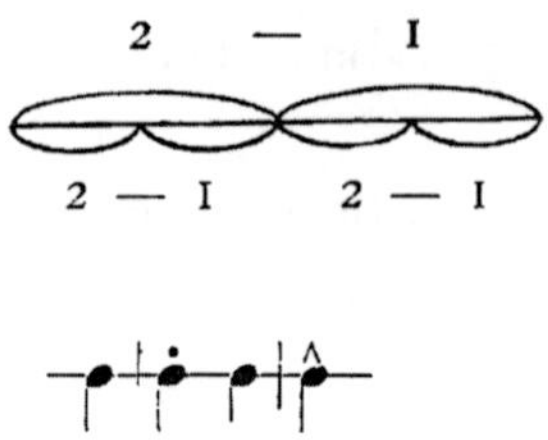

Three-timed.

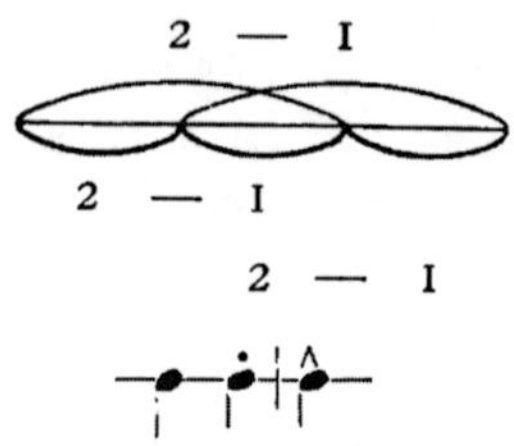

53. The third of these determinations of accent in the three-timed metre, *B* (*a*), has, like the second, *A* (*b*), the principal accent upon its middle member. But it has at its beginning the accented member of the unaccented pair, and cannot therefore, like the second, begin with the up beat. Here the first part of the bar has the subordinate accent, and the second part has the principal one. This accentuation under proper metrical conditions is also in practice found to be not unnatural. Yet if the metrical figure be long-continued, entering as member into a formation of higher order, the position of the accent upon the second time of the bar will soon become doubtful in its effect. The accented member will require to be heard as first in the bar, that is, to determine itself as the beginning of it. The accentuation

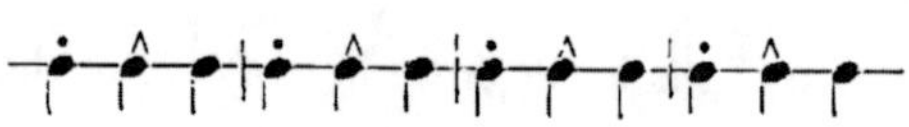

will soon come to be heard as one in which the first member bears the principal accent, and the member with the up beat the inferior accent:

54. We find here an analogy to what was previously ('Harm.' par. 38) said of the minor triad in reference to the construction of the minor key; namely, that a minor key can never be determined from a series of minor chords only, in the way in which the

major key is determined from a series of joined major chords. In the chain of minor triads

G—b♭—D—f—A—c—E—g—B—d—F♯
II — I   II — I
II — I   II — I   II — I

the positive

g—B♭—d—F—a—C—e—G—b—D—f♯
I — II   I — II
I — II   I — II

will always have a tendency to put itself forward so long as the negative, which is intended for the principal determination, is deprived of the positive presupposed in it. Since in the minor triad

II—III—I
A c E

the negative Third *c—E* is in fact also the positive Third *C—e*, while the note *c* finds its positive Fifth in *g*; and since similarly every note which is a Third in the minor series can be assigned its positive determinations in the same series, therefore the positive altogether will come to prevail in the series and will make the series itself appear a positive one. Only by the major triad on *E* can the minor triad on *A* be determined as a tonic principal element, and only by the major triad on *B* can the minor triad on *E* be so determined.

Hence too the rhythm

must be united with one of the other rhythms that accent the first member of the bar:

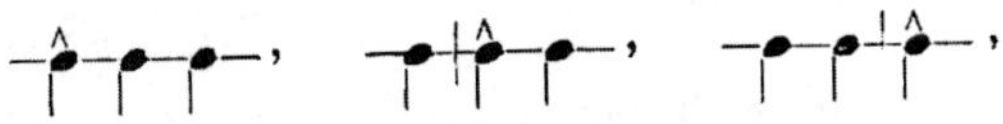

before it can carry on its metrical meaning in a prolonged succession. We are now speaking only of a prolonged accentuation of the second element. A single minor triad, e.g. *a—C—e*, would neither awake the adjacent major triads *F—a—C* and *C—e—G*, nor lose its independence through them ; nor would a single metrical unity having the principal accent upon its second member call up at once the determination of the up beat. It might even persist without ambiguity through several repetitions. Only it does not admit of being carried on as uninterruptedly as those rhythms which are accented upon the first member of the beat. Accentuation of the second time in three-timed metre is characteristic of many dance rhythms, e.g. of the *Mazurka*. Yet even here it is not kept up steadily, but alternates with other forms of accentuation.

55. Besides the four differently determined forms of accent in the three-timed metre which are derived from those of the twice-two-timed, there are yet four more to be added, whose determination is indeed to be referred to a double two-timed metrical formation, but which can never appear in double two-time, because their nature is to pass at once into three-time. These are the forms of accent which arise from union of pairs of opposite kind, and that within the same metrical order. For hitherto the opposition of positive and negative determination has been contained only in the different orders superposed. The positive pair of the superior order could have for its contents negative pairs of the inferior order ; or inversely the negative pair of the superior order could be filled out with positive pairs of the inferior order.

56. But if in the lower order itself a negative pair is set to follow a positive, or a positive to follow a negative :

1 — 2 2 — 1 2 — 1 1 — 2

then in the middle of such formations there arises a contradiction against the condition of succession ; for they set **equals** after one another :

2 — 2, 1 — 1.

Now '**after one another**,' agreeably to its notion as well as to its verbal expression, requires after **one, another**: after a second, a first; after a first, a second. The elements which meet in the middle of the formation above, 2—2, 1—1, belong as the same elements to **different** pairs; and in **this** meaning they certainly have so far their difference. But in themselves they are alike. They are not **one** and **another**, but in fact **one** and the **same**, and will also want to take up one and the same place. In this sense these formations at once of their own accord take the shape of three-timed metre:

1 — 2
    2 — 1,

2 — 1
    1 — 2;

for the second member of the first pair is not different from the first member of the second pair; the same metrical element, a relative or a positive, is presented in both. A succession, a division and consequent union, could only arise here if these places should contain relative and positive one after the other.

57. In what way two and three accents of members can follow in immediate succession, we are taught by the positive three- and four-timed metres. There the accent-elements get a difference among themselves through the accentuation of members of higher orders. But unaccented members cannot present any difference of accent; moreover no kind of metrical combination yet considered shows a succession of several unaccented members. If the twice-two-timed metrical formations just shown, with opposite pairs, are wanted expressed as four-membered, it can only be by the first, 1—2—2—1, taking the metrical shape:

1—2 2—1

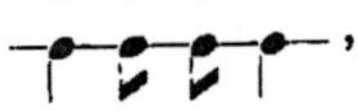

and the second, 2—1—1—2, the shape:

2—1 1—2

Then, in the first case, the second element is relative to the first and the third relative to the fourth, and at the same time there is brought in a relation between the second and the third; for the second, without detriment to its relativity to the first, is a positive to the third. In the second form, 2—1—1—2, which does no more than place in succession two positive and differently accented members, the first rhythmical figure would also be brought to light, were the metre to be continued; for the same succession of unaccented elements enters again, on the boundaries of the members of higher order:

2—1—1—2 | 2—1—1—2

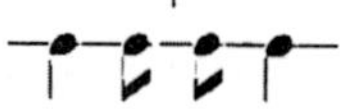

Thus these rhythmically four-membered determinations pass of their own accord into three-timed metre. But the distinction here taken in the relative elements which meet together vanishes in the three-timed form of the metre with opposite pairs, and with it also the small accent which emphasises the first of the contracted members as against the second. And there arise for the three-timed metre four accent-determinations different from those already given.

A. (*a*) Positive-negative of the lower order in positive of the higher:

Twice-two-timed.	Three-timed.
1 — 2	1 — 2
	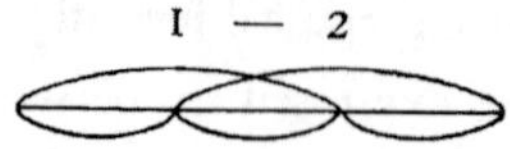
1 — 2 2 — 1	1 — 2 2 — 1
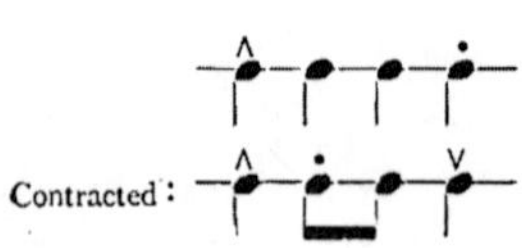	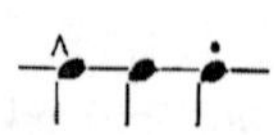

(*b*) Negative-positive of the lower order in positive of the higher :

Twice-two-timed. Three-timed.

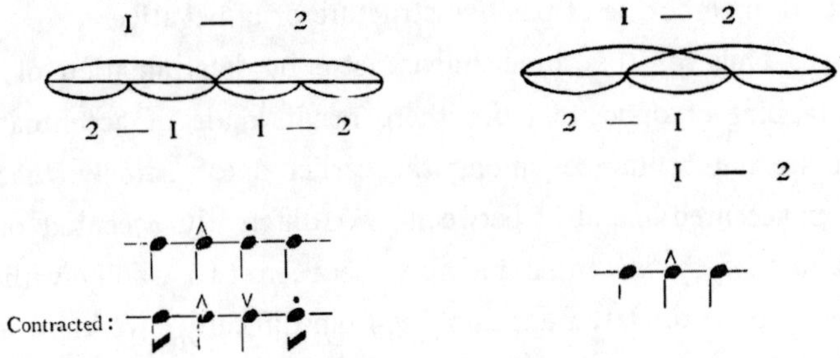

B. (*a*) Positive-negative of the lower order in negative of the higher :

Twice-two-timed. Three-timed.

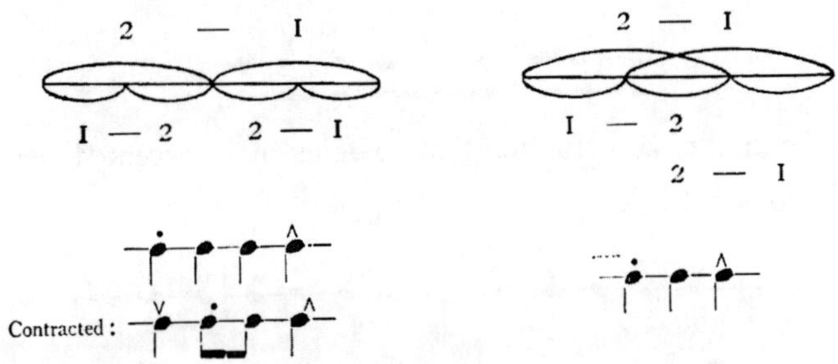

(*b*) Negative-positive of the lower order in negative of the higher :

Twice-two-timed. Three-timed.

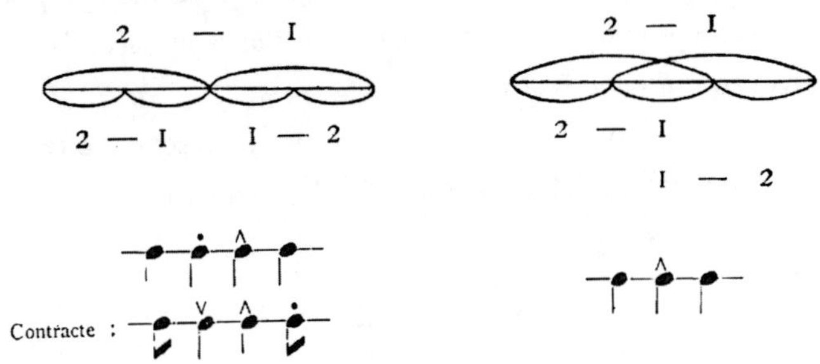

The difference that there is in the twice-two-timed accentuation of the metres *A* (*b*) and *B* (*b*) disappears in the three-timed metrical forms that correspond; because there the two differently accented positive elements coalesce into one. For the accent of this metre it therefore comes to the same thing, whether the order of the superior members is of positive structure or of negative.

58. Thus for the three-timed metre by determination of the overlapping of opposite pairs there result kinds of accentuation that are not contained among the earlier ones; namely, that of the unaccented member between two differently accented ones, and that of the accented member between two wholly without accent. Now the latter appears free from difficulty; we know it as the triple bar accented only in one element, where the accented element is preceded by one unaccented element and followed by another:

But the kind of accentuation that contains the unaccented element in the middle:

is far less able to be used without violence to rhythmical feeling. The accented end of the formation will not easily be followed by an accented beginning; a shock is felt, as of a beginning repeated. Here are two primary elements relating to the same secondary, two positives to the same relative.

In this case too we have to look for, and represent, the relationship of the metrical determination with the harmonic.

A series of **major** chords:

F—a—C—e—G—b—D

I — II

I — II I — II

is to be identified with the metrical **positive** construction :

1 — 2

1 — 2   1 — 2.

A series of **minor** chords :

D—f—A—c—E—g—B,

II — I   II — I

II — I

answers to the metrical **negative** construction :

2 — 1   2 — 1.

2 — 1

Here a steady, continuous transformation of the relative element into a positive is always proceeding.

The manner in which a harmonic element can subsist at one time in double determination of unity is seen in the system of the minor key, which contains the major triad of the dominant joined to the tonic minor triad by the Root of the former, so that both triad-determinations originate from that one note. E.g. in the system of the key of A minor :

A—c—E—g♯—B,

I — II

II — I

the note *E* is at once positive Root and negative : it is Root in two opposite directions.

To this double determination corresponds metrically the form :

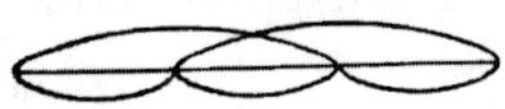

2 — 1

1 — 2,

namely, accentuation of the second time without any subordinate accent upon the first and third ; for the formation contains only one (differently determined) positive place and two relative, unaccented places.

In triad-construction an element may occur as at once positive and negative Root, but never as at once positive and negative Fifth. And similarly in metrical construction, while the coexistence of a positive and negative First is allowed, a positive and negative Second cannot coexist in the same element.

The following is an attempt to establish this metrical principle.

59. We may imagine the metrical notion of **major** as a relation of **present** to **future**, and the metrical notion of **minor** as a relation of **present** to **past**.

The present is in both cases the positive (I); past and future are the two relatives (II).

The metrical **positive** succession, 1—2, joins **to-day** and **to-morrow**; the metrical **negative** succession, 2—1, joins **to-day** and **yesterday**. It goes, not from to-day to yesterday, but from yesterday to to-day; beginning, not with the positive, but with the relative: it begins with that which is presupposed in the positive **present**, i.e. with the **up beat**; and it reaches the positive present only with its second element. That this succession takes for beginning what positively is **not** beginning, what to the positive present is a relative, and that it places the positive itself as relative, is the negative element in it, its essence as the notion of minor.

In the harmonic notion of minor, which has precisely the same contents, there can be no expression of a negative by a single interval; for that remains the same, whether it be called positive or negative. But when the Third placed inside the interval of Fifth, instead of being joined on to the Root, is joined on to the Fifth—issues negatively from it—then the Root may also be regarded as a negative Fifth to the Fifth as a negative Root.

Similarly with the two beats which in the beginning we assumed to denote a first metrical determination. If they are of equal strength, if one is not accented above the other, it is left undecided whether their mutual relation shall be metrically positive or negative. For in the succession one after the other of two equally strong beats we can imagine the one meaning

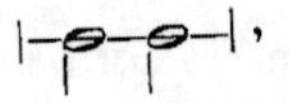

just as well as the other

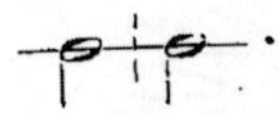

But with the accent, either can be established decidedly in metrical first, or positive, value.

60. Now the metrical determination :

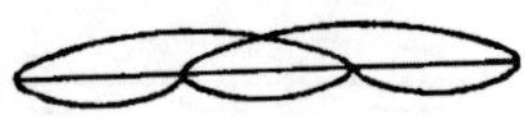

2 — I

I — 2,

is thoroughly natural and consistent. It places in the **middle** the **to-day**, to which a **yesterday** and a **to-morrow** relate. As has already been said, it is in every respect to be identified with the harmonic determination :

A—c—E—g♯—B.

I — II

II — I

But the other :

I — 2

2 — I,

places a **to-morrow** as **yesterday**; the first referring to a foregone, the other to a future **to-day**. This is the same contradiction already met with in the **Fifth**-, or separating, element of key-construction, when the triad is determined in self-opposition as dominant chord and as subdominant:

F—a—C—e—G, I — V   C—e—G—b—D, IV — I

a contradiction which is afterwards resolved in the **Third**-element, when the triad determines, instead of being determined, on two sides, and has therefore become a tonic triad.

The form

1 — 2
1 — 2

expresses a natural relation of time; as also does the opposite form

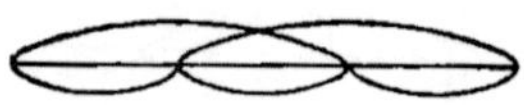

2 — 1
2 — 1.

The first places **to-morrow** as **to-day** to another to-morrow: the **day after to-morrow**;—the second places **yesterday** as **to-day** to another yesterday: the **day before yesterday**. The former begins with the positive (to-day), and transforms its relative (to-morrow) again to positive (to-day). The latter begins with the relative (yesterday), and makes its positive (to-day) again into relative (yesterday).

In neither determination is any contradiction contained; the middle element in both is a positive towards one of the two sides, to-day to a to-morrow **or** yesterday.

In the negative-positive succession:

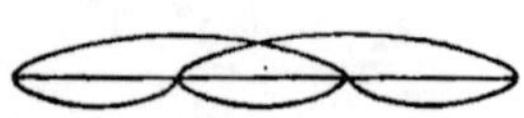

2 — 1
1 — 2,

it is to-day to a to-morrow **and** yesterday.

In each of these three cases the change of meaning in the middle element is in intelligible succession.

But in the form

1 — 2

2 — 1

the middle element, from being **future**, must immediately become **past**. This it cannot do, unless during the passage it becomes **present** (as must also the tonic triad in the key-system, when it is to pass from the dominant meaning, which it has to the subdominant triad, into the subdominant meaning, which it has to the dominant triad). The abrupt transformation, or unreal metrical succession, is the **untruth**, and therefore too, in this direct sense, the **impossibility** of the rhythmical form. It may also be shown to be untrue in harmony, in its application to the union of triads. For if we try to take the Fifth of a major triad as Root of a minor triad, i.e. change the positive Fifth to negative:

C—e—G—b♭—D,

I — II

II — I

the immediate result is an organic impossibility, viz. the minor triad on *G* in a key that contains the major triad on *C*. In the key of F major the triad on *G* would be, not *G—b♭—D*, but *G|B♭—d*; consequently not a minor, but a diminished, triad.

61. The form

1 — 2

2 — 1

contains two positive elements, which give rise in the relative which lies between them to the contradiction of being past and future. It is therefore precluded from passing immediately into Three-time; because its middle element is not truly a single element. The middle member can be applied in its relative meaning only to one or other of the positive members; either to the first, 1—2 | 1, or to the second, 1 | 2—1. Thus either the second positive element or the first remains solitary. Then in the first case the second positive element will seek its relation in the future, in the second case the first positive element will seek a relation out of the past; but in both cases twice-two-timed construction will arise, a distinct pair of pairs, of positive nature or of negative:

1 — 2
2 — 1
1 — 2 | 1 is filled out as 1 — 2 | 1 — 2;

1 — 2
2 — 1
1 | 2 — 1 is filled out as 2 — 1 | 2 — 1.

Moreover we feel plainly, that the first time and the third being accented, and the middle time absolutely without accent, the third cannot at once be followed again by an accented first; but that an unaccented time must either, as last, conclude the form, or else, as first, begin it.

62. In order to link the succession we might also have recourse to that separation of the middle element into one and another relative,

1—2

1 — 2 — 1,

by which a relation of positive and relative is formed within the middle element itself. But now, in so far as the middle time is a time separated and united, it is no longer absolutely without accent. Its first half receives the accent that must fall to it in this lower order:

,

whereupon this three-timed rhythm has again returned to the point from which it started, and appears as what it really is, contracted four-timed.

63. That a four-timed metre can sometimes be used with the accent upon the first and fourth times ought not to be found in contradiction with the statements just made; since the explanation of such rhythms is not derived at all from this source, and will be given later on in considering **syncopation.** But moreover, in the following accentuation:

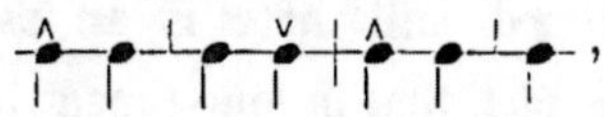

the third member is by no means wholly without accent. If it were without accent, it could not occupy a first place in the twice-two-timed metre. Its accent of lower order is merely overshadowed by the syncopated accent.

If, then, we proceed presently to rank the metrical formation:

1 — 2
2 — 1,

among the three-timed, yet so far as the organic structure and accentuation of it are concerned, it must not be supposed that we have lost sight of the explanation just given of this metre.

(*d*) In the Four-timed Metre.

64. The essentially four-timed metre—i.e. that which consists, not merely of a repetition of two-timed, but of a formation that has passed through three-time—must also make apparent in its accentuation the conditions through which it has come into existence. That is, it must be distinguished in its accentuation from the twice-two-timed.

The twice-two-timed formation consists merely of a pair of pairs:

If we assume positive nature of memberment throughout, it bears the accent of the member on the first time and the third, and the accent of the pair upon the first.

The four-timed formation is something more than a pair of pairs. Even if we could consider it, in accordance with its mere extent, as twice-two-timed, still there is an essential difference between the two in the fact, that in four-timed the second half of the whole is not a member of opposite quality to the first, or at least is not so necessarily. On the contrary, those determinations which are most natural to the metre, viz. those which contain no unusual accentuations, are derived from the following form.

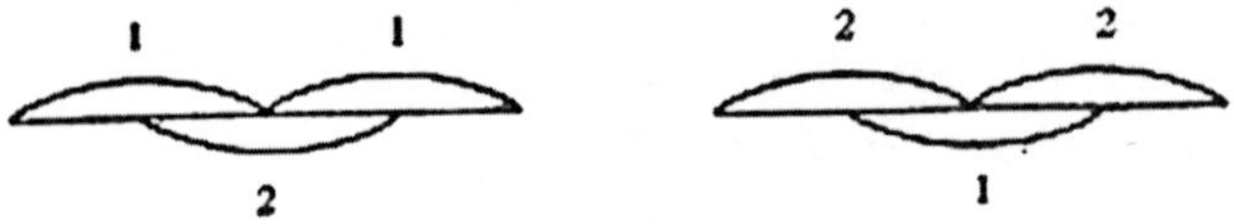

And even if hereafter we shall see the forms

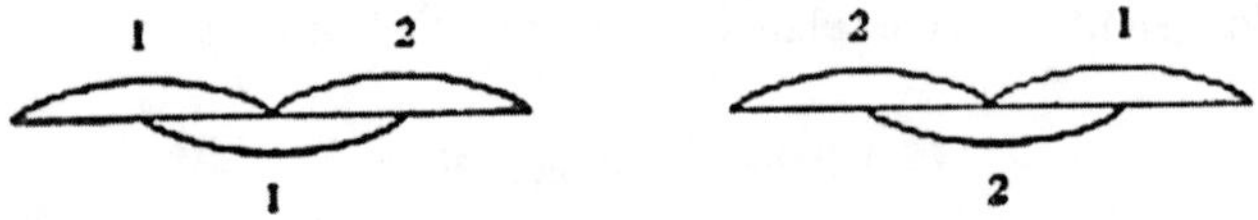

maintaining themselves as admissible, yet we shall observe that from them arise only such formations as accentuate that part of the bar which in the natural order is without accent: the so-called **weak** part.

65. In the four-timed metre the two halves of the whole do not stand to one another in immediate succession. The supreme opposition here is that of a first and second of **three-time**.

In this twice-three-timed whole, the third two-timed member, i.e. the second half of the whole, has direct relation only to the second, and may be related indirectly to the first as 1—1, 1—2,

2—1, 2—2; while in the twice-two-timed metre the two halves can only stand to one another in the relation 1—2 or 2—1.

If, then, the succession is the first of those given above:

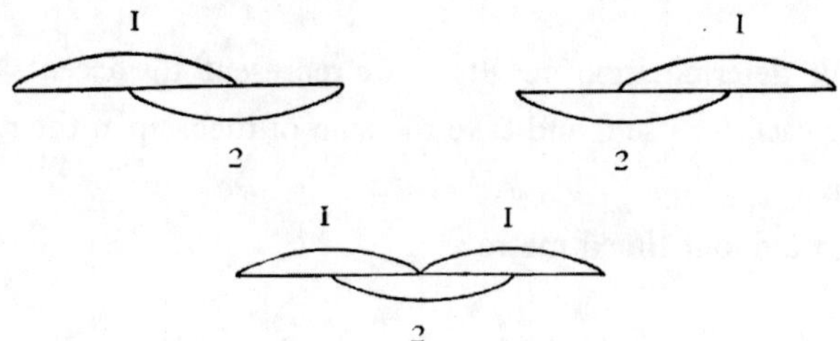

the second half (the third two-timed member) has, like the first, the accent of the pair, which therefore falls upon the third member, as well as upon the first member; the second member, as first in the second pair, has, like the first and third, the accent of the member; but the first member, in addition to the two former accents, has also the accent of highest order, that of the first of the two overlapping three-timed parts.

66. If we denote the accent of the three-timed part by 3, that of the pair by 2, and that of the member by 1, without intending by these numbers to indicate the specific strength of the different accents; then upon the first member of the four-timed metre will fall the accents 3, 2, and 1, upon the second the accent 1, upon the third the accents 2 and 1, and the fourth will remain without accent. If we assume that the accent of the lower order is absorbed in the accent of the higher order, the accentuation of the four-timed metre will be:

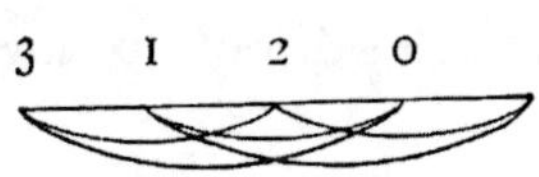

Represented in the same way, the three-timed metre has the accents:

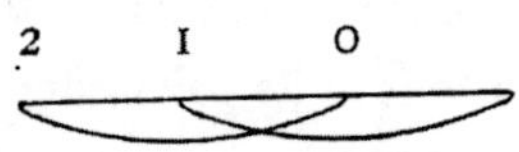

and the twice-two-timed:

2 0 1 0

A like determination results if we represent the accents of every order each for itself, and take the sum of them upon the respective places.

In the four-timed metre:

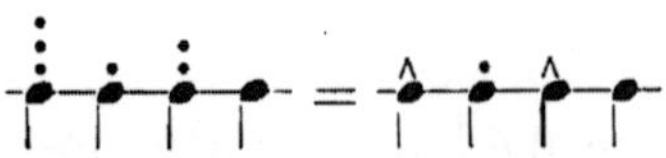

In the three-timed metre:

In the twice-two-timed metre:

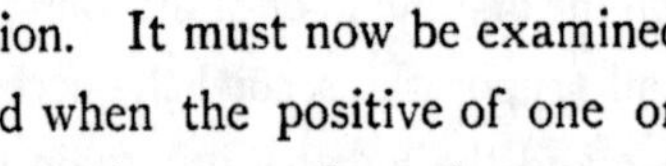

This is the accent-determination of the four-timed metre, as it results when the succession in every order is taken as 1—2, i.e. in positive progression. It must now be examined how these accents will be presented when the positive of one order combines with the negative of another, or when the succession in every order is negative.

67. The **two-timed** metre admits only of a **twofold** form of accentuation; it can consist either of a positive or of a negative succession of members:

1 — 2 2 — 1

68. The **three-timed** metre follows the **twice-two-timed**, in so far as it can be referred to it in its pairs; and in the first place can have, like the latter, **fourfold** form:

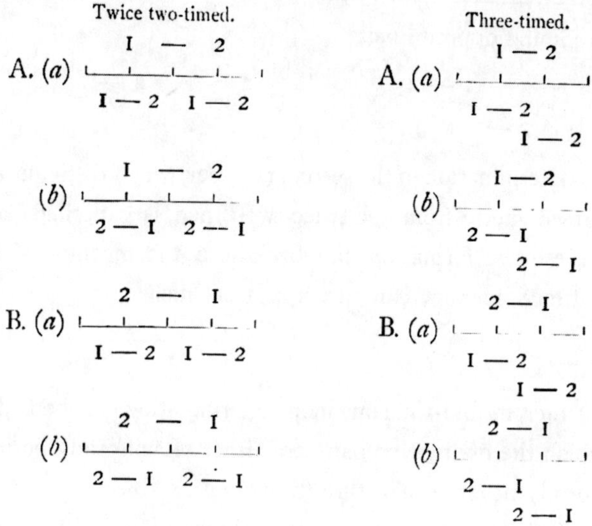

69. The **four-timed** metre, consisting as it does in the highest order of two overlapping three-membered parts, will contain double the number of the formations of the three-timed metre ; because the succession of the two three-membered parts may be either positive or negative. Hence arise eight different determinations for the accentuation of the four-timed metre.

70. But to the accent-determinations of the three-timed metre, besides those which it takes corresponding to the accents of the twice-two-timed, must be added also those which arise from combination of opposite pairs ; these consist of a positive-negative or negative-positive succession of the pairs of the lower order combined with either positive or negative of the pair of higher order, and form four other determinations, as previously detailed.

These will now be transferred also into the four-timed metre, and that in double number ; because the succession of the two three-timed members of the four-timed metre may be either positive or negative. Hence arise eight new accent-determinations for the four-timed metre.

But in joining opposite pairs:

1 — 2 1 — 2 2 — 1 2 — 1

2 — 1 1 — 2

the double determination of the second member, which distinguishes the four-timed metre from the twice-two-timed, is cancelled; and in accent these two formations fall back into the meaning of the twice-two-timed, for they can only appear as such:

1 — 2 1 — 2 2 — 1 2 — 1

71. Further, in four-time one more determination is to be added, that in which the interwoven pairs are either of uniformly positive or of uniformly negative structure throughout.

When all three orders take positive shape, we see the accents hence decreasing step by step:

3 2 1 0

If negative throughout, the accents increase step by step:

0 1 2 3

72. One last possible determination remains: that in which the pairs follow one another in like succession, but are related oppositely in their members. Hence there are again produced eight modes of accentuation different to the previous ones. Nevertheless, as in the construction last but one discussed, the result of the accentuation is only as if it belonged to twice-two-time; for in this case, as in the former, the second member is deprived of double determination.

73. That we should obtain sixteen accent-determinations in the four-timed metre coinciding with those of the twice-two-timed, while the latter can only show four different forms in all, ought not to be looked upon as a contradiction. Those sixteen forms may be like the four in their result, and again may show a fourfold

difference in the inner conditions which give rise to them. In the twice-two-timed metre, as in the four-timed with opposite pairs overlapping, the accents will fall upon the first and third or upon the second and fourth members, and the intermediate members will remain without accent ; one of the accented members receives the principal, the other the inferior accent. In this the likeness of the two metrical species consists. But the conditions from which these like external results are produced show in the twice-two-timed metre a fourfold, and in the four-timed metre a sixteenfold difference. By negative elements the sixteenfold difference is reduced to fourfold. But the conditions of the negation here belong no less to the organic determination of the four-timed metre, than do the conditions which pass positively into the final result. Accordingly the accent-forms of four-time which agree with the twice-two-timed must also be drawn out fully in the description below.

RÉSUMÉ OF ALL ACCENT-DETERMINATIONS IN THE TWO-TIMED, TWICE-TWO-TIMED, THREE-TIMED, AND FOUR-TIMED METRES.

74. It appears from the preceding that there result

for the **two-timed metre** . . . . **two,**
" " **twice-two-timed** . . . . **four,**
" " **three-timed** . . . . . . **eight,**
" " **four-timed** . . . . **thirty-two**

different determinations of accent. Of the last of these, half the number coincide with those of the twice-two-timed metre and are absorbed in them, which leaves **sixteen** properly belonging to four-time. Consequently the accent-forms for the four metres named stand with regard to their number in the relation of 2 : 4 : 8 : 16, or $2^1 : 2^2 : 2^3 : 2^4$. In order to obtain a comprehensive and systematic review of the whole of them, we shall now set them down in their connexion by metrical and musical notation. Not to interrupt the tabular form of the description, any observations that may seem required by particular rhythmical examples will find room at the end, with a reference back to the examples in question.

I. Accents of the Two-timed Metre.

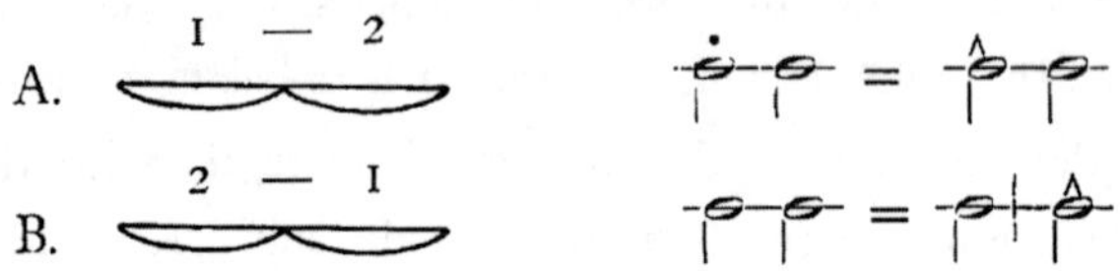

II. Accents of the Twice-two-timed Metre.

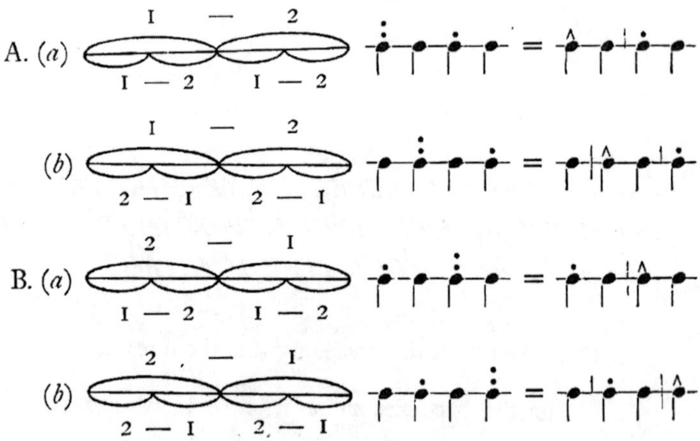

III. Accents of the Three-timed Metre.

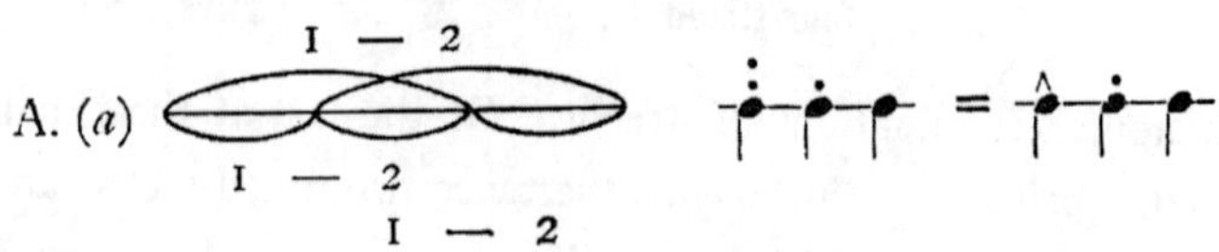

(*b*) 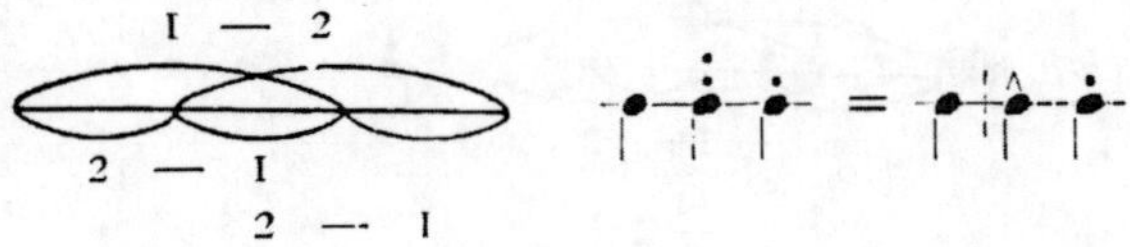

B. (*a*) 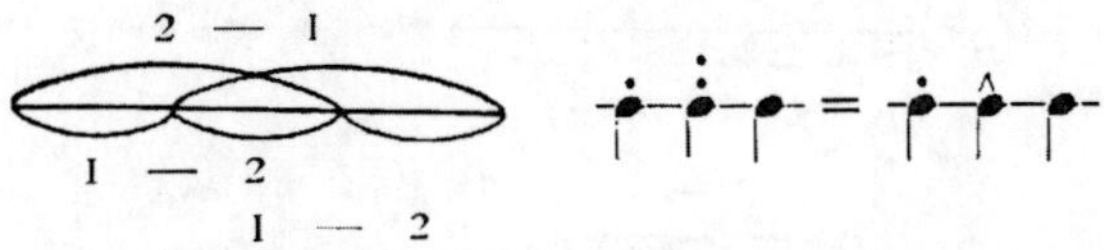

(*b*) 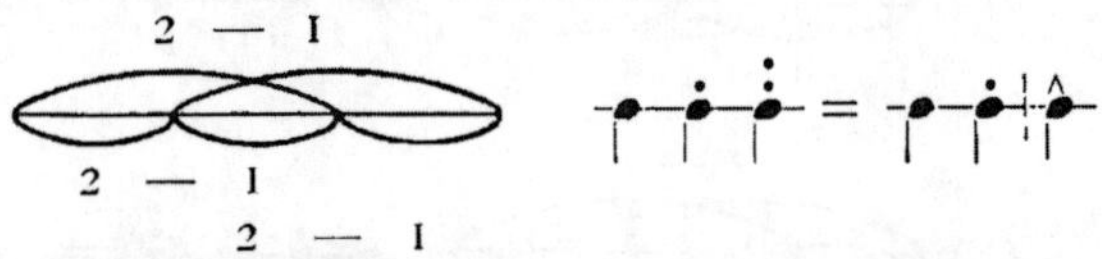

A. (*a-b*) 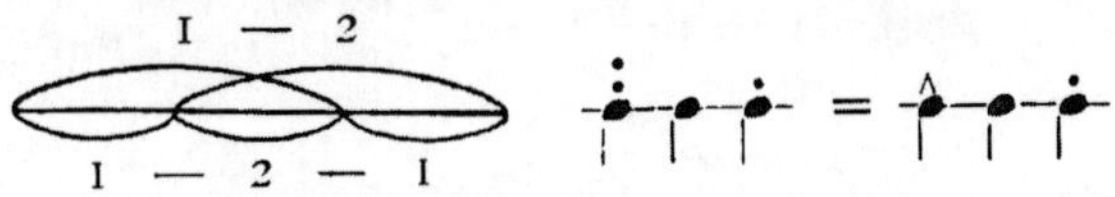

(*b-a*) 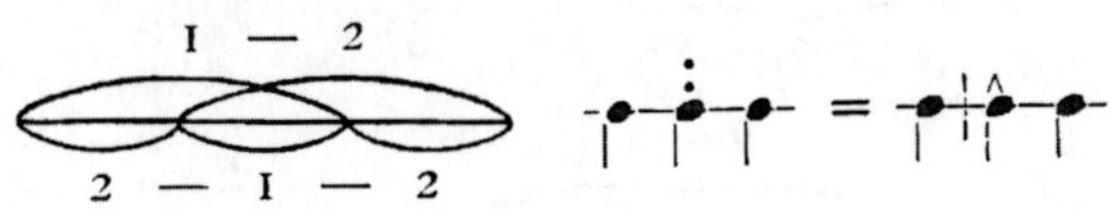

B. (*a-b*) 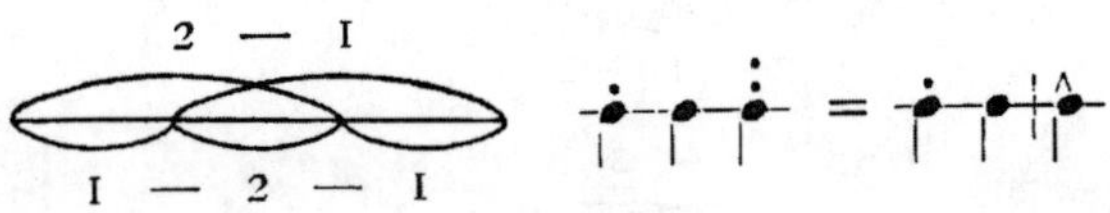

(*b-a*) 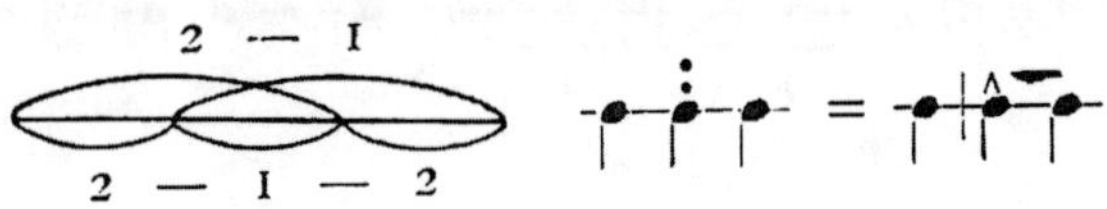

IV. Accents of the Four-timed Metre.

A. (*a-b*, *a*) 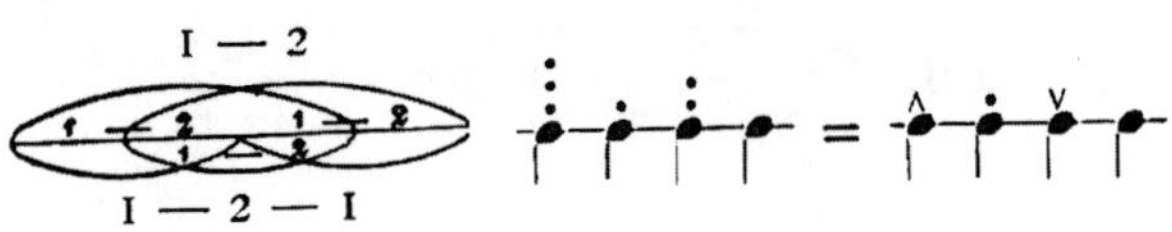

(*β*) 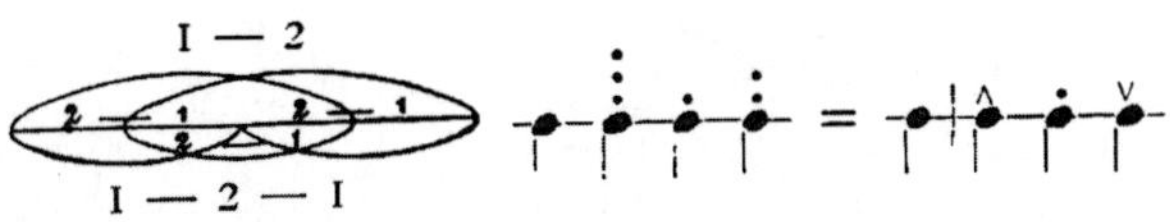

(*b*-*a*, *a*)

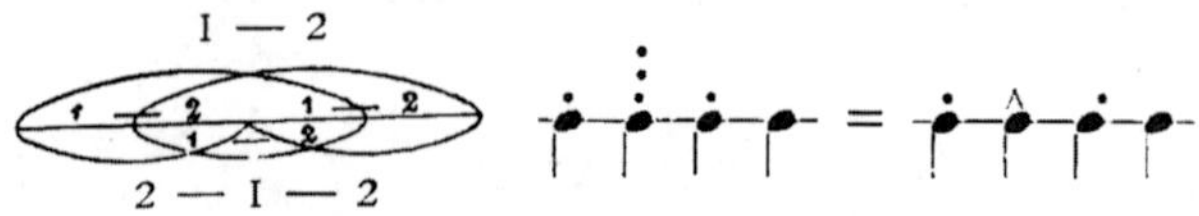

(β)

B. (*a*-*b*, *a*)

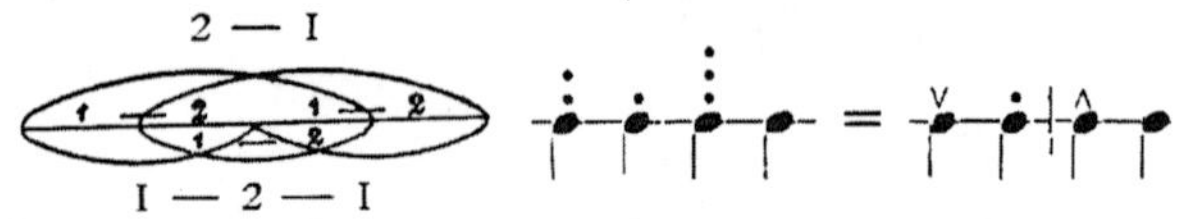

(β)

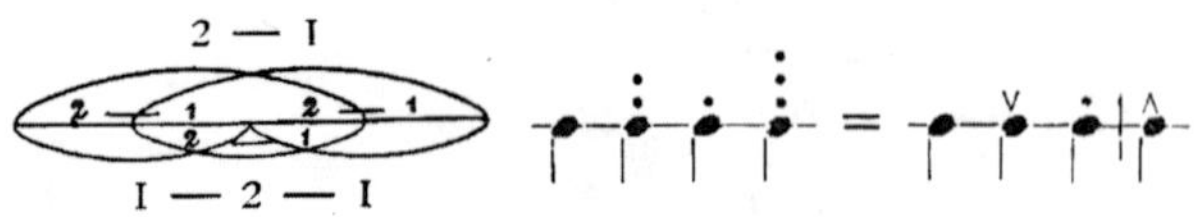

(*b*-*a*, *a*)

(β)

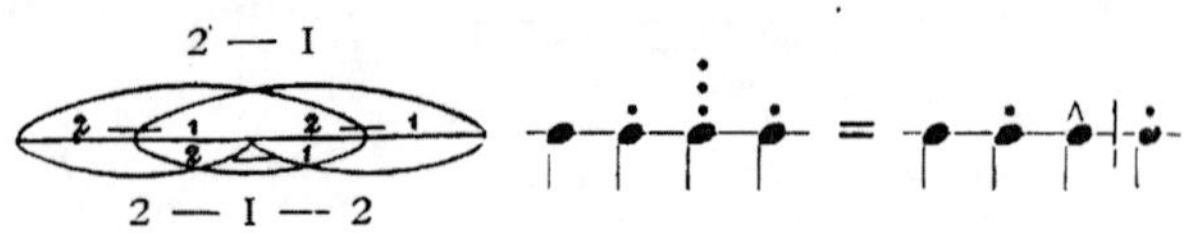

A. (*a*-*b*, *a*-β)

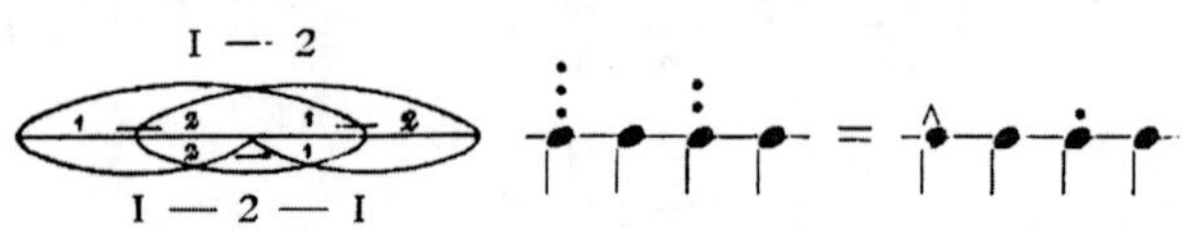

(β-*a*)

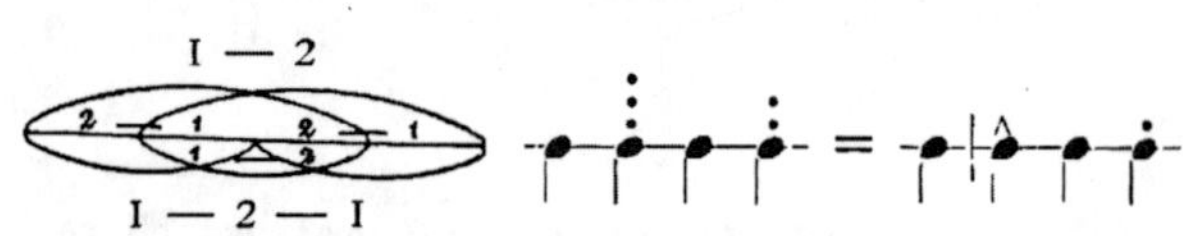

(*b*-*a*, *a*-β)

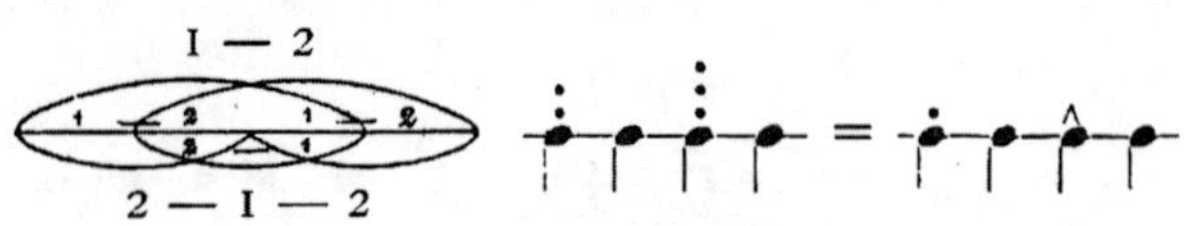

(β-*a*)

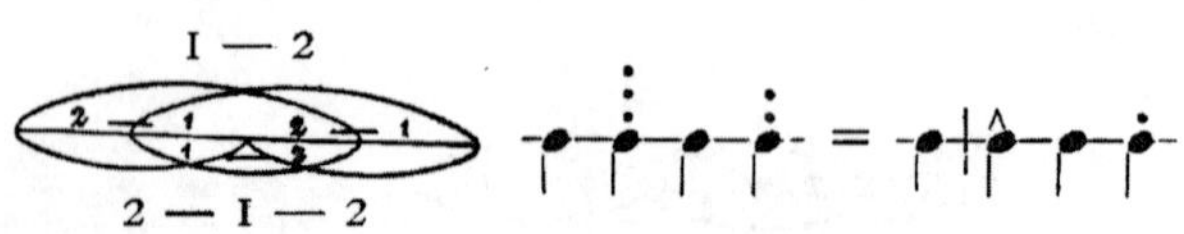

B. $(a\text{-}b, \alpha\text{-}\beta)$

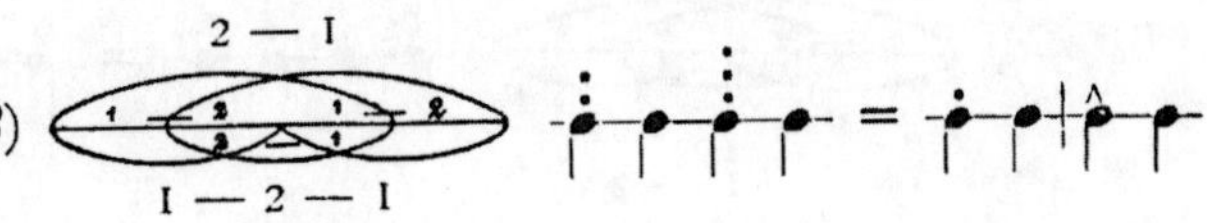

$(\beta\text{-}\alpha)$

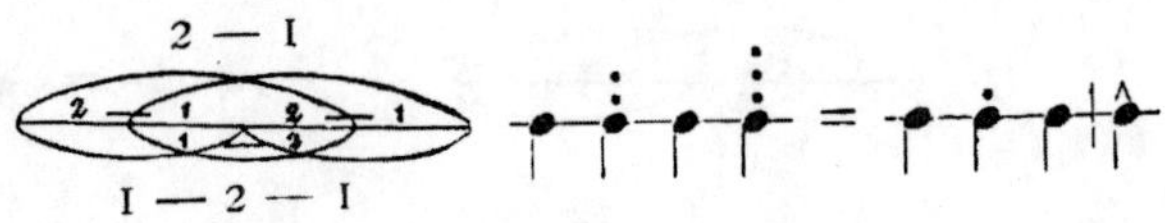

$(b\text{-}a, \alpha\text{-}\beta)$

$(\beta\text{-}\alpha)$

A. (a, α)

(β)

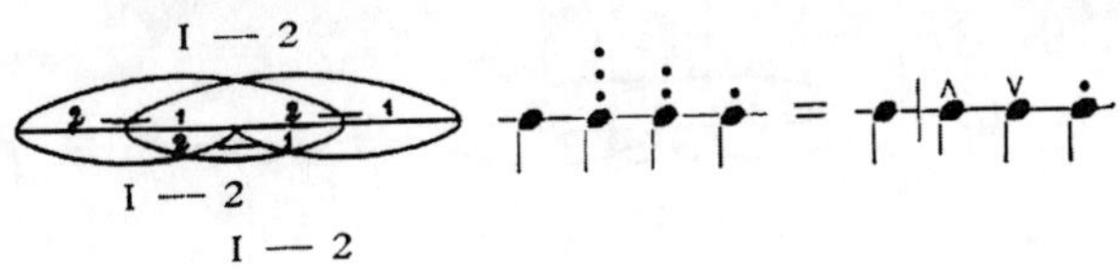

(b, α)

(β)

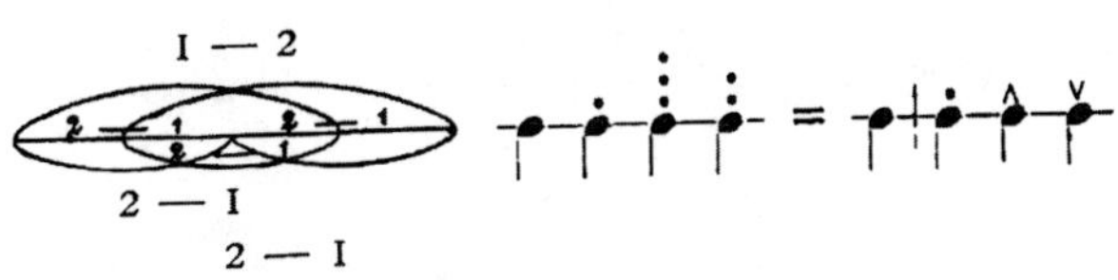

B. (*a*, **a**)

(β)

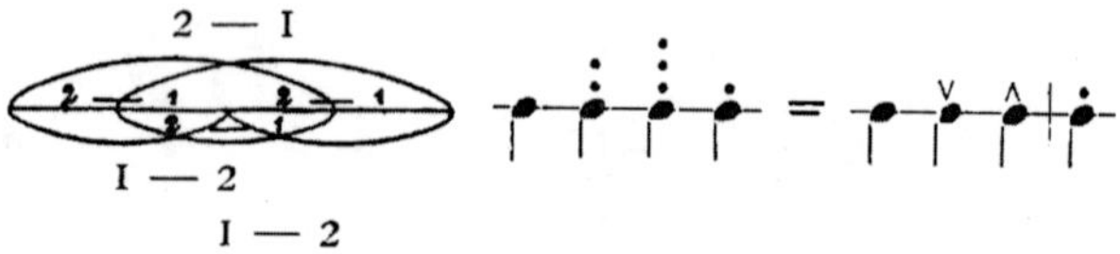

(*b*, **a**)

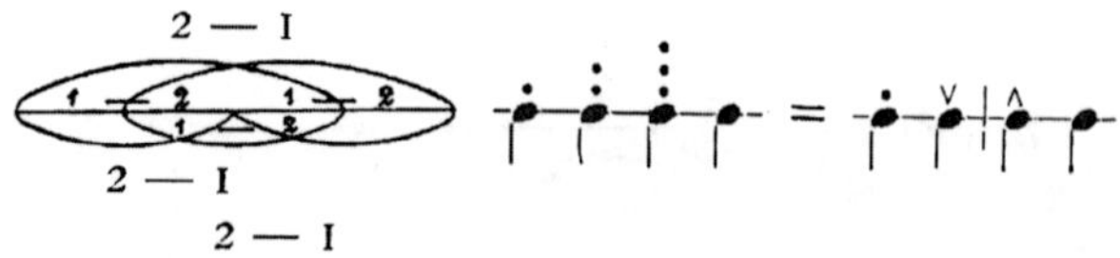

(β)

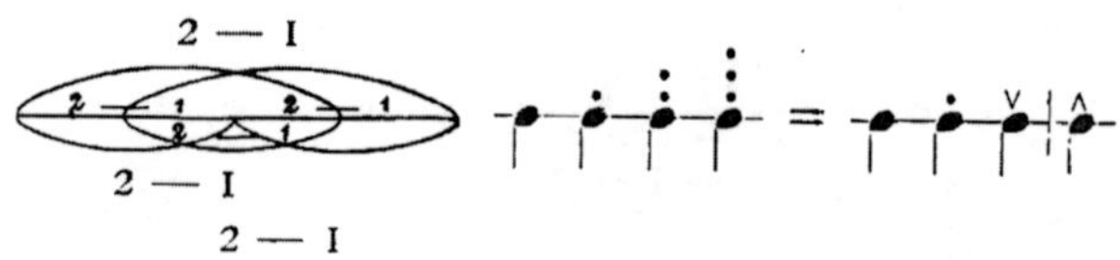

A. (*a*, *a*-β)

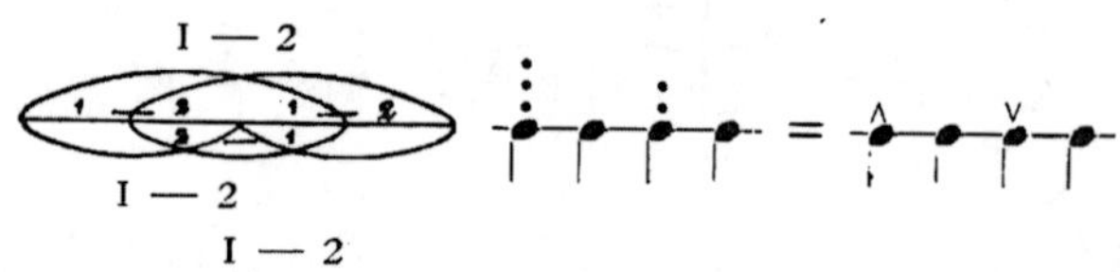

(β-*a*)

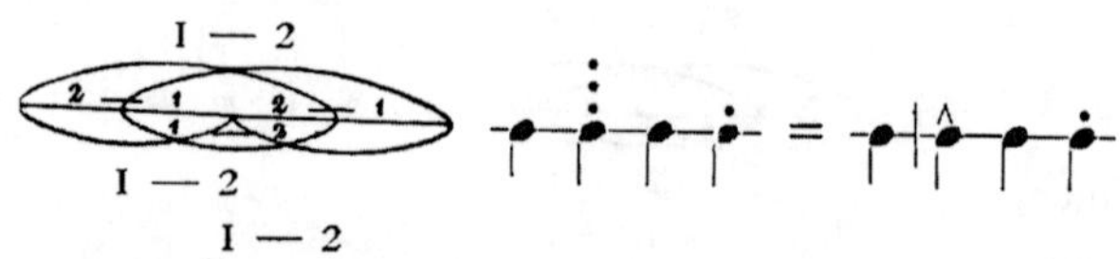

(*b*, *a*-β)

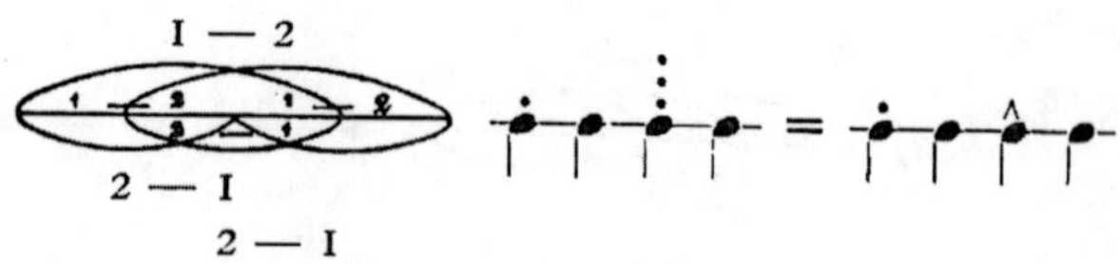

(β-*a*)

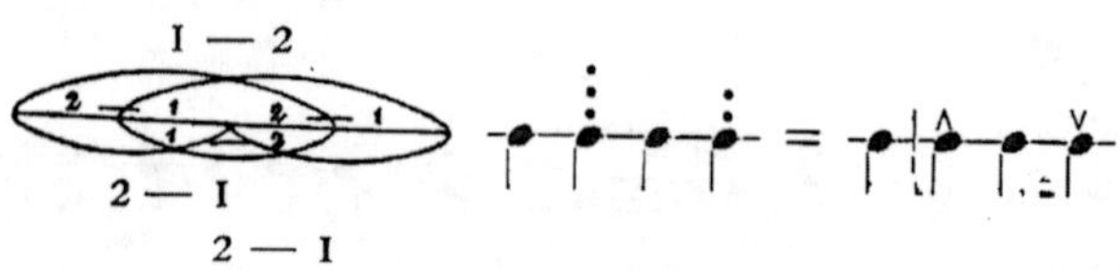

B. (a, a-β)

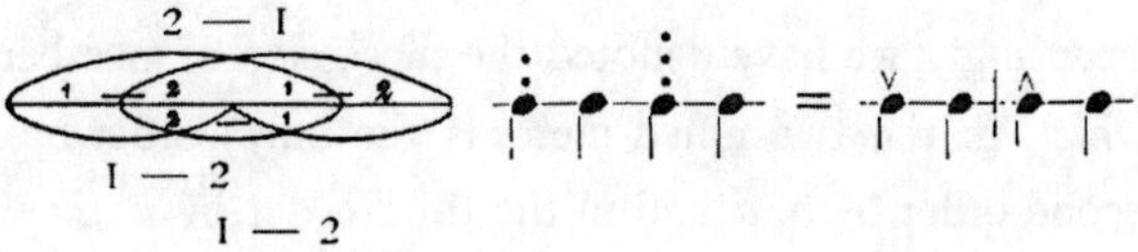

(β-a)

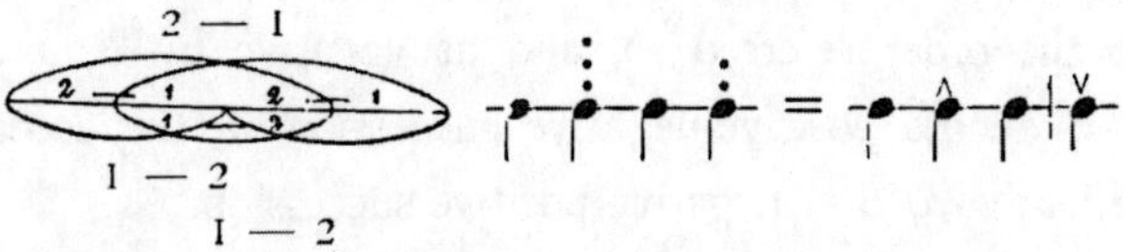

(b, a-β)

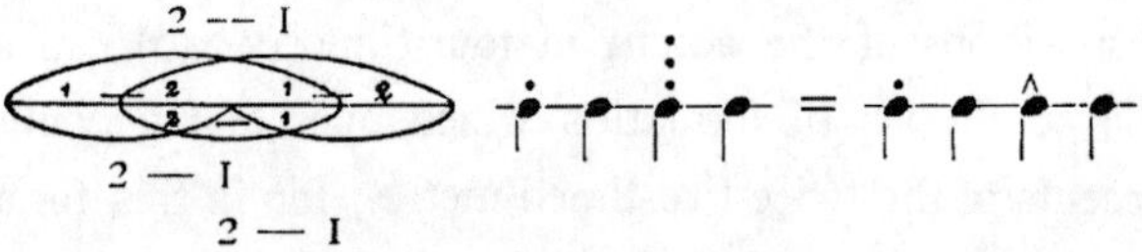

(β-a)

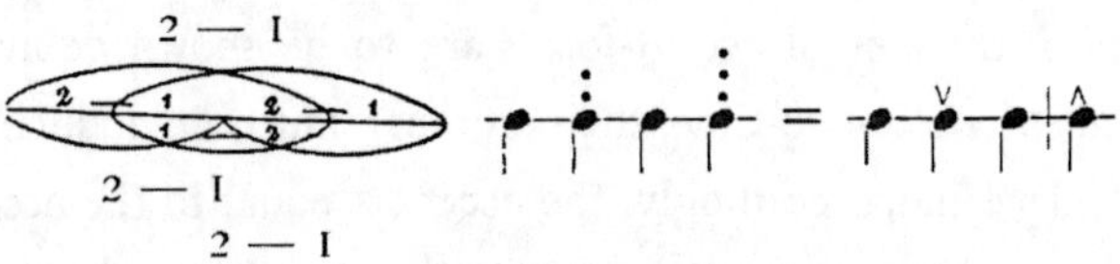

The accents of **two-time** and of **twice-two-time** in the foregoing description need no remark. From what has been said before, they are perfectly intelligible as they stand in the notation.

The eight different kinds of accentuation of the **three-timed** metre are in their four first numbers taken from the twice-two-timed, whence is explained their arrangement with regard to the chief emphasis and the beginning of the bar.

Of the four last accent-determinations of this metre, which result from the succession of opposite pairs within the lower order, we have before spoken particularly.

The thirty-two accent-determinations of the **four-timed** metre are comprehended in four divisions or groups, each of which contains eight differently intended kinds of accentuation.

In the two-timed metre there is contained only **one** metrical order, in the twice-two-timed and in the three-timed **two** orders, while in the four-timed three orders of metrical pairs are combined; accordingly, we have denoted the succession of members in the first (which in the two-timed metre is the only) order by *A*, *B*, in the second order by *a*, *b*, and in the third order by *α*, *β*.

The succession is marked as positive by *A*, *a*, and *α*, according to the order referred to, and as negative by *B*, *b*, and *β*; *a–b*, *α–β* denote positive-negative succession in the second or third order; *b·a*, *β–α* negative-positive succession.

The second group, consisting of eight differently determined dispositions of the accent in four-time (p. 240), can, according to the conditions of formation which operate here, only repeat the accents of the twice-two-timed metre; for in this form the second member has lost all trace of the double meaning attributed to it. But if these eight accent-forms are to be shown equivalent to the four of twice-two-time, their number must be reducible one-half. And we find, accordingly, the accent 2 equal to the accents 4 and 8, and further the accent 3 equal to the accents 5 and 7; consequently the numbers 4, 5, 7, and 8 fall out as repetitions, and there remain over the accentuations 1, 2, 3, and 6, corresponding to 1, 2, 3, and 4 of twice-two-time.

Similarly the fourth group of the four-timed accent-forms (p. 242) being also without double determination of the second member, is, like the second just spoken of, only twice-two-timed in accentuation. Here too the resulting accents, 2, 4, 6, are alike, and also 3, 5, and 7. The difference to be noted, that 2, 3, and 7 carry the secondary accent as simple emphasis of the member, while in 4, 5, and 6 it is the accent of the pair at those places, is not one that affects the result; because in this metre there is only room for a discrimination of accents into principal and secondary. Accordingly these eight modes of accentuation also are reduced to the four accents of twice-two-time.

In the third group of four-timed accents (p. 241), in which the second two-timed member has its determination changed (in the preceding formations it remained unaltered), we notice a succession of accents increasing or decreasing step by step, such as can only arise under the following conditions: when all orders are positive in structure,

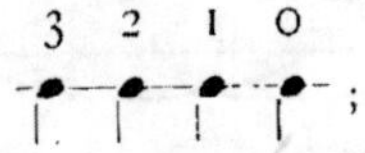

and when all are negative,

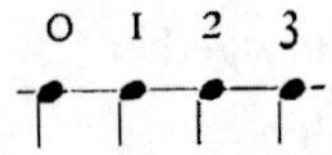

This is the most complicated combination in respect of the determination of accent. Nevertheless the result will not be otherwise than clear and unambiguous even here, if we consider, both singly and also in combination, the causes which co-operate in bringing about the several determinations of accent.

In the formation

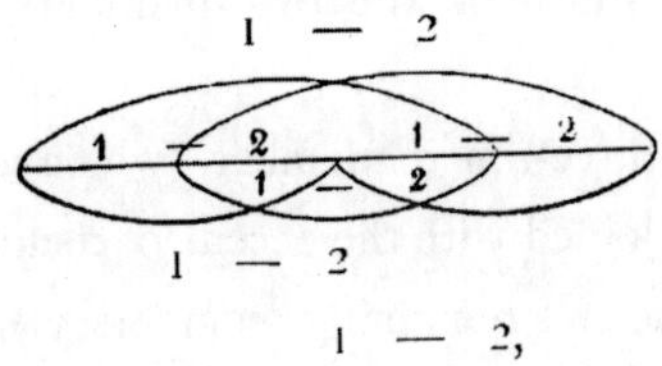

as in all others, we have first to consider each order by itself as a succession of an accented and an unaccented part, and to reckon as adding to the effect of every member of higher order only that part of the lower order which fully belongs and is proper to it. Thus this formation contains in the accented three-timed member

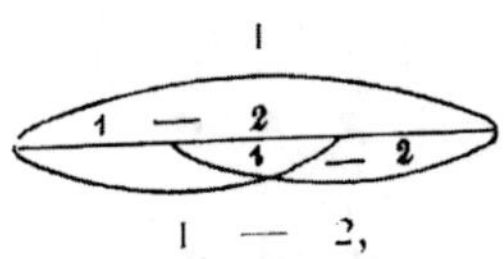

one accented and one unaccented two-timed member. The second two-timed member has, it is true, an accent; but only in virtue of belonging, not to the first accented, but to the second unaccented three-timed part.

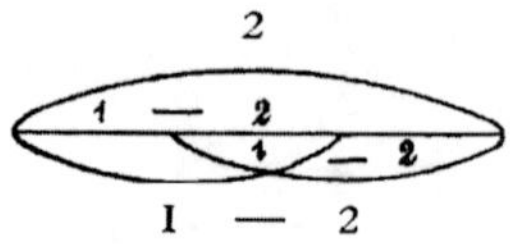

Hence the accent of the second two-timed member, although in taking the whole construction together

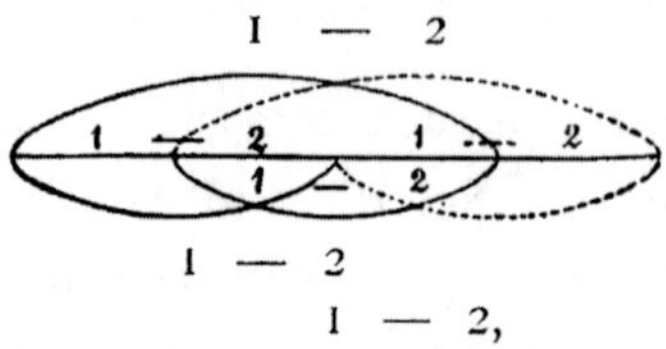

it falls within the compass of the accented three-timed part, nevertheless does not receive triple emphasis like the first, nor can there be a doubt, which of the two members it should be assigned to.

In the second three-timed member (which as such is without accent) this accent joined with the accent of member ranks only as double, and with the two remaining members yields the succession

But the first, the accented three-timed part, receives the accentuation

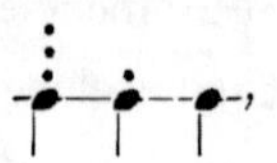

and both three-timed members together

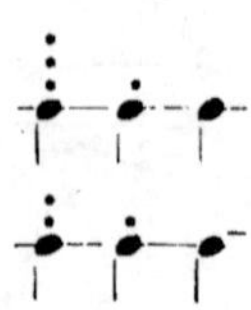

combine to produce the figure

The member-accent of the second time of the first three-timed part is the same which in the first time of the second three-timed part was added to the pair-accent belonging to that member, and thus gave it a double emphasis. This accent therefore, being already reckoned in the double emphasis, is not to be added to it again to make it triple.

In this way each of the accent-determinations here represented may be accounted for, and justified as brought about naturally on rhythmical metrical lines.

What we have marked as the beginning of the bar is always an accented element. But the accents of second and third order, that of the pair and that of the member, may also be found as first time in the bar. For a formation positive in the highest order, the beginning of the bar can fall only in the first half of the four-timed metre; for a formation negative in the highest order, the beginning of the bar can fall only in the second half. But moreover, an accented first time must be answered by an accented third time; for four-time is always also twice-two-time, its two-timed half will always be apparent. That the whole is of twice-two-times is its Third-condition; just as the three-times of its two overlapping highest parts constitute its Fifth-condition, and the two-times of its three overlapping parts its Octave-condition.

Accordingly metrical forms such as  (p. 240, *B*, *b–a*, *β*),  (p. 242, *B*, *a*, *β*) cannot be distributed in bars thus:

even though in this way the beginning of the bar falls, agreeably to the first condition, in the second half. If the beginning of the bar were placed thus, the third member, which corresponds metrically with the first, would be without accent:

and so in contradiction to the twice-two-time of the four-timed metre. The determination of the bar for these two formations can therefore take place only as denoted in the scheme above. That is to say, it must take place so that the member-accent of the fourth element may form the beginning:

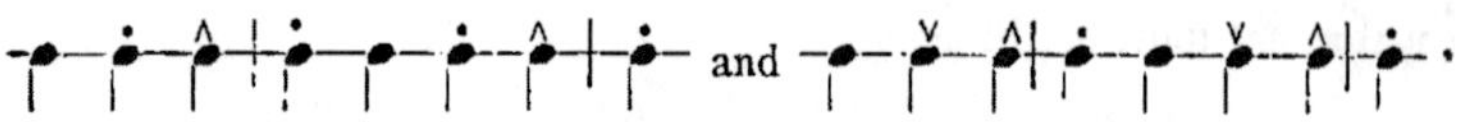

A member determined in the twice-two-timed metre as unaccented can through the meaning which it assumes in the four-timed receive single, double, or triple emphasis. But a member which in the twice-two-timed metre is accented, even though it be but singly, cannot in the four-timed become unaccented.

ACCENTS IN COMBINED METRE.

75. The combined metres, in which any one of the formations drawn out above with their accent-determinations may be taken up as member in a formation like it or different to it and of higher order, are, as may easily be imagined, of the utmost manifoldness of construction; but still the emphasis must always be subject to the conditions here exhausted. In structures of greater compass the chief accent must still fall always upon an element that is in all orders emphasised or positive. This might have been seen already in the twice-two-timed metre, which is really a combined one, and

was here taken in anticipation, partly because of its kinship with the three-timed, and partly in order that by it might be elucidated the peculiarity and independence of the four-timed.

76. The reciprocal combination of the two-, three-, and four-timed formations has been investigated already ('Metre,' par. 25) and represented metrically. It would be a useless as well as lengthy undertaking, were we to draw out in detail the arrangement of accent in these nine forms of combination, as was done for the simple two-, three-, and four-membered metres; were we to exhibit in metrical and musical notation the twice-three-timed and the twice-two-timed with their 2 × 8 or 8 × 2 = 16 different accent-determinations, the thrice-three-timed with its 8 × 8 = 64, the thrice-four-timed and the four-times-three-timed with their 8 × 32 or 32 × 8 = 256, and, lastly, the four-times-four-timed with its 32 × 32 = 1024. By what has preceded, the accentuation for each individual case of higher metrical combination may be found without difficulty, even for one crossed repeatedly with positive and negative determinations, by taking the sum of the accents of every order upon the element in question, whereby the chief as well as the subordinate accents will manifest themselves in their proper degrees. So, e.g., the thrice-three-timed metre with negative pair of the lowest order, positive of the second and third, and negative of the highest, will take the following shape and emphasis:

2 — 1

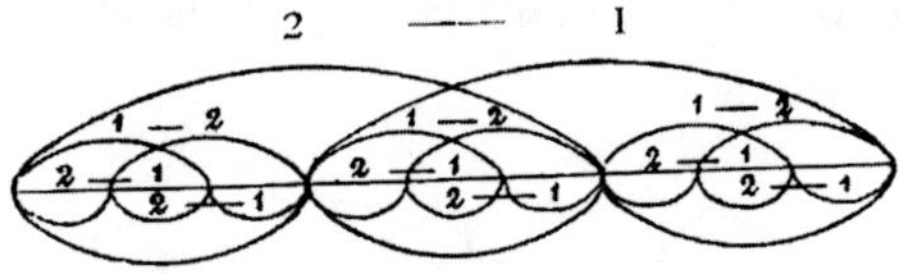

1 — 2

1 — 2;

The same with positive pair of the highest order :

I —— 2

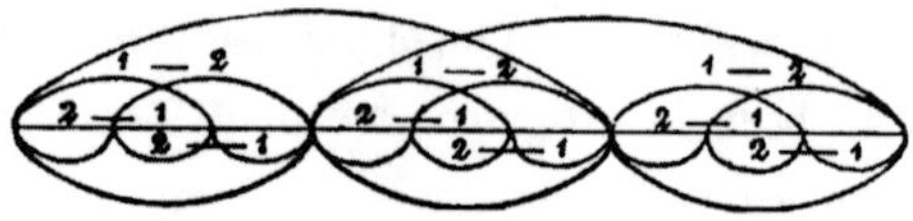

I —— 2

I —— 2.

In the first case the principal accent falls upon the fifth member, the principal secondary accent upon the second ; in the second case this is reversed, and the secondary accent falls upon the fifth, the principal accent upon the second member.

77. Suppose it is required to throw the principal accent upon an element of time previously determined on, e.g. upon the fourth member of the thrice-three-timed metre. First the place must be fixed as being emphasised in all orders :

I ——

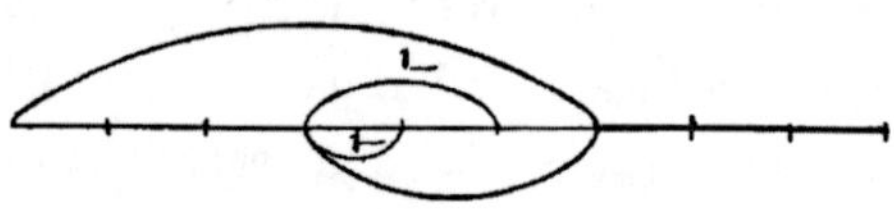

I ——

and then the formation will in the rest of its members be necessarily determined as :

I —— 2

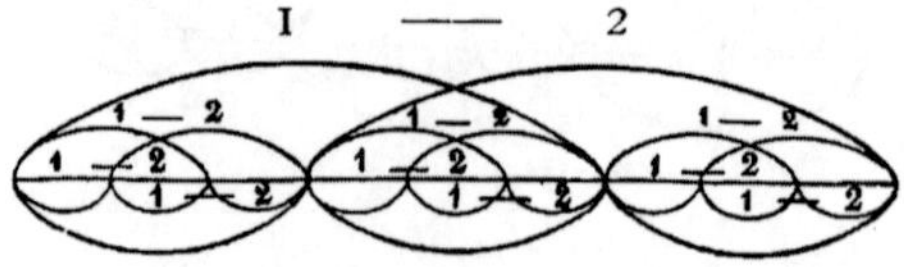

2 —— I

2 —— I,

which produces this accentuation :

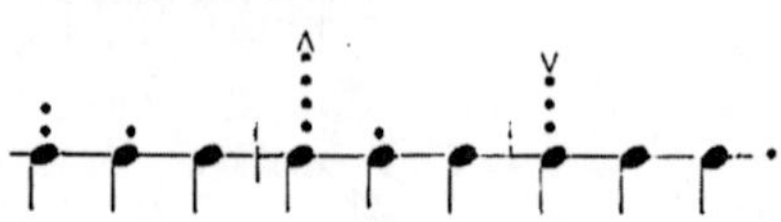

Here if we assume the highest order negative, and then the first three-timed member positive:

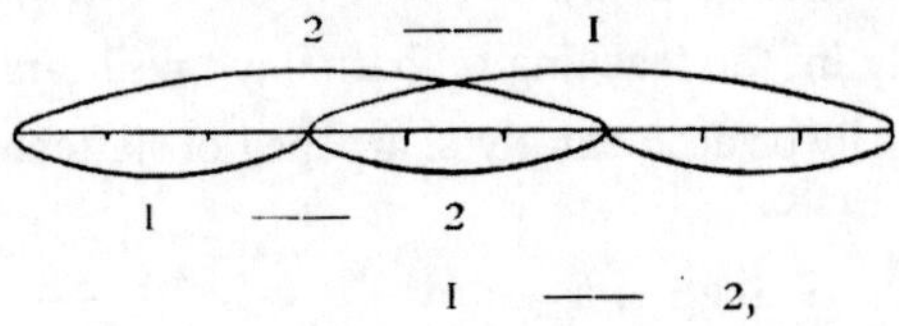

whereby the second acquires positive value in the **second pair** of three-timed members, then the principal accent will indeed fall upon the same fourth member, but cannot form the beginning of the bar. For there arises for the whole the formation:

which begins with the full bar, and carries the principal accent upon the second three-timed member:

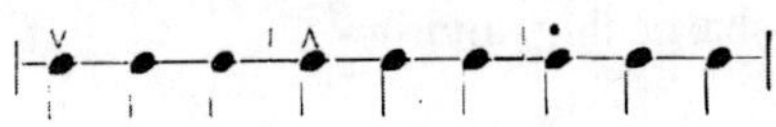

The first metre rests in its highest order upon the determination:

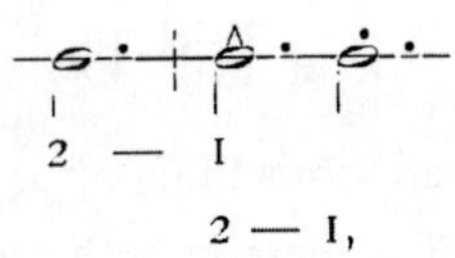

and therefore in that order begins without accent.

78. Thus all accentuations possible to feeling, manifoldly different as they can be, will always be found rooted in the organic metrical forms treated of. And on the other hand every accentuation that conflicts with nature is also self-excluded from those forms. In metre, what harmony has already laid down is but repeated. There it is on the one hand impossible for systematic harmonic construction of chords to produce a combination of sound unfitted for practical use, and incapable of being justified to hearing, and on the other hand every chord perceived as correct in

practice must allow of its derivation, its nature, being traced in the organic system of harmony.

Certainly in the teaching of harmony one hears notes spoken of as arbitrarily or accidentally sharpened or flattened. In the two successions:

G ··g♯·· a   G ———
e ———   e♭ ———
C ———   C ··c♭·· B♭,

the *g*♯ of the first is called a sharpened Fifth, and the *c*♭ of the second a flattened Root. But why in the collocation

G ·· g♯ ·· a
e♭ ———
C ———

does the same sharpening, and in

G ———
e ———
C ··c♭·· B♭

the same flattening, seem something altogether repugnant to feeling and inadmissible, if, as here in both successions, the first chord indeed stands in intelligible connexion with the last, and if the progression from one to the other means nothing more than that the note which progresses is drawn upwards or downwards, being arbitrarily sharpened or flattened? But we know that the so-called augmented triad, which may here be recognised in the middle chord of both successions, and which has been spoken of in its place (' Harm.' par. 234), is one that can be systematically accounted for; that it exists in a natural system; and that, when the chord appears, the system must be able to be present connectedly. The subsequent course of the harmony may either remain in that system or pass into another.

In like manner no accent can be an isolated determination, nor occur in a single portion of time as a solitary element not standing in an arrangement of accents and not in reciprocal relation with all the other parts of time in a metrical unity. Each single accent is always rooted in the metrical system; in its order it is conditioned by the whole system, or conditions a whole metrical system present at its entrance or arising with it; which afterwards may pass into another related system, from which again new accents may be determined; just as in harmony every change of meaning in a chord, or chromatic alteration of a note of a chord, is founded upon, or founds, a transformation of the key-system.

RHYTHM IN METRE.

79. The system of accents, their order, and their change, is that which in the chief sense we shall name **rhythmical** in metre. Hitherto this expression has been avoided; for it was necessary first to become acquainted with the conditions upon which this order and this change depend. These must always be metrical determinations, just as the notes of melody must always be parts of harmonies. For in this meaning **rhythmical** in opposition to **metrical** may justly be compared to **melody** in opposition to **harmony**.

As the melodic succession called the **scale** resting upon harmonic basis, joins together opposite triads in each element of its progression:

C ·· D ·· e ·· F ·· G ·· a ·· b ·· C
C G C F C F
a e a

so also the rhythmical formation unites what is metrically opposite, **related**, i.e. diverging one from the other: it goes on beyond the end of the metrical positive unity and holds that and the beginning of a following one together in a **close.**

THE RHYTHMICAL CLOSE.

80. The notion of the close is, that something separated becomes united, that it is closed up, joined together.

Union always presupposes a separation, and separation unity ('Harm.' par. 11). Thus the close is the contentment of recovered unity.

By itself the positive metrical pair forms no close. It is one in itself, and therefore has nothing to unite. Thus the magnet with its positive and negative poles cannot by itself exhibit any attractive force. But as the opposite poles of two magnets seek each other, and as the **minus** of the one tries to attach itself to the **plus** of the other and to close on to it, so we see too that in the metrical negative form, ··2—1··, the two members cleave together all the more firmly for being as yet decidedly **not** metrical unity.

In a continued positive series:

1—2   1—2   1—2   1—2,

one may easily see that it is the negative series also contained in it

that with cohesive force couples together the double members of the first series, effecting a close between them.

81. Thus from the very notion of union it follows that a positive metrical second member cannot be rhythmical closing element. The close will at all times fall upon a positive first, to which a second has gone before; upon the beginning, not upon the end of

a metrical positive duality: the last member of a positive pair will always postulate the first of another following pair to form with it a close. In the negative metrical formation the last member is last also rhythmically; for negative last is in fact positive first.

82. When the rhythmical close coincides with a metrical second member, that happens in so far as every **one** of a higher order within itself is, or can be, **one and another** again of a lower order. If in the simple positive two-timed form the rhythmical close falls upon the second time, then the second half of the first time has united with the first half of the second time:

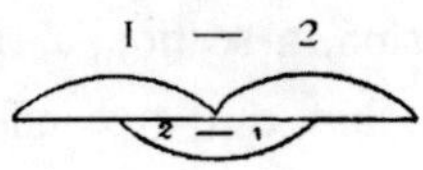

for in its quality of two-timed the form cannot with its first and second give rise within itself to any close, since the close presupposes being divided, which cannot yet be said here. So that here too the closing element is in its rhythmical meaning the first of a second and not the second of a first.

Only try to have the close fall upon an absolute last, or, since that is impossible because every unity may always be divided again into halves, upon a second member that may be accounted small in comparison with the whole, and the impossibility of considering such a form as a rhythmically closed one will at once make itself felt:

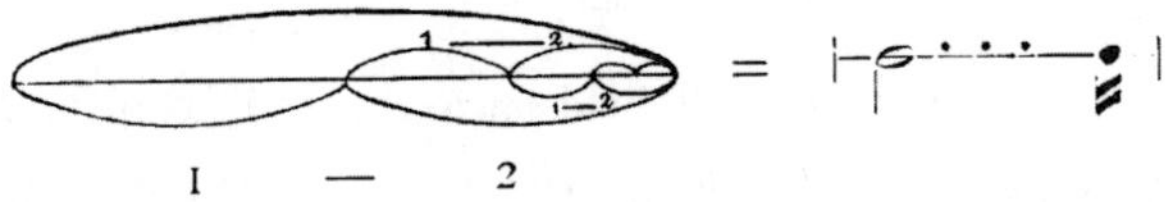

On the other hand the smallest second member will always easily unite with a first of highest order following it into a rhythmically closed figure:

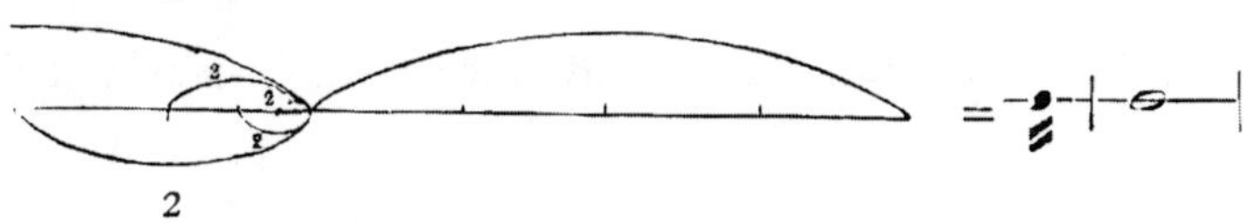

83. In this sense rhythmical unity is something opposite to metrical unity. That which in the positive metre is separated and would fall asunder is by the rhythmical close united and held together. To be rhythmically united is to be metrically separated, and to be rhythmically separated is to be metrically united. By this it is not said that what is metrically at unity has to be divided rhythmically, and that what is rhythmically at unity has to be divided metrically: not, that the positive of the one determination is cancelled by the negative of the other; but only that the negative of the one is everywhere covered by the positive of the other. Thus wherever metrical union exists, and just because it exists, there a rhythmical division, a section, a **cæsura**, is possible. And every metrical element that can give effect to the meaning of a first may, in so far as it can do this, be a rhythmical last, a closing element.

84. If, then, in the positive two-timed unity:

1 — 2

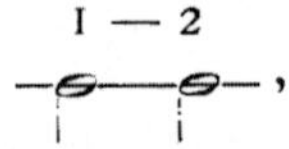

the second time is to become the rhythmical closing element, that can happen only by understanding rhythmical union between the second half of the first member and the first half of the second member:

1 — 2

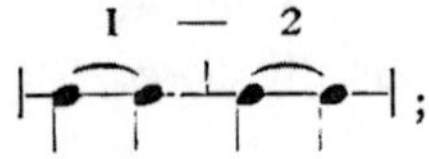

2 — 1

and the second time here, if held on to the end, i.e. given its full contents, would seem too long, heavy, and dragging. The close is in fact completed in the figure:

2 — 1

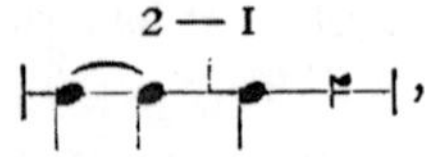

and the last, fourth part, if appended to the closing member, would be a useless burden to it, for it stands here, not in the meaning of second half of the whole, but only in that of first part of the second half. The close is therefore

not 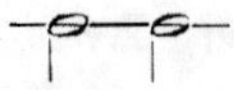 but  ;

as indeed it would naturally be performed in practice.

85. In the rhythmical closing figure just given:

2—1

1—2 1—2

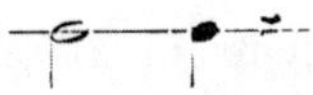

fulfilment of the condition of the close has turned the simple two-timed formation into a twice-two-timed one. The last member, however, of the latter, the second time of the second half of the metrical whole, has not been called into the rhythm. Supposing the close to fall upon the second half, and that with the second member of that half no new rhythmical figure is to open, then the place remains empty, void of contents; it becomes a metrical **rest**.

FILLING-UP OF THE METRICAL FORM. REST.

86. The metrical form cannot of itself make manifest the elements belonging to its determination; for this it needs contents to fill it out. From the beginning we have taken audible beats to represent the metrical sections; and little as these may be considered as filling out a space of time in the way in which the sound of a continuous note would fill it, yet even they must be thought of as absent from the abstract formal determination. Of itself the metrical form is still only an empty space of time, a metrically determined rest, and the membered form is only a rest conceived as membered.

This form, then, in all its different metrical determinations of memberment, may be filled out with contents either as a whole, or as divided, either in its parts collectively, or in individual parts.

(*a*) In the Two-timed Metre.

87. The **two-timed** metre, which has in it the two determinations of containing once twofold and twice single:

$$1 \times 2$$
$$2 \times 1,$$

can be filled out with contents in a fourfold manner: (1) as a whole, (2) as divided; as such (*a*) in both parts, (*b*) in the first part, (*c*) in the second part:

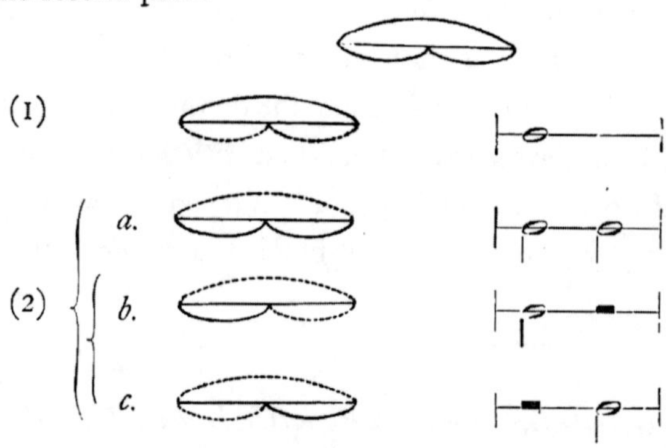

(*b*) In the Three-timed Metre.

88. The **three-timed** metre has in it the determinations of containing once threefold, twice twofold, thrice single:

$$1 \times 3$$
$$2 \times 2$$
$$3 \times 1.$$

It can be filled out with contents in a twelvefold manner.

This takes place here with wider scope of combination than in the two-timed metre, but its inward process follows the same plan. The metrical and musical notation will now suffice to represent this process clearly enough, without its being necessary to append further explanations.

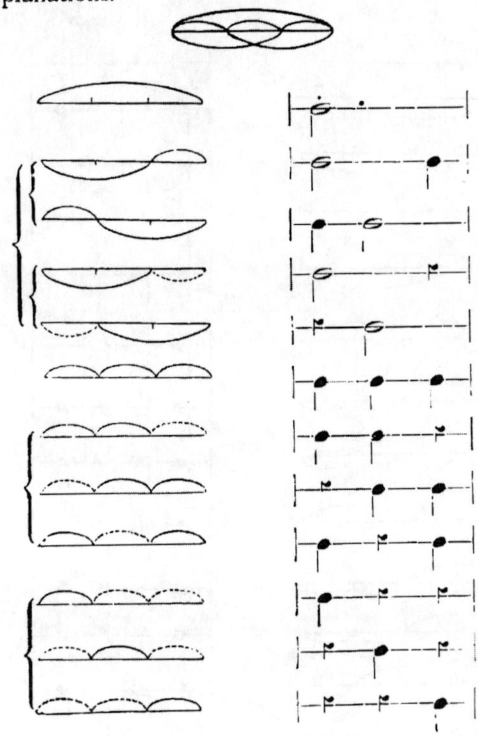

(*c*) In the Four-timed Metre.

89. The **four-timed** metre has in it the determinations of containing once fourfold, twice threefold, thrice twofold, and four times single :

$$
\begin{array}{c}
1 \times 4 \\
2 \times 3 \\
3 \times 2 \\
4 \times 1.
\end{array}
$$

It affords thirty-two different ways of filling it out with contents :

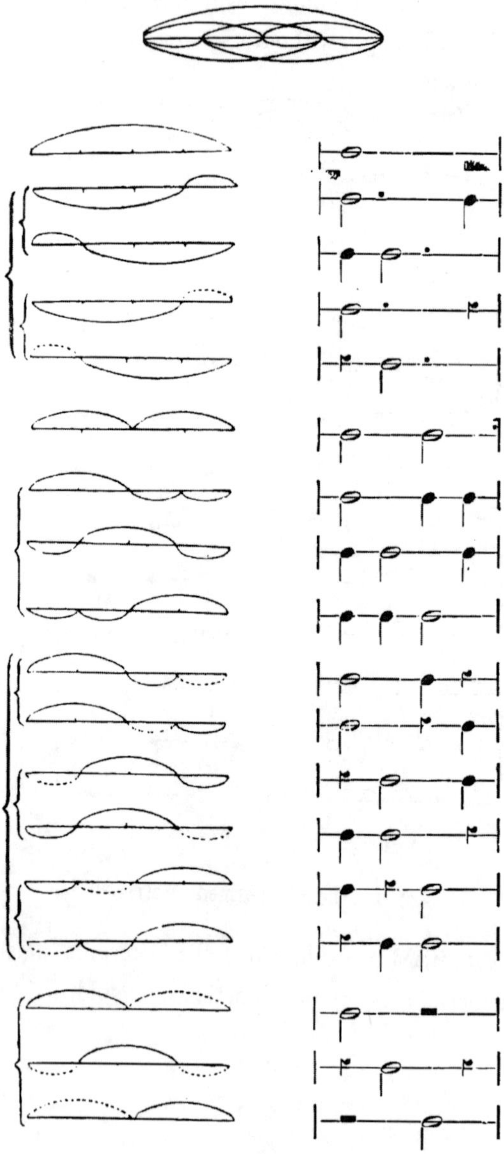

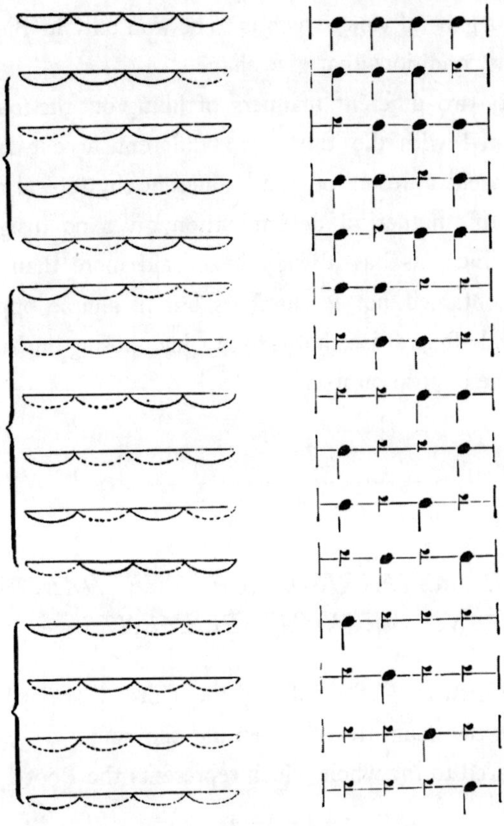

90. In these filled-out metrical forms there is assumed only positive determination of accent for all orders; as may be seen from the musical notation, in which they begin throughout with the beginning of the bar.

How they would combine either as wholly or as partially filled out under all other determinations of accent, and how far the latter would be able to be discerned in the forms partially filled out, it would be a vain undertaking to represent particularly. For it would lead us on into the unlimited, and therefore could not afterwards afford a general view, which is to be won only in the notion embracing the conditions that give shape.

The thirty-two different manners of filling out the four-timed metre combined with the thirty-two different accent-determinations of it yield a result of 1024 different rhythmical metrical figures; but this numerical determination gives no insight into the notion, which, as has already been said more than once, is everywhere contained, not in numbers, but in simple opposition, and its removal afterwards: that is to say, in opposing the **being** and **not being** of the opposition itself.

FURTHER COMPARISON OF THE HARMONIC AND METRICAL ELEMENTS.

91. If the Octave, $\frac{1}{2}$, the Fifth, $\frac{2}{3}$, the Third, $\frac{4}{5}$, are opposed to the Root, then the quantities representing the sound, $\frac{1}{2}, \frac{2}{3}, \frac{4}{5}$, must first be compared to the whole which represents the Root:

$$1 = \frac{2}{2} = \frac{3}{3} = \frac{5}{5};$$

they must enter into a relation of equality with it:

$$\frac{1}{2} + \frac{1}{2} = \frac{2}{2},\ \frac{2}{3} + \frac{1}{3} = \frac{3}{3},\ \frac{4}{5} + \frac{1}{5} = \frac{5}{5}.$$

The Octave is opposed to the Root in $\pm\frac{1}{2}$,
the Fifth " " $\pm\frac{1}{3}$,
the Third " " $\pm\frac{1}{5}$;

for the same that must be added to the quantity of the Octave to make it equal to that of the Root, must be taken from the quantity of the Root to make it equal to that of the Octave. That which produces equality is in the first case $+\frac{1}{2}$, in the second $-\frac{1}{2}$; and consequently is the same, opposed to itself as positive and negative, i.e.

posited and annulled. In the same way we have for the Fifth $+\frac{1}{3}$ and $-\frac{1}{3}$; for the Third $+\frac{1}{5}$ and $-\frac{1}{5}$.

With these elements of comparison,

$$\pm\tfrac{1}{2},\ \pm\tfrac{1}{3},\ \pm\tfrac{1}{5},$$

the Octave, $\frac{1}{2}$, is found to be simply equivalent to the element in question $(1 \times \frac{1}{2} = \frac{1}{2})$; the Fifth, $\frac{2}{3}$, to be double of its element $(2 \times \frac{1}{3} = \frac{2}{3})$; the Third, $\frac{4}{5}$, to be fourfold $(4 \times \frac{1}{5} = \frac{4}{5})$, i.e. twice double of its element. And as in the first interval there is unity; in the second, duality set asunder, i.e. doubling; in the last, duality simultaneously as doubling and as halving, and therefore in the latter sense brought under unity, or, we may say, duality simultaneously posited and annulled; so the Fifth in the Octave acts as the interval that separates, and the Third in the Fifth as the interval that annuls separation and unites.

92. The same meaning is contained in the metrical determinations of the twofold, threefold, and fourfold metres: in the first the simple meaning of the Octave, in the second the double meaning of the Fifth, in the third the fourfold meaning of the Third.

93. But further, in the intervals the positive may be put negative, so that we think of the determining element in the relations as determined; i.e.

for	C—C,	put	C—C,
	$1 : \frac{1}{2}$		$\frac{2}{1} : 1$
„	C—G,	„	F—C,
	$1 : \frac{2}{3}$		$\frac{3}{2} : 1$
„	C—e,	„	a♭—C,
	$1 : \frac{4}{5}$		$\frac{5}{4} : 1$

whereby in the Octave $\frac{2}{1} : 1$, in the Fifth $\frac{3}{2} : 1$, in the Third $\frac{5}{4} : 1$, the lower note appears as a determination from the unity of the higher. And so too in the metrical relations the sense of something 'determined' will be substituted for 'determining,' if the negative succession of members (2—1) be put instead of the positive (1—2):

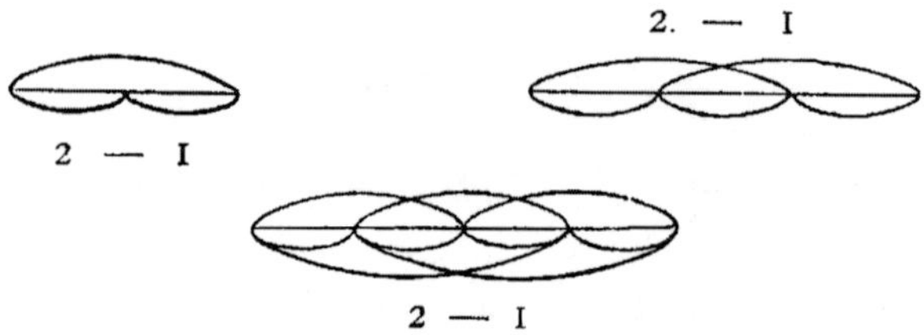

94. Without acknowledgment of the opposition of positive or negative unity in the metrical twofold, of positive or negative duality in the metrical threefold, and of positive or negative triplicity in the metrical fourfold, the nature of these metrical formations cannot be comprehended. But the notion of their organic essence goes past the determination of opposition on to that of the removal again of it; inasmuch as it collects the two, three, or four members into a membered whole and fuses them into a unity. This unity, moreover, finds further determination in its own opposition and the negation of it.

95. Here we may meet an objection that might be started against these comparisons of metrical with harmonic determinations of relation. For harmony, in the three intervals $\frac{1}{2}$, $\frac{2}{3}$, $\frac{4}{5}$, groups together **simple, double,** and **fourfold** in the meaning which we know; but metre groups together **double, triple,** and **fourfold.** Here, then, the difference from the twofold to the fourfold, as the twice-twofold, is not present in metre, at least in the outward structure of the determination of quantity, in the way in which it is present in the interval-relations of harmony. For in metre the determinations that we have described as answering to those of the Fifth and Third, stand in the relation of 3 : 4, instead of fourfold against twofold, as in harmony.

But, in comparing the outward differences of the harmonic and metrical determinations, we must take notice of the nature of the respective spheres in which they occur, and the manner of their springing into form in each.

96. The musical relations of the intervals are dynamic: they are relations of tension. The Octave has double tension to the Root; double force in the same inertia or weight; the Root compared with the Octave opposes double inertia to the same force. In the Fifth $\frac{2}{3}$ of the same inertia, in the Third $\frac{4}{5}$ of the same inertia, is overcome by an equal force. And apart from the meaning of the ratios there is in the higher note less heaviness, it is lighter and brighter; the lower is dragged down by weight less matched by force, and is heavier and more sombre. The positive intervals are determined in the direction of height; they are force-determinations. The negative are determined downwards; these are weight-determinations. The rational meaning of their relations, simple, double, and quadruple, is contained in them in the sense already known to us.

97. The metrical determinations are extensive in space of time. But their rational meaning does not lie in the number which gives the sum of their successive parts in time. It is contained intensively in the transformation which such succession produces in a time-unity posited in the beginning. This time-unity is by a second in time determined to be first of that second; by a third it is separated from its second; and by a fourth united to its second.

The sense of these three elements of metrical construction is completely the same as the sense of the Octave, Fifth, and Third in harmonic construction. The latter is no more contained in the numerical ratios by themselves, than the former is contained in the mere number of the metrical members. A third and a fourth member have no metrical meaning as being third and fourth, either in the most complicated or in the simplest metrical combinations; everywhere we find only a first and a second, a determining element and a determined, in positive or negative succession. And so too the fourfold in the quantity of the Third has reasonable acoustical meaning only as a twice-twofold, and the fourth part only as half of the half.

98. As anything in metre that extends beyond the fourth member, i.e. beyond the pair of pairs, no longer exerts influence within the first pair, and cannot therefore be comprehended in a metrical unity of an order in which the first pair stands as such; so too in harmony that which exceeds the fourfold ceases to be directly and immediately intelligible as an interval-determination. In the ratio 4 : 5 or $\frac{4}{5}$, that of the Third, the complementary part $\frac{1}{5}$ has no meaning in relation to the number 5, but only to the number 1; for the quantity of the Third, $\frac{4}{5}$, is predicated fourfold, i.e. twice-twofold of the numerator, which alone is what here determines. Precisely as the complementary $\frac{1}{3}$ of the ratio of the Fifth, $\frac{2}{3}$, determines the quantity as twofold; and the complementary $\frac{1}{2}$ of the Octave-ratio, $\frac{1}{2}$, determines the quantity as simple of its measure.

In the ratio $\frac{3}{4}$ the quantity compared with the complementary part $\frac{1}{4}$ would appear threefold, and consequently beyond the directly intelligible opposition of duality. Similarly in the ratio $\frac{5}{6}$, which to the complementary part is fivefold, we have a quantity extending beyond the twice-twofold.

99. Such ratios as differ in their numbers by more than unity, as $\frac{1}{3}$, $\frac{3}{5}$, can therefore afford no directly intelligible determination. For here the element which compares between the whole and the thing compared, $\frac{2}{3}$, $\frac{2}{5}$, is itself not unity, not a measure but measured, not determining but determined.

100. Hence there are left for directly intelligible harmonic determinations the ratios $\frac{1}{2}$, $\frac{2}{3}$, $\frac{4}{5}$; for metrical, the two-, three-, and fourfold, in their metrical meaning agreeing with the former, as being those that can be comprehended in a membered whole, and that determine the whole in its members by opposition and by opposition of opposition.

METRICAL CONSTRUCTION INWARDS AND OUTWARDS.

101. Every simple metre may become combined by subdivision of its parts. A part is unity in the order within which it is subdivided.

In the so-called semibreve bar with motion in semiquavers the crotchet is, in respect of the whole, a **part**, half of the half; in respect of the semiquaver it is a **whole**, containing halved halves.

102. But division into sixteen parts, which is here comprised in one bar, may also be comprised in a series of sixteen bars; and each of the bars may again be divided into sixteen. It is the same in the combination of different metrical determinations, the two-, three-, and four-parted, which readily explain themselves. So that a thing of six parts, made up of two three-parted or three two-parted unities, is in its highest order twofold or threefold, in its second order threefold or twofold, and may be further determined as a member in larger formations, as well as more minutely articulated in its own members.

103. The division into parts, so far as it is still conceived as metrical determination, remains always subject to the principles of metre.

A memberment into 5, 7, 11, 13 equal parts is not conceivable. It is otherwise with the formation which is grouped together and constructed by augmentation, so that a whole becomes part, or by diminution, where the part becomes a whole.

If when to one single another single has been joined, to this twofold then another twofold, to the fourfold a fourfold, to the eightfold an eightfold, and so on, and if to the sixteenfold, thirty-twofold, sixty-fourfold, &c., there must always be added, as necessarily following member, the equal of the whole that has preceded, then (still apart from all æsthetic conditions and only considering formal admissibility) such a progression would very soon extend beyond any possibility of being seen through or grasped.

Both in extreme height and in extreme depth sound has a limit of being audible and determinate. So also the comprehensibility of metrical relations in both directions, that of diminution and that of augmentation, has its limits. Now in the first direction the aggregate of the members is held together by a whole already formally determined; if division be carried too far, the clearness of parts may be endangered, but the whole of its order remains secure. But the combination which augments must determine the whole by means of the part, and here the too long lapse of time demanded by the progression of the members would soon pass beyond the bounds of a unity able to be reviewed and comprehended in beginning and end. In things visible in space, a whole that stands before the eyes as unity can be reviewed at once in all its elements. In things audible in time, only one element of the train is present, which, though it leaves its impression behind it, is liable to be pushed back into the past and obscured by the following element, and by others following that, and the more other elements follow it the more its definiteness diminishes.

Supposing a musical period could be lengthened out intelligibly to an extent of thirty-two bars, slow movement, yet it would not by any means require a second equal to it as necessary answer. Even a first phrase of sixteen or of eight bars need not always be followed by an after phrase of equal number.

The two-, three-, and four-part kinds of bar do not admit of being joined into an agreeable course of rhythm. But in more advanced metrical forms, two-, three-, and fourfold combinations, explained and governed by their contents, may very well be brought together in an æsthetically satisfactory construction. And it ought not to be regarded as showing a want of the sense for regular construction, or an incapacity for the review or comprehension of a whole of any considerable size, if it should seem to us that a metrical formation not strictly to be called regular nevertheless fulfils our æsthetic requirements. In reality the form is everywhere only the form of the contents. The artistic work that is richer in contents and higher of purpose is precisely that which contains such deviations from the absolute transparent regularity of pure metrical structure, and which can make them approved oftener than we should be willing to tolerate in productions of lesser rank. So too the organic structures of nature upon the lower levels show a more comprehensible regularity of form, appear to follow a stricter law, than the more highly organised; in which the richer and more individual life passes too into their formal existence, shaping it more completely: not less by law, but under multiplied conditions.

Only in pieces of music of the smallest compass shall we find the metrical parts arranged in the simple regularity with which metre by itself makes them follow, or be produced from, one another. Thus metrical dance-forms keep up, as a rule, a constant number of bars, two, four, or eight; for there regular metrical division is the first requirement, they being intended to lead the figures and steps of the dance and lend them metrical support.

Now as already in simple three-timed metre a metrical second element receives the value of a first, is first second, and then becomes first; so it happens too in broader formation that a larger metrical group may be related in one direction as after phrase and in the other as fore phrase. This is the same as a change of meaning of a chord with reference to the key, or modulation: as when a dominant chord (II) is used as a tonic (I),

I — II
        I — II,

and we find ourselves thereby carried from the tonic into the dominant key. And such a change of meaning in metre, according as its sense is expressed decidedly or doubtfully, clearly or unclearly, will prove easy to understand and correct in effect, or appear incorrect and a mere mutilation of rhythm.

Should it be attempted to represent throughout a whole large composition its formal metrical web apart from all reference to the contents, there would always, even in the most regular of the classical masters, be found much that is not with clearness metrically self-evolved; although with the context it appears easy of comprehension, unambiguous, and altogether such that an educated sense of rhythm cannot perceive in it anything conflicting with good order. As in all things healthy and natural, theoretical conditions will not once occur to the mind.

But in many productions of newer and the newest music deviations from the directly intelligible metrical regularity do not always imply masterly twisting of the web. More often it is nothing but a tumult of sound, in which the composer has himself not arrived at clear metrical perception, and now inflicts the unclearness upon us also. The defect in such an artist—if a composer with this defect can still be called an artist—is the not being able to comprehend, or not wishing to comprehend, a whole as whole in its members. It is thus at bottom a defect of proper artistic sense, which demands, not a piece in isolated fragments, but a body of healthy coherent members.

Music in its rhythmically moving course cannot do without metrically regulated support. The rhythmical phrase derives its meaning in art from metre, in vocal music as well as instrumental.

Prose speech is also made up of rhythmical phrases. Recitative is rhythmical without being metrical. Now as recitative is distinguished from melody proper, from the metrically periodic composition, with which the sphere of musical art in the narrower sense is first entered upon, it is a great error in a composer to suppose that in setting a text to music he need only follow the course of its rhythm, and is exempted from conceiving it musically in metre. Even the words of psalms, being in themselves unmetrical, can be handled in musical art only in a metrical conception of independent value. For music must always be music in itself, apart from the words sung, and carry its own determination of form. Had music no other task than that of emphasising the words agreeably to their accents and logical import, then the first things to be thrown aside would be bar- and part-singing. Music must then be confined to declamation in recitative. For even measured verse is not spoken by bar; and it is impossible for several melodies sung at one time, under the condition in part phrase of being different, to be in equal measure adapted to the logical emphasis.

UNEQUAL-TIMED DIVISION OF THE METRICAL MEMBER.

The Metrical Determinations compared with the Spacial.

104. Architecture has been called frozen music; in the same way music might be called fluid architecture. Things of time have a notion of **symmetry** like things of space. Architecturally we might call bilateral **breadth** the **space** of space, and **height** the **time** of space. Symmetry is to be found only in the space of space, in the sides opposite one another of the dimension of breadth. Height is a **progression**, is evolution, and cannot oppose like parts to one another. It has in it no opposition at all; by itself it is absolute unity, just as breadth by itself is absolute duality; then the one in the other is real determined space.

105. Hitherto in the metrical determinations we have only seen what may be compared to the **space** of space: namely, the **space** of time; which, agreeably to that, has in it too its notion of symmetry meant of time, its things of like form in opposition. To this **space** of time must be opposed a **time** of time: a notion in time answering to the notion in space of time of space, or height-unity; just as the space of time, the metrical determinations up to now, may be put answering to space of space, the bilateral opposition of duality, i.e. breadth.

This side of metrical determination we have now to consider in its notion and in its manifestation. But at the same time it will not be going out of our way, having already found for it a counterpart in the notion of space, also to investigate its relation to one aspect of the notion of harmony. Such an aspect there must be; for there could not be musical metre and metrical music, were not the musical and metrical determinations rooted in the same nature and principles.

106. Metrical determinations, as heretofore given, with all their manifoldness of accentuation, are nevertheless always made up of parts equal in time. They rest upon the opposition of a first and second in direct or inverted succession. The single may be put double or halved; yet in the double as well as in the halves only equal is set against equal, never the part against the whole or the whole against its double. Everywhere the only difference made is between accented and unaccented of equal quantity.

107. So is horizontal symmetry in ruled space: it demands like to like on both sides. In this determination of equality, in space as in time, single produces double, and double fourfold; for the same is always put against the same:

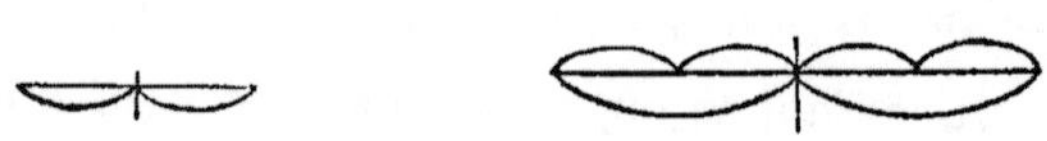

Our metrical three-timed formation, too, contains only opposition of like determinations, and if we represent it in its notion in space it must not be drawn as a symmetrical figure, made up of two halves in themselves unequally divided,

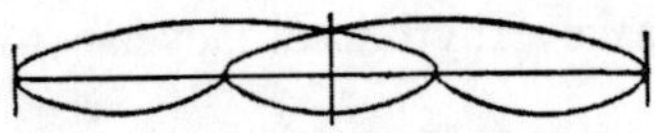

but as a horizontal space-determination with **two** middles.

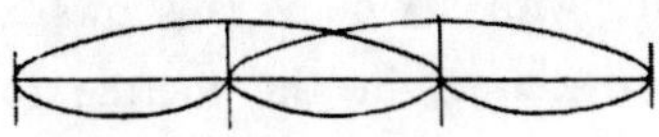

This corresponds again to the notion of Fifth, and in an abstract sense to the dissonance-notion of a double unity, such as might be pictured architecturally by a building with two porticos or two main entrances placed side by side.

108. What gives rise to the Gothic pointed arch is a similar duality of centre; since the centre of the arch of one side falls upon the periphery of the other,

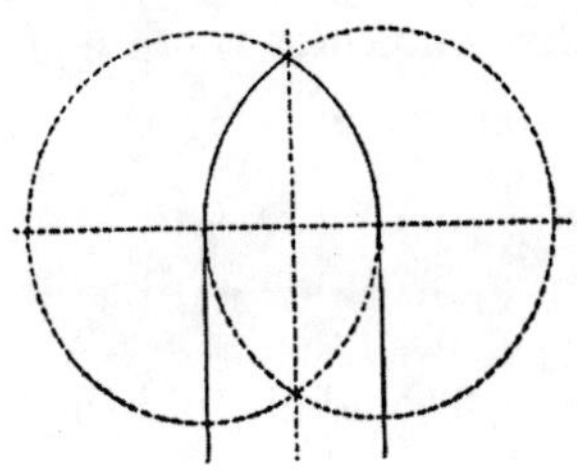

in contradistinction to the round arch, which is produced from a single centre.

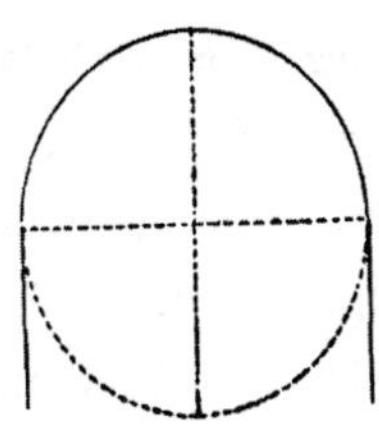

The Gothic arch contains in its point, in the middle that has come to be, the resolution of its dissonance, its Fifth-duality. The round arch cannot show a determinate middle in itself, because it is only unity and every part in it passes into its other.

109. In all symmetrical determinations, as such, equal will only enter into union with equal, quantitatively.

But if we now take a rhythmical movement like

,

then, as the marking with six quavers shows, a twice-three-times may certainly be discerned in the metre; for the three-timed may appear in the filled-out form (' Metre,' par. 88) of a whole pair and a single member. But it makes a difference, whether in a unity we have to consider the whole as the principal determination, or the parts.

In the figure

occurring in the three-timed metre, the first double time is two-part brought together; wholeness is not its first determination; it has come originally from the growing together of the parts. The figure

,

from the rhythm above, also admits of being resolved into a three-membered one:

;

but if we think of this rhythm in quick movement and many times repeated, the twopartedness of the first double time seems, not its original determination, but division of a length originally determined as undivided; and the whole figure therefore consists of the succession of an undivided double and a single, or of a time-unity and its half.

110. This same determination is also contained already in the

equal-timed metrical formation, namely in the second or **Fifth** element of it: in the **three-timed** metre. The fundamental metrical determination is two-timed **unity**. This in the three-timed metre becomes **doubleness**; it is divided, the halves stand out in it. In the meaning of equal-timed metre, whole and part here subsist in one another.

111. The unequal-timed rhythmical formation causes the whole, on ceasing, to be followed by the half of that whole. It places **one after the other** in time, that which the equal-timed metrical contains **one in the other** (in the meaning of rest) in space. The same notion lies at the bottom of both, in positive meaning and negative, posited and annulled. Rhythmical determination is the 'not being at once' of the 'being at once' in the metrical: the **coming to be** of **being** in time: **time in time.**

112. In the metrical three-timed there has arisen an extension by enlargement of the metre. The rhythmical unequal-timed determination does not admit of being increased in the same way, for it originates within the metrically determined member. The member must therefore contain both elements of the determination, and they must be formed in it successively; for rhythm is essentially **successive**, just as metre is essentially **simultaneous.**

113. Certainly, nothing can take shape in time without being successive. But we have pointed out that there is space in time and time in time; and similarly in space, that there is time of space and space of space, picturing by the latter the stationary and simultaneous horizontal determination of space, and by the former the vertical and progressive.

If the notion of a determination of time thought of as space could not be conceived, then we could form no picture at all of shape in time. For only one element of what passes is ever really present; and not until this is taken together with the element that has gone before and the element that follows after—therefore with something that is no longer and with something that is not yet—can the notion of an image in time be realised.

114. In determination of space symmetrical relations of equality are natural to the horizontal dimension when considered as base, and progressive relations, increasing or decreasing, to the vertical dimension. If we look at a building, it seems to us a construction which has arisen from below upwards, out of the ground-plan presupposed in its whole breadth. In its horizontal proportions it is a two-sided equal, symmetrically measured together and at once; it is in space. In its vertical proportions it is successive, progressive, growing: it **comes to be** in space.

115. In the sphere of determination of sound the same opposition which in the notion of space is presented by the determination of horizontal and vertical, that namely of 'being at once' and 'not being at once,' or of being and coming-to-be, is found again as the opposition of harmony and melody: that is, of simultaneous sound and successive, if they are contrasted independently, or of harmony of melodies and melody, i.e. succession, of harmonies, if they are considered in combination.

116. The notion of harmony places Root and Fifth, *C*——*G*, sounding together as simultaneity or space-interval. The notion of melody places Root and Fifth as time-succession or interval. In the melodic progression, *C*··*D*, *C* is Root to *G* and *D* is Fifth to *G*; that which therefore was itself at first Fifth, then became Root, and if its two meanings are taken together forms the unity by which the difference of the two successive notes *C*··*D* becomes intelligible and by which their combined sound exists as an intelligible dissonance. *C* and *D* sounding together in harmony contain the same contradiction that we should obtain if we placed a whole and a half in architectural symmetry, i.e. a whole on one side and a half on the other; a contradiction that would demand resolution into one or the other, to one side or to the other in symmetrical equality. On

the other hand this proportion of 2 : 1 or 1 : 2 in the vertical line is quite suitable as an architectural arrangement.

117. Thus in the notion of space equals are situated as equal in time, or horizontally symmetrical; unequals are produced successively, or vertically, increasing or decreasing in their proportions; nevertheless the vertical determination first comes to reality in and with the horizontal determination, i.e. ascent can only become real and perceptible by reference to something that ascends. Further, in the notion of sound the Fifth *C*——*G* as an interval is simultaneous in sound, and therefore is as it were in space; while the Fifth of the Fifth, the Second *C*··*D*, has only a relation of succession, and is therefore an interval in time, yet again, as being in time, it has the foundation of its intelligibility only in something which persists (*G*). And so too the metrically unequal, which we compare to the ascending in space and to the progressing in melody, can come to real existence only upon a metrical basis, only within the equal-timed form of metrical unity. Thus the rhythmical figure

belongs to the unity-determination of **time** in time, and not to that of **space** in time. The latter is **double**, the former **single**. It belongs therefore to the **single** in **double**, to the part in the whole, and can therefore be realised only in repetition.

A $\frac{3}{8}$ bar is but the half of a metrical unity; a unity that can be either of positive form or of negative, 1—2 or 2—1, whereby the unequal-timed division begins either with the beginning of the bar,

or on the up beat.

A two-, three-, or four-timed metrical basis is always required, just as a harmonic basis is necessary to melodic progression.

For the unequal-timed is not in itself an independent metrical construction in the sense in which the equal-timed is.

118. A member that carries the unequal-timed metrical determination cannot at the same time contain the equal-timed. For so it would itself be a double unity, a metrical one-and-other, and as such it could not have the unequal-timed articulation, which can only be formed in a member which is single.

POSITIVE AND NEGATIVE FORM OF THE UNEQUAL-TIMED DIVISION.

119. The unequal-timed determination having in its rhythmical meaning to be identified with the metrical three-membered formation, its parts, its long and short, must next be shown to be correlative to the metrical first and second of the two-membered: the rhythmical long to the metrical accented member, and the short to the unaccented. Then all that has been described and contrasted as metrically positive and negative and metrically major and minor will find its corresponding application also in the unequal-timed division. The metrical equal-timed unity contains a **first** and **second**, an accented member and an unaccented, and places them one after the other in direct or inverted succession; in the unequal-timed division of the member these are replaced by a **long** and a **short**: the **accent**-determination by a **quantity**-determination; the accented member by the long, the unaccented by the short.

120. The equal-timed positive succession,

1 — 2

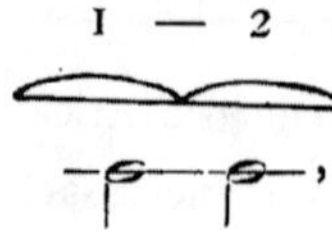

appears in unequal time as a succession of long and short,

the equal-timed negative,

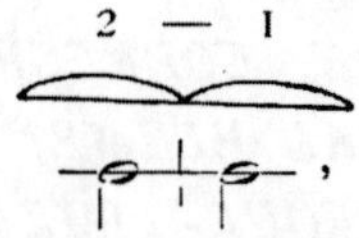

in unequal time as a succession of short and long,

121. The long, as such, has no accent; for a metrical element receives the accent only as being first to a second which is **equal** to it. Without the condition of equality a succession cannot, in this meaning, be comprehended. But the long as against the short is in itself a double: and is, moreover, of decidedly positive nature, seeing it appears unseparated; for negative succession would have separated it. And thus the beginning of the long is accented in that member by reason of its double and positive nature, but the short in its quality of single can have no accent.

122. According to the two possible accentuations of the metrical dual unity, in which dual unity alone the unequal-timed division is determined into a whole, the latter is capable of being emphasised in four different ways. It can be contained: (*A*, *a*) as positive in metrical positive, (*b*) as negative in metrical positive, (*B*, *a*) as positive in metrical negative, and (*b*) as negative in metrical negative.

A. (*a*)  (*b*) 

B. (*a*)  (*b*) 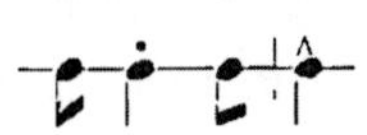

THE THREE ELEMENTS OF THE UNEQUAL-TIMED DIVISION, CORRESPONDING TO THE THREE METRICAL ELEMENTS OF THE TWO-, THREE-, AND FOUR-TIMED UNITIES; AND LIKEWISE TO THE HARMONIC ELEMENTS OF OCTAVE, FIFTH, AND THIRD.

123. Since the unequal-timed division can only develope in a given member of the metrical equal-timed determination, it is bounded, extensively, by the latter: the unequal-timed construction can take place only within the member. Now the unequal-timed division of the metrical member being identified for rhythmical meaning with three-timed metre, we know that the metrical determination does not cease with the three-timed formation, the element of duality or Fifth in metrical meaning, but that it goes on to reach repose of unity and completion in the four-timed. Therefore for the unequal-timed memberment there must likewise still be left an element of determination wherein it shall find the finish of its process of memberment.

124. The element of the unequal division, in its present aspect, corresponds with the notion of duality in rhythm. The two-timed metre contains first and second still only as unity, while the three-timed calls up decided separation in the pair, and the four-timed brings about union of the separated pair; in the unequal-timed division, the first of these three elements of the notion is contained in the undividedness of the metrical member, and the second is contained in its unequal division, according to which one part has the determination of being **whole** as against the other, and this other has the determination of being **part** as against the first.

125. The metrical equal-timed determination now proceeds to its third and last element essentially as follows: It makes the **whole** become **part** or **half**; the membered pair it places as member in a pair of higher order. The advance in this, as formerly with the three-timed, is by enlargement in extension: the formation now claiming twice the space of time occupied by the two-timed.

126. But division of the member cannot be carried beyond its extent; it must be completed within it. In the unequal division the **whole**, i.e. the long, cannot, as in the equal, become **part**, i.e. rhythmical short. For that by which the long could appear short, or half, would be greater than the member, or more extended than the space of time within which the determination must take effect. But the short can appear long by a shorter than it within the member, i.e. by the half of the short; consequently the **part** may appear as **whole**. And thus, as the equal-timed metrical formation, in the completion of its notion, puts the whole as part, and thereby removes the opposition of one and other; so the unequal-timed formation, by putting the part as whole, thereby arrives, agreeably to the nature of its method of construction, at the same completion of its notion.

127. The short is made to appear long by a part preceding it, of which it is itself the double. Consequently the second element of the unequal division is determined as short against the long which precedes it, and as long against the short which precedes it, and thus contains united in itself both opposite determinations of the unequal division.

The rhythmical figure that is produced from this determination is one well known to us from the seventh symphony of **Beethoven**:

where it is kept up so consistently in its peculiarity and essential difference from a real double three-timed bar, that though the bar is marked, as is customary, with $\frac{6}{8}$, yet a division of the half-bar into three equal parts instead of the two unequal parts, or a combination of the two kinds, never once appears in the whole long phrase. The first alteration would make a variety in the rhythm, but the second would change its whole character.

128. It is easy to perceive that in a spirited performance the middle element in this rhythm does not receive quite the full value of third part of the first: that it is taken shorter, and in fact is not connected with the first, but with the third. For the third member as against the second receives the opposite meaning to that which it takes as against the first, and therefore comprehends within itself the double meaning of short and long, and there is a tendency to put stress upon the latter meaning by more sharply marking as short the middle element. In this sense there is also imparted a proportionate degree of accent to the last element, in so far as against the immediately preceding member it is a **double**; although against the first it is a **half**, being thus opposite in itself, $\frac{1}{2}$ and $\frac{2}{1}$.

129. With the three elements of the unequal-timed division of members:

I. 

II. 

III. 

this rhythmical determination closes, just as the metrical determination ceased with the two-, three-, and fourfold, and the harmonic with Octave, Fifth, and Third. Further division of the member can only proceed as in equal-timed metre, or by a repetition within a smaller equal-timed member of the unequal-timed division in the second or third element of its notion.

130. As the unequal-timed division of the member is also, in a sense, equal three-timed metre, being marked $\frac{3}{8}$, $\frac{6}{8}$, $\frac{9}{8}$, $\frac{12}{8}$, even when, as in the phrase from the symphony just given, a real division of the half-bar into three equal parts does not occur; so, on the other hand, the three-timed metre will also offer a point of view from which it may be regarded as unequal two-timed, as a succession of long and short or of short and long. The first pair of members of the three-timed formation can take effect as an undivided unity; then the single member, the half of the other pair of members, remains over as the complementary part, and we get at once a long and a short. Then, further, the short here may be made to appear long by a half put before it; so that an unequal-timed determination, like that of time in time, arises also in larger measure in the real three-timed metre.

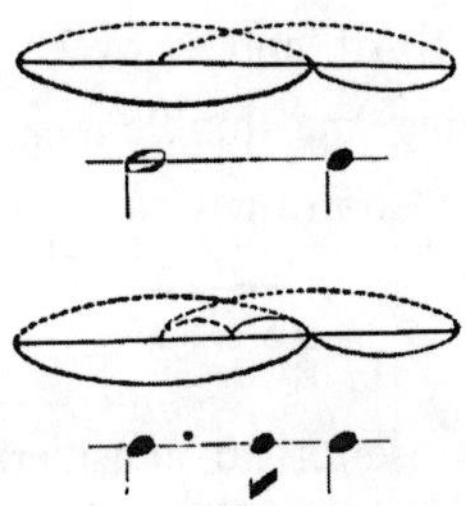

The difference between this metrical figure and the rhythmical one before noticed will not be overlooked. Wherever a strict metrical behaviour of the parts to one another remains perceptible, especially of the long long and short short, there the sharply accented, elastic nature of the rhythmical formation is missing. For those two elements cannot enter into direct relation to one another; the second is only a relative to the third.

131. A relative should always be referred to its positive alone. To another positive it stands in no intelligible relation; moreover it

does not hinder the relation of this other positive to its relative from being truly presented. In the rhythmical figure

the two determinations

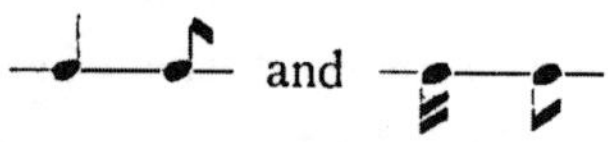

stand together, and at once,

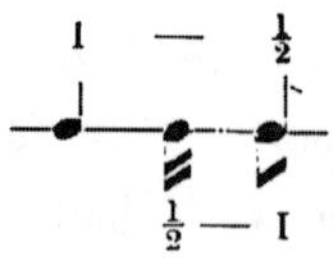

in such a manner that no relation between the long long and the short short comes into question. A direct relation is only found between the first and third and between the second and third elements, the third having the double meaning of long short and short long. Therefore also in the figure

the middle member presents no considerable proportion to the first—it would be represented here by 1 : 3—but the first long has its duration and metrical meaning, irrespective of the entrance of the intermediate member, and lasts up to the beginning of the second principal element of the formation.

So also between two notes that do not form the interval of an Octave, Fifth, or (major) Third, no direct harmonic relation can exist. The concord of the minor Third, e.g. *e*—*G*, will always merely point to a third note, *C* or *b*, in which the two notes *e* and *G* may then attain to relation in unity, as Fifth and Third of positive or negative determination.

132. The expression for the negative form of the third element of the unequal-timed division must likewise be completed within

the compass of the member. It must also, like the positive, fulfil the determination of opposite meanings being contained at once without contradiction. It can therefore be no other than that represented below—the rhythm of the **quail's cry.**

As the positive form must at the same time comprehend in it the negative:

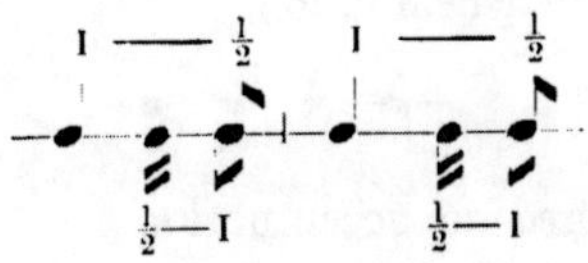

so too in the negative there must at the same time be contained the positive:

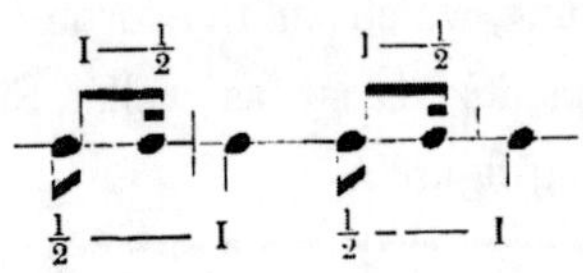

the figure beginning with the short of the up beat, which also takes to itself the meaning of long.

THE DOTTED MOVEMENT.

133. By these rhythmical figures we are led to the so-called dotted movement in general; which is also to be considered as an independent determination, for it can be produced from metrical formations of every kind.

It has already been seen in the unequal-timed dotted rhythm that the little short has no influence upon the effect of the great long, and that it exerts an influence only upon the intensive quality of the second principal element, the longer short; which, from being wholly without accent, it strengthens into being accented in due proportion. And so generally, to this intermediate element metrical meaning ought not to be ascribed, at all events not such as would claim for it a measured portion of time determined or determinable in duration. It is an element of absolute shortness, joined on to the next following, relatively long, element.

134. The metrical figure

has as four-timed the accentuation

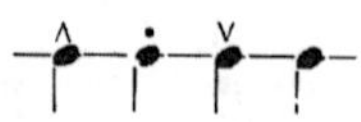

but as twice-two-timed the accentuation

Besides the fourth time, which in the former is without accent, the second now drops its accent as well. Similarly the dotted rhythm of the following figure:

,

will make the difference of accent, both in the fourfold of the four-timed and in the threefold of the three-timed metre, far less noticeable; because, on account of the short prefixed to the second, third, and fourth times, each of these elements has an accent imparted to it, and thereby an accent-determination of four equally emphasised elements arises,

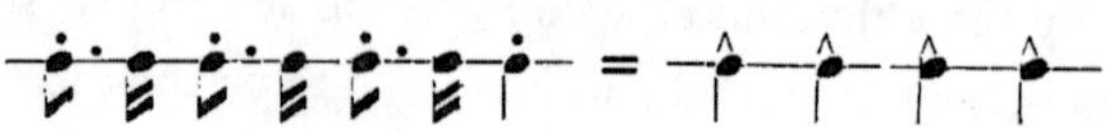

in place of the four-timed,

or of the twice-two-timed.

135. As has already been observed, the short in the dotted movement has no metrical quantity. As soon as quantity can be recognised in it, and it thereby becomes determinable for duration, the rhythm loses its character; this movement requiring a sharp contraction of the intermediate element, in consequence of which the following portion of time always appears accented, apart from its metrical duration and other metrical meaning. In this manner the accent-determination stands by itself, and does not essentially change, whether the time following upon such a short is metrically long or short, emphasised or not emphasised.

Analogy in Harmonic Melodic Determination.

136. This rhythmical division, which has not and cannot have metrical meaning, because here as well as in the unequal-timed rhythm it is concerned with the member only as a finished metrical determination, we may compare to melodic passing notes struck before or after a chord-note. These indeed have their origin and existence in harmonic determination alone—the only way of writing them is as notes thus determined—yet it is not in their chord-relation that they are used, but, on the exact contrary, as **not** harmonic notes, notes not belonging to the subsisting chord. Having this negative meaning in harmony, they are positive for melody; they are notes of union in melody, because they are notes of separation in harmony.

137. The succession of two chord-notes, e.g. *C··e* over the stationary major triad on C or minor triad on *a*, is melodic, inasmuch as the notes enter successively. But they might also sound at once, or the first might be prolonged to sound with the second: they make a successive harmony.

138. The passage *C··D··e* over a stationary triad prevents the first chord-note of the melody from sounding on into the second;

it separates their harmonic unity. The third note of this melodic figure, which in the immediate succession of *C··e* is merely a harmonic echo of the first, and has therefore but a secondary meaning to it, is after the second unharmonic note to be regarded as a newly entering chord-element, and so gets a primary meaning. It is exactly like the short of the unequal-timed division appearing as a new long against the smaller short prefixed to it, i.e. acquiring a primary meaning without giving up its secondary meaning against the first long. And as in that case the intermediate element has reference only to the last and is joined on to it, so too in melody the passing note is attached closely to the next following. Between it and the next following note no division can be placed; and it is no more possible to close with the passing note than with the short of the short in the unequal-timed or with a decided metrical second element in the equal-timed metre.

Analogy in the Determination of Space.

139. If we want to discover in the determination of space something analogous to the unequal-timed rhythmical division, corresponding to the analogy between the equal-timed metrical division and the bilateral symmetrical base, it will have to be sought among dimensions of height and other determinations drawn from the nature of progression. Now in general the proportions of height in constructions which shall correspond to a reasonable free determination of space must not be uniform, but increasing or decreasing; and will in the first order be made out of single and double. And if this principal proportion corresponds in the first instance to our Fifth-notion of the unequal-timed rhythmical determination, then the Third-notion, which is to show the half also as whole, the secondary also as primary, the unaccented also as accented, and to present the separated elements of the opposition determinately in their state of union as well as in their state of

independence, will find a place here also as last determination in the distribution of space.

140. First height is unity, or whole. Then it is divided within itself into an unequal duality, of positive or negative succession. Next the two immediately contiguous elements of this determination must be separated, that they may be able to be united; and this is effected by the interposition of smaller intermediate members, just as it was effected in the melodic succession of *C··e* by means of the passing-note *D*, and in the unequal-timed rhythmical form by means of the intermediate member of the smaller short. The principal proportions lying one above the other might so far be viewed as produced immediately one from the other, but with intermediate members interspersed they seem continuous, united, and knit together just by reason of the separation that they thus have.

However attractive it might otherwise be to pursue further the principle of the laws of harmony and metre as applied to the determination, by law, of space, especially with reference to architectural formation, yet to attempt it here would take us too far out of our way; wherefore with these general indications the subject must rest.

METRE OF SPEECH.

FOOT. VERSE-MEASURE.

Dipody—Tripody—Tetrapody. Dimeter—Trimeter—Tetrameter.

141. In the art of scansion a single member of a verse is named **a foot**: the parts of a verse are called after the number of the feet contained in them, and the whole verse after the number of such parts.

In speaking of verses with **six** or **five feet**, of **hexameters, pentameters,** or of **five-footed iambics**, no more is indicated than the mere superficial counting up of the members; the inner structure of the metrical form is quite left out. For names like these tell us little more of that than might be learned from reckoning the number of syllables; and so they must be regarded merely as names for things which in their contents and properties are already known to us.

142. But the name of **foot** for the single member is very well adapted to the matter, because it brings out the natural necessity for a **pair** of such members. For there is no going with **one** foot: it wants a pair, and a pair with right foot and left, one to step out and one to be brought after.

143. Such a pair of feet, or the pair of steps which it is engaged in taking, corresponds to our first metrical determination, the two-timed. If we picture the step of the right foot as the stronger, it will then count for the accented member, and the step of the left foot brought after for the unaccented. Stepping out with the right foot

will make the accent fall upon the first step, and stepping out with the left will make it fall upon the second; the former to be regarded as the metrical positive succession, 1—2, the latter as the negative, 2—1.

144. This metrical duality of members is commonly called a **dipody.** If we wished to substitute the expression '**two-foot,**' yet the three-membered unity, the **tripody**, could not properly be called a '**three-foot**' member. Walking on three feet is in itself hard to imagine; and besides we know that the three-membered metrical unity is in truth also a formation by pairs—that is to say, pairs of higher power. Here it would have to be regarded as the function of a pair of pairs of feet, the second pair commencing with the second step of the first pair. To pursue further the comparison of metrical members with the action of these members of our body, would probably prove generally inappropriate, and might even become laughable. So, e.g., if we wished to compare a combined metre, such as the twice-two-timed, to the gait of a father walking in long slow steps, and holding his little son by the hand, who must take two steps to one of his father's, so that the child's right foot treads once with his father's right and once with his left. Yet the three-membered metre no longer admits of such apportionment of step between two persons, at any rate not in continued succession, because the third member brings to a stand the person who first steps out. And even the last comparison of the twice-two-timed metre is wanting in inner truth. For every metrical formation, even the most complicated, ought always to be regarded as one sole organism with members proceeding from itself; the conditions of its memberment may not be apportioned between two or more individuals; to make it single, they must have their ground in one and the same individual.

145. The memberment of speech-metre can in essentials be no other than that of metre in general, as we have seen it up to now;

namely, **equal-timed**, consisting of opposition of equal members, and **unequal-timed**, opposed within the member. But now let us call the first determination, occurring in what order it may, the **metrical**, as pre-eminently such, and the other the **rhythmical**.

146. The metrical determinations are:

A. *Lower Order.*

1. The **dipody**; two-membered.
2. The **tripody**; three-membered.
3. The **tetrapody**; four-membered.

B. *Higher Order.*

1. The **dimeter**; twofold.
2. The **trimeter**; threefold.
3. The **tetrameter**; fourfold.

From combining the determinations of both orders there arise the thrice-three formations before demonstrated ('Metre,' par. 26), which by reference to the former description we may now name for speech-metre—

I.	(*a*)	2×2.	**Dipodic dimeter.**
	(*b*)	2×3.	**Tripodic dimeter.**
	(*c*)	2×4.	**Tetrapodic dimeter.**
II.	(*a*)	3×2.	**Dipodic trimeter.**
	(*b*)	3×3.	**Tripodic trimeter.**
	(*c*)	3×4.	**Tetrapodic trimeter.**
III.	(*a*)	4×2.	**Dipodic tetrameter.**
	(*b*)	4×3.	**Tripodic tetrameter.**
	(*c*)	4×4.	**Tetrapodic tetrameter.**

Tetrametric formation in practice occurs only dipodically; but here the tripodic and tetrapodic are included for the sake of systematic completeness.

In general, the system of possible formations may be gathered into an easier view, if we combine only the two- and threefold of both orders, for this purpose allowing the four-timed to count as twice-two-timed. The practical metres, with the exception of the tetrameter, are contained in these forms.

This combination is fourfold :

A.	(*a*)	2 × 2.	Dipodic dimeter.
	(*b*)	2 × 3.	Tripodic dimeter.
B.	(*a*)	3 × 2.	Dipodic trimeter.
	(*b*)	3 × 3.	Tripodic trimeter.

147. Every metrical shape will depend upon one of these determinations. But only the outline of its principal division is thus given. The manner of dividing the member gives the character and colour to the metre.

148. Here the only rhythmical division of the member that can be considered is the unequal-timed. The equal-timed would only repeat the metrical determination in another order, e.g. would make the two times of the dipody appear twice-two times. But if the dipody is to remain two-timed, its member must not become two-timed. So, then, for further enlivenment we must come to that division of the member which puts not equals as **first** and **second** one after the other, but **long** and **short.** In scansion we know this form, as rhythmical **positive**, under the name of **trochee** — ◡, and as rhythmical **negative**, under the name of **iambus** ◡ —.

149. This rhythmical dual determination, which has been denoted as corresponding in its sphere to the **Fifth**-notion, is preceded by another element of determination; and it is also followed by another. The first, corresponding to the **Octave**, is that of unity, that of the undivided member. The last is that of the **Third,** corresponding to unified duality, that of the short determined to long in unequal division.

150. The dipody with its members undivided appears as the **spondee**. (— —).

This takes up a **pair** of members. It is not a foot like the trochee or iambus; it consists of a pair of such feet, which may become trochees or iambuses.

151. The short determined as long (by means of a smaller short prefixed to it) produces the **dactyl** in the single member, the trochee.

–̆◡ = 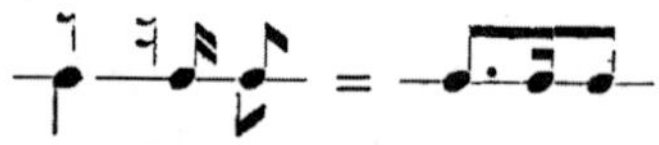

The dactyl contains the iambus in the trochee. What was rhythmically opposed as positive and negative, it has merged one in the other; and in this sense has formed the rhythmical **Third**. The short of the trochee appears here as at the same time the long of the iambus.

152. The opposite of the dactyl is the **anapæst**.

◡–̆ = 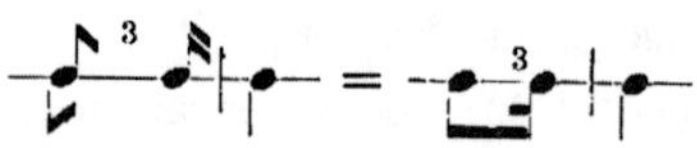

It contains the trochee in the iambus. The determination corresponding to the rhythmical Third-notion with regard to the negative trochee, that is, to the iambus, consists in this, that the short of the iambus becomes the long of the trochee.

153. Accordingly the metrical two-timed unity may be rhythmically divided, according to the elements of the unequal-timed determination :—

(a) In Rhythmically Positive Form.

1. — — as **spondaic**
2. —◡—◡ „ **trochaic**
3. –̆◡ –̆◡ „ **dactylic**

} **dipody** 

(b) In Rhythmically Negative Form.

1. — — as **spondaic**
2. ⏑—⏑— „ **iambic**
3. ⏑⏑—⏑⏑— „ **anapæstic**

} **dipody**

154. In this the difference of positive and negative quality is put in the **rhythmical** determination alone; the metrical is taken only **positive.** Hence the spondee is the same in both forms, **sinking.**

—́ —

The **metrical** negative determination would throw the accent upon the second member of the spondee, **rising**:

— —́

whereby the principal accent of the **rhythmically**-membered formations must also find its place on the second principal metrical element.

155. In metrical **negative** meaning the above rhythmical determinations will be as follows:

(a) Rhythmically Positive.

(b) Rhythmically Negative.

156. Of these rhythmical forms with positive and negative meaning, the first stands in notion inwardly akin to the Octave and to the metrical two-timed division; the second to the Fifth and to the metrical three-timed division; the third to the Third and to the metrical four-timed division.

157. Metrical determination by itself requires only equality of the members in the whole of their duration. Rhythmical determination is completed within the member. It may be different in the single members of the metrical unity; and therefore suffers combination **dipodically** in $3 \times 3 = 9$ ways. These we now draw out in positive meaning only, metrical and rhythmical:

Tripodically the combination happens in $(3 \times 3) \times 3 = 27$ ways.

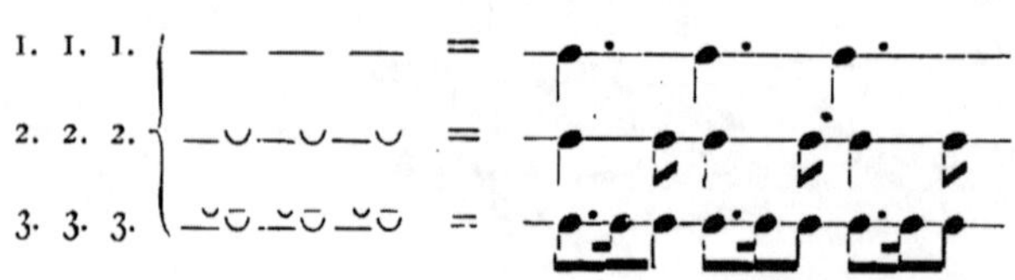

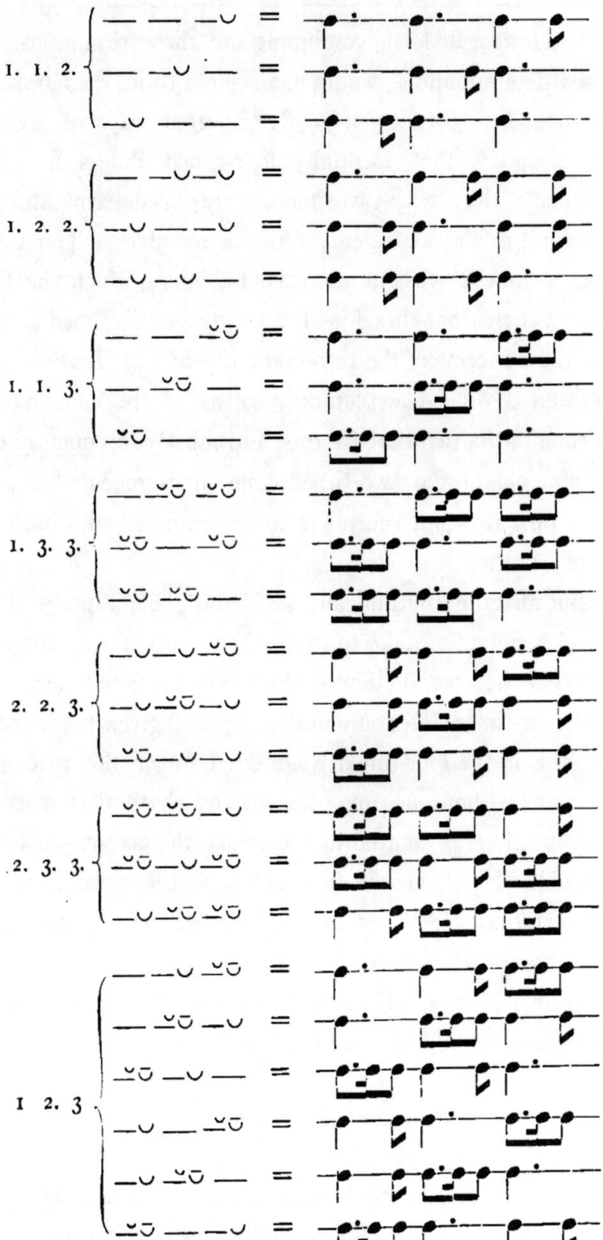
1. 1. 2.
1. 2. 2.
1. 1. 3.
1. 3. 3.
2. 2. 3.
2. 3. 3.
1 2. 3

158. The **tetrapodic** form, combining the three rhythmical unequal-timed determinations, would again yield thrice the number of the preceding, i.e. $(3 \times 3 \times 3) \times 3 = 81$ different ways of division. But the tetrapody, the essentially four-timed, differs from the double dipody, the twice-two-timed, only in determination of accent, and not in the arrangement of its members. The twice-two-timed is indeed without an accent-element, which the four-timed has; yet the four-timed is always a twice-two-timed as well. Therefore the 81 forms of the tetrapodic rhythmical division need not be written down. They can only consist of the combinations two at a time of the two-timed forms, and must consequently contain the ninefold of the two-timed nine times repeated, because each of the nine two-timed forms is to be combined with itself and with the eight others.

159. But also the rhythmically divided double dipody will in its accent-determination take to itself the nature of the tetrapody. We know that the accentuation of the twice-two-timed metre and that of the four-timed differ only in the emphasis given to the second member; this in the four-timed is accented, but in the twice-two-timed remains without accent. But in the rhythmical unequal-timed division there is allotted to every long the accent which falls to it as double short. Hence in every case the metrical second element, though as such it is unaccented, receives rhythmically a proportional emphasis.

The double dipody, which, when undivided, is without accent upon the second as well as upon the fourth time,

$$\overset{\wedge}{—}\ —\ \Big|\ \overset{\vee}{—}\ —$$

will, when divided, receive rhythmical emphasis upon both elements; thereby appearing, as far as the second element is concerned, also tetrapodically accented:

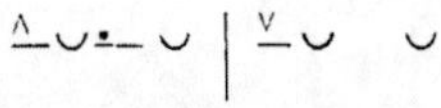

Thus the rhythmically divided dipodic tetrameter passes easily into the tetrapodic dimeter, or may be conceived as such.

160. The rhythmical negative form of division of the members, which begins with the short, would reproduce with **iambuses** and **anapæsts** what in the foregoing description of the positive appears with **trochees** and **dactyls**. The trochaic figure

is transformed into the iambic;

and the dactylic

into the anapæstic.

161. Moreover rhythmical divisions of positive and negative meaning will readily unite in the same metre ; as, e.g., the anapæstic with the dactylic :

the dactylic with the anapæstic :

without imperilling metrical order and unity, for these have nothing to do with the rhythmical structure of the members. The members are regarded for metrical determination merely as wholes of time.

DIFFERENCE BETWEEN THE METRICAL DACTYL AND THE RHYTHMICAL, OR BETWEEN THE SPONDAIC DACTYL AND THE TROCHAIC.

162. The third element of the unequal-timed positive rhythmical division, where the short of the trochee appears also long in respect of a smaller short prefixed to it,

–̆ ◡̄ = 

has been named by us a dactyl. But the rhythmical structure of this foot, as also the representation of it thereon founded, does not coincide with what in the science of metre is commonly called a dactyl and with the way of representing it, namely, as a long followed by two equal shorts.

– ◡ ◡ = 

If, then, both forms of the dactyl

 and 

are to exist side by side, we have in the first place to make the distinction, that the latter is not to be named a **foot** in the sense in which the first is. For that comes from dividing a single member, while the other plainly embraces, like the spondee, a pair of members. Let us call the first construction the **trochaic** or **rhythmical**, the latter the **spondaic** or **metrical** dactyl. The rhythmical dactyl is formed in the member, it stands for the trochee; the metrical dactyl is a form of dipody, and stands for the spondee. The latter cannot find place in a series of trochees, any more than in music the figure

can occur in a bar of $\frac{3}{8}$ or $\frac{6}{8}$ without changing the nature of the time.

Although, then, both forms of the dactyl exist, yet the customary way of representing metre knows but of one, the dactyl with equal times:

I — 2

—∪∪

and conjoins it, not only with spondees, but also with trochees. With the latter, however, the rhythmical dactyl, —̆∪̄ , alone can be combined,

—∪ —̆∪̄ —∪— = 

while the metrical dactyl finds its place only in the series of spondees.

—́ — | —́ ∪∪ | —́ — | —́ = 

In the latter the division is all of metrical equal-timed structure.

163. But then this marking is used (and that not only where the dactyl is concerned, but also for the other members) when trochaic rhythm is proper to the metre, as, e.g., in the so-called **æolic** and **logaœdic** verses.

We find series such as

—∪ —̆∪̄ —∪ —

denoted only by

— — —∪∪ —∪ —

where the first trochee, that which precedes the dactyl, appears as a spondee, its short as a spondaic long; while the short of the third trochee, that which follows the dactyl, remains unchanged in value.

Whereby, if the metre were to be performed as it is denoted, the following unmetrical formation would be produced.

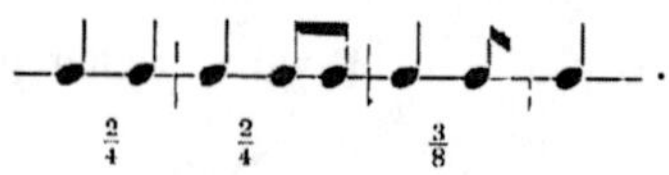

And if, notwithstanding, this marking should be allowed to represent the rhythm

then the question arises, how should a spondee stand for the first trochee, an undivided pair of feet for a divided foot?

The unlawfulness of putting one for the other is obvious. The first foot marked with two longs cannot, if a trochaic dactyl follows, be a real spondee, and the second long cannot be a metrical long.

164. It is well known that in the dipodic trochaic series the short of every second trochee is written over with a long.

—∪ —∪̄ —∪ —∪̄ —∪ —

The iambic series has the long marked upon the short of the first foot of every dipody.

∪̄— ∪— ∪̄— ∪— ∪̄— ∪—

The trochaic dipody forms by itself a metrical whole; it has its metrical first and second, and should the second die away in a weak echo, there it will want to end. If another dipody is to be produced out of the first, then the first must not end with weakness, the sound dying away; on the contrary it must show generative energy at that place. For this the short of the second trochee must receive a more generous, a superabundant fulness, swelling it out and joining it tighter to the following element; so that the boundaries of the dipodies are pressed together, and they pass into one another, and appear joined undividedly into a whole. The place contains a prosodic long in a metrical short, a fulness of syllable in a narrowly determined but extensible space of time. If these places are furnished with logically closing but prosodically trivial contents, then the series of dipodies is deprived of the tie to unite and cover the joins.

165. Moreover it is the same reason that requires the rhythmical or trochaic dactyl to be preceded always by this kind of seeming spondee, a trochee with more-than-filled short. When trochees and trochaic dactyls are joined, the dactyl will always require to keep the positive first place in the dipody.

1—2
—̆⏑̄ —⏑

It has the greatest energy of memberment, has more weight in the whole, is the stronger member, so that the trochee can follow as its weaker echo. A dactyl cannot, on the other hand, be produced after a trochee. In this latter succession the formation would merely tend to assume negative dipodic meaning;

2—1
—⏑ | —̆⏑̄

but then the trochee has in fact become second member, and the dactyl is first in positive meaning:

1 — 2   1 — 2
(—⏑) —⏑ | —̆⏑̄ (—⏑)

and the short before the dactyl is exactly that of the trochaic series, which has to unite two dipodies and therefore pretends to greater fulness. The difficulty of closing a metre with a dactyl is readily perceived; the dactyl always requires one more element to follow it.

—̆⏑̄ —

166. This must not by any means be taken as insisting that in metrical series the dactyl should occupy only the first place in the dipody. Most metres would be found to contradict that condition. But the dactyl cannot be an unaccented member in the series, as a second trochee can (disregarding the small accent which every long carries on its beginning).

Thus in the three-timed metre, whenever the second time is divided as a dactyl, it has rested upon its meaning of being first to the time which follows:

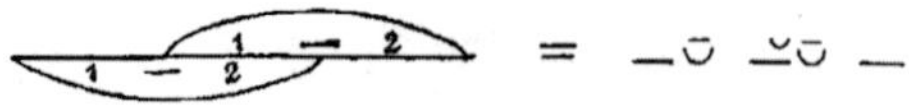

for the three-timed formation allows this increase of weight upon the second time as forerunner of the third. In four-timed formation

the third is the important time as against the fourth. Only this last remains unaccented in four-timed metre, as the third time in three-timed metre, and the second in two-timed. Accordingly the dactyl, with the condition of having to be **first** to a second member, may always be formed in any member of the metrical series with the exception of the last, which alone is a decided **second.** And so too the prosodically filled out short must precede the dactyl in every position, inasmuch as the latter begins a dipody, and the preceding trochee enters to it in metrical secondary meaning.

167. In the scheme previously given of the trochaic dactylic memberment for the two- and three-timed metres—the four-timed being considered as twice-two-timed for the purpose in hand, it was not found necessary to draw it out in its 81 forms—the combination of the three elements of unequal-timed division was shown to the full number of all possible cases. But in those forms which

close with a dactyl, in which, therefore, a decided second foot of a dipody has received dactylic division, a continuation is always felt to be necessary. Otherwise the metre, leaving off so, seems broken off, suspended. Dactylic memberment always requires to end with a non-dactylic member or part of a member following the dactyl.

168. Dactylic verses are measured by scansionists monopodically, i.e. the measure of the verse is named after the direct number of dactyls, and not reckoned by dactylic dipodies or tripodies, as trochaic and iambic verses are by dipodies and tripodies. If under the dactylic form the spondaic dactyl alone is to be understood, then, inasmuch as the real spondee embraces by itself a whole dipody, no objection could be made to this measurement. Only it must seem strange that anapæstic verses are not then measured likewise by the number of anapæsts, but in dipodies like iambics.

169. Whether all dactylic movement in spoken metre does not at bottom belong to the trochaic rhythm, might at any rate still be debated. Not that the spoken dactyl is obliged always to move exactly in the trochaic rhythm

For with equal justice might the strict spondaic rhythm

be deemed to suit all words of dactylic form. It seems, however, as if rhythmical enlivenment has its first origin in the trochaic element, to which the spondaic is ordained to form merely the metrical substructure. The metrical equal-timed formation, presented as two-, three-, and four-timed, lacks the rhythmical tension, the elastic nature, which first comes into the metre with the unequal-timed, or animating, distribution of the member; because then it contains the metrical opposition of first and second rhythmically united as single and double in one, whereby the divergence of metre is at last wholly negatived.

170. In the metamorphosis of plants, blossom-forming goes on the principle that the leaves, standing opposite one another on the stalk, are at the same time gathered round a centre or axis; from being separate in opposition, upon this side and that, they are congregated into the circle, into the unity of union. Thus the equal-timed metrical may be compared to the diametrically separated position of the leaves; the unequal-timed rhythmical to the centrally united. Similarly, trochaic in its abstract meaning may be put as the melody of metre, and spondaic as its harmony.

171. By the natural rhythm of words the strict metrical quantity of the spondaic dactyl must nevertheless be subject progressively to the most manifold modification; because, without forcing the metre very harshly, it is not practicable to continue speaking dactylic movement in the time of

Similarly the trochaic dactylic form too must always be ready to give way freely to the conditions of language. Although metrical quantity is determined independently in itself, yet in its reciprocal relation with the spoken contents which fill it out it nevertheless acquiesces in the rhythmical modifications which are the demands laid upon it by the latter. And it is the union of both together that gives the finished picture, metrically ordered and rhythmically animated, in form and contents correlated and made one.

172. If all dactylic movement is of trochaic nature, there will then have been obtained an explanation why trochees are rightly admitted in dactylic series as well as dactyls in trochaic series. On the other hand, it might then seem that the spondee is wrongly joined with the dactyl. But in places that may be regarded as

joining dipodies the spondaic form of word does not stand in the meaning of metrical spondee ; it then represents the trochee with the accented short, which in trochaic series may stand before every dactyl, consequently in every place except the last and the last but one.

173. All that has been said here about the difference between the spondaic and trochaic form of **dactyl**, will apply also to the **anapæst**, which we must accordingly distinguish into spondaic and iambic.

METRE-MARKING.

174. The customary way of marking verse-metre is wanting in means to discriminate accurately the fine shades of rhythm ; nor is it employed to disclose the inner metrical structure of verses. By the scheme which it presents we are taught only the order of succession of long and short syllables ; which taken by itself is but the surface, the outside of the edifice of verse.

We may pass by the circumstance that it makes trochees and iambuses with accented short equal to the real spondee, which embraces a trochaic or iambic dipody, and that it thereby represents doubtfully the total contents of the metre. But even then single metrical quantities strung nakedly together will give us no image of the inner conditions, on which a metrical formation as a whole rests ; the latter being always, not aggregated, but expanded from the metrical unity, an unfolding of the metrical notion that underlies the whole.

175. Thus, e.g., the **hexameter** is laid before us schematically in the following shape :

—⏔ —⏔ —⏔ —⏔ —⏔ —⏓.

From this series we cannot in the first place see whether the sixfold of its members consists of a twice-threefold or of a thrice-twofold. Nor yet is it evident whether the parts of the highest order shall be taken in positive succession or negative. Further, in lower order the pairs of members may be positive or negative, and thus doubly different, in themselves and in their succession. From all these different possible determinations, even if we have decided for one or the other assumption with regard to the highest order—viz. that the metre is a twice-twofold one, or a thrice-twofold—there will still result a sixfold difference in the metrical organic form: in fact any one of the six members may appear principally emphasised.

We must not confound what here is only doubtful multiplicity of meaning, nor even bring it into connexion, with what is called eth **rhythmical cæsura of the verse**:—which receives its determination from the logical contents, and, as is known, can in the hexameter enter at sixteen different places, namely after every single member of the dactyl. For now we are speaking only of the metrical form in itself, within which the shaping of the rhythm has afterwards its own special determinations. In metrical sense the question here, expressed in empiric musical fashion, is merely whether the sixfold of the metre is a $\frac{6}{8}$ bar or a $\frac{3}{4}$; further, whether it begins with the full bar, with the down beat, or with the up beat; and in the latter case, how many members belong to the up beat.

176. The six-membered metre as a twice-threefold,

I — 2

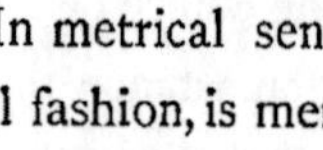

can be shown metrically in the six forms:

I —— 2,

2 —— I,

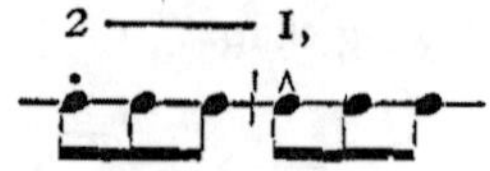

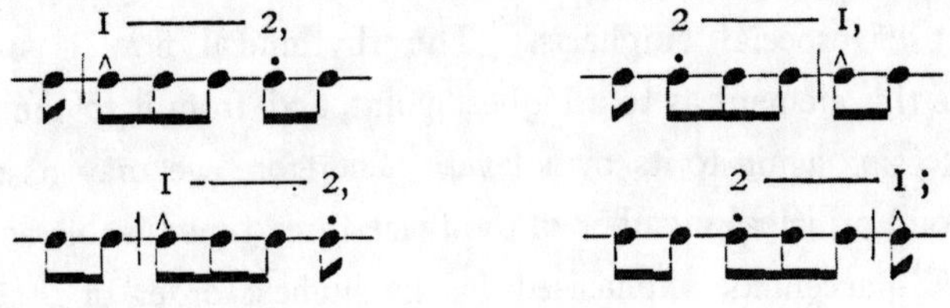

but as thrice-twofold,

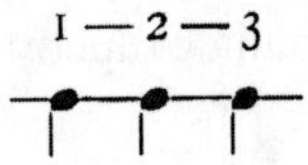

in the six forms:

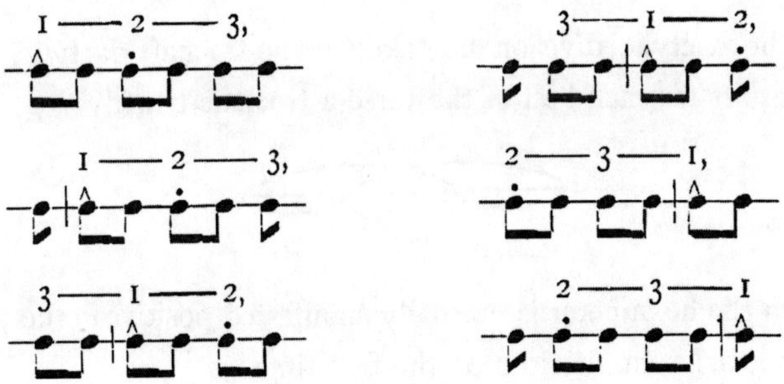

In these different metrical constructions, the organic conditions of which are known to us from what has gone before, the rhythmical determination, as given by the spoken contents according to logical meaning and independently of the metrical, may still be most manifold; for it is only in the accent-determination that it comes in contact with the metrical.

177. The possible meaning that such a series of members can assume being thus various, a closer representation is needed before metrical definiteness can be recognised in it. Knowledge of metre can come to us only from its practical use; here from the hexameter itself. Of this we know from experience that it has its principal section in the middle, consequently that it consists of a twice-three-timed formation; i.e. that it is a **tripodic dimeter.** Further, the beginning of the second half is perceived to be an

element of especial emphasis. The rhythmical flow is urged towards this element as to a highest point, and from it to the end seems to sink again to its own level. Therefore we may assume the second principal member of the twice-three-timed whole as the principally accented, emphasised in the highest order, or positive of that highest order. Thus the principal formation of the metre is determined as a rising spondaic dipody :

2 — I.

If the dactylic division be taken to be trochaic dactylic, then there results for each half of the verse a trochaic tripody:

–◡◡ –◡◡ –◡◡,

which in the hexameter is normally manifested positive in the pairs of members, i.e. emphasised on the first time.

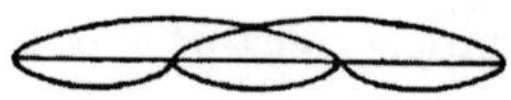

I — 2
I — 2.

But the dipodies themselves in the **first** half-verse are related oppositely to the emphasis of the members ; the second dipody is the accented one.

2 — I.

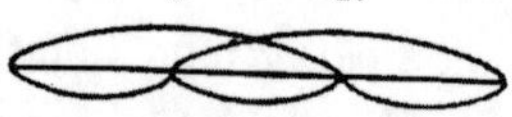

In the **second** half-verse the first dipody is accented :

I — 2;

the accent of the first half lies upon the second time, in the second half it is borne by the first time.

Accordingly the scheme of the whole appears in this shape:

2 — I I — 2.

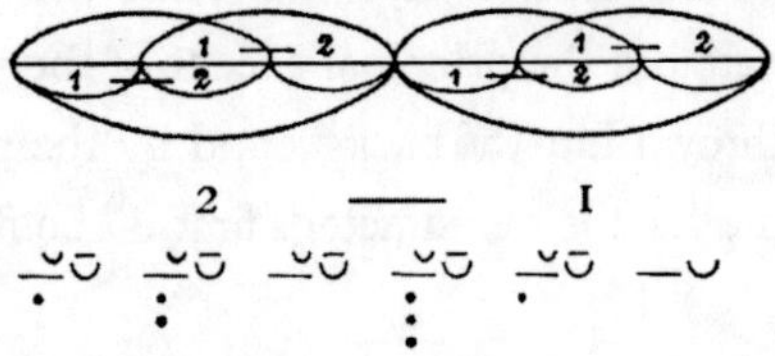

That dactylic division is not given to every trochee is known. The last but one will hardly do without it; on the other hand the third will the more readily, that in it the principal cæsura enters normally, whereby the short of this trochee unites with the long of that following, forming an iambic beginning to the second half of the verse, which contrasts as iambic with the trochaic first half.

178. To the hexameter is joined in elegiac metre the **pentameter.** It is the female hexameter. Like to the first verse in tripodic dimetric structure, the pentameter is contrary to it in carrying the principal weight upon the first half; the separated second half is a weaker echo of the first. In its principal formation the pentameter is a sinking spondaic dipody:

I — 2.

The other relations of memberment are the same in the pentameter as in the hexameter, and its scheme accordingly:

2 — I I — 2;

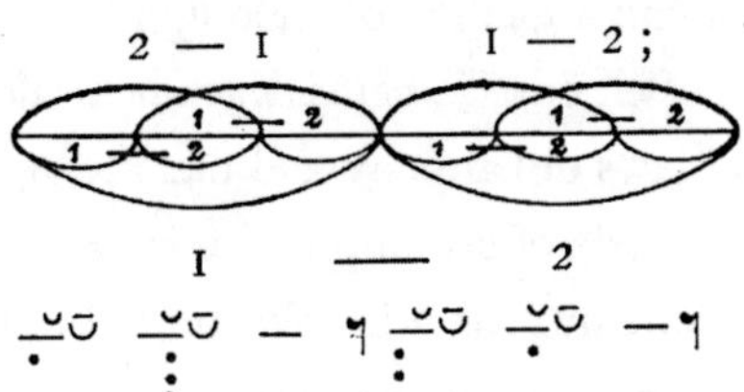

the positive half, which ends in the hexameter, begins in the pentameter.

179. Again, in the union of both verses into a **distich** the hexameter is itself the first half of the whole, and the pentameter the second half. Therefore the principal accent of the pentameter is a secondary one, thrown into the background by the principal accent of the hexameter; for the pentameter's first is the first in a second:

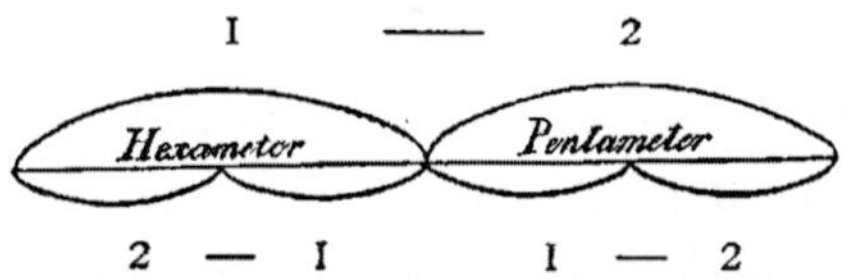

'In the Hexămeter rises the foûntain's silvery column;
In the Pentâmeter aye făllling in melody back.'

(Coleridge's Translation of Schiller.)

180. More might be said about the æsthetic conditions and requirements, as well as about the rhythmical cæsuras of this verse; but it must be withheld here, where a nearer consideration of this particular kind of metrical formation was undertaken altogether by way of example, as illustrating the general principle in a concrete form supposed familiar to us. To draw up a method of verse, theoretical and practical, an elucidation of the customary verse-measures with their specific peculiarities, again, does not lie within the scope of these investigations, any more than the preceding part, on Harmony, was meant to contain a method of thorough bass or instruction in the practical use of chords. There it was undertaken to investigate alone the natural laws of harmony and melody, upon which everything that can be made of use in practice is grounded. So here we have to set out alone in their principles the natural laws of rhythm and metre, which are the same in metre of music and of speech. We are dealing only with the rational ground of the phenomena, not with the phenomena themselves; these we must dismiss as soon as the firm basis is found for them. Everywhere threads of connexion

are left standing, which would have to be taken up in carrying out further the particular parts. But if the principle has been preserved, then it will be less difficult to follow out the intricacy of the numerous branches, and to see that the particular things of the phenomena are organically determined. If considered singly, or only outwardly placed together, they might easily seem to us arbitrary formations, which yet they in no wise are or can be.

CATALECTIC AND ACATALECTIC METRE.

Examples both in Spoken Metre and in Musical.

181. In the foregoing we have marked with a rest the termination of the two tripodies of the pentameter ; they end with the first member of the foot and leave the second unfilled :

–⏑⏑ –⏑⏑ –⏑̣ .

whereby the two halves of the verse appear separated, the tie which should unite them is wanting.

In scansion generally a distinction is made between **catalectic** and **acatalectic** metres : verses or parts of verses which leave a rhythmical member or even a foot unfilled at the end of their metre, and such as fill their measure quite up.

The verse, e.g., of the ancient drama, the **trimeter** :

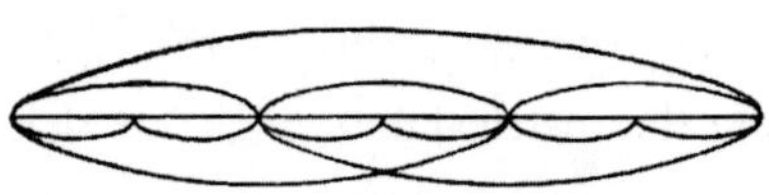

⏓–⏑–|⏓–⏑–|⏓–⏑–,

is **acatalectic** ; its three iambic dipodies are completely filled up.

The newer dramatic verse, the metre of the so-called five-footed iambics :

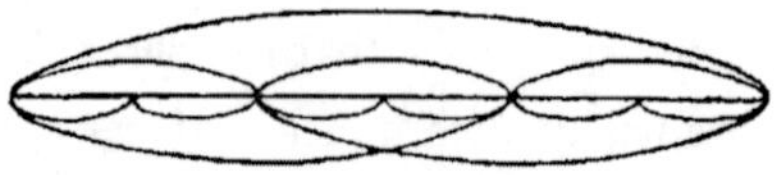

⏑ — ⏑ — | ⏑ — ⏑ — | ⏑ — ⏑ 𝄽

or :

⏑ — ⏑ — | ⏑ — ⏑ — | ⏑ — 𝄾

is of the **catalectic** kind. It is an iambic dipodic trimeter, like the former ; but it leaves one or two places empty at its end, either the last iambic long or the whole last iambus. According to the notion of musical time these places ought to bear rests before the beginning of the following verse. That, however, would only be practicable in cases where a logical cæsura, a break or breaking off in the thought, takes place ; which again precisely in this place ought not to occur too often, in order that the verses may not be detached lyrically, but joined into continued oration. Therefore a catalectic metre in its continuance is kept up more by shading the emphasis (which in itself has the power of betokening one rhythmical element against the others in its metrical meaning—i.e. as first, second, third, or fourth) than by progressive movement in bar.

182. Here at any rate is found an essential difference between the metre of music and that of speech ; for the former is not at liberty to begin a new bar before the last has quite run out. But also from the quality of its contents the necessity for its so doing can never arise ; since, being wholly bound to the metrical determination, and not subject to other conditions, the contents receive their shape in time from the metrical determination alone.

183. Yet another difference between spoken metre and musical consists in the former not offering the larger contrasts in the duration of its rhythmical elements that the latter does, in joining into metrical figures members of any length and any shortness. The

former combines metrically only single and double time-differences, modified variously, it is true, in practical use, but not so as to be capable of determination, and still only in the meaning of the above proportions.

Of the overlapping of several orders in the arrangement of the metre itself, in so far as it is twice-threefold, thrice-twofold, and so on, no mention is here necessary—for spoken metre has this in common with musical—but only of the differences of quantity which reach expression in the spoken syllables.

184. Vocal rhythm by itself, apart from metre, is in its shades of quantity comparable to the melody of speech, in which height and depth of sound are regarded as lending emphasis to words and syllables. The latter could hardly be represented in a determination by harmonic intervals, although it makes the vocal note rise and fall; nor would it be easier to establish a determination for the infinite gradations and transitions in which the rhythm of the parts of speech approaches the pure metrical forms, coincides with them, and again deviates from them; because in measured speech the rhythm preserves measure in the whole, and also is seemingly at one with it in the members.

But it would deserve to be called downright absurdity, to let oneself imagine that a poetically animated delivery must or could everywhere conform exactly to the mathematically determined forms of a rigid metrical system, or reflect it in all strictness. The metrical form is the solid skeleton, the bony framework, round which the soft parts, which the life inhabits, grow in rounded, mutually re-entrant forms, and, while they cannot do without the firm determined support, yet let it appear not at all, or only in veiled, softened, and apparently self-determining outlines.

QUANTITY AND ACCENT.

Difference between Ancient and Modern Verse.

185. The art of ancient verse has the determinations of vocal quantity for its formal elements: length and shortness of syllable. Modern verse substitutes for the long the accented or logically emphatic syllable, and for the short the unemphatic and unaccented. The modelling of the former art stands upon its own merits, is not directly affected by the emotional or mental life of the thing represented. For syllabic quantity is not determined by logical meaning. The short may be the logically emphatic syllable in a word, the long may be logically without accent.

So far therefore as the construction of verse follows determination of quantity, its metrical structure is quite independent of the sense contained. The form is therefore more self-sufficient; it can in itself be of metrical artistic importance. In modern verse, which seeks its accents in the logical meaning of syllables, the formal construction has not this self-sufficiency. Here the form is merged and lost in the contents; it is, if we compare the modern verse-metres with the ancient, altogether of less consequence artistically. Where the latter in their strophes afford an inexhaustible variety of rhythmical division, our verse in strophes for the most part consists merely of an alternation of rising and falling, measured in two, three, or four times. The metrical art-element plays so small a part, and is so much absorbed by the poetical contents, the logical meaning of the words, that now, to prevent the verse from being quite inartificial, another element is needed besides the metrical: such as, being again formally self-sufficient, is fit to carry the contents without being their slave. Such are **rhyme, assonance, alliteration.** These conditions of sound have no more interest in the contents than metre by quantity has. The inner references which creep in sometimes between rhyming words, as when **heart** and **smart, sweet** and **greet** are made to rhyme, are quite accidental; it is by no means the business of rhyme to hunt for them. Rhyme consists in pure and simple likeness of sound, and is in itself artistic form. So too with assonance, beginning with the same vowel, and alliteration (in German **Stabreim**), beginning with the same consonant, of which the most elaborate use is found in Scandinavian poetry.

186. To verse ruled by quantity we might ascribe more of a **plastic**, to modern accented and rhymed verse more of a **musical** nature; or in the former meet rather the principle of **form**, and in the latter rather the principle of **colour**. The accented strophe will hardly do without rhyme; to the strophe with quantity rhyme would be quite an unsuitable, even an unwelcome addition. Rhymed endings to the ancient strophe might be compared to colour upon a statue.

Then, again, verse by quantity is compared to polyphony in music, and accented verse to homophony. As verse by quantity tries to avoid coincidence of the logical cæsura with the metrical, so too the polyphonic phrase spins a web over its metrical form, and covers the cæsura of one part by the progression of another; while the homophonic phrase holds its parts in metrical unison, and accented metre, especially in verse destined for song, need not avoid the lyrical cæsura, but rather courts it.

Historically we see among the Greeks poetry by quantity and homophonic music, among the old Italians poetry by accent and polyphonic music standing together. In our time homophonic music and accented poetry are the more natural growth; polyphonic music and poetry by quantity belong more to the nursery of art.

187. But where, in the alliance of poetry and music, the latter is to have full play, there the poetry can only be controlled by **accent**;

for it must have the lyrical cæsura. The newer attempts to set ancient poetry to music have never fallen out otherwise than to the detriment of the poetry. The delicate distribution of the ancient metre is crushed under the weight of our self-sufficient musical forms; or else the music, in trying for a more intimate connexion, must make surrender of its own most special nature, because our song is less the emphasised word, than the contents of the words set to music in forms of independent musical value.

188. It has been said by a writer upon art, doubtless between jest and earnest, that in music poetry seems to have but one privilege; it may be bad with impunity. Poetic both in contents and expression it must always be, if it is to be capable of being represented musically. **Mattheson** pledged himself to set a placard to music. But the contents of a placard or a bill of fare could not be reached in the musical expression; though certainly joy at famous names in the first and at favourite dishes in the other would admit of being expressed musically. But to emphasise speech according to its verbal expression, to tint it in its single elements, cannot be the task of music, which by its nature has to do the precise opposite. Music has to express in the language of feeling **unitedly**, what intellectual language of words can only put **dividedly**, successively. Where the latter speaks of **gladness** and **sorrow**, and must name them separately, first one and then the other, there music can express, and ought to express, **sorrow in gladness**, and **gladness in sorrow**; but not to emphasise one word joyfully and the other mournfully.

Herein musical expression leaves the speech of poetry far behind; and the music, where not merely declamatory, not merely lending emphasis to words, will always take rank above the poetry. The verbal expression can make good no other demand upon the musical, than that it shall not be injured by unintelligent emphasis conflicting with the sense; but not that the music shall enter into all its particulars and try to express them by notes. For music emphasises the complex of feeling contained in the words, and not the words themselves.

Music may be compared to **algebra**, speech to **arithmetic.** What music contains in a general expression, language can only express as particular. An algebraical formula shows the factors in their mutual dependence and operation: the factors and the product in one. Arithmetic shows either the factors alone or the product alone. Algebra gives the universal meaning for infinitely many particular values that may be taken. Music is like it in this. One has often seen the experiment made of expressing the contents of a piece of instrumental music in words, in a poem. The result can never be satisfactory. If the algebraical expression makes $a+b=c$, and one chooses to replace this by $2+3=5$ with arithmetical values, this application of the formula is certainly quite a correct one. But there is an infinite number of other values to be put for *a* and *b*, which yield *c* as another sum, and where the combination of factors fulfils the purport of the formula just as correctly. So too the same music might be expounded verbally in the most different ways, and of none of them could it be said that it was exhaustive or that it contained the proper and the whole meaning of the music; for that is contained with the utmost definiteness only in the music itself. Music has not an indefinite sense; it tells the same tale to everyone; it speaks to men, and says only what men feel. But ambiguity comes to light when each in his own way seeks to comprehend in a particular thought the impression of feeling that he receives, trying to fix the fluid element of music and to utter the unutterable.

189. We see that as used in music metrical forms are not followed with mechanical strictness; because by conditions of harmony and melody, as well as of animated performance, they continually suffer small deviations from exact mathematical definiteness, which yet never seem like losing the time. But the metre of speech is in the

relative quantities of its members still far more given up to modifications by the conditions, logical and phonetical, of its contents—the words that fill it. The unequal-timed feet, the trochee and the iambus, with a sonorous or logically important syllable in their short, will often pass almost into equal-timed ; the trochaic dactyl may, by reason of syllabic contents and emphasis, assume the form of the spondaic dactyl or even of the tribrach, the form of equal-timed three-membered division ; thus it may appear as trochee with metrically divided long :

or even as trochee with metrically divided short :

and yet not give up its meaning of dactyl in rhythmical metrical determination. In like manner the iambic anapæstic form too will bend to the quality of its verbal contents and submit to manifold modification.

190. Not to be confounded with these rhythmical modifications arising from particular verbal contents, is the rhythm which in itself progresses only by equal times, such as arises from metrical construction without quantity, but with accent alone. Here the difference of long and short is in fact not present ; the change consists only in the succession of emphasised and unemphasised members, in rising and falling. Our rhymed verses are mostly of this kind.

191. But these are not alone in passing over the difference of long and short parts of time. Even in verses marked trochaic and iambic it is only brought out noticeably, where dactylic or anapæstic movement accompanies the trochaic and iambic. In pure trochaic or iambic lines there would be difficulty in continuously doing justice to rhythmical quantity, by double and single duration

of time. With the trochaic dactyl especially (and also, but less decidedly, with the iambic anapæst), if it follows soon after the beginning of the line, rhythm by quantity may make its appearance, and, being once started, it is then kept up through several members. Conversely, after a longish series of accented rhythm the dactyl may easily take the metrical equal-timed form; and then the succession is also further continued as equal-timed.

192. Musical metre always makes a much more definite distinction between equal- and unequal-timed movement. The $\frac{6}{8}$ bar cannot be changed for the $\frac{2}{4}$ bar without causing an interruption in the rhythm. In passing from one to the other a break is always felt, a change of the prime rhythmical condition.

In speech-metre, where the distribution of members has to be impressed upon the syllables of words, the rhythm adapts itself on the whole to the metrical relations; these, on the other hand, accept their modifications in particular from the rhythm. Here form and matter are both of elastic nature; they spread and contract according to the claims which the one enforces upon the other. Too small a syllable, however, is ill suited for filling the metrical long; while too heavy a syllable will resist being crowded into the metrical unaccented short. But in modern languages the logical accent, above all, is that which determines the metrical position of syllables; not only in accented, but also in quantitied metre.

193. In scansion the metrical positive first element is named the **arsis**, and the second the **thesis**. In musical meaning this is reversed; for the first part of the bar, the so-called 'strong' time, is called thesis, and the second part, the so-called 'weak' time, is called arsis. The expression **thesis** in music points to the down beat, with which the beginning of the bar is marked; the expression **arsis** in scansion for the same element of time to the lifting force with which the positive metrical determination begins. This difference might indeed have been assumed to be already known

to the reader; but for our purpose it seemed best to avoid these names altogether, because of their opposite meaning in music and prosody; lest the metrical notion, which is the same in both spheres, should, through these different names applied to the same thing, be brought into seeming contradiction with itself. Knowledge of technical names, as well as of the outward appearance of the things called by the names, has always been assumed in our treatise hitherto, and so we have used the names as known; our business being less with the outward appearance of the things named, than with their inner entity and connexion in unity.

III.

METRICAL HARMONY. HARMONIC METRE.

HARMONIC METRICAL DETERMINATION.

1. HAVING considered by themselves the process of harmonic melodic construction in the first place, and the metrical rhythmical in the second, it now remains to unite the two double factors into concrete unity as they exist in music, so wrapt up in one another that every element of harmony must have its meaning also as an element of melody, and at the same time also as an element of metre and of rhythm.

But melodic rhythmical does not admit of being gathered up into an abstract system, or of being developed in the way that harmonic metrical does. With the former, in the infinite multiplicity of the possible phenomena, nothing could be discussed except what is most general or most particular. With the latter, the particular can be comprehended in the universal, and from the whole can be deduced the explanation of each single thing.

The following contains only harmonic metrical investigation.

In the notion of a succession of notes or chords an advance in time is already expressed ; but still it has only the general meaning of sequence without any metrical determination necessarily being connected with it.

2. Now the first metrical determination is that of the succession of a first and second, a positive and relative, an accented and unaccented :

I — 2.

Its opposite is the same in inverted order:

2 — I.

3. Harmony also has its positive and relative in the notion of succession. We have similarly denoted it by I and II, as the relation of a dominant or subdominant triad to its tonic triad: I—V, I—IV, both included generally under the above expression: I—II.

Here again the 'other,' the opposite of these successions, is their inversion: V—I, IV—I, under the general expression: II—I.

4. In uniting the harmonic with the metrical notion—that is to say, in the harmonic metrical or metrical harmonic notion—we get, as in every twice-twofold combination, a fourfold possible relation of the harmonic determination to the metrical: *A* (*a*) harmonic positive in metrical positive; (*b*) harmonic positive in metrical negative; *B* (*a*) harmonic negative in metrical positive; (*b*) harmonic negative in metrical negative:

A. (*a*)	I—II 1—2,	(*b*)	I—II 2—1.
B. (*a*)	II—I 1—2,	(*b*)	II—I 2—1.

5. The positions in which the harmonic positive counts as metrical negative are not contradictory to rational meaning. Their sense is, that something **that has a relative**, harmonically, becomes something **that is a relative**, metrically; that in them a harmonic active is found as a metrical passive. A chord cannot be at the same time harmonically positive and harmonically negative: the triad *C—e—G* cannot at once be tonic and dominant; but it can, being tonic, occupy metrically positive or metrically relative position, just as a metrically positive element, though it cannot at the same time

be metrically relative, may have for its contents harmonic positive or relative.

6. Thus succession of consonant harmony is in itself as yet without determination for the metrical position of its successive members. The same series of consonant chords may take most different shape metrically, and thereby also become most manifoldly different in inner meaning. For even the succession of the triads *C—e—G*··· *G—b—D*, according as it is placed in metrically positive or negative order:

C—e—G b—D—G, C—e—G | b—D—G,
1 —— 2 2 —— 1

according therefore as it has its metrically positive, accented element upon the tonic chord or the dominant, lends expression in the first case to the notion of major, and in the second to the notion of minor; that is, to the notion of independence or to the notion of dependence, thus with the same harmony expressing opposite meanings; and if we continue with further triads in more advanced metrical formation, in three-timed or four-timed and in combined metre, we may be led to the greatest diversity of harmonic metrical meaning.

7. As with the triad, so also with its first inversion, the chord of the Sixth; which in itself contains no determination for metrical position. Among triad forms the Six-Four position alone in many cases is limited metrically to only one place or the other; the same position whose occurrence in harmony was subjected to multiplied conditions. Thus the Six-Four position of the tonic triad, when following the subdominant it passes into the dominant chord and leads to the close, will always require a metrically accented place, while its resolution into the dominant chord takes a second, unaccented place. Here it is the succession involved in the nature of the chord-position, and the condition of the closing element having

to be a metrical first, that imparts to the chord its metrical determination.

8. Otherwise it can only be said generally of groups of triads in this respect that no kind of metrical succession is unconditionally impossible in them. For as the successions of the triads:

1—2	1—2	2—1	2—1
C—G,	G—C;	C / G,	G / C;
I—V	V—I	I—V	V—I

contain united what is metrically and harmonically similar and also what is metrically and harmonically opposite; and as the unconnected dominant and subdominant chords may also succeed one another in a fourfold harmonic metrical sense, as:

1—2	1—2	2—1	2—1
F—G,	G—F;	F / G,	G / F;
IV—V	V—IV	IV—V	V—IV

so too every passage from the tonic triad into the conjunct minor triads:

$$\overset{1\,-\,2}{C-\begin{cases}a\\ e,\end{cases}}\qquad \overset{1\,-\,2}{\begin{rcases}a\\ e\end{rcases}-C;}\qquad \overset{2\,-\,1}{C/\begin{cases}a\\ e,\end{cases}}\qquad \overset{2\,-\,1}{\begin{rcases}a\\ e\end{rcases}/C;}$$

or into the disjunct diminished triads:

$$\overset{1\,-\,2}{C-\begin{cases}D^{\circ}\\ b^{\circ},\end{cases}}\qquad \overset{1\,-\,2}{\begin{rcases}D^{\circ}\\ b^{\circ}\end{rcases}-C;}\qquad \overset{2\,-\,1}{C/\begin{cases}D\\ b^{\circ},\end{cases}}\qquad \overset{2\,-\,1}{\begin{rcases}D^{\circ}\\ b^{\circ}\end{rcases}/C;}$$

may be placed in all the various metrical determinations of succession.

9. In these successions the chord in the position of relative, if it belongs to the subdominant side, will also seem akin to the subdominant chord; and if it belongs to the dominant side, akin to the dominant chord. So that the successions

$$\begin{matrix}\text{I—VI}\\ \text{C—a}\end{matrix}\ \text{and}\ \begin{matrix}\text{I—II°}\\ \text{C—D°}\end{matrix}$$

veil the meaning

$$\begin{matrix}\text{I—IV}\\ \text{C—F,}\end{matrix}$$

and the successions

$$\begin{matrix}\text{I—III}\\ \text{C—e}\end{matrix}\ \text{and}\ \begin{matrix}\text{I—VII°}\\ \text{C—b°}\end{matrix}$$

the meaning

$$\begin{matrix}\text{I—V}\\ \text{C—G.}\end{matrix}$$

Now, since it is principally the Third that in these secondary chords suggests the subdominant or the dominant, because the subdominant chord here is touched by *a*, and the dominant by *b*; therefore the minor triad on the subdominant side, because it contains both Root and Third of the tonic triad, is also fit to represent the tonic triad itself. So much depends here upon the particular position, upon the prominence of one or another interval of the chord, that to establish an abstract, universally valid, determination for the substitution of secondary for principal chords, is not possible. In concrete cases it will always be easy to perceive, and express, the meaning.

10. In the scale, whose degrees, as before was shown, are determined in the major key by the three notes of the tonic triad, a change always takes place between tonic and dominant or subdominant chords :

C ·· D ·· e ·· F ·· G ·· a ·· b ·· C
I — V — I, IV — I — IV
(VI—III—VI)
I — V — I.

To a tonic chord, I, answers directly the metrical positive, 1 ;

to the chord of the Fifth above or below, II, answers the metrical relative, 2.

According to this the metrical position of the scale notes up to the sixth degree will be:

I — V I — IV I — IV
C ·· D ·· e ·· F ·· G ·· a
1 — 2, 1 — 2, 1 — 2.

But from the sixth degree onwards it is:

I—V I
a ·· b ·· C
1—2, 1.

Therefore the sixth degree has metrically relative meaning to the fifth degree, metrically positive meaning to the seventh degree. In every sense at this place there will always be found a drag upon the progression, rhythmical as well as harmonic. Here, if metrical positive is to coincide with harmonic positive, this sixth degree in changing its harmonical determination must also receive metrically twofold determination, first relative and then positive. This can be done by doubling or halving the metrical value of the place, letting it be repeated or else conjoining it with the seventh degree:

G — a | a — b | C, or G — a — b | C.
1 — 2 | 1 — 2 | 1 1 — 2
  1 — 2 | 1

In both ways the sixth degree counts as relative to the fifth degree and positive to the seventh degree, and the metrical determination squares fully with the harmonic.

11. It is now plain that here in the scale, as in the beforementioned triad successions, the metrical determination may in every

way come into opposition with the harmonic, in every sense go chequer with it; because the scale can only have degrees determined by the interconnexion of triads. They are determined, however, not by most nearly related triads connected in the Third, but only by triads connected in the Fifth, related in the second degree. The former imply melodic quiescence principally, advance only secondarily. In the latter melodic advance is the principal thing; the harmonic support is secondary, subordinate.

METRICAL POSITION OF DISSONANCE.

12. With the entrance of dissonance there also comes in a more definite appointment of metrical position in the harmonic phrase.

We know dissonance in two principally distinguished kinds: **suspension** and **Seventh-harmony.**

The resolution of the suspension follows, or may follow, without alteration of the Root-harmony of the chord in which it is contained dissonantly.

By the resolution of the Seventh chord a new Root-harmony is necessarily brought about.

(*a*) **In the Chord of Suspension.**

13. The passage from one triad into another closely connected with it does not give rise to a chord of suspension; this can result only from passage into a triad that is principally **not** connected, more separated than connected. Hence suspension can never arise but with the appearance of a triad essentially different to the preceding one, related to it in the Fifth or altogether separate. Moreover, its resolution is not upon an essentially different harmony, but upon the Root-harmony of the chord of suspension itself. With this,

then, is given the determination that this dissonance must be a metrical First and its resolution a metrical Second; that the dissonance must stand upon the accented part of the bar, and the resolution upon the unaccented part. For with the dissonance a new harmony has entered, which is not altered in the resolution and merely draws after it a necessarily following second element. Dissonance and resolution belong to the same Root-harmony, and so stand in metrical positive unity as a first and second member. Every suspension has the metrical **first** place, and its resolution the metrical **second.**

(*b*) **In the Seventh Chord.**

(*a*) *In the Untransposed Key-System.*

14. The dissonance of the Seventh chord is introduced in two different ways: it is prepared either in the Seventh or else in the Root, according as the Seventh chord contains in simultaneous sound the passage into a triad lying above or into a triad lying below.

Thus from the passage of *C—e—G* to *a—C—e* arises the Seventh-harmony *a—C—e—G* in the position *C—e—G—a*, for the Fifth of the major triad on *C* has progressed to the Root of the minor triad on *a*, and has at the same time remained stationary as Fifth: the dissonance in *C—e—G—a* is prepared by the Seventh *G*. And this *G* becomes Seventh by the entrance of the **Root** *a*.

15. The opposite passage, from the triad *a—C—e* to the triad *C—e—G*, gives rise, when framed as harmony, to the same Seventh chord *a—C—e—G*; and in the position *G—a—C—e*, for here *a* has progressed to *G*. But in this succession it is the **Fifth** of the new triad that enters dissonantly to the Root of the first.

The succession *a—C—e···G—C—e* = *G—a—C—e* determines no new basis with its second element; but the succession

C—e—G···C—e—a = C—e—G—a does. The Seventh chord of the last succession, as arising from the entrance of the Root, will require to have the metrical **first** place, the accented element. But in the Seventh chord of the succession *a—C—e···G—C—e* the basis of the second triad is already contained in the first; it does not enter with a new Root, it only brings the Fifth to a Root already present, and the Fifth is a harmonic secondary or relative. Therefore metrically it will not take a primary, positive, first, or accented position, but rather that which corresponds to its harmonic meaning, i.e. relative or secondary: it will find its place upon the **second**, unaccented metrical element. Thus the prepared Seventh stands normally upon the 'strong' part of the bar, and the passing Seventh upon the 'weak' part.

This harmonic metrical determination is valid for all Seventh-harmonies which are combined within the untransposed system from two real triads, one major and one minor, i.e. for all those in which, as we have earlier seen, the Seventh could not enter ascending to the Root.

(β) *In the Transposed Key-System.*

16. There are also the Seventh chords that contain the joined limits of the system. We were then able to consider the system as transposed within itself, having its middle divided up and taken for limits, and its limits joined and taken for middle. Thus the systems of the C major and C minor keys:

(e) G—b—FF—a—C (e)
(e♭) G—b—FF—a♭—C (e♭)

are characterised by the element *FF*, the Root of the subdominant sounding with the Fifth of the dominant. In these Seventh chords the Seventh might move upwards to the Root. Unlike those contained within the untransposed system, they do not consist of a union of two overlapping triads; they are combined out of the dominant and subdominant chords, that is, from triads that are decidedly separate. Also their production, unlike that of the others, is not governed by conditions of passage, for they are not necessarily produced only from the succession of the two triads contained in the Seventh-harmony: in fact, one at least of these is here a diminished triad and therefore not truly a triad.

17. What was earlier said of the nature of these Seventh-harmonies need not be repeated in this place, nor how that special character is contained in them which they have over those of the untransposed system. We will here lay stress only upon one characteristic; that in the Seventh chords of the transposed system we have elements of like harmonic meaning sounding together to form the dissonance, while in the Seventh chords of the untransposed system there is always the Fifth of one triad sounding dissonantly with the Root of another.

In the Seventh chords:

I I
G—b—D/F,

III III
b—D/F—a,

II II
D/F—a—C,

there are in the first the Roots of the subdominant and dominant *F* and *G*, in the second the Thirds of the subdominant and dominant *a* and *b*, in the third the Fifths of the subdominant and dominant *C* and *D*, confronting one another and forming dissonance.

The Seventh chords:

I II
F—a—C—e,

I II
a—C—e—G,

I II
C—e—G—b,

I II
e—G—b—D,

on the other hand, all of them mean by their dissonance, that the Fifth of the upper triad stands in contradiction with the Root of the lower, or rather that sounding together they give rise to the contradiction in the interval that lies between.

18. Now in every case, since the dissonant notes cannot come together simultaneously, for that would lie beyond all interpretation, they can only bring about the dissonance by entering successively, coming one after the other. The notes must enter successively in the order either of Root and Fifth, or of Fifth and Root. The metrical equivalent meaning is then plainly found in the order of first and second, or of second and first: to the Root as Seventh belongs the first metrical place, and to the Fifth the second:

But those Seventh chords which are contained in the transposed system oppose as elements of dissonance, not a Root against a Fifth, but two harmonic elements of like determination: Root against Root, Fifth against Fifth, Third against Third. Here, then, a self-evident metrical determination for the position of the dissonance-chord, according as it is prepared in the Seventh or in the Root, is no longer to be found. At least it is not given in the difference of the dissonant notes according to their harmonic meaning, as it is in those Seventh chords in which Root and Fifth are dissonant; for here the Seventh is of like harmonic meaning with the Root. Both confront one another as the same elements of the subdominant and dominant chords, and may, at any rate according to the harmonical meaning which they have with respect to their own triads, with equal right lay claim to equal places. And so in fact we see the Seventh chords of the transposed system, i.e. those which contain its limits joined as middle—in the key of C major:

G—b—D | F, b—D | F—a, D | F—a—C;

and in the key of C minor:

G—b—D | F, b—D | F—a♭, D | F—a♭—C,

with prepared Seventh, occupying the metrical second time with good, irreproachable effect, and having both their preparation and their resolution upon metrical firsts.

19. A sequence of prepared Seventh chords with their resolutions into the corresponding triads, where the Seventh chord is taken upon the second time and the resolution upon the first, cannot but prove strained and unnatural in the dissonance-harmonies of the untransposed system. But in the dissonance-harmonies of the transposed system, nothing faulty is perceived. For there the metrical arrangement with preparation of the Seventh on the first time and entrance of the Root on the second is as well founded as the reverse. Root and Seventh being harmonically of equal dignity, neither is preferred before the other.

20. The following series:

$$C \mid F_{\natural} - b^{\circ} \mid e_{7} - a \mid D^{\circ}_{7} - G \mid C_{\natural} - F \mid b^{\circ}_{7} - e \mid a_{7} - D^{\circ} \mid G_{7} - C,$$

which with this metrical arrangement contains the dissonance-chord upon the first time, cannot seem otherwise than unexceptionably correct in each element. If the same series is placed in metrically opposite order:

$$\mathrm{C} - \mathrm{F}_{\not 7} \mid \mathrm{b}^{\circ} - \mathrm{e}_{7} \mid \mathrm{a} - \mathrm{D}^{\circ}_{7} \mid \mathrm{G} - \mathrm{C}_{\not 7} \mid \mathrm{F} - \mathrm{b}^{\circ}_{7} \mid \mathrm{e} - \mathrm{a}_{7} \mid \mathrm{D}^{\circ} - \mathrm{G}_{7} \mid \mathrm{C},$$

we then see the dissonances fall upon the second, unaccented time, and this cannot correspond to the weight with which the Seventh chords of the untransposed system enter. The Seventh chords *F—a—C—e*, *a—C—e—G*, *C—e—G—b*, *e—G—b—D* find their fitting place only upon the metrical first time.

21. On the other hand the Seventh chords *G—b—D|F*, *b—D|F—a*, *D|F—a—C* quite readily adapt themselves to the unaccented place. With the chords *G—b—D|F*, *b—D|F—a* there is unmistakably felt the entrance into the other region of dissonance, different to that in which the rest of the Seventh chords have their being. With the Seventh chord *D|F—a—C* this is less noticeable; because, as has already been remarked in cases where it has occurred, the diminished triad *D|F—a* may easily be confounded with the minor triad *d—F—A*, or the latter may really be substituted for the former; and then the chord appears, like the Seventh chords *a—C—e—G* and *e—G—b—D*, as one of those that must fall upon the metrical first time.

In the minor key no ambiguity is found at this place: the chord *D|F—a♭—C* is in relation to the minor key-system of precisely the same nature as *D|F—a—C* in the major; in its effect, however, it is of a more decided kind, and is not liable to be confounded with a Seventh chord of the untransposed system. Hence also it can be placed metrically second with less hesitation than can the chord corresponding to it in the major key.

SUMMARY OF THE FOREGOING CHAPTER ON THE METRICAL POSITION OF DISSONANCE.

22. As existing in harmony, every dissonance-chord is at once a first and a second. It is second in consequence of the previous preparation of the dissonance, and first in respect of its resolution, which necessarily follows. But, metrically, prominence is given to one harmonic relation or to the other, according as the dissonance is either determined by a Root newly added to the chord, or as it enters against a Root already present.

In constructing the dissonance of the chord of suspension, the dissonant element is always metrically first, accented; for here the dissonance arises by a new Root entering. Its resolution is metrically second and unaccented; it ensues without essential alteration of harmony.

In the construction of the Seventh chord the dissonant element is metrically first if the dissonance is prepared in the Fifth of the upper triad, and metrically second if in the Root of the lower triad. But it may be first or second, if the dissonance is not between a Root and Fifth, but between chord-elements of equal order, which then can only be equal elements of the opposed dominant and subdominant chords.

Suppose that the harmonic process of dissonance-construction may again be represented generally under the form

I — II
    I — II,

in which the middle doubly determined member is to signify the chord of dissonance, the first member the chord of preparation, and the last the chord of resolution. Then the metrical determination joined with the harmonic will give a twofold result. It must take as accented either the first harmonic member or the second, the element of preparation or the element of dissonance ; then the third member, the element of resolution, is, in consequence of the determination of the second, at once determined as accented or not accented.

The harmonic metrical determination is accordingly either :

I—II
I—II or I—II
I—II
1—2 | 1 ··, ··2 | 1—2.

Under the first of these forms appears the so-called passing Seventh ; and such Seventh-formations as have their origin in the transposed system will also be adapted to it : pre-eminently the dominant Seventh chord and the Seventh chord upon the Third of the dominant ; less unrestrictedly the Seventh chord upon the Fifth of the dominant in the major key, for reasons previously discussed.

Under the second form the dissonance of suspension is always represented ; also Seventh chords of the untransposed system when not prepared in the Root ; while those of the transposed system may thus appear, and in tied harmony they mostly will.

DISSONANCE IN THREE- AND FOUR-TIMED METRE.

23. Hitherto, in its bearing upon combined harmony and metre, the behaviour of first and second time has alone been taken into consideration. Now two-timed metre is but the beginning of metrical construction, which goes on to three- and four-timed, finding in these two elements its development and completion.

By this further formation the accent-determination becomes combined. In the three-timed, as well as in the four-timed metre, the second time is no longer unaccented; in the three-timed only the third, and in the four-timed only the fourth is without accent. But now the accents appear in different orders. The two-timed metre contains only one simple order of accents; but in the three-timed we find them doubly, and in the four-timed triply superposed. And a metrical member, which in a higher order is without accent, but in a lower order is accented, may claim this accent for the harmonic meaning in its order.

Thus a harmonically accented element, which in the positive two-timed metre can only coincide with the first time, may in the three-timed coincide with the first and second times, and in the four-timed with the first, second, and third.

24. In the three-timed metre the first time is doubly accented, the second is singly accented, and the third is without accent. Hence on the last time can stand only the unaccented dissonance, or passing Seventh, which is prepared in the Root, and also the dissonance-chords belonging to the union of the dominant and subdominant. But the suspension and the Seventh prepared in the upper Fifth may occur on the second time just as well as on the first. The preparation then happens, in the first case upon the first time, in the second case upon the preceding third time.

25. In the four-timed metre, in which only the fourth time is wholly without accent, everything holds true of it that was said of the third time in the three-timed. But what was true of the first two times of the three-timed metre cannot without restriction be applied to the first three times of the four-timed. In the four-timed the first time is triply accented, the second singly, and the third doubly. Therefore the four-timed metre lays stress principally upon its first time and its third as accented; while on the other hand the second with its single accent, that of the member,

certainly not seem fitted to carry an element of heavy harmonic emphasis. On this account the harmonically accented dissonance-elements, the suspension and the tied Seventh in the real combination of triads, will fall only to the first and third members of the four-timed metre; but the second, feebly accented, member, coming after the triply accented first, and also the unaccented fourth, following the doubly accented third, can only receive the harmonically unaccented passing Seventh.

In place of the latter the other not necessarily accented dissonance-harmonies may also enter, as is manifest, since they may even occupy wholly unaccented metrical places.

SYNCOPATION.

26. In the three- and four-timed metres, in closed formation, the weak member of one pair is covered by the strong member of another, and is in its turn made prominent by accent; and such an arrangement of members in linked positive pairs may also be carried further and continued in a series.

27. Every series of progressive formation necessarily affords already a double point of view. A series of major chords contains in it at the same time a series of minor chords; and similarly in the metrically positive series a negative series is simultaneously contained:

B♭ — d — F — a — C — e — G — b — D — f♯ — A

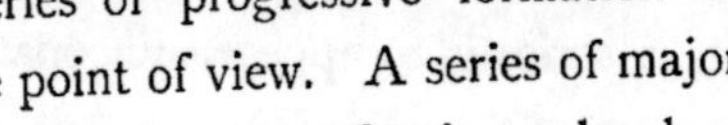

The metrically separated pairs of the positive series are united by the pairs of members of the negative series; and here we must refer the reader to what has been said in its place about the notion of the close and about the difference between metrical and rhythmical unity.

28. But the linking of members now to be considered is of another kind. The second member of one pair is here joined with the first of the pair following, not as having the meaning that belongs to them already as members in the positive series, i.e. not as a negative pair, but as a positive pair again.

In music this proceeding is known to us under the name of **syncopation**, which joins a metrically second member to the following first member in positive undivided unity, and lends an accent to the unaccented member:

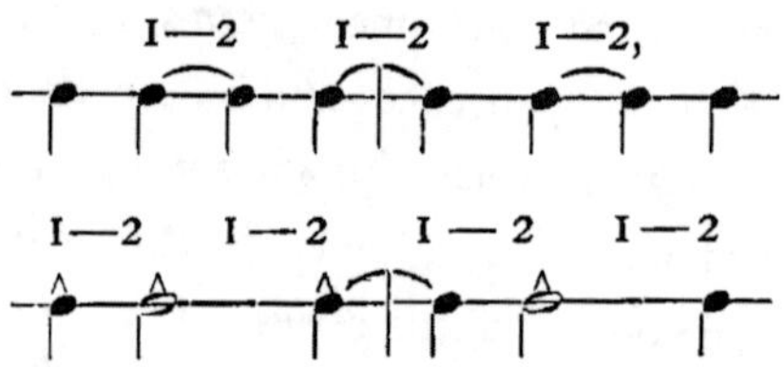

29. If, however, a series is to appear syncopated, then the unsyncopated series must at the same time be present with it; for without the normal series, of which the syncopated forms the metrical contradiction, the syncopated would itself be shown normally accented. The above would seem a series commencing with an up beat.

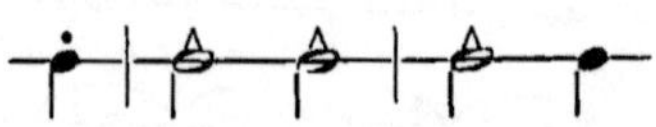

The syncopated movement will be yielded as such only if the accented elements of the normal series are marked at the same time with it.

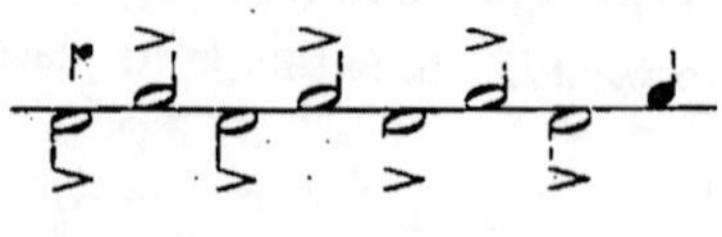

Consequently, to exhibit syncopation, two parts at least are required, of which one contains the normal, the other the syncopated emphasis. But this condition of two-partedness is only absolute where the syncopation enters undivided, without distinction of a second element. Otherwise a phrase might have syncopated emphasis, and yet in its memberment always allow the normal metrical structure to show through, as we have before seen many times in rhythms accented upon the second metrical element.

30. In such syncopations, ligatures, and ties from a second time-element to a first, the latter cannot have longer duration than the former; as is seen to be the natural conclusion when we consider that both elements here stand to one another in the relation of a first member to a second, just as in the two-timed metrical unity by itself. Starting from a metrical beginning, there is nothing to prevent us from lengthening the duration of the member put first; for its duration from the beginning is self-determining, and not determined, as is that of the second element. But where the latter, being already determined in its duration, is taken as positive first, there its relative second cannot be more than equal to it. It may indeed have shorter duration, because the actual filling up of the measure need not be complete; but not longer, because the contents cannot exceed the measure.

31. Consequently a tie from a shorter to a longer portion of time:

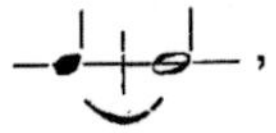

is on the face of it always something metrically untrue. The syncopated first time can only have a second of equal or less duration united with it; a longer would be, relatively to the preceding member, more than single, and being then related within itself as first and second, it breaks up the inner unity of the tie: it makes an accent felt.

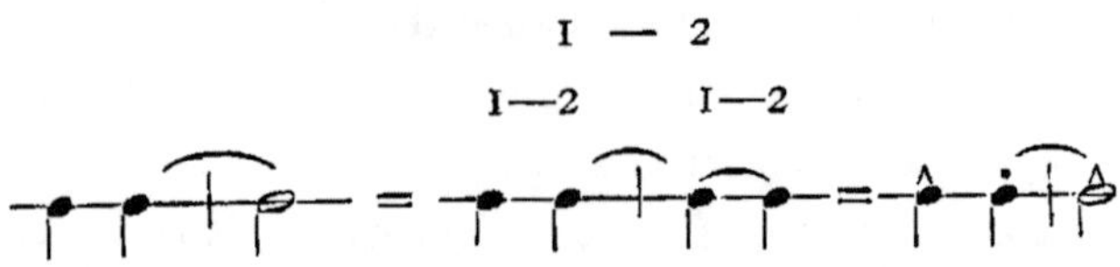

From this it follows that those forms (included above with the others) of filling up the four-timed metre, in which an undivided triple follows the single time,

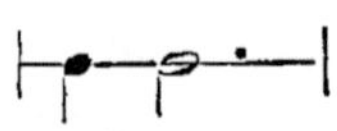 and 

are not metrically justified, which is why they are instinctively rejected. For in them a double containing the third and fourth is tied to the single second member.

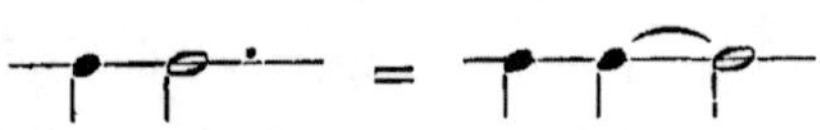

32. All such rhythmical arrangements, in places where they occur (as they can occur) with excellent effect, are intelligible as something out of the common way, the expression of particularity, or of that which is not of universal validity; and may therefore act as rhythmical passionate excitement or as rhythmical stimulus. But where such particularity is not intended, or not given in the structure of the phrase, there they seem mere lawlessness, a diseased rhythm in a healthy metre.

33. What has just been discussed is only connected with the metrical conditions for the treatment of dissonance in the requirement by which the tied dissonance in general has a claim to a metrically accented element. But it is not by any means insisted upon, that the duration of the chord of preparation shall be equal to the duration of the chord of dissonance; only that the tied dissonant note itself must not be longer than the consonant note which prepares and precedes it. The resolution of the dissonance

may equally well follow later on, after other harmonic intermediate notes; for the law of the tie, which requires the length of the preparing note to be equal to that of the note tied to it, is a rhythmical metrical law on its own account: it is the same for consonant and dissonant harmony, and is no more touched by particular harmonic conditions than, in its turn, it imposes particular conditions on them.

HARMONICAL CORRESPONDENCE OF THE SUCCESSION OF LINKED SEVENTH CHORDS WITH THE METRICALLY SYNCOPATED SERIES.

34. Now if a syncopated series in union with the normal one contains in each of its metrical members an accented element—with alternate normal and syncopated accent—then in this view every member of such a series should also be able to bear an accented dissonance-harmony. A succession of linked Seventh chords, such as we have previously seen formed with three kinds of passages, in the two first running on, in the third periodically interrupted ('Harmony,' pars. 155–160), answers in harmonic sense to the metrically syncopated series. Each of the dissonance-elements immediately following one another is at once a harmonic First and Second; in the meaning of First (I) it is dissonance, in the meaning of Second (II) it is resolution and preparation.

35. But the syncopated progressive series is metrically intelligible only as periodic, as numbered in two, three, or four times; and the accents of higher orders will prevail in it above the accents of members emphasised with equal strength. Hence particular elements of the series are put forward as places of principal accent and as principally suitable for the tied dissonance. Thus in the

three-timed metre the second member as compared with the first, in the four-timed the third member as compared with the first, or the second with the third, will seem always of slight metrical weight; while, as compared with the rest, the fourth in the four-timed, or the third in the three-timed—being wholly without accent in the formation by itself, and having only the syncopated accent—will have the weakest emphasis of all, and therefore will be the least fit to receive heavily emphasised dissonances. To these places will be allotted by preference one of the Seventh-harmonies that may stand even upon an unaccented time. Such are the Seventh chords of the transposed system, and among them pre-eminently that chord of the dominant Seventh which leads irresistibly to the tonic close, and next to it the Seventh chord upon the Third of the dominant.

36. But in the succession of linked Sevenths, in the sense of syncopation, every metrical place may bear an accented dissonance. The dissonance of suspension alone cannot acquiesce in removal from normal into syncopated accent; for its resolution must necessarily fall upon the normally unaccented place.

37. And here it must be called to mind that the determination of first and second metrical element, so often named, is repeated in every order, and no other is conceivable, and therefore everything that has been said relating to syncopation and position of dissonances is equally true for all orders. Thus in distribution by bars the application is the same, whether made to members of the simplest or of the most complicated uniform partition. The first member of the two-part division, the first and third of the four-part, the first, third, fifth, and seventh of the eight-part, and so on, receive with respect to their order the meaning of a normal First; the uneven numbers marking the normal accents, and the even, 2, 4, 6, 8 ···, denoting what is without accent or has to be accented by syncopation.

38. In all organic existence the mutual interaction of opposite factors has always to be recognised in the notion of unity; and here too, when harmonic and metrical determinations are contrasted, it should not escape us, that in essence both are really but one and the same thing seen as determined from one side or from the other, and that in the concrete whole the one ought only to be intellectually distinguished, but not separated from the other. The prepared chord of dissonance does not seek for a metrical place that shall be in itself accented; but itself determines the place on which it stands as a metrical first or accented. Because, harmonically, it must have a second to follow it, therefore it must of itself be a first in time. Yet, as spoken metre has to unite logical and metrical accent, and cannot let heavily emphasised syllables fall upon light times; so too will musical metre demand that first-timed and heavily emphasised dissonance shall not be given a place that should by the natural metrical order be unaccented.

APPENDIX.

A SHORT ANALYSIS OF HAUPTMANN'S TREATISE.

HAUPTMANN'S book is divided into three parts, treating respectively of Harmony, of Metre, and of Harmony and Metre combined.

I. The first part begins with a short deduction of the triad from acoustical notions. The triad is shown to be made up of three factors or elements, whereof two are in their nature antithetical, and the third is such as to bring about reconciliation of the other two, and to stand as a link between them, so that the three elements stand together in a unity that both contains and is made up of them. Also the three elements are not utterly distinct and as it were disjoined from one another, but connected organically and fused together.

These are the *Root*, the *Fifth*, and the *Third* ; and if regarded as generated successively (which yet in reality they are not) the Root is the original unity that generates or gives rise to the triad ; but with respect to the acoustical notions the Root—that is, the musical sound—is a derived or generated unity.

Now the fundamental idea of the philosophy is that every notion—as key, scale, Seventh chord, resolution, and so on—is made up after this fashion ; i.e. that it possesses three elements involving an antithesis and a reconcilement, and that one of the three elements is the Root from which the other two, and so the whole construction, springs. This Hauptmann regards as self-evident, and it is the basis of Hegelian metaphysics.

Thus from the triad posited as unity springs the key, a triad of triads ; and from the key as unity springs the system of modulation, comprising the tonic, the dominant, and the subdominant keys, or we may say modulation in general.

Again, the chord is of its nature simultaneous ; but the key can only be manifested in succession. This antithesis of 'simultaneous' and 'successive' is identified with the antithesis of harmony and melody, which are opposed, though one involves the other. As the chord represents simultaneous sound, harmony, so the scale, the diatonic succession, represents successive sound, melody.

Now if successive sound, i.e. the diatonic interval, be taken as simultaneous, this is a contradiction, successive and simultaneous being antithetical. And it is this contradiction that is the essence of *dissonance*, which in this light, i.e. as involving a contradiction or unreality, is a *Fifth*-notion. The other two elements are the chord of preparation, from which springs the dissonance, and the chord of resolution, which produces reconcilement of dissonance with consonance, and so is the *Third*-element.

Dissonance is treated in two kinds : the chord of suspension and the Seventh chord. Both contain succession taken as simultaneous ; but in the Seventh chord it is a succession of adjacent chords, in the chord of suspension it is a succession only of adjacent notes. The dissonance of the Seventh chord is the completer notion, and historically is later. It is the complete antithesis of consonance, and only by its antithesis of dissonance is the notion of consonance completed.

Another antithesis or opposition that occurs frequently is that of *major* and *minor*. The minor triad is a major triad measured in the opposite direction, an inverted major triad. Thus the notion of major and minor in music corresponds to that general one of positive and negative ; as, e.g., when a straight line is reckoned positive if measured in one direction, and negative if measured in the opposite direction. The major or positive is the primitive notion and is presupposed in the negative or minor, of which it is the positive premise.

There are also to be noticed two special phases of the key-system. One is when a key tends to pass into its dominant key and yet not fully accomplishes the transition ; when it takes as it were but half a step. Then there is subsisting a key-system intermediate between that of the original key and that of the dominant. For example, *f*♯ appearing in the key of C major does not necessarily indicate a complete modulation into the key of G major, which the chord *D—f*♯*—A* would indicate. In half-closes upon the dominant it often happens that e.g. in the key of C major an *f* sharp occurs without a modulation being effected into the dominant.

Hauptmann names this the system *stretching out* or *in extension*, and several chords are to be referred to it.

In the other phase the key-system is regarded as passing, not into another key-system but into itself, whereby it becomes inverted. The uninverted and the inverted states of the key-system are principally discriminated by the Seventh chords that arise in them. The uninverted state is the primitive one, in which the tonic triad lies between the subdominant and the dominant, thus :

F—a—C—e—G—b—D.

Here the system is bounded on the two sides by *F* and *D*. To express that the system passes into itself, the boundaries *F* and *D* must be brought together in a chord. But then the system becomes

(e)—G—b—D | F—a—C—(e),

which is named the closed, otherwise the transposed or inverted system. By closing its ends the system is in fact rendered circular :

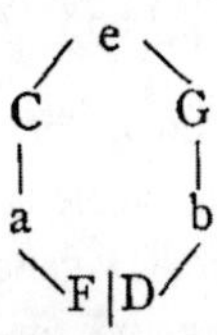

i.e. infinite in the Hegelian sense.

II. The second part treats of Metre and Rhythm, of which the first, the measure, is compared to harmony, while rhythm, the kind of motion in the measure, is analogous to melody.

The metrical unit is shown to be a two-parted unity. This, as two-timed metre, is identified with the Octave (or Root) in harmony ; then three-timed metre, which contains two overlapping metrical units, is identified with the Fifth, and four-timed, which is the last of the uncompounded metres and includes the other two, with the Third. The four-timed metre is the metrical triad.

Next, accent is considered as attaching to the first member of the metrical dual unit ; and hence are derived the various accentuations possible in all metres, simple or compounded.

The notion of major and minor is then shown to have its analogy in metre; viz. the metre that begins with its first or accented member is analogous to the triad that issues or is measured from its Root, while the metre that begins with its unaccented member (as, e.g., a metre beginning with an up beat) is analogous to the minor triad that issues downwards from its Fifth.

The metre is the measure, but rhythm is the filling out of the measure. The rhythm that fills out a metre may be *equal-timed* or *unequal-timed.* A rhythm is equal-timed when the members of the dual unities that make it up are equal in duration, as | ♩ ♩ | ♩ ♩ | . . . The equal-timed rhythm is identified with the Octave.

The unequal-timed rhythm in which the least element is a whole followed by its half, e.g. ♩. ♪, is identified with the Fifth; and the unequal-timed rhythm in which the least element is ♩. ♬ ♩, such that the last quaver is the half of the whole ♫ that has gone before, but also the whole to its half ♬ that immediately precedes, and so at once half and whole, is identified with the Third.

These three elements, the equal-timed and the two unequal-timed divisions, together constitute the determination of rhythm. The two last have also their minor forms: ♪ | ♩ and ♫ | ♩.

III. The last part of the book considers the union of Metre and Harmony; that is, harmony and melody in concrete combination with metre and rhythm. In this the few general principles that can be laid down regard only harmony and metre, for these elements are more fixed and determinate than melody and rhythm. Thus the metrical position of dissonance is discussed, both of suspension and of the Seventh chord. Also continued accent by syncopation is shown to correspond with the series of linked Seventh chords.